CISTERCIAN STUDIES SERIES: NUMBER EIGHTY

A.J. Krailsheimer

THE LETTERS OF ARMAND-JEAN DE RANCÉ

CISTERCIAN STUDIES SERIES: NUMBER EIGHTY

THE LETTERS OF ARMAND-JEAN DE RANCÉ
Abbot and Reformer of la Trappe

presented by

A.J. Krailsheimer

comprising 365 letters translated in full
together with some 1700 others
calendared with notes

Volume One

1641–1682

Cistercian Publications
Kalamazoo, Michigan
1984

© Copyright, Cistercian Publications, Inc., 1984

Available in Britain and Europe from
A.R. Mowbray & Co Ltd
St Thomas House Becket Street
Oxford OX1 1SJ

Available elsewhere from the publishers
Cistercian Publications, Inc.
WMU Station
Kalamazoo, Michigan 49008

All rights reserved

The work of Cistercian Publications is made possible
in part by support from Western Michigan University.

Typeset by the Carmelites of Indianapolis

Library of Congress Cataloging in Publication Data

Rancé, Armand Jean Le Bouthillier de, 1626–1700.
   The letters of Armand-Jean de Rancé, abbot and reformer of la Trappe.

   (Cistercian studies series; 80–81)
   Includes index.
   1. Rancé, Armand Jean Le Bouthillier de, 1626–1700.
2. Cistercians—France—Correspondence.   3. Trappists—
France—Correspondence.   I. Krailsheimer, A.J.   II. Title.   III. Series.
BX4705.R3A4   1984   271'.125'024   [B]   82-19837
ISBN 0-87907-880-4 (v. 1)
ISBN 0-87907-881-2 (v. 2)

TABLE OF CONTENTS

Acknowledgements	vii
Introduction	ix
A Note on the Letters	xxiii
Source Key	xxv
The Letters, 1641–1682	1

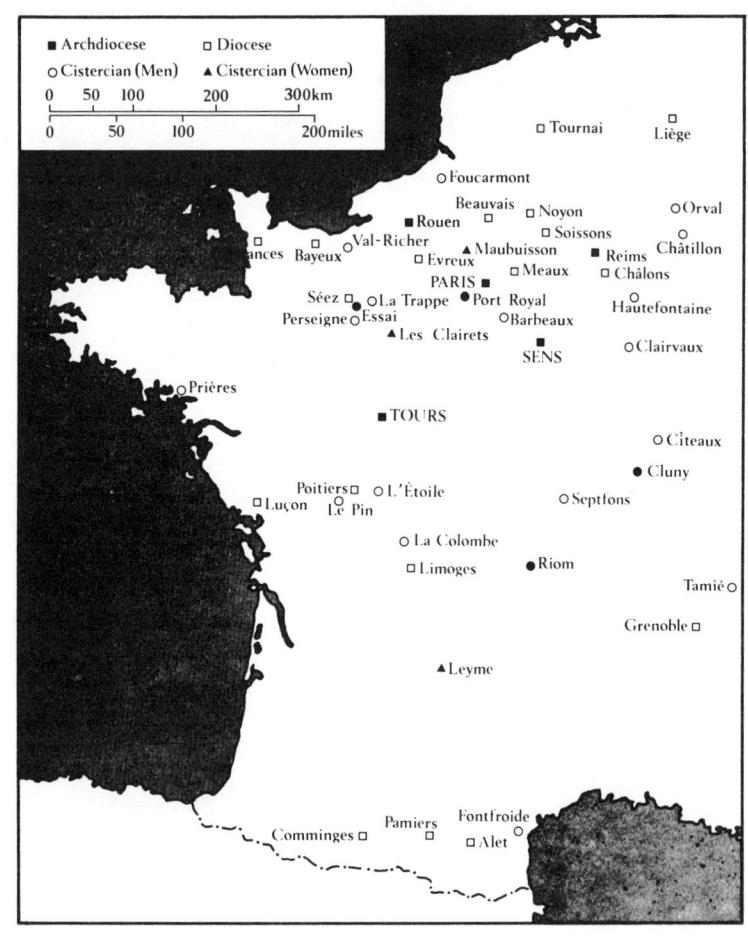

Places mentioned in the text

ACKNOWLEDGMENTS

I OWE A DEBT of gratitude to all those people already mentioned in my earlier book*, but I am sure they will forgive me for not repeating all their names here. Some, however, have responded to further requests with the same kindness and efficiency as before, notably Sister Marie-Patricia (formerly Agathe) Burns of the Visitation Monastery at Annecy and Mlle S. Montagne of Clermont-Ferrand, and I am happy to record my thanks. M. Thierry Bodin of Paris was courteous enough to make me a copy of a previously unknown Rancé autograph; M. André de Villenoisy, also of Paris, took immense trouble to send me abundant documentation on the Chalvet-Rochemonteix family, into which Rancé's sister married, and my old friend, M. Joël Dupont gave me invaluable information about his fellow Norman, the maréchal de Bellefonds, and his home. A special word is due to RM Marie-Agnès, Prioress of the Annonciades at Langres, for great kindness and hospitality; the precious information found in her archives enabled me once and for all to solve the problem of Rancé's Annonciade sisters.

As before, this work could never have been produced but for the generosity of my college, Christ Church, Oxford, and the ceaseless kindness of the community of la Trappe, now headed by dom Gérard Dubois, and including Père Lucien Aubry (now prior) and Père Eric de Jessé, to whom I owe more than I can ever say. Finally, my thanks are due to Dr Rozanne Elder of Cistercian Publications for a degree of cooperation and friendliness which made this arduous task almost enjoyable. Descartes maintained that the work of a single person was superior to that of many; having transcribed, translated, typed, indexed, and checked this all by myself I am convinced that he was wrong, but at least no one but myself can be held accountable for the defects of this volume.

OXFORD   AJK

*Armand-Jean de Rancé, Abbot of La Trappe. His Influence in the Cloister and the World Oxford: Clarendon, 1974.

INTRODUCTION

THIS EDITION of the letters of Rancé, together with my earlier book,[1] represents the fruits of many years of research and is intended to make available previously inaccesible source material essential to any definitive study of Rancé. I never considered producing a complete edition of the letters, nor could such an enterprise be justified on its merits. Far too many of them are repetitious, problems of identifying date and address are insuperable, and for the great majority of even specialist readers the cost in time, effort, and money would be quite disproportionate to the gain. On the other hand, no selection can satisfy all interests, and this one can only be offered as the best compromise I could achieve. Throughout the task I have had three main aims in view. First, I have tried to provide as complete a bibliography as possible of the rather more than two thousand letters extant and identified in my researches. Compare this with the 1529 MS items listed in 1905 by Tournouër[2] (who did not itemise printed letters); several hundred of these turn out to be duplicates which he failed to collate and thus eliminate. It should be noted that the total of extant letters for any one year only twice (1680 and 1682) exceeds one hundred, twice the overall average, and it is likely that no more than ten per cent of Rancé's letters survives—an impressive number, none the less. More letters will certainly turn up, especially from private collections; some of my identifications of date or address will inevitably be proved false. But in the nature of the case no Rancé bibliography can claim to be final, and my only hope is that in quantity and quality this one will stand the test of time.

Secondly, I have calendared each letter as fully as the contents demanded. I have tried to provide such historical and other notes as will enable the letters to be read as a kind of logbook of Rancé's contacts and preoccupations over the years. In addition, I have quoted *verbatim* whatever judgement or turn of phrase seemed to warrant it.

Thirdly, I have translated in full rather more than three hundred sixty letters, and since these make up the greater part of this volume, the principles governing my selection need a word of explanation. While the whole point of translating and editing the letters in English is to make them accessible to readers who are not at home in French, it did not seem right, within the constraints of available space, to translate in full those letters which have already been published in French in works generally available in libraries. Solely for that reason I have not translated the more than two hundred letters to Favier, Nicaise, and Mme de Guise published by Gonod[3] although they are of the highest interest, or the fifteen from the *Autographes de Troussures*[4] (especially valuable are those to Perseigne), or the more than forty, all to Quesnel, excellently edited by Tans.[5] All these are publications of original letters, almost all in complete series to a single addressee, and, following that example, I have combined these two elements.

Virtually all extant original letters not previously published are translated here, as are all the longer unpublished series to a single addressee, whether originals, copies, or mixed. Thus the letters to the maréchal de Bellefonds, to Henri Barillon, Bishop of Luçon, to Rancé's sister Marie-Louise, to Guillaume Le Roy, staunch Jansenist and one-time close friend, to the Bishop of Limoges, to the Cistercian Abbess of Leyme and the Abbot of Châtillon make up about three hundred of the total, and enable one to follow Rancé's relationships with these widely differing persons either over an extended period of years or in detail over a shorter time. The remainder consist of letters to close friends, unpublished originals or copies of special interest. One or two have been included purely for their subject matter.

The content of these letters naturally varies a great deal according to the recipient, and taken together they give a good idea of Rancé's interests over the years. He writes to Bellefonds, general, diplomat and courtier, about exile from court and disgrace, twice incurred by imprudently offending the king, about war, and especially the threatened English invasion following the expulsion of James II, but he also writes about Bellefonds' saintly Carmelite aunt, about attacks from both Jansenists and Jesuits, about the retreat house constructed on Bellefonds' Norman estate; and into every letter the twin themes of friendship and deep faith are woven together. The even longer series to Barillon, extending over more than thirty years, deals with pastoral problems in a diocese which contained large numbers of Protestants, discusses publication of *De la Sainteté* and subsequent works, commends priests and religious who need help, and is full of personal notes regarding the bishop's health, Rancé's longing to see him, and the fatal illness of Rancé's old friend, the bishop's brother. The letters to his Annonciade sister, Marie-Louise, are naturally the most spiritual, since neither he nor she left their enclosure, and show his affectionate concern over nearly forty years. The cooling off of his once warm friendship with Guillaume Le Roy can be followed in the firm, but courteous, series of letters provoked by the quarrel over humiliations as practiced at la Trappe. The few extant letters to the Bishop of Limoges are included for the light they shed on the nature of the advice Rancé gave to those who sought it, and may be compared with the similar letters he wrote to Bishop Le Camus of Grenoble (not translated in full because of numerous gaps in the series). Of particular interest are the letters to the two Cistercian superiors. Unlike the other correspondents just mentioned, the Abbess of Leyme never met Rancé, but in the face of discouragement and even persecution from the Common Observance authorities, she turned to him for help and advice. His letters to her show a characteristic combination of wisdom, piety, and personal rancour (soon dissipated) directed at faithless friends. The Abbot of Châtillon was a trusted friend and one of the more effective leaders of the Strict Observance, and in writing to him Rancé comments with often devastating candour on persons and houses known to them both, on the gloomy prospects facing their observance, and, rather unexpectedly, on specific questions of discipline at Châtillon.

Among some of the other letters given in full are several to Mlle de Goëllo, sister of the duchesse de Montbazon whose death precipitated Rancé's conversion, to M. Duhamel, a once-militant Jansenist who submitted to authority in later life and read Rancé's last letter of consolation on his deathbed, and a remarkable letter to the Oratorian Nicolas Malebranche, after Descartes the most distinguished French philosopher of the century, who had applied to be a postulant at la Trappe.

Even those letters presented only in summary afford a fascinating insight into the world—or worlds—with which Rancé was in contact. Kings and nobles, men and women of distinction or total obscurity, monks, nuns, bishops, and priests, all add up to a varied pagent of the age, no less absorbing for being depicted through the narrow focus of la Trappe.

The interest and value of Rancé's correspondence taken as a whole derives from the human dimension which it provides, and which is largely lacking, or distorted, in his published work. If he was at his worst in public dispute, he was at his best in personal relationships, and since these were perforce conducted for the most part through correspondence, it is only in the letters that we can today come anywhere near to understanding the personal magnetism felt by his contemporaries. Above all his letters reveal an aspect of his character absent from every other source; the stability and fidelity of his friendship. Like a broad, majestic stream, interrupted from time to time by the whirlpools and cataracts of controversy, his basic qualities—affection, loyalty, and compassion—flow on. Unfortunately it is precisely the interruptions which are recorded in print, but to infer from them the character of the whole man is no longer excusable now that the letters are available to prove quite different qualities.

In addition to the historical and biographical notes, I have included (in square brackets within the text) references to the relatively small number of direct quotations (mostly from the Bible), but I have not attempted to annotate the very frequent indirect allusions to the Bible, the Rule, and similar sources. And while a fuller selection would have been even better, I believe that this considerable sample gives a very good idea of what Rancé was like as a person dealing with close friends, relatives, and those seeking advice.

My translation tries to be close rather than free, but in the interests of clarity I have had to introduce much more punctuation than Rancé or his secretaries tended to use.

One or two letters are carefully prepared set pieces (notably the much published one of 1678 to Bellefonds) but most were written or dictated in a hurry, and cannot be held up as models of French prose style. I have translated the integral text of each letter omitting only the concluding compliments.

The only major element I have omitted from the notes is any detailed reference to Rancé's spirituality and its sources. As I said in my earlier book, I am not competent to discuss these things properly, and in any case I believe that the letters speak for themselves to those who know what to look for. The formal presentation of Rancé's spirituality in *De la Sainteté et des Devoirs de la Vie Monastique* and later works (of which the letters give many echoes) needs to be supplemented with what might be called the spontaneous spirituality of correspondence, but the task calls for a study of its own.

If the now much needed full study of Rancé's life and works ever comes to be written, it will have to draw on much material besides the letters, which, despite big gaps in chronology and content, remain the single most informative and reliable source. I would not wish to revise in my earlier book anything but detail (including some dates unaccountably transcribed wrongly),[6] but equally I do not wish merely to repeat and paraphrase the same story. Specifically as an introduction to the letters, therefore, the following summary of Rancé's life and some conclusions regarding his place in history may be of use.

Rancé's upbringing and development up to the time of his conversion in April 1657 was no different from that of most boys of his class at the time. His tutors, Bellérophon and Favier, gave him an excellent grounding in Latin, and the Faculty of Theology at Paris added a sound grasp of that subject. Reports of Rancé's early sermons and speeches imply that his gifts of oratory matched his learning and intelligence. His father's death in 1650 left him head of the family at a relatively early age (24) and his uncle, the Archbishop of Tours, soon charged him with diocesan responsibilities which could no doubt have remained largely nominal, but which in fact Rancé seems to have performed with some zeal. Though Mazarin in 1657 rejected the proposal to make the young archdeacon coadjutor to his uncle, such a career in the long term remained entirely consistent with his talents and family background. Indeed, his nomination as chaplain to Gaston, duc d'Orléans, Louis XIV's uncle, only months before his conversion, marked a further step up the ladder to high office. What sort of bishop he might have made is an idle question, but in later years Rancé would point to his boyhood friends Barillon at Luçon and LeCamus at Grenoble as model pastors.

All this concerns the outer man, talents rather than character. If one looks more deeply into Rancé's family and personal background the picture grows more sombre. The boy can hardly have felt a sense of loss when his eldest sister, Claude, entered the Annonciades at age about nine, never to emerge (he was about five). The death of his elder brother, Denis, in 1637, aged barely 17, his mother's death in 1638, the murder of his sister Charlotte's husband in 1642 after less than three years of marriage, finally

Introduction

his father's death in 1650 were successive intimations of mortality likely to increase the young Rancé's natural human need for security and affection. His early success in society, due to a natural charm attested by all witnesses, and his ambition were accompanied by a restless and impetuous temperament expressed in fondness for riding and hunting, and by a capacity and need for affection expressed in close friendships with men of his own age and with at least one woman, Mme de Montbazon. Concerning this last relationship the truth is as elusive today as it was three centuries ago. It is relevant that it was to women, notably his aunt, Mme Bouthillier, and the Visitandine RM Louise Rogier, as well as to men, to whom he turned immediately after his conversion and they must be assumed therefore to have enjoyed his confidence for some time before it. A similar trait is his devoted loyalty to his tutor, Favier, whose approval clearly meant much to him throughout his life. Except for the few surviving letters to Favier, almost all Rancé's life up to 1657 is either a matter of public record or of conjecture based on hearsay or of later reference by Rancé himself.

The seven years (1657–64) between his conversion and his installation as regular abbot of la Trappe is very much better documented, above all in a remarkable series of autograph letters to the Jansenist scholar Arnauld d'Andilly and copies of letters to RM Louise. The most obvious and immediate change was total revulsion against the pointless life of Paris society, to which he never returned, and a sustained effort to identify and attain a spiritual goal. Through RM Louise, Rancé put himself under the direction of Oratorians, with whom he maintained the closest links thereafter, and probably through his aunt he sought guidance from Andilly, whose main advice seems to have been that Rancé should steep himself in Church history and the Fathers.

The death of Gaston d'Orléans in 1660 ended Rancé's nominal duties as chaplain and left him a free hand to find his own way; but if freedom was an essential part of his programme, the next step was anything but clear. The whole of this period could be called the consultation of oracles: RM Louise, several Oratorians, Andilly, Mme Bouthillier, the Bishops of Châlons, Comminges, Pamiers, and Alet, and finally the Cistercian authorities, in particular Abbot Jouaud of Prières, chief of the reform movement or Strict Observance, inaugurated earlier in the century. To all these, and no doubt others too, he deferred with a respect amounting to humility, but if he took every possible care to seek the best advice available, in the end he made his final choice of career in solitude and not at the urging of any of his advisers. It must be added that Rancé's patience and respect did not extend to those who, deliberately or otherwise, thwarted his aims, like his archiepiscopal uncle (later reconciled) or those who caused delay in his transfer of benefices or interrupted his country retreat. To this period belongs his acquaintance with the Desert Fathers, especially St John Climacus, translated by Andilly in 1652 and again in 1658.

Towards the end of these seven years Rancé's ideas crystallised, and he was swept away by the logic of events. His decision in August 1662 to introduce the Reform into his ruined abbey of la Trappe was a recognition of his personal responsibility for the welfare of the houses whose commendatory abbot he was, in the same way as the transfer of his other benefices to trusted friends like Barillon and Favier had been. The commendatory system, whereby anyone, even a child, could be appointed by the king titular superior of any number of abbeys or priories as a purely financial transaction, was a universal abuse in France generalised since the previous century. Rancé's brother, Denis, had from an early age enjoyed the titles and revenues of three abbeys and two priories which devolved on Rancé at the age of twelve, when Denis died. Only now did it occur to Rancé that financial benefit might entail moral, even spiritual obligations. Similarly the material restoration of the abbey, whose revenues he had enjoyed since boyhood, was no more than the discharge of a long overdue moral debt. All this changed in the course of the next few months. Living in conditions of discomfort and even danger from crumbling buildings, Rancé spent the winter 1662–63 observing the half dozen monks sent from Perseigne to introduce the Reform. It cannot have been a very attractive assignment for them, uprooted from their spiritual family and bidden to restore monastic life among ruins, but what Rancé saw and heard during those months cleared his mind more than all the books he had so far read or the discussions he had had. It was no longer enough for him to put the house in order and preside as commendatory abbot, he felt impelled to bind himself by vows—to do penance, in his own words,—for many and grievous sins.

His resolve to enter the Cistercian order at Perseigne as a novice was the direct consequence of spending the previous months watching, and to some extent sharing, the regular monastic life reintroduced at la Trappe. He must have done some reading that winter, perhaps making some acquaintance with the Rule of St Benedict and the basic Cistercian texts, but what mattered to him was practice, not theory. For someone undergoing an emotional and spiritual crisis as protracted as Rancé's, this direct monastic experience, at that time, at that place, had an intensity which proved decisive.

The specific nature of the experience also explains why Rancé finally decided not to remain an ordinary monk but to become a regular abbot. His critics later accused him of assuming command without ever having served in the ranks but, while this is true, it misses the point. Intellectually and socially, if not spiritually, Rancé stood far above most of his Cistercian contemporaries, let alone the monks of la Trappe or Perseigne. Richelieu's godson, nephew of an archbishop, friend of the highest in the land, Rancé could get things done by exercising an influence which no amount of monastic training could supply. Moreover, it was as commendatory abbot of la Trappe and other benefices that Rancé had for years, as he now saw it, cheated God and the Church; it had to be as regular abbot that he should make reparation. In theory he could have ended his days as a simple monk, in practice he knew he could contribute much more as abbot by wielding his long abused power and influence for the benefit of the community and Order he had exploited. It is absurd to deny a born leader the right, even the duty, to lead, and in seventeenth-century France the course Rancé chose was the only proper one. It would be even more absurd to suggest that the monastic vocation which Rancé finally acknowledged was in any way separable from the specific vocation to la Trappe. There is no evidence in 1664, or later, that he was ever led by ambition or any other motive to consider leaving the place which he so often said he regarded as his tomb. His commitment to his abbey and his Order was for life, and only if regular observance, as he defined it, had ceased to be possible at la Trappe would he ever have contemplated moving.

When in July 1664 Rancé took over the government of his abbey, then a community of nine, he already had clear ideas of how he intended to conduct affairs. The reform movement which affected most religious orders in the seventeenth century was primarily a reaction against mitigations accumulated down the ages as a result of which many monks enjoyed material conditions superior to those of the ordinary layman. The Strict Observance which Rancé introduced to la Trappe was a return to a regular discipline conducive to spiritual health. However, it was not the Cistercian source as such to which Rancé wished to return, because at that stage he hardly knew it, but rather to the Desert Fathers, who at the time of his profession already represented his monastic ideal. Their spirituality, above all that of St John Climacus, lay behind all Rancé's subsequent, very personal, interpretation of Benedictine and Cistercian tradition and usage.

He had had only a few weeks to set things going when he was despatched, most reluctantly, to Rome to plead the cause of the Strict Observance. Having taken over as abbot in July 1664 he had at once made clear enough what he wanted, and he left oral and written instructions when he set off for Rome in September. Between his departure from la Trappe and his return in May 1666 he remained in contact with his monks by letter, but was evidently unable to rule his flock effectively at long range. His mission came at a good time in that any latent ambition he may ever have had was decisively checked by what he saw of power politics in Rome. Moreover, the endless lobbying and pleading required of him in his mission gave him in a few months a more intense and thorough acquaintance with the legal and historical arguments underlying the Reform than he could ever have acquired by staying at la Trappe. Disgusted and disillusioned by the failure of his mission to win victory for the Strict Observance, he returned at last to his abbey, more impatient than ever to start building on the modest foundations already laid there. Much of this story appears from the letters to RM Louise.

From 1666–75 Rancé took a prominent, but ever more reluctant, part in the Strict Observance's campaign against the brief *In suprema*, which had essentially given victory to the Common Observance. He made a formal protest at the General Chapter held at Cîteaux in 1667, (the only one he ever attended), he sought support from influential friends, he wrote directly to the King and attended frequent meetings in Paris, until finally, in April 1675, a royal commission found against the Strict Observance and Rancé returned from Paris for the last time. By French law no edict from Rome was effective in France until it had been registered and approved by King and

Parlement (acting as a supreme court). What the Strict Observance had failed to achieve in Rome, they hoped to achieve in France, but their delaying tactics could not survive the findings of the royal commission, which Rancé (and others) had tried so hard to sway. Throughout this period recruitment at la Trappe, after a slow start, was growing apace. Most of those who wanted to come (probably nine out of ten) found conditions too hard; some returned whence they had come, and a number of others went on to Strict Observance houses where life was less demanding. By 1675 the original nine had become twenty-five monks, plus seven lay brothers, but then six professions were matched by six deaths in the same year, and in 1676 there were again four deaths to balance four professions, though numbers soon recovered and greatly increased. As the community grew and prospered, so did responsibility for the 'souls committed to his charge' (a favourite phrase of Rancé), and preoccupation with his own feelings of guilt gave way to care and concern for his monks. For example, he gave as a reason for not going to Paris for the final meeting of Strict Observance superiors that one of his monks was dying and that it was the abbot's duty to be with him at the end. Only the order of his diocesan bishop prevailed on him to go. The community formed Rancé no less than he formed them.

The first decade of Rancé's abbatial rule proved therefore critical in two ways: he was constantly involved with his fellow abbots in the struggle to achieve autonomy from the Common Observance, and thus came to know them, and they him, during ten years of collective stress; secondly the actual implementation of his programme at la Trappe, originally judged chimerical by Jouaud and other senior abbots, was proceeding, though at a cost in the goodwill of Orders and communities which felt threatened by wholesale defection, and also, inescapably, in the health and even the lives of himself and his monks. Friends and enemies alike criticised the unprecedented austerity of the regime, and Rancé was forced on to the defensive. La Trappe was at once a magnet for those whose piety, or desire for penitence, was of heroic stamp, and an inevitable point of comparison with houses, even of the Strict Observance, where much less, or no, austerity prevailed. The question was constantly asked: why go further than the rule of life observed in houses where devotion and discipline were already exemplary?

From an early stage Rancé and la Trappe were acknowledged as being special within (just within) the Strict Observance, and no case can be made for the view that he believed Trappist life to be normative, or sought to impose it on others. A recent article[7] spells out in detail the explanation of what Trappist reform aimed at and why: Rancé's work of reform was the direct and logical outcome of his personal conversion, which in turn took the Desert Fathers as the ideal to which modern monks should aspire with what strength they could muster. As to why he remained loyal, in his fashion, to the Cistercian Order, the answer is most probably to be found in the sincere respect for established authority, above all for that of the king and the bishops, which he shared with such men as Bossuet, in his acute sensitivity to what was or was not legal, and, not least, to the realisation acquired over the years that the Rule of St

Benedict as adapted by the first Cistercians furnished the best available institutional framework in which his own community could thrive. His relations with other Cistercian houses more than compensated for his absence from Chapters and refusal of office in the Order (e.g. visitor); at different times religious were sent to or came from Hautefontaine, l'Etoile, Foucarmont, la Colombe, Orval, Tamié, Septfons, Barbeaux, Champagne, Perseigne, les Clairets, and Maubuisson (he sent chaplains to the last two) with the full agreement, and often at the urgent request, of their superiors. In such practical ways his contribution to the Order was considerable, and though few, if any, of those houses approached Trappist rigour, something of Trappist spirit must have been communicated. To take a military analogy, such elite forces as the U.S. Rangers, or the British Guards Brigade are passionately proud of their own identity, and never allow themselves to be merged in other formations, but they serve as a model to other troops, often train them, and fight alongside them, while remaining unmistakably themselves and excelling in heroism.

From 1675 until his retirement just twenty years later, the image of Rancé best known to posterity was formed. In essence it is the consolidation and reemphasising of all that has been said so far. He himself had become an oracle, consulted from far and wide, and the great expansion of his correspondence reflects this. Publications like the first *Relations*, then *De la Sainteté* and the long series of supplementary volumes exchanged with Mabillon on monastic studies, drew approval from some and loud disapproval from others. All of them encouraged critics to portray an aggressive and authoritarian fanatic who imposed inhuman silence on his monks while ceaselessly shouting from the housetops himself. The bitter dispute over humiliations with the Jansenist commendatory abbot of Hautefontaine, Guillaume Le Roy (1672-77), had at least been principally conducted by letter; from 1683 onwards those behind Rancé saw to it that all was published.

At different times Rancé had gravely offended the highest authorities in other Orders by refusing to send back their members who presented themselves at la Trappe, and he usually justified his action on the ground that la Trappe offered a more regular observance than other houses. The Generals of the Celestines, Maurists, Feuillants, Premonstratensians, all at various times resorted to legal action to prevent further depletion of their ranks, though the total number involved was, except for the Celestines, only two or three. The Jesuits had always disliked him (not surprisingly no member of the Society ever applied for admission to la Trappe), the Carthusians actually lost no members (transfer was illegal for them), but had to contend with restless monks who talked of going and their General, dom Le Masson, bitterly resented Rancé's claim that the spirit of their Order was no longer what it was. Rancé further incurred increasing hostility from Jansenists, orginally drawn in his quarrel with Le Roy, exacerbated by his letter of 1678 to Bellefonds disclaiming Jansenist sympathies, and intensified to a pitch of real fury by his mildly dismissive comments on their leader Antoine Arnauld's death in 1694.

Once *De la Sainteté* was published, and ran into second and third editions, making Rancé's monastic ideals unignorably public, polemical publications multiplied praising or condemning Rancé's view of contemporary monasticism and the model offered at la Trappe. Supporters like Maupeou and Thiers, both parish priests, enemies like the Protestant Larroque and the Maurist Sainte-Marthe, created a climate of controversy even more tempestuous than that which Rancé himself generated by his own writings. In an age when only the pulpit came near to what we call mass media, pamphlet warfare of a virulent kind took the place of modern press campaigns. Most of his opponents Rancé never met, and when he did, as happened with Abbot Somont of Tamié or Mabillon, the usual result was reconciliation. He relied far too much on hearsay, mostly from interested parties, he was repeatedly indiscreet when experience had shown how few of his confidences were respected, and in his concern for the preservation of what had been achieved at la Trappe he was excessively sensitive to reactions from above, especially from Louis XIV, on whose protection he wholly depended, and perhaps to a lesser degree on reactions from the Pope and hierarchy in general. All this is reflected in letters written from 1683 onwards, many of which seem almost obsessively concerned with public reaction to his book.

His very frequent references to calumny and misrepresentation, from which he claimed to derive more spiritual benefit than from praise, fall short of a persecution complex, but show a defensive stance curiously combining the aggressive and the melancholy. The respect and affection in which he was held by many friends saved him from adopting the purely negative attitude of a man misunderstood, but also led him fiercely to assert that he was right and others were wrong. The problem was never as black and white as he saw it, and only in the context of la Trappe can Rancé's point of view be appreciated.

It must be remembered that the large and thriving community which Rancé eventually established owed nothing to his influential connexions. Admittedly, successive concessions from the King and from Rome for the future conduct of the abbey after Rancé's death were the result of his personal standing, but this hardly affected the community so long as he was there. It was Rancé himself who created and nurtured the abbey. Against all the predictions of those, like Jouaud, qualified to judge, the programme drawn up by Rancé, based on his reading of the Desert Fathers applied to the Rule, had been fully realised. Far more postulants came than could be received, and were of the highest quality. As abbot, Rancé appointed the novice master and other officers, he alone addressed the monks on their calling and duties, he alone acted as their confessor (though they were free to choose another); in a word la Trappe was from first to last his creation and survived because he and his monks, selected by him for that reason, were of one mind. It was by any standards a very good community, vindicating the principles on which it was founded and implicitly inviting other communities to aim as high. In looking at what had come to pass since 1664 Rancé could believe only that he had, against all odds, been right all the time. In the most fundamental sense he and his community were one, inspiring and justifying each other.

When outsiders, even monks like Abbot Le Maître of Châtillon, saw Rancé's monastery in operation, it was only natural that they should seek to extract from this practical success lessons which could be passed on to others. The conferences on monastic life delivered by Rancé both defined and contributed to what he was trying to do, and it was reasonable to suppose that other religious and other superiors might profit from the same lessons. Even individual monks and nuns, feeling isolated in an indifferent community or under a mediocre superior, might feel encouraged in their spiritual toil by meditating on the principles underlying life at la Trappe. So ran the reasoning of those like Abbot Le Maître, and eventually Bossuet, who urged Rancé to publish what had orginally been domestic talks. When the book, *De la Sainteté et des Devoirs de la Vie Monastique*, came out in 1683, some twenty years of history lay behind the Trappist reform, but many still doubted whether it would outlast its initiator. Rancé in part answered these doubts by supplying an ample documentation to show that the basis for life at la Trappe was no different from that laid down by the Desert Fathers and mediæval monastic leaders like St Bernard. All subsequent changes and mitigations were signs of decadence. Such monastic fundamentalism derives from the same spirit as the uncompromising biblical fundamentalism also professed by Rancé, as by most Catholics and Protestants of the time. It is hardly surprising that it appealed to a generation undergoing the 'crisis of the European conscience'[8] in science, philosophy, and religion. Rancé would have fought hard enough if the issue had concerned la Trappe alone, but in the event he saw himself as the lonely champion of true monastic values.

The decade (1683–1695) between the appearance of *De la Sainteté* and Rancé's resignation saw more publicity and more polemic than all the twenty years preceding it. By that time, too, Rancé's secretary and trusted agent was no longer a monk, but a secular, Charles Maisne. Whatever Maisne's motives may have been, and sincere loyalty to his master may possibly have come before pure self-interest, the surviving evidence does not inspire trust in him. He often wrote on his own account to Rancé's correspondents, he willingly joined in, and even instigated, intrigue in the outside world, he very probably pushed Rancé to more, rather than less, publicity. In the last years leading up to Rancé's resignation, and in the pathetic final phase after it, one can never be too sure that the hand that wrote the letter was not also recording the voice of Maisne rather than Rancé. Bossuet too was a major influence towards the end of Rancé's life (from about 1682) and while he toned down many of the excesses in Rancé's published work, his undoubtedly sincere friendship further polarised Rancé against those who thought and lived differently. Anyone who wished to see Rancé had to come to la Trappe; Rancé himself had no direct contact with any other way of life, private or public, religious or secular, for twenty-five years. Relying wholly on correspondence and hearsay he could hardly form a balanced view of the world outside of la Trappe. For his part he regarded all worldly values as so empty and ephemeral that la Trappe in any case represented a higher reality.

Long before his death Rancé had become a living legend, and la Trappe a magnet for the pious and curious alike. It is difficult to assess the objective truth, but quite likely that Louis XIV regarded him as one of the holiest and most exemplary religious in his kingdom. The Pope and the Abbot of Cîteaux equally came to look on him as an institution and were no doubt thankful that only one such existed. *De la Sainteté* was certainly influential, and remained so well into the nineteenth century, but none of his other writings was widely read. It is not possible to assess in any way the abiding effect of his letters on their countless recipients, but that influence lasted no longer than the generation in question. In one respect alone his influence remained decisive for two centuries after his death: through la Trappe.

To say, as some critics do, that Rancé was essentially a secondary figure in his age is to say that enclosed religious in any age are secondary figures, which in a sense they are, but if monastic life is at its highest the essence and distillation of Christian life, the total love and service of God, then one can see that a monk or nun whose life and teaching attracts as many men and women as did Rancé's may be important out of all proportion to the duration of each individual contact. A retreat of a week or two each year may well mark the retreatant more than the remaining fifty weeks of normal life. Contact with Rancé, especially when repeated and extended over many years, may well have been the most intense spiritual experience in hundreds of lives. Even a visit to la Trappe, without personal contact with Rancé, is known to have deeply impressed innumerable visitors through the years. Cost-effective calculations count for little in the spiritual life, but leaving aside active religious, preachers, writers and the like, the only community or individuals to compare with la Trappe and Rancé is Port-Royal and its solitaries. The destruction of that community, and the dispersal of the solitaries, the survival of the community of la Trappe and the rebuilding of their abbey offers at least one gauge by which to measure their respective importance in the long term.

The revival of monastic life in Western Europe after the French Revolution was a widespread phenomenon, but it was dom Augustin Lestrange, inspired by Rancé's teaching, who enabled the community, and then the Congregation, of la Trappe to survive and propagate the Cistercian Order throughout the world. For a century at least Trappist and Cistercian were synonymous in popular speech, and even today, when Cistercians show little enthusiasm for the reformer of la Trappe, they might do well to ponder the chain of historical causation. Just as St Bonaventure is often called the second founder of the Franciscans, so Rancé, for all his faults, has more claim to be called second founder of the Cistercians than any of his contemporaries in the Order, not one of whom is remembered except by specialists.

What Mabillon and the Maurists did for the glory of God and Benedictine scholarship, Rancé did equally for the glory of God and the silent witness of his monks and their Trappist successors in what he called the solitary life. His teaching and personality had grave defects, but the community he built endures and his good lives after him. His all too human faults must not be forgotten, but he should be remembered for his spiritual legacy. To know what manner of man he was, the letters that follow offer the richest source.

NOTES TO INTRODUCTION

1. A.J. Krailsheimer, *A-J de Rancé, Abbot of la Trappe*, (Oxford; Clarendon, 1974).
2. H. Tournouër, *Bibliographie . . . de la Trappe. Documents sur la Province du Perche*, 4e série, 2 (Mortagne, 1905-6).
3. B. Gonod, *Lettres de A-J de Rancé* (Paris, 1846).
4. Dom Paul Denis (ed.), *Lettres autographes de Troussures* (Paris, 1912).
5. J.A.G Tans, 'Un dialogue monologué: lettres à P. Quesnel', *Augustiniana*, 13 (1963).
6. The most glaring of these are: p. 3: Rancé was born on 9 (and not 26) January 1626; p. 18: Félibien took possession on 30 June (not 3 July); and Rancé was blessed on 13 (not 19) July 1664.
7. Lucien Aubry [Prior of la Trappe], 'Les Pères des Déserts à la Trappe', *Cîteaux* 32 (1981) 166-214.
8. P. Hazard, *La Crise de la conscience européenne 1685-1715*, (Paris, 1934, revised 1961) E.T. *The European Mind* (1952).

A NOTE ON THE LETTERS

Numbering and dating

Each letter has been given a reference number based on its date. Where the full date is known (or can be reasonably conjectured) this is given in conventional six figure form: year, month, day; and when more than one letter is attributed to the same day the second and subsequent such letters are distinguished by alphabetical serials (e.g. 821102, 821102a: letters written in 1682 on November second). When the month, but not the day, is known, the last two figures are given as '00' and letters attributed to the same month are similarly distinguished, after the first, by the use of alphabetical serials (e.g. 821100, 821100a), which have no chronological significance. Where only the year is known or can be conjectured, only the two figures for the year are used, followed by a stroke and a numerical serial for each letter (e.g. 82/1, 82/2), which also has no chronological significance.

Dates are either given in the form in which they appear in the letter, or in square brackets when the date has been established through internal or external evidence. Where a figure is wrong in the copy (a frequent occurrence) the correct figure is given in square brackets, and the incorrect one noted below. All doubtful dates, especially those involving two or more years or months, are prefixed by a query (?). Undated letters are listed separately at the end of the dated series. Minor variations have not usually been noted; many copies of surviving originals systematically give a date one day later than the original.

An asterisk (*) denotes a letter translated in full. Bold face entries are given for chronological orientation.

Styling of addressees

In most cases the original French style has been used in giving addresses, with a few exceptions (such as bishops) where translation is unambiguous. Wherever possible the full name of addressees is given, and the names of incumbents given in square brackets after their title. The form of title is often the only way in which an incomplete address can be filled out, and the distinction between M *l'abbé* (used both as courtesy title for clergy in general and also, more correctly, for commendatory abbots or priors) and RP *abbé* (used solely for regulars) cannot be adequately rendered in English. Similarly RP for regular clergy and M. or M. *l'abbé* for seculars has no English equivalent. M was used almost universally for clergy, laity, and even bishops (e.g. M. *de Meaux* for Bossuet, M. *de la Trappe* for Rancé), and *Mme* applied from royal princesses, like *Mme de Guise*, down to ordinary married women of the bourgeoisie. In the circumstances, and despite the radical inconsistency of copyists and even original correspondents, a uniform style has been used throughout for the same person. The many letters addressed simply to *religieux* or *religieuse* pose an intractable problem; some copies actually change RM into *ma soeur* (or vice versa); the same person may be addressed on one occasion as *prieure* and on another as *supérieure*, and so on. Abbesses, and abbots, are sometimes given the honorific *très-révérend(e)* or TRM, TRP, sometimes not. With the exception of the Abbot of Cîteaux (addressed as *Révérendissime* and here distinguished by being given in English) all heads of abbeys have been uniformly described as RP *abbé*, RM *abbesse*, and likewise with lesser superiors. Titles of nobility, public offices and so on have been left in the original and often have no comparable description in English. It is worth noting that Rancé reserved *très chère* for his sisters and niece, and *très cher Monsieur* or *père* for such intimates as Favier or Monchy.

Bibliographical references and abbreviations

Whenever an original ('orig.') or autograph ('aut.') has survived, this is given first and followed by references to copies in all the principal series used; when only copies survive, references are given to all the main series, but not to further single copies made from them. Printed sources, especially modern, are normally given after the MS copy, and in one or two cases only a printed source is known. MS sources have always been preferred, but it should be noted that even the best copies often omit personal postscripts found in the original, and can be shown to differ, not usually very much, from each other. In particular there is a tendency for copies to conflate or split up original letters (particularly marked in A 2606). It should be noted that MS Df 49 at the Bibliothèque Sainte-Geneviève, Paris, is a duplicate of M 1214, differing only in having correct numbering for all the letters where M 1214 has two letters 26 with consequential error thereafter; to avoid repeating 106 entries, references have been given only to M 1214.

Source Key

Manuscript

A	Bibliothèque de l'Arsenal, Paris
BN	Bibliothèque Nationale, Paris (*fonds français* unless otherwise stated)
Carp	Carpentras, Bibliothèque Municipale, MS 625,626 (the two volumes of a copy made of dom Le Nain's *Vie de Rancé* before editorial excisions, and the sole source for several letters unknown elsewhere)
CF	Clermont-Ferrand, Bibliothèque Municipale et Universitaire
L	Luçon, Archives diocésaines
M	Bibliothèque Mazarine, Paris
P	Poitiers, Bibliothèque Municipale, MS Fontaneau 65
SS	Bibliothèque de Saint-Sulpice, Paris
T	Troyes, Bibliothèque Municipale
TA	La Trappe, *Lettres originales*
TB	La Trappe, *Lettres à imprimer* (reference to page)
TC	La Trappe, *Lettres de piété* (reference to number of letter)
TD	La Trappe, *Lettres diverses* (series A,B,C)
Tour	Collection Henri Tournouër (in private hands near Alençon)
U	Utrecht, *ancien fonds d'Amersfoort, Port-Royal*
W	Windsor Castle, Royal Library, Stuart Papers

Printed Works

Autographes Troussures	*Lettres autographes de Troussures* [château near Beauvais], ed. dom Paul Denis, 1912
J-B Bossuet:	references are to the edition of his correspondence by Ch. Urbain and E. Levesque, 15 vols. Paris, 1909–12
Burnier, *Hist. de Tamié*	E. Burnier, *Histoire de l'abbaye de Tamié*. Chambéry, 1865 (contains letters, numbered serially, to Cornuty, copied from MS *Chronique de Tamié*, kept at the abbey)
Charavay	The sales catalogues of Maison Charavay, Paris, specialist dealers in autographs, still issued. An index of these, and other sales up to about 1900, can be found in the BN, MSS Department, under Fichiers Charavay (Rancé RAI-RAZ).

DBF	*Dictionnaire de Biographie française.*
Dubois	Abbé Dubois, *Histoire de l'abbé de Rancé.* 1866
Gonod	B. Gonod, *Lettres de A-J le B de Rancé.* 1846
Mug	*Lettres de piété écrites à différentes personnes par... Rancé*, vol. 1, 1701; vol. 2, 1702, published by F. Muguet
Mme de Sévigné	references are to the edition of her letters in 3 vols, éd. de la Pléiade. 1953
Sol, *ND de Saint-Bernard de Comminges*	abbé Sol, *Notre Dame de Saint-Bernard de Comminges.* Toulouse, 1923
SP	*Stuart Papers*, vol. 1, ed. F.H. Blackburne Daniell. 1902
Tans	J.A.G. Tans, 'Un Dialogue monologué; lettres à P. Quesnel, *Augustiniana*, 13. 1963 (reference to letters by serial number)

A Note on Rancé's Signature:

Up to 25 March 1643 Rancé signed his extant letters to Favier *Ab. Bouthillier de Rancé*. His signature then changed to *l'abbé de Rancé*, but starting with the letter of 14 May 1658 (after his conversion) none of his letters to Favier is signed, nor are any of those to Arnauld d'Andilly, but a letter to Andilly's son, Pomponne, of 18 February 1662 is signed *l'abbé de Rancé* and is the only signed letter from this period known to survive. After his profession he always signed *fr Armand-Jean, abbé de la Trappe*, never again using his family name, and after his resignation in 1695, when he could no longer use his hand, letters are always signed for him *fr Armand-Jean anc.[ien] abbé de la Trappe.*

THE LETTERS OF ARMAND-JEAN DE RANCÉ

Armand-Jean Bouthillier de Rancé born in Paris   9 January 1626

410110   RP SIRMOND, SJ, CONFESSOR TO THE KING   10 January 1641
Tour. aut. (Greek)
Sends edition of Anacreon.

This edition, of some one hundred-fifty pages with commentary, was dedicated to Cardinal de Richelieu, the boy's godfather, and printed in Paris in 1639. It is not necessary to believe that it is all, or mostly, R's own work, but it played a part in developing the legend of later years.

420904   M. FAVIER (SENIOR)   4 September 1642
CF 344,f.1 aut.; Gonod 1
Respects. M's son, R's tutor, has gone, but is keeping himself free in case needed again.

420926   JEAN FAVIER   26 September 1642
CF 344,f.3 aut.; Gonod 2
R. will always keep his promises to Favier; 'the affection which I have so often sworn . . . will never diminish.'

421011   JEAN FAVIER   11 October 1642
CF 344,f.5 aut.; Gonod 3
Has written three or four times without reply. Began physics two weeks ago.

421200   JEAN FAVIER   [December 1642]
CF 344,f.7 aut.; Gonod 4
Describes murder on 6 December of comte de Belin [husband of R's sister Charlotte] by Bonnivet [Belin's brother-in-law]; would avenge crime if he could.

430325   JEAN FAVIER   25 March 1643
CF 344,f.9 aut.; Gonod 5
R's father better disposed to Favier than latter thinks. R. finished philosophy six weeks ago, should defend thesis in two months.

430900   JEAN FAVIER   [September 1643]
CF 344,f.103 aut.; Gonod 6

Defended thesis six weeks ago. Has seen Favier's brother. Has resolved, with his father's agreement, to devote himself to the Church. Starting theology on 15 [September] with M. Le Moine [a doctor of the Sorbonne with Jansenist sympathies, who resigned in 1654 and died in 1659].

431100   JEAN FAVIER   [after 11 November 1643]
CF 344,f.11 aut.; Gonod 7

His theological studies; hopes to start preaching soon.

440213   JEAN FAVIER   13 February 1644
CF 344,f.13 aut.; Gonod 8

Rarely sees Favier's brother and is anxious for news.

440317   JEAN FAVIER   17 March 1644
CF 344,f.15 aut.; Gonod 9

Will talk to Favier about Arnauld's *De la Fréquente Communion* and dispute in university over Jansenism and Jesuit casuists.

When Jansen's Augustinus *appeared posthumously in 1640, Antoine Arnauld soon became the chief defender of the doctrines contained therein. His own book (on the necessity for proper preparation before receiving communion) was published in 1643. Jesuit moral theology, and especially casuistry, was the object of bitter attacks by traditionalists and was to form the main subject of Pascal's* Provincial Letters *(1656-8).*

441019   JEAN FAVIER   19 October 1644
CF 344,f.17 aut.; Gonod 10

Favier's case is under review and promises well.

451125   JEAN FAVIER   25 November 1645
CF 344,f.19 aut.; Gonod 11

Not true that the only sign of R's friendship is his sister's kindness to Favier.

Charlotte had married again, Gilbert, comte d'Albon, and apparently employed Favier in some capacity.

Rancé awarded Master of Arts degree   18 May 1646

461000 JEAN FAVIER   [October 1646]
CF 344,f.21 aut.; Gonod 12

Has sent copies of his thesis to Favier and Bellérophon [his other tutor].

461016 JEAN FAVIER   16 October 1646
CF 344,f.22 aut.; (fragment) Gonod 13

R. has just returned from a disastrous trip to Touraine, where his father has been ill.

470516 JEAN FAVIER   16 May 1647
CF 344,f.24 aut.; Gonod 14

Has been a month at les Claies (near Versailles), since the day after his Easter sermon at the Discalced Carmelites (men).

His first sermon is said to have been at his sister's clothing at the Annonciades, in 1647, but this one must have come soon afterwards. The Carmelites had a house in the rue de Vaugirard.

470730 JEAN FAVIER   30 July 1647
CF 344,f.26 aut.; Gonod 15

Favier's health still worrying.

481222 JEAN FAVIER   22 December 1648
CF 344,f.28 aut.; Gonod 16

Had made a retreat of twelve days alone at Saint-Lazare before receiving on successive days minor orders, sub-diaconate, and diaconate from the Abp-Coadjutor [Retz].

Many Paris clergy made a retreat under Vincent de Paul at Saint-Lazare before ordination, as Retz himself had done in 1643.

500219 JEAN FAVIER   19 February 1650
CF 344,f.30 aut.; Gonod 17

Has been three times to Touraine in past four months; continues licence in theology.

His father died in May, and the visits may have been to do with his father's illness.

510212 JEAN FAVIER   12 February 1651
CF 344,f.32 aut.; Gonod 18

Defended his thesis on 10 February. Ordained priest by Abp of Tours [his uncle] three weeks earlier [22 January].

510312 M. FOY CONSEILLER DU ROI, BEAUVAIS   12 March 1651
aut. (offered for sale April 1981 by M. Thierry Bodin, who was kind enough to let
me inspect it and take a copy.)
Brief note asking for help in conveyancing property at Beauvais.

This is probably Raoul Foy, whose son, also Raoul (1653–91), became a canon of Beauvais, and died on the scaffold after falsely accusing his fellow canons of treason in 1689. The case indirectly involved R.

Rancé placed first in Licence in Theology.   1652

Rancé takes Doctorate.   1654 (?)

Attends as delegate the Assembly of Clergy in Paris;   1655–57
appointed chaplain to Gaston d'Orleans.

Death of Mme de Montbazon; Rancé retires to   24 April 1657
his country house at Véretz, near Tours.

570604   [RM LOUISE ROGIER]   4 June 1657
M 1214,4
'I will never join any cabal whatever in religious matters.'

58/1   [RM LOUISE ROGIER]   1658
M 1214,1
Would have liked to make retreat near her, but not possible. Séguenot wrong to praise R. for giving up plurality of benefices; 'I simply gave up crime.'

Claude Séguenot (1596–1676) joined the Oratory in 1624. He got into trouble for alleged Jansenism, but held high office in the order and was superior in Paris from 1666–73. He was the first director proposed to R. by RM Louise after his conversion.

58/2   [RM LOUISE ROGIER]   1658
M 1214,2
Had to go back to Paris without seeing her. Abp of Tours angry with him, but R. will not change his mind, even if this means going to Canada. Was offered, but refused, direction of all feminine communities in diocese.

58/3 [RM LOUISE ROGIER] 1658
M 1214,3

'It is not enough to endure the afflictions and bitter events sent by God . . . we must do so in his way, not in ours, and in the places to which his providence seems to assign us.'

58/4 [RM LOUISE ROGIER] 1658
M 1214,5

Mme de Saint-Loup has just spent the whole day with him; 'a very pious woman who always has the best intentions.' His health better, but still uncertain.

58/5 ARCHBISHOP OF TOURS [VICTOR BOUTHILLIER] [? July] 1658
A 6035,f.290

Would have obeyed order to go to Paris, had it been on Abp's service, but it was not. Hopes Abp does not think R's way of life is motivated by 'caprice or oddity'.

58/6 RELIGIEUSE [1658]
M 1214,9; Mug I/6

It is as wrong to grieve over God's conduct to others as it is to resist his conduct to us.

58/7 RELIGIEUX 1658
Mug I/4

God will not abandon him now any more than before.

580104 ROBERT ARNAULD D'ANDILLY 4 January 1658
A 6035,f.191 aut.

From Véretz. Sympathy on death in battle of Andilly's son [Jules Arnauld de Villeneuve]. Reference to a visit six months earlier to Port-Royal. [R. visited Andilly in July 1657].

580303 ROBERT ARNAULD D'ANDILLY 3 March 1658
A 6035,f.203 aut.

From Véretz. R. going to inspect his abbey at Beauvais and hopes for two or three hours talk with Andilly on the way.

580404 ROBERT ARNAULD D'ANDILLY 4 April 1658
A 6035,f.205 aut.

From Cuny [near Ponts-sur-Seine]. Grateful for Andilly's kindness. Impatient to return home and start rule of life. Duc de Luynes has remembered R.

Louis, duc de Luynes (1621–90) was a fervent supporter of Port-Royal and lived at Vaumurier nearby.

580514 JEAN FAVIER 14 May 1658
CF 344,f.34 aut.; Gonod 19

From Véretz. 'I shall try to find peace in the attitudes and employment appropriate to a man of my calling.'

580626 ROBERT ARNAULD D'ANDILLY 26 June 1658
A 6035,f.218 aut.

Almost no visitors now. Has been at Blois on duty [with Gaston d'Orléans] for two days. Is reading *Petrus Aurelius* with enjoyment, asks for pamphlets against Jesuits. Has to go and inspect the ruined church of one of his abbeys thirty leagues away [= la T.]

Petrus Aurelius, *a treatise on episcopal authority, was written in 1631 by Saint-Cyran, Jansen's closest friend. With the end of Pascal's* Provincial Letters, *the fight went on in a pamphlet war, in which Pascal was involved. R's reading programme could hardly have been more Jansenist.*

580710 ROBERT ARNAULD D'ANDILLY 10 July 1658
A 6035,f.223 aut.

Has returned from visit to Perche [= la T.] Still reading *Petrus Aurelius*, in mornings, and Eusebius (church history) in afternoons. Has translated a letter of St Basil. Almost no visitors.

This seems to have been R's first sight of la T.

580718 ROBERT ARNAULD D'ANDILLY 18 July 1658
A 6035,f.227 aut.

Glad that Andilly approves of his recent journey [to la T.] Asks for another pamphlet from *curés* of Paris and copy of Bp of Orléans' censure of the Jesuits' apology [of their moral theology].

580727 JEAN FAVIER 27 July 1658
CF 344,f.36 aut.; Gonod 20

Troubles of M. Bellérophon, father and son. 'I am applying myself wholly to my books and what I imagine belongs to my calling.'

R. continued to interest himself in his former tutor, Bellérophon, an Auvergnat like Favier.

580730   ROBERT ARNAULD D'ANDILLY   30 July 1658
A 6035,f.228 aut.

Pamphlets arrived. *Petrus Aurelius* just finished. R. will send his translation of St Basil for criticism; lives in almost total seclusion.

580820   ROBERT ARNAULD D'ANDILLY   20 August 1658
A 6035,f.230 aut.

R's respect for Bp of Angers [Henri Arnauld, Andilly's brother]. Letters sent via Visitation at Tours cause great joy to R's friend, 'a most intelligent and virtuous woman.'
The final reference seems to be to RM Louise Rogier.

580824   ROBERT ARNAULD D'ANDILLY   24 August 1658
A 2035,f.235 aut.

R. has a poor opinion of most of the French bishops.

580910   ROBERT ARNAULD D'ANDILLY   10 September 1658
A 6035,f.244 aut.

Has been in Poitou seeing a benefice [Saint-Clémentin]. Reading Eusebius, feels he is doing God's will. Barillon has just arrived; Caumartin expected.
Henri Barillon was to receive one of R's benefices; Caumartin, Retz's agent, was an old friend of R.

580920   ROBERT ARNAULD D'ANDILLY   20 September 1658
A 6035,f.244 aut.

Andilly has criticised some points in R's translation of Basil. Sorry to have missed the duc de Luynes when he came to Touraine. Many visitors.

581006   ROBERT ARNAULD D'ANDILLY   6 October 1658
A 6035,f.251 aut.

Hopes that the Church will not continue to be rent by controversy [over Jansenism].

581024   ROBERT ARNAULD D'ANDILLY   24 October 1658
A 6035,f.266 aut.

Just back from visiting Mme Bouthillier [his aunt] at Chavigny. Spent two hours with duc de Luynes. Reading du Perron [church history].

581031   M. BELLÉROPHON   31 October 1658
CF 344,f.38 (copied by Favier): Gonod 21

Latin letter of congratulations on work on Canticles.

581109 ROBERT ARNAULD D'ANDILLY   9 November 1658
A 6035,f.268 aut.

Glad that bad weather will now keep visitors away.

581126 ROBERT ARNAULD D'ANDILLY   26 November 1658
A 6035,f.274 aut.

Bp of Angers has sent his censure of Jesuit casuists. Still reading du Perron.

581214 ROBERT ARNAULD D'ANDILLY   14 December 1658
A 6035,f.279 aut.

Has had a bad cold and fever. Left in peace thanks to the weather. Has annotated *Petrus Aurelius*, finished Eusebius, should finish du Perron next day.

581227 ROBERT ARNAULD D'ANDILLY   27 December 1658
A 6035,f.287 aut.

Pastoral letter received. Question of having to sign Sorbonne's censure [of Jansenism].

59/1   [RM LOUISE ROGIER]   1659
M 1214,6

Desires still stricter retreat. Has avoided answering someone who disapproves of his signing [a formulary against Jansenism].

This formulary required all clergy and religious to accept the official view of what was contained in Jansen's book. Arnauld and his friends denied that the incriminated doctrines were in it, and signed at first with that reservation, but then refused unconditional signature.

59/2   [RM LOUISE ROGIER]   1659
M 1214,7

R. getting rid of his benefices. 'We live in perpetual illusion and ignorance of truths, from which death alone draws the veil.'

590126 ROBERT ARNAULD D'ANDILLY   26 January 1659
A 6035,f.299 aut.

Quite content with his present life when he compares it with that which he led in the world.

590211 ROBERT ARNAULD D'ANDILLY   5 February 1659
A 6035,f.303 aut.

Has read the two latest episcopal censures [of casuistry]. Has begun Baronius [church history up to 1198.]

590302   ROBERT ARNAULD D'ANDILLY   2 March 1659
A 6035,f.305 aut.

Discusses censure issued by five bishops [against Jesuits].

590319   ROBERT ARNAULD D'ANDILLY   19 March 1659
A 6035,f.307 aut.

Condemns attack on five bishops.

590409   ROBERT ARNAULD D'ANDILLY   9 April 1659
A 6035,f.316 aut.

Praises book sent by Andilly, especially its explanation of *Pater noster*. Still receiving episcopal letters of censure. Hopes to see him in May at Port-Royal.

590616   ROBERT ARNAULD D'ANDILLY   16 June 1659
A 6035,f.340 aut.

Was at Ponts-sur-Seine a few days earlier and talked about Andilly with Mme Bouthillier. Going to see Bp of Alet.

590712   ROBERT ARNAULD D'ANDILLY   12 July 1659
A 6035,f.347 aut.

Has been at [? Véretz] for past ten days, enjoying great peace.

590804   ROBERT ARNAULD D'ANDILLY   4 August 1659
A 6035,f.357 aut.

From Châlons. Had to go to Ponts on his uncle's orders, and then to Paris to see the comte de Rochefort [later known as prince de Soubise], who was very ill.

590822   ROBERT ARNAULD D'ANDILLY   22 August 1659
A 6035,f.365 aut.

At Véretz. Has been undeservedly praised by a prelate.

590916   [RM LOUISE ROGIER]   16 September 1659
M 1214,13; A 2106,f.11

Bp of Comminges visited two days ago, tried to take R. with him to see Bp of Alet, 'the holiest man there is'.

The Bp of Comminges was Gilbert de Choiseul, of Alet Nicolas Pavillon.

590917   ROBERT ARNAULD D'ANDILLY   17 September 1659
A 6035,f.370 aut.
A friend [G. le Roy] is now sharing his solitude; 'his views delight me'.

590900   [RM LOUISE ROGIER]   [? September] 1659
M 1214,10
Leaving Boulogne, near Chambord, the next day with much regret.

591026   ROBERT ARNAULD D'ANDILLY   26 October 1659
A 6035,f.384 aut.
Had to go to Blois five or six days earlier. Warmly praises Le Roy, who adds a PS himself.
Gaston d'Orléans resided at Blois, where R. had to do a tour of duty as chaplain.

591108   ROBERT ARNAULD D'ANDILLY   8 November 1659
A 6035,f.386 aut.
Had not known duc de Luynes was in Touraine. Asks Andilly's help in action Luynes has taken against one of R's former employees for poaching. Le Roy has been very ill, now better.

591122   ROBERT ARNAULD D'ANDILLY   22 November 1659
A 6035,f.394 aut.
Has written to thank Luynes for kindness. Le Roy better.

591225   ROBERT ARNAULD D'ANDILLY   25 December 1659
A 6035,f.402 aut.
Glad that Andilly escaped an accident. Le Roy obliged to return to Paris; trouble with an eye, and also chest.

591228   ROBERT ARNAULD D'ANDILLY   28 December 1659
A 6035,f.404 aut.
R. now all alone.

60/1   RELIGIEUSE   [? 1660]
M 1214,11
R. expected difficulties and disapproval, but is indifferent to mens' judgment.

60/2   RELIGIEUSE   [? 1660]
M 1214,26; Mug I/8
Importance of a pure heart.

600208 ROBERT ARNAULD D'ANDILLY   8 February 1660
A 6035,f.420 aut.

Illness and death of Gaston d'Orléans kept R. from writing sooner.
He died on 2 February, with R. in attendance.

600222 ROBERT ARNAULD D'ANDILLY   22 February 1660
Charavay, Oct. 1967, no. 32018, aut.
Death of Gaston d'Orléans.

600303 ROBERT ARNAULD D'ANDILLY   3 March 1660
Aut: sold at auction 30 October 1980

R. has had a bad cold; assures Andilly of sincere friendship.

600310 ROBERT ARNAULD D'ANDILLY   10 March 1660
Charavay, April 1891, no. 130, aut.
Expression of thanks.

600405 ROBERT ARNAULD D'ANDILLY   5 April 1660
Tour. aut.; Gonod 200

Intends to leave Véretz in five or six days for Normandy.

600400 [RM LOUISE ROGIER]   [April] 1660
M 1214,15; A 2106,f.11

After visiting Normandy [Abbaye du Val], leaving la T. next day for Paris. Beginning to have doubts about his decision, but will try to carry it through.

600500 RELIGIEUSE   [May 1660?]
M 1214,12; Mug I/2

His stay in Paris has strengthened his dislike of all that is not Christ.

600501 [RM LOUISE ROGIER]   1 May 1660
M 1214,16; A 2106,f.

Has been three days in Paris; must wait for the court to leave before beginning journey to Alet.

600509 [RM LOUISE ROGIER]   9 May 1660
M 1214,17

At Ponts; will go to Touraine after Pentecost [16 May], then to Alet. Has been three days at Fresnes.

600510 [JEAN FAVIER] 10 May 1660
A 2106,f.12 vo.; TC II/17

Death of Gaston d'Orléans very sad but Christian. Greetings to Bellérophon. Trip to Chartreuse put off, but R. still wants to go.

600600 [RM LOUISE ROGIER] [June] 1660
M 1214,14

Obliged to go for some days to Châlons.

600601 [RM LOUISE ROGIER] 1 June 1660
M 1214,18; A 2106,f.8 (dated 3 January 1657)

Has been waiting for Abp of Tours to come to Paris for past week; excessive heat. Leaving in the evening for Châlons.

600620 [RM LOUISE ROGIER] 20 June 1660
M 1214,19

Leaving for Pyrenees next day. Has been warned of Bp of Alet's severity.

600705 [RM LOUISE ROGIER] 5 July 1660
M 1214,20; A 2106,f.13

Arrived at Comminges, praises Bp. Leaving soon for Alet. Already used to Pyrenees.

600708 [RM LOUISE ROGIER] 8 July 1660
M 1214,21; A 2106,f.13 vo.

Frightening country; admires Bp of Comminges more and more 'governing a wild and hard people'.

600723 [RM LOUISE ROGIER] 23 July 1660
M 1214,22; A 2106,f.14

Still at Comminges, waiting for Bp of Alet to return from pastoral visits.

600730 ROBERT ARNAULD D'ANDILLY 30 July 1660
Charavay, Dec. 1883, no. 155, aut.

Praises Bps of Comminges and Alet.

600816 [RM LOUISE ROGIER]   16 August 1660
M 1214,23; A 2106,f.14 vo.

At Alet. Sanctity, kindness and strictness of Bp.; ruggedness of site.

600822 ROBERT ARNAULD D'ANDILLY   22 August 1660
A 6626,f.422 aut.

Had written from Comminges, now at Alet. Admires Bp.

600902 [RM LOUISE ROGIER]   2 September 1660
M 1214,24; A 2106,f.15

Still at Alet. Hopes to be home by 20 October, and will miss Séguenot [his former director, an Oratorian].

600908 ROBERT ARNAULD D'ANDILLY   8 September 1660
TA aut.; Gonod 201

At Alet. Bp's friendship for Andilly. Congratulations on marriage of Andilly's son. Praises Bp of Comminges. Will be still some time in Pyrenees and will then return to Véretz.

601017 ROBERT ARNAULD D'ANDILLY   17 October 1660
A 6626,f.424 aut.

At Véretz. Praises Bp of Alet.

* 601116 RM MARIE-LOUISE [BOUTHILLIER]   16 November 1660
TD/A

'My dear sister, I do not need to say much to you to convince you that it gives me real joy every time I have news from you, for I am sure that you have a sufficiently high opinion of my sincerity to believe that I should not speak like that unless I were expressing the feelings in my heart. I am most concerned that you should believe me genuine, so that, appreciating that fact, you should think a little more often of me before God, since there is some justice in the order of charity, and some obligation to wish the good of those who love us in preference to others. I beg you to be persuaded of this truth, and to ask God for me to show me his will, and at the same time give me grace to submit to it. I promise to pray to him as much as I can for you, wretched though I am. I am besides scandalised at all your formality in your letters. Such ceremonial is not for either of us, and I beg you to cut it out when you write to me. Do not doubt that I am entirely yours with all imaginable affection and charity.'

The copyist has noted that 'he was not yet regular abbot' and his sister had no doubt addressed him as Monsieur l'abbé or by some such formula.

601208   ROBERT ARNAULD D'ANDILLY   8 December 1660
A 6626,f.426 aut.; Gonod,p.202

In Paris since some days; hoping to see Andilly at Port-Royal.

601217   [RM LOUISE ROGIER]   17 December 1660
M 1214,25

In Paris, affairs blocked, has still failed to find a good man for one of his benefices. Abp of Tours more cordial than expected.

601228   [RM LOUISE ROGIER]   28 December 1660
M 1214,28; A 2106,f.15 vo.

Still in Paris, looking for a good man. On good terms with Abp of Tours. Spent Christmas in retreat with Discalced Carmelites of Charenton. Still uncertain where he will live.

Charenton was then a village just outside Paris.

610105   [RM LOUISE ROGIER]   5 January 1661
M 1214,29; A 2106,f.16

Still held up by business in Paris.

610113   [RM LOUISE ROGIER]   13 January 1661
M 1214,30; A 2106,f.17 vo.

Still in Paris; will stop complaining in letters. Waiting 'for Pyrenees to decide'.

610120   ROBERT ARNAULD D'ANDILLY   20 January 1661
A 6626,f.428 aut.

Leaving next day for Champagne, where he will visit two places where Andilly is known.

Hautefontaine, where Le Roy was commendatory abbot, and Retz's home at Commercy.

610202   [RM LOUISE ROGIER]   2 February 1661
M 1214,31; A 2106,f.18

At Ponts-sur-Seine. Still undecided where to live. Dismisses rumour that he is to be appointed Coadjutor to Abp of Tours.

Mazarin had already squashed proposals for the coadjutorship in 1657, but he was on his deathbed (he was to die in March), which may have prompted the rumour.

610211   [RM LOUISE ROGIER]   11 February 1661
M 1214,32; A 2106,f.18 vo.

Will be at Châlons only two or three days, then back to Touraine. If Abp of Tours is still in Paris will discuss plans with him; not right to keep them secret.

610228   [RM LOUISE ROGIER]   28 February 1661
M 1214,35; A 2106,f.20

Has not yet told Abp of Tours his plans; due back next week.

610328   ROBERT ARNAULD D'ANDILLY   28 March 1661
Charavay, aut.

On the death of Mazarin [9 March].

610408   [? JEAN FAVIER]   8 April 1661
A 2106,f.19

Glad to know that [? Favier] agrees with intentions regarding benefice and will accept it.

610728   [RM LOUISE ROGIER]   28 July 1661
M 1214,36

Returns some letters she has sent. Particularly moved by those of RM Agnès on God's judgements.

RM Agnès is probably Agnès Arnauld, Abbess of Port-Royal, (1593–1671), Andilly's sister, who wrote many widely circulated letters.

610928   BISHOP OF ALET [NICOLAS PAVILLON]   28 September 1661
U 4281

Would write more often but for fear of being importunate. No regrets on decisions taken at Alet. One abbey [Beauvais] disposed of, another [Val] soon will be; intends to give a third benefice [Boulogne] to Oratorians of Tours before retiring to remaining abbey [la T.] for the rest of his life; sale of Véretz delayed for family reasons. Hopes to consult with Bp in person when all is in order.

This is the first record of R's decision to settle at la T. as commendatory abbot (like Le Roy at Hautefontaine).

611211   [RM LOUISE ROGIER]   11 December 1661
M 1214,37; A 2106,f.20 vo.

Véretz still not sold, and affair of Val still blocked. Warm greetings to his niece.

This is R's first reference to Louise-Henriette d'Albon, educated at Tours from about 1652, and evidently just about to embark on a religious life.

611217   [RM LOUISE ROGIER]   17 December 1661
M 1214,38; A 2106,f.21; Mug. I/9
Still struggling with impatience at so many delays.

*620214   RM [MARIE-LOUISE BOUTHILLIER]   14 February 1662
TA aut.
'My dear sister. Your letter reached me in Paris, from whence I had not gone as I had hoped, being prevented by business. It is always a consolation for me to learn your news and to see from that that I am still in your mind. I beg you always to keep for me there the share I imagine I ought to have, especially before God, where Christians are obliged to remember each other in relation to Christ, to whom they belong by a bond even more intimate than that which unites us naturally and by blood. In that I am asking you what I intend to do for you throughout my life, praying God in his mercy that the lives of each of us should be entirely for him and that we should be able to give them to him up to the last moment, since there is not one which does not belong to him and for which he will not demand strict account. Please assure the Mother Superior of my very humble respect. I commend myself to my sister with all my heart.'

Although on profession she had taken the name Marie-Louise, in this letter R. addressed her in his own hand as 'Louise-Isabelle', her previous given name. The sister referred to in the last line was Marie-Dorothée (Claude), born 1621, professed in 1637, died 14 May 1680. She had lived at the Annonciades from about the age of nine and took the veil only after overcoming her father's objections on grounds of her delicate health. R. can hardly have known her and no letters to her are known.

62/1   CARDINAL DE RETZ   [1662]
Retz, Œuvres, 1887, vol.VIII, p. 640
Material fortune an obstacle to the true good R. desires for the cardinal.

620211   [RM LOUISE ROGIER]   11 February 1662
M 1214,39
She has had a long illness. His obstacles remain in his way.

620218   MARQUIS DE POMPONNE   18 February 1662
Tour. aut.
Sympathy on Pomponne's disgrace.

Following the disgrace of the minister Fouquet, Pomponne had been exiled to Verdun.

620419   BISHOP OF ALET [NICOLAS PAVILLON]   19 April 1662
TC I/16; U 4281

Recommends Henri Barillon to him.

Like R., and for the same reasons, Barillon made a trip to the Pyrenees for advice about his future.

620501   [RM LOUISE ROGIER]   1 May 1662
M 1214,40

In Paris, still deadlocked.

620522   RELIGIEUSE   22 May 1662
M 1214,27; A 2106,f.48 (dated 30 Jan. 1667); Mug I/12 (Dated 27 Sep. 1662)

Still falling short of his intentions of leading a life of penitence.

620600   [RM LOUISE ROGIER]   [? June] 1662
M 1214,41

She has sent on a letter from the Abbot of Grandmont, regretting that he cannot accept R's nomination of a prior to succeed him at Boulogne. 'In an endless state of uncertainty over the main business'.

Boulogne was a Grandmontine house.

620600a   [RM LOUISE ROGIER]   [? June] 1662
M 1214,43

Endless difficulties.

620703   [RM LOUISE ROGIER]   3 July 1662
M 1214,44

In Paris. Plans to supervise building work at Boulogne. Disgusted at world's insincerity. Séguenot and other Oratorians have been exiled on royal orders for alleged Jansenism, though quite innocent. Saw Séguenot previous day and found him resigned and indifferent to human actions.

620720   [RM LOUISE ROGIER]   20 July 1662
M 1214,45; A 2106,f.26

In Paris. Expected her to be distressed at treatment of Séguenot, but his innocence should console his friends. Paris intolerable; R. longs for retreat.

620816   [RM LOUISE ROGIER]   16 August 1662
M 1214,46; A 2106,f.27

No longer able to contribute to a seminary at Tours; the benefice [Boulogne] has gone to someone falsely accused of Jansenism [Barillon], like the equally innocent recipient [Favier] of his abbey at Beauvais. Delighted at reinstatement of Séguenot. After four days in Paris now back in his solitude for winter; very foggy and isolated by forests.

R. had once thought of giving Boulogne to the Oratorians for a seminary. The solitude is la T.

620818   [RM LOUISE ROGIER]   18 August 1662
M1214,47; A 2106,f.27

Condolences on a loss she has suffered. 'I have established the Reform at la T.' Will be there a few days, then to Boulogne.

Six monks from the abbey of Perseigne had been installed to reform la T.

620818a   [JEAN FAVIER]   18 August 1662
A 2106,f.23

Sorry to have missed him in Paris. Has now been nearly three months in his abbey [la T.] but is obliged to go to Paris on business. Favier's health is poor. Visitors limited to three days, unless close friends, and only allowed into refectory once, so as not to interrupt the monastic regularity.

620822   RELIGIEUSE   22 August 1662
M 1214,33; Mug I/10 (dated 3 July 1662)

Longs to wind up his affairs and start a life of solitude and silence.

620829   [RM LOUISE ROGIER]   29 August 1662
M 1214,48; A 2106,f.27 vo.

At Boulogne, but not now for winter. Work of reform at la T. so important that he wants to stay there some months to ensure its permanence. Work going on at Boulogne, and R. still intends to stay there eventually.

620922   [RM LOUISE ROGIER]   22 September 1662
M 1214,49

At la T. No longer interested in seminary at Tours. Obliged to spend winter with family of bailiff with several children, but tries to accept impaired solitude as God's will. Refers to loss of 'P.M. de L' who had too high an opinion of him.

R. had to stay with the bailiff because the abbot's lodging was not available, and major building went on all through the winter. The 'P.M. de L' is probably Gaston's daughter, Princess Marguerite-Louise de Lorraine, who married Grand Duke Cosmo III of Tuscany in 1661 and left France then.

620922a RELIGIEUSE   22 September 1662
M 1214,34; A 2106,f. 49 vo. (dated 22 May 1667)
Her union with Christ must be total and exclusive.

620927 RELIGIEUSE   27 September 1662
M 1214,26 a: Mug I/8
However holy our desires, God disposes as he wills. She will find God in retreat. Only perishable friendships suffer from separation, not those inspired by Providence.

621101 [RM LOUISE ROGIER]   1 November 1662
M 1214,50; A 2106,f.28: Mug I/12
At la T. She has suffered a new loss, but all human attachments are subject to loss and should be seen as bonds preventing full attachment to God. Missed a bad accident previous day when a beam broke, and whole ceiling collapsed in a room he had just left.

621104 RM THÉRÈSE BOUTHILLIER   4 November 1662
TB 1
He is back from Boulogne, longs for retreat.

621222 RELIGIEUSE   22 December 1662
M 1214,8; Mug I/11
'We must be solitary in spirit and desire if we wish to possess God in our solitudes.'

This, and earlier letters simply addressed to 'une religieuse', could well be to his sister Thérèse, but there is no evidence, and they could have been to any of several persons.

630400 RELIGIEUSE   [? April 1663]
M 1214,52
Glad to hear of harmony in her community.

630416 [RM LOUISE ROGIER]   16 April 1663
M 1214,51
In Paris on business. Abp of Tours well disposed; R. glad.

630428   PERSONNE RETIRÉE (SOMEONE IN RETREAT)   28 April 1663
Mug I/15

'I have not promised God to live in solitude like those . . . who withdraw to monasteries.'

The date must be wrong, perhaps it should be 1662. See next letter.

630430   [RM LOUISE ROGIER]   30 April 1663
M 1214,53

Preparing to give himself solely to God, who has guided him for seven years.

*630430   A SUPERIOR [RM LOUISE ROGIER]   30 April 1663
M 1214,54, This letter has also, more plausibly, been assigned to Mme Bouthillier and the date 12 May 1663 proposed.

'I am quite sure that you will be surprised to learn of my decision to give the rest of my life up to penitence in the habit and the reform of St Bernard. God led me by ways quite unknown to me for several years, but finally for some eight or ten months, since his mercy inspired in me the sentiments I now have, I have begun to see things more clearly than I did, and I am convinced at present that the state in which he wishes me to engage is that of the regular life. That will seem strange to those who measure everything by the customs and usual behaviour of men, and who think that what is established by the majority is what should be practised by all. In truth, if one thinks seriously and objectively of the necessity for all Christians to live in penitence, and of the obligations of those who have been involved in the world, there is much more reason to be amazed at the fact that there are those who imagine that they are giving themselves to God with qualifications and reservations which offend his justice, do not pacify his anger, and in no way accord with the state of a sinner who should return to God by way of a sincere conversion and genuine and total renunciation.

May God be content with the little I do and my desire to do more were I not held back by the weight of my sins. I know that many centuries of the life I intend to embrace cannot for a moment make satisfaction for the life I led in the world, and if I did not find in the ample mercies of God what I cannot find in my actions, however much my person might change, I should live comfortless on earth; but I confess that as the confidence I have in his goodness keeps me from falling into that temptation, it also impels me to abandon myself completely to his providence, so that I submit to his guidance in all things and leave it to him for ever to dispose of my person and all I am. From this you will easily judge how much I need the support and prayers of my friends to obtain a faithful response to the grace God shows me. The world is full of people who have intended, but not executed, things. It is even very rare for those who begin to persevere, yet perseverance alone will be reckoned at God's judgement, and intentions which remain unfulfilled, however holy they may be, will produce nothing but confusion for those who have not completed them. Pray Our Lord therefore, I beseech you, to strengthen my vocation, and give me the spirit of those holy solitaries whose actions, as you know, once delighted me, since I am consecrating myself to retreat and solitude for the rest of my days.'

The holy solitaries of the final sentence are the Desert Fathers, whose Lives had been translated by Arnauld d'Andilly.

630530   RELIGIEUSE   30 May 1663
Mug I/16
He is going to embrace the life of a regular.

630530a   BISHOP OF ALET [NICHOLAS PAVILLON]   30 May 1663
U 4281

Had felt obliged to introduce the 'Reform of St Bernard' into the abbey he retained, and living on the spot thought it useful and perhaps a good example to share the life of the reformed monks: 'After living some months in this way I felt moved to embrace the regular life. The feeling did not last, but very shortly afterwards I felt it much more strongly than before. I felt like that for more than two months without saying a word to anyone, and what I proposed was to devote the rest of my life to penitence.' Then he went to Paris to seek advice from a wise and pious priest, who told him to rest for a while. Three months later returned to la T., where, after six weeks, he felt 'a burning desire to delay no more'. Returned to Paris to seek royal permission to take abbey out of commend and make it regular and is persevering against opposition. 'I see that the life I am undertaking is beyond my strength . . . but I know that nothing is beyond God's power.'

The visit to Paris for advice was in January 1663, when he met the Bp of Comminges at the Institution de l'Oratoire and told him his plan. The priest was probably Bouchard. In mid-April he met Jouaud, leader of the Reform, in Paris and asked for the habit, and on 10 May received royal permission to make la T. regular.

Rancé takes the habit at Perseigne.   13 June 1663

630615   [RM LOUISE ROGIER]   15 June 1663
M 1214,55

Six weeks after he decided to change his dress. 'By God's mercy the yoke I have accepted seems to me such as I hope to bear until my death.'

630805   [RM LOUISE ROGIER]   5 August 1663
M 1214,56

At Perseigne. So far coping with new life. Last benefice [Boulogne] has gone to the brother of his best friend. This 'most virtuous and learned ecclesiastic', though only 22, has been four months with the Bp of Alet, who judges him capable of any post in the Church.

This praise of Henri Barillon, brother of Paul (the best friend) was to be justified subsequently at Luçcon.

630816   [RM LOUISE ROGIER]   16 August 1663
M 1214,57

Thanks her for praying so long for his conversion.

630903   [JEAN FAVIER]   3 September 1663
A 2106,f.31

At Perseigne. Surprised that Favier learned of his entry into religion only through rumor; wrote three months earlier, but letter went astray. His only aim now is a life of penitence. Wholly convinced of his vocation. Bp of Alet has written, giving full approval.

631129   JEAN FAVIER   29 November 1663
CF 344,f.40 aut.; Gonod 22

Has been very ill, still weak. 'I was never more determined . . . to spend my life in solitude and penitence.'

640116   [JEAN FAVIER]   16 January 1664
A 2106,f.33 vo.

At la Trappe. Life there not so extraordinary in its austerity as people say. Regrets difficulties at Beauvais.

Favier had nothing but trouble at Beauvais, with the buildings, with the monks, disinclined to reform, and from the site, some distance from the town. If the date is correct, R. wrote this while recuperating at la T. just before returning to Perseigne to complete his novitiate.

640210   RM LOUISE-HENRIETTE D'ALBON   10 February 1664
M 1214,58; A 2106,f. 45 vo. (dated 10 Feb. 1666)

She has been ill, must accept God's will and live in charity with those around her.

640227 JEAN FAVIER   27 February 1664
CF 344,f.41 aut.; A 2106,f.34

Favier with the Albons, who are causing financial difficulties. R's pension from the abbey of Beauvais will soon be transferred to Favier. 'It is much easier to abandon outward things than to abandon one's own self.'

640430 RM THÉRÈSE [BOUTHILLIER]   30 April 1664
TB 7

Obligations of vocation.

640504 MADAME   4 May 1664
TD; Mug I/17

His feelings.

640527 BISHOP OF ALET [NICHOLAS PAVILLON]   27 May 1664
U 4281

Bp had approved news of his clothing in letter sent by R. a year ago (30 May 1663). R. fell seriously ill three months after entering the novitiate, but never weakened in his resolve to become a monk. Taking vows in three weeks. Prays 'that having so often broken my baptismal vows, God will give me grace to keep those that I am going to make'.

640614 [RM LOUISE ROGIER]   14 June 1664
M 1214,59

Only waiting for his bulls [as regular abbot] to be professed.

Rancé professed at Perseigne.   26 June 1664.

*640630 A SUPERIOR [RM LOUISE ROGIER].   30 June 1664
M 1214,60; A 2106

'This note is to confirm your presentiment of my profession. It took place three days ago, when I dedicated myself to God for the rest of my days in a state which seemed to me very lowly and contemptible and thus very well suited to doing penance for my sins. You ask me what feelings were in my heart at that moment, and in reply I will tell you in a word that I saw myself as a man condemned to hell by the number and gravity of his sins, and believed at the same time that the only way to appease God's wrath was to engage myself in penitence which would finish only with my death, and that the calling I embrace was entirely suitable for someone full of such feelings. Although I saw it as the only way remaining open to me, I did not on that account think that it made my salvation sure, because God often finds our sacrifices unacceptable because we personally are unacceptable, and it happens only too often that his judgements are opposed to those that men have concerning our conduct and our life. I do not know whether mine will be pleasing to him, or whether the public satisfaction I wish to make will find grace in his eyes, but I do know that I have knocked at the only door open to me, and that there was no other way of entering into the peace of Jesus Christ. I still see all the reasons I had for doubting that God's mercy would extend to miseries and aberrations as great as mine, but with all that I am full of hope, and the confidence that God gives me is such that I surrender myself blindly. I leave to him the decision about my eternity; I will try to keep with constant fidelity what my heart promised him countless times before my mouth professed it outwardly. My peace of mind comes from serving a Master who never abandons those who persevere in his service. Finally, he will do as he pleases, he is the lord, and no one has a right to complain, but I will do my duty until I die, at least I will not cease to ask him for grace to do so. That, in a few words, is my present disposition, entire resignation before God's providence and entire surrender to his eternal designs. I remember having read in St John Climacus that a creature who has been unfortunate enough to lose the good graces of his God must not stop the flow of his tears until God tells him, by himself or one of his angels, that his sins are forgiven.' [*The Ladder of Divine Ascent*, First Degree, art.7].

640704   [JEAN FAVIER]   4 July 166[4]
A 2106,f.23 vo. (wrongly dated 1662)

On his recent profession and forthcoming lifelong retreat. Presses Favier to visit him.

640809   [RM LOUISE ROGIER]   9 August 1664
M 1214,63; A 2106,f.35 vo.; Mug I/19

Gradually accepting some of the cares demanded by his new establishment, but has not had a free moment for three weeks. Essential to avoid outside contacts. Quotes St John Climacus.

640900   [RM LOUISE ROGIER]   September 1664
M 1214,64; A 2106,f.35 vo.; Mug I/20

Never enough time for all he wants to do. Too many curious visitors.

641030   [RM LOUISE ROGIER]   30 October 1664
M 1214,67

Obliged to go to Rome; only obedience makes him accept. No time to write to his niece but she should give herself up to God unreservedly.

His niece *(Louise-Henriette d'Albon)* has just been professed at Tours.

641113   [RM LOUISE ROGIER]   13 November 1664
M 1214,68

In Rome. Saw ailing Grand Duke in Florence. He feels unsuited to present task, but obedience is his rule.

At the end of August, R., after barely six weeks at la T., went to Paris to a meeting of Abstinent abbots, and to his dismay was nominated, together with Dominique Georges, Abbot of Val-Richer, to go to Rome to press the case for the Reform, then at a crucial stage. After a few days back at la T., he set off on 19 September, seeing Retz at Commecy on his way and meeting Abbot Georges at Châlons on 8 October. By way of Lyon the party arrived in Florence, where R. was handsomely received, through his connexions with Gaston's daughter, who had married the reigning Grand Duke's son. R.'s friend, Pierre Félibien, accompanied him and kept a diary, but that has perished, and these letters are all that is left to confirm or check extant biographies.

641207   [RM LOUISE ROGIER]   7 December 1664
M 1214,69

Spent an hour and a half with the Pope [Alexander VII] five or six days ago. Well received. The sights of Rome do not interest him, but the churches are more majestic than in France, and inspiring because of so many relics of martyrs.

650608   [RM LOUISE ROGIER]   8 June 1665
M 1214,71 (wrongly dated 7 Dec. 1664); A 2106,f.38 vo.

Justifies his sudden departure from Rome as prompted by advice of others and as causing Abbot of Cîteaux to return to France. Once ordered back left Lyon at once, though ill. Has secured delay of judgement until Retz arrives. Says mass daily at Oratorians' church, though they are not friendly.

R. had very suddenly left Rome in February, and got as far as Lyon before being ordered back. He was back in Rome on 1 April. While it is true that Abbot Vaussin of Cîteaux also returned to France, R. could hardly have anticipated this reaction; he probably fled at what he judged to be imminent defeat.

650619   [RM LOUISE ROGIER]   19 June 1665
M 1214,72

Curia more friendly since his return. Retz's arrival two days ago a great consolation.

Retz in fact arrived in Rome on 13 June.

650715   [RM LOUISE ROGIER]   15 July 1665
M 1214,73; A 2106,f. 39 (only part)
Missing retreat, but tries to accept God's orders. Retz helping his cause. People still criticise his flight from Rome.

Retz, urged specially by the Queen Mother, made a good impression, but changed nothing.

650818   [RM LOUISE ROGIER]   18 August 1665
M 1214,74
Affairs making no progress; tries to accept exile.

650820   [MONKS OF LA TRAPPE]   20 August 1665
Dub I/305
Reminds them of their duties; they must observe the rule as laid down.

Some of the monks had protested when the prior allowed fish to be eaten in the refectory (permitted in Reform houses).

650904   [RM LOUISE ROGIER]   4 September 1665
M 1214,75
Rome no more favourable to the good than any other court. His brothers-in-law, MM. d'Albon and Vernassal, are causing his brother Henri great trouble over settling father's estate.

*650904a   HENRI BARILLON   4 September 1665
P f.761

'If I have given you no sign of my distress at your illness and its continuation, it is not because I failed to feel as I ought about someone as dear to me as you are, but I thought that such outward signs would be no help to you and that you do not doubt how I am disposed towards you. I am sure that God made you ill, consoled you in your sickness, and that the same hand that lay heavy on you sustained you. When God speaks, men cannot do better than [hear?] him. He will have taught you that the time of sickness is precious and that it is then that the souls in whom he has put holy and christian preparation make great progress. I will ask him for the continuation of his grace towards you, and the increase in you of the blessings he has given you so early to esteem and particularly your desire, which I well know, for my conversion. Monasteries are not made for sinners like me unless they work more faithfully than I do to satisfy God's justice with their penitence. Always love me, I beg you, and rest assured that for no one in the world do I have more affection and esteem than for you.

I am waiting for the Boulogne papers to come from Touraine at any moment. I will send you a proxy to receive a year's income, due to me at All Saints', which you will use on the spot for the church and to go on with it, according to a little note I shall send you.

Please assure Monsieur de Morangis of my continuing respects and see that I always retain some share of his honoured favour.

What Monsieur d'Oron tells me of the Dean amazes me so much that I still cannot imagine that it is true.'

It was to Barillon that R. transferred his Grandmontine priory of Boulogne, near Chambord. Morangis was Barillon's uncle and brought him up after his father's death. The transfer had been arranged in May 1663, but took two years to complete. Barillon was ordained deacon on 19 September 1665. The last sentence remains wholly mysterious.

650925 JEAN FAVIER   25 September 1665
CF 344,f.43 aut.; Gonod 24

Had hoped to return from Rome sooner. Financial problems at Beauvais.

650929 [RM LOUISE ROGIER]   29 September 1665
M 1214,76; A 2106,f.40 (dated 22 Sep.)

Totally frustrated by affairs. Withdraws whenever possible to tombs of martyrs and apostles, and yesterday visited nine churches prescribed for pilgrims. Retz well considered in Rome.

651015 [RM LOUISE ROGIER]   15 October 1665
M 1214,77; A 2106,f.39 vo. (dated 15 August)

'Rome as insupportable as court once was'; only visits to holy places consoles him. Death of much younger sister.

Marie, comtesse de Vernassal, had died in Auvergne, aged about thirty-six, leaving two sons and a daughter all under seven.

651201 [RM LOUISE ROGIER]   1 December 1665
M 1214,78

Asks her to convey respects to Bp of Angers, through whom he had sent letter. His health not bad in Rome. As pleased as she at completion of convent church [of the Visitation].

Henri Arnauld, Andilly's brother, was Bp of Angers.

651229 RELIGIEUSE   29 December 1665
M 1214,80; A 2106,f.41

She is fortunate in her detachment from creatures. R. does not expect to see her again, as only obedience will move him from la T., but 'those who serve Christ are united by his divine spirit so that physical distance cannot separate them'.

*66/1 RM MARIE-LOUISE [BOUTHILLIER]   [BEFORE 1667]
TD/A

'My very dear sister. We shall not fail to do as you wish, and feeble and wretched though our prayers may be, we shall offer them to Our Lord Jesus Christ for your holy community. We should have much to gain if you grant us the same grace, and if we share in some way in the holy and withdrawn life you lead, which, being wholly freed from worldly contacts and conversations with men, brings you close to God and lets you find in a state which is still mortal the blessed peace enjoyed by the angels in the bosom of the divine majesty. Praise God, my dear sister, praise him without ceasing for setting you apart in his mercy and as it were hiding you in the secret of his countenance; praise him for the fact that one of your chief obligations is no longer to see anything which might distract you from the continual assiduity with which souls consecrated to him must incessantly look on him. I pray him with all my heart to give you ever renewed grace and make you more and more worthy of his goodness towards you in preferring you to an almost infinite number of persons whom he leaves committed to the vanity of the outside world. I am in Christ with all possible affection' [your . . .].

66/2 RELIGIEUSE   [?1666]
M 1214,62

In the cloister one must follow God's, not one's own, spirit. No advantage of birth must count and at la T. all most menial tasks go to those of gentle birth.

660104 RM LOUISE-HENRIETTE D'ALBON   4 January 1666
M 1214,83

Warm encouragement in her vocation.

660111 RELIGIEUSE [? RM LOUISE ROGIER]   11 January 1666
M 1214,81; A 2106,f.43

She has praised his patience, he must try to live up to it.

660119 JEAN-FRANÇOIS CORNUTY   19 January 1666
MS *Chronique de Tamié*, Burnier, *Hist. de Tamié*

In Rome. Welcomes Cornuty as recruit to la T.

The Letters of Armand-Jean de Rancé 29

Cornuty, a student at Collège des Bernardins in Paris, had left without warning and arrived at la T., asking to be stabilised there instead of Tamié. This caused much annoyance to the Abbot of Tamié, a fellow student of Cornuty, but R. took Cornuty, on the unique condition that he promised to return to Tamié if that monastery were ever reformed; it was, and he did return.

660202 RELIGIEUSE[? RM LOUISE ROGIER]   2 February 1666
M 1214,82; A 2106,f.43 vo.

Hopes at last to leave Rome and to be back at la T. by early April.

Alexander VII issues Brief *In Suprema*.   **19 April 1666.**

660622 RM LOUISE-HENRIETTE D'ALBON   22 June 1666
M 1214,85

She shows right sentiments about religious life.

660819 [RM LOUISE ROGIER]   19 August 1666
M 1214,86; A 2106,f.45

Reform defeated [by *In Suprema*], but penitential life at la T. safe from threat.

660915 [RM LOUISE ROGIER]   15 September 1666
M 1214,87; A 2106,f.45 vo.

R. will go on writing to her as she is not of the world. Difficulties of his brother [Henri] over inheritance.

661022 [JEAN FAVIER]   22 October 1666
A2106,f.46

Benefices must be given only to persons of proven piety. Favier's duty is to supervise the abbey at Beauvais, and reside there if possible. Only gives advice because Favier insists.

*661120 [? RM LOUISE ROGIER]   20 November 1666
M 1214,61

'My life passes by so rapidly that the days last only for moments, although I do not include any contact with people from outside, write only very rarely and apart from necessity, we speak to each other only three times a week in our monastery. Everyone lives in strict silence. Presence in choir, manual labour, a little solitude, and some business that superiors cannot avoid take up all the time and often make me say that life is not long enough for the service we owe to God, although it is too long for the great number of infidelities I commit. The reversal I see in our observance might well upset me and disturb the peace of my solitude, but so far God has given me such resignation to his will that I preserve my peace amid the agitation of our Order. I resume my life in a stricter penitence than before; we have added something to our accustomed silence and retreat, and we abandon ourselves unreservedly into God's hands.'

670215   DAME DE PIÉTÉ (PIOUS LADY)   15 February 1667
Mug I/21

Sorry she is in such poor health.

670422   RELIGIEUSE   22 April 1667
Mug I/23

Visit of an abbot [? Beaufort]. Bread better than it ought to be. Religious vocation a special grace.

Rancé attends General Chapter at Cîteaux for first
and only time, reports on negotiations in Rome
and registers his formal protest.   9–16 May 1667

670709   RELIGIEUSE   9 July 1667
M 1214,79

All the practices of religious life are empty and hypocritical without complete surrender of oneself to God.

670828   RELIGIEUSE   28 August 1667
M 1214,42 (undated); A2106,f.49; Mug I/26

'Religious life must be always progressing and advancing; . . . Persevere in hating the world.'

670903   [JEAN FAVIER]   3 September 1667
A2106,f.50

Regrets distress caused by his letter. As Favier cannot reside at Beauvais, he should resign in favour of someone who can, keeping enough for a pension, as he has no private means.

* 670910   RM MARIE-LOUISE [BOUTHILLIER]   10 September 1667
TD/A

'My dear sister. I cannot fail at the beginning of this new year to tell you that I pray Our Lord to make it a happy one for you and to fill you more and more with his blessings and gifts of grace. I am not speaking thus as a mere compliment, but from my innermost heart. I beg you too for your part to respond to my sentiments and help me with your prayers. That is the only mark of friendship we can render each other, all the more as God usually listens to those who have some interest in praying for each other. We are about to begin lenten penitence, that is, to live for forty days as we should live our whole life, yours and mine, my dear sister, being wholly devoted to works of penitence and exercises of mortification, especially fasting, solitude and silence. As you will be very much present to me in the course of this holy career, I beg you too to pay serious attention before God to my needs and wretchedness at this same time, so that we may meet at the feet of the One who must be our judge, and that you may prepare him through your lamentations to treat me with mercy when he comes to judge the world in his justice. I hope for this grace from your charity. Do me the grace of also believing that I am most affectionately and truly yours etc.

PS I am sending by Father Prior to you and my sister two Camaldolese in oak with two medals. I take the liberty of assuring Madame de Rancé of my humble respects and commending myself to her prayers, and I am also sending her a Camaldolese with indulgences. She will still remember my name. Commend me to my sister; I am not writing to her and she can apply to herself everything I tell you.'

The new year is the monastic year, beginning on Holy Cross day (14 September). Carved figures of Camaldolese are often referred to as presents from la Trappe, but it remains a mystery why these should have been chosen. Madame de 'Rancé' is clearly a scribal error for Rantzau; Elizabeth de Rantzau (1627–1706) at the age of twelve married her cousin, who became maréchal de France (1609–50); she was converted from Lutheranism in 1644. When she lost her husband she decided to take the veil, and entered the Annonciades in 1652, being professed next year as Marie-Elizabeth. She signed as prioress in 1660, and in September 1666 left with three other nuns to found a priory at Hildesheim, in her native Germany, where she died at an advanced age. From this letter it would seem that she had returned, at least on a visit, to Paris.

671106 [SEBASTIEN CAMBOUT DE PONTCHÂTEAU]   6 November 1667
PR 47, f.111

Agrees with proposal of retreat for a friend. Praises letter from Pontchâteau to Le Camus, who has also written to fr[ère] Benoît [Deschamps, whose brother was at Port-Royal].

The letter was sent under the pseudonym Montfrein.

680200   SEBASTIEN CAMBOUT DE PONTCHÂTIEU   [? February 1668]
PR 47,f.114

Thanks him for recipe for broth. Sends seeds requested. M. Deschamps now fr Benoît, clothed fifteen days before. Boxwood forks enclosed. Respects to M. Arnauld.

Pontchâteau was a keen gardener. Boxwood objects were standard souvenirs of la T. Benoît was professed on 23 February 1669, and must therefore have been clothed a year earlier.

680305   SEBASTIEN CAMBOUT DE PONTCHÂTEAU   5 March 1668
PR 47,f.112

Glad that Pontchâteau had a favourable impression from his visit.

680819   RP PROVINCIAL, CELESTINES [LOUIS TERTORIN]   19 August 1668
TC I/60

Denies soliciting Jacques Puiperrou to leave the Celestines, and only allowed him to visit after a year, but when he insisted on leaving his order, R. thought he must accept him. Asks Provincial to drop opposition to this translation.

Jacques was the first of several Celestines to come to la T., partly at least to avoid persecution for alleged Jansenist sympathies.

680828   [SEBASTIEN CAMBOUT DE PONTCHÂTEAU]   28 August 1668
U 863,orig.;PR47,f.113

Touched at Pontchâteau's sympathy. 'I should not like M. Le C[amus] to wish to be a bishop. . but he should not be so reluctant as to be excluded.' Hopes to see him appointed.

He had to wait until 1671.

681024   ROBERT ARNAULD D'ANDILLY   24 October 1668
A 6073,f.134 aut.

Comforted at restoration of peace in the Church and to learn from Andilly's letter 'that you are still what you were six or seven years ago as far as I am concerned'.

This is the first extant letter after 20 January 1661, and almost certainly none was written in the meantime. The reason was clearly the persecution of Port-Royal, as is proved by the resumption of relations so soon after the conclusion of peace negotiations.

681027   RP PROVINCIAL, CELESTINES [LOUIS TERTORIN]   27 October 1668
TC I/61

The prior of the Celestines in Paris will have brought the Provincial up to date. R. maintains his defence. Jacques Puiperrou will always be grateful to the Order in which he began religious life.

681030   RP PRIEUR [? BARBEAUX]   30 October 1668
Autographes Troussure, p. 533

If the prior's official duties threaten his salvation he should resign, but otherwise do his duty. Read Scripture, St Augustine on the Psalms, St John etc. Avoid 'anciens' (unreformed members of the community). R. apologises for venturing to give advice at all.

In many reformed houses the existing members who would not accept reform stayed on in their former way of life, and this duality led to much friction.

681119   ARCHBISHOP OF PARIS [HARDOUIN DE PÉRÉFIE]   19 November 1668
TC I/14

R. defends his acceptance of a priest from Saint-Victor, who is writing to Abp himself and begging approval.

This is the future dom Le Nain.

681119a   RP PRIEUR, SAINT-VICTOR [EUSTACHE DE BLÉMUR]   19 November 1668
TC I/15

If the religious [Le Nain] neglected formalities in leaving Saint-Victor, the demands of his salvation excuse him.

681227   BISHOP OF EVREUX [HENRI DE MAUPAS DE TOUR]   27 December 1668
TD A

Louis Guérout, professed at la T. before introduction of reform and condemned by Abbot of Clairvaux, has been a vagabond in diocese of Evreux, saying mass at St-Martin, Laigle.

69/1　[GUILLAUME LE ROY]　[? 1669]
TC I/67; Dubois I p.365

He should resign his abbey, but not keep income of 2000 livres from land. He is more concerned with his own welfare than that of religious. He should live modestly with fewer servants.

690130　[RM LOUISE ROGIER]　30 January 1669
M 1214,88; A 2106,f.54 vo. (dated 20 January)

Responsibilities of a superior.

690225　RELIGIEUSE　25 February 1669
Mug I/22

R. should be asking her advice on the duties of a superior.

690324　RP ABBÉ [OF ORVAL: CHARLES DE BENZERADT]　24 March 1669
Carp, p. 236; Mug I/24

Delighted to know of abbot's intention to introduce reform; willing to travel to meet him.

R. met him at Châtillon in April.

690326　BISHOP OF PAMIERS [ETIENNE CAULET]　26 March 1669
TD A

Sends a note of some practices they are trying to introduce at la T. Dom Pierre le Nain took the habit four months ago.

Caulet had close connexions with Saint-Victor, hence his interest in dom le Nain.

690523　HENRI BOUTHILLIER, CHEVALIER DE RANCÉ　23 May 1669
Tour. aut.

Greetings

690529　[RM LOUISE ROGIER]　29 May 1669
M 1214,89; A 2106,f.54 vo. (partial)

Happy to know that peace now reigns in her community. Her recent loss of a friend should teach her to despise the things of this world.

690611   JEAN FAVIER   11 June 1669
CF 344,f.45 aut.; Gonod 25

Favier is in Paris with M. d'Albon, who still delays. Urges him to come on a visit soon.

Favier remained on close terms with the Albons to the end of his life.

690717   FR. ALEXANDRE [DE PATROS], SEPTFONS   17 July 1669
TD B: TC II/41 (dated 14 April 1669)

Alexandre had spent his novitiate at la T. and is now treating his own abbot badly on the pretext that what he learned at la T. was not done at Septfons. He must obey.

While proper buildings were being constructed at Septfons novices were sent to la T. for a year or two. Alexandre came in 1668, and was then aged forty-four, perhaps a source of friction with an abbot ten years younger.

690817   RP PROVINCIAL, CELESTINES [LOUIS TERTORIN]   17 August 1669
TC I/62

Jacques Puiperrou has written critically about the Celestines to a former confrère. R. disclaims responsibility, and now that the Celestines have excommunicated Jacques and censured R., he has to defend himself against false rumours.

*691218   RM MARIE-LOUISE [BOUTHILLIER]   18 December 1669
TA orig.; Mug I/25

'I have read your letter, my very dear sister, and it was most consoling for me to see in it the fear you have of displeasing God, and your holy resolve never to have a hand in anything contrary to the fidelity you owe him. Having thought a lot about your present difficulty, and how you should behave in the actual state of your monastery, I will simply say that you cannot in conscience consent to any changes in the strictness prescribed by your rule in maintaining your grills and enclosures. First of all, you promised God by a solemn vow to maintain them as they were established in the institution of your Order. I can see no reason which might free you from so pressing an obligation, or dispense you from so important a commitment, taken at the foot of the altar. The preservation of your monastery should carry no weight in your mind to the prejudice of what you owe to God. He does not want us to do good, however great it may appear to us, by ways which are illicit. And it is an obvious sign that he does not demand that from us when he gives us legitimate means of doing it. If the universe were about to perish I must not take a step to prevent its destruction which is not in God's order and according to his law. That is the view of the saints; and can you imagine that you are acting according to God's law by violating a most holy law? And that your conduct is according to his order when you break an important promise publicly made to him, as your rule lays down? If your observance is destroyed, and only way you can prevent it perishing is illegitimate, its ruin will not be imputed to you. But if you break the vow you made to God, you must believe that he will call you to account for it, and will judge your action in the severity of his justice. There are rules and laws of external discipline which may suffer changes and modifications as times vary, but as for those which aim essentially at the preservation of holiness, and are, as it were, guardians of the spirit with which every observance should be animated, it is never permitted to deviate from them; they must at all times be inviolable in our hearts. They are like the vital defences which no consideration should make us abandon. You cannot doubt that the rule in question is of that nature, if you regard yourselves in the divine plan and that of your Institution as chosen souls, whom he has hidden in the secret of his countenance, like chaste brides, to whom he has forbidden all contact with the children of men, in order to make you more worthy of that holy familiarity which he wishes to have with you.

The particular difference and characteristic distinguishing you from other observances is separation from the world. You were mainly founded to follow in the footsteps of the Blessed Virgin, to imitate her in the very strict retreat in which she lived; and your observance only took the name of the Annunciation because the Virgin was never more alone, more cut off from men, than when she received the visit of the blessed archangel. That is so expressly pointed out in the story of Blessed Mother Victoria, your foundress, that you cannot fail to know it. It is in that intention that you publicly take a fourth vow to open your grills only four times a year to your fathers, mothers, brothers and sisters, and never to bring about, either by yourselves or through others, any alteration whatsoever in the integrity of that vow. Your superiors pledge themselves to it afresh before the whole community after their election. You are even allowed to take a fifth vow, to commit yourself never to see anyone, as your foundress did. All that clearly shows that the vow, which it is now maintained you should abolish, is something so essential and primordial in your Institution that you cannot break it without doing a mortal injury. That separation from men is so much your spirit that the Jesuit Father Bernardino, to whom God had given special knowledge of matters affecting your observance, when consulted by your Mothers, who wanted to know what was the main point of your vocation, answered that this lay in detachment and distance from the world. That can be seen again in the same life, written in Italian, by Father Fabius Ambrosius Spinola and is worthy of note. He calls this vow the "apple of your observance's eye", he says it is like the seal and defence of the Order, and exhorts you all to maintain it with unshakable fidelity, not only in its substance but in all that concerns it. I am not afraid to say that if there were no other expedient for preserving your community than that of departing from that fourth vow, which I would never agree to, such preservation, implying the destruction of your spirit, could only be external, and of brief duration. It would be plain that God would not want it to last longer, and that it would be within the order of his providence that it should not be extended; and you would be obliged to acquiesce and suffer in resignation what you could not prevent by right and legitimate means.

Secondly, you should be persuaded, my dear sister, that nothing is more liable to bring about the ruin of your house and bring on your monastery the misfortune you seek to avoid than to abolish holy principles and introduce relaxation in their place. The only reason regular observances are destroyed is that God withdraws the protection he gave them at the time of their original fidelity. What estranges him is when he is constrained to withdraw either by blatant disorders or hidden faults and secret infidelities. Thus the main care of religious souls, when they realize that God is no longer looking upon them in his usual way, should be to examine with special attention what defect there may be in their conduct, to repair any evil they may find, and if it should happen that they can observe nothing to account for the change, to groan at errors and wretchedness unknown to them, to make themselves still more faithful than they were, and to ask God with fervent prayers not to turn away from them the face of his mercy; finally to appease his wrath by groans and tears. These are the ways the saints have followed in times of affliction. This is how they seem often to have obliged heaven to change from rigour to favourable attitudes. But if, instead of behaving in the same way and using the same remedies, one seeks to cure the ills by human skills, one mitigates rules which appear too hard, one lessens their austerity so as to make them accord better with the supposed weakness of men, and one tries to moderate what one imagines to be too difficult, on the pretext of allowing more people to practise them, then there is no doubt that such carnal prudence harms the trust we should have in divine providence, that such precautions are contrary to his commandment to put our hope in him alone, and that this laxity which we adopt through false wisdom gives him good cause to withdraw from us and deprive us more and more of the effects of his mercy.

I will say, my dear sister, that God formed regular observances through the intermediary of his saints; the laws by which they should be guided are not human inventions, but holy rules written by his hand, which is the Holy Spirit, who has engraved them in the hearts of those who left them to us. It is beyond doubt that to abolish them is to oppose God's plan; it is to elevate one's own opinion above his wisdom, it is to prefer one's own feelings to his guidance, it is to try to destroy what he has made. For your special preservation God has wished that you should have only very little contact with the world, and do you think that you cannot survive unless this contact is greater than what he set up? God closes your gates and grills so that you should persevere in fidelity and in the purity you owe him, and you claim that in order to remain in being you must open the same gates and the same grills that he closed? It is hardly likely that you should reach the same ends by such different ways, and it must necessarily be either that he is wrong or that you are mistaken. Note, however, that there is more reason than ever for staying away from the world, since its corruption is infinitely more dangerous than when the rules separating you from it were made and human weakness is much greater than at the time of your foundation.

To conclude, my dear sister, my view is that you should remain within your obligations, keep with constant fidelity the vows you made to God, declare that you cannot consent to any contravention of those vows, oppose it with all your might; but in all things behave with such moderation and charity that those who do not share your views know from the simplicity and gentleness of your conduct that you are only acting under the impulse of the true spirit and the urgent prompting of your conscience. If your view prevails, remain in peace, whatever may be the consequences, and give God eternal thanks for not permitting so specious a temptation as that which may have arisen for the preservation of your house to prevail over your fidelity. If the contrary opinion wins, endure without protest or murmur the establishment of these supposed dispensations, pray hard for those who have contributed to having them introduced, because they will be in much need of prayer, but take care never to approve them, consent to them, or use them. Do not heed the thoughts of those who try to persuade you that your conscience obliges you to help your community by deserting your vows. You cannot owe or render it any assistance by methods which are forbidden to you. I repeat yet again, it is by God's order that you have broken off contact with the world; approaching it again and renewing links with it is clearly acting against God's will, destroying Christ's invisible temple on the pretext of preserving the visible one. We shall pray him with all the force at our command to give you the necessary discernment and firmness to do nothing at the present juncture which is unworthy of the honour you enjoy of being solely consecrated to him. I am in him, my dearest sister, as he knows and as I cannot sufficiently express, yours etc.

PS I beg you, my dearest sister, to assure the Mother Superior of my humble service and my gratitude at the honour she does me of remembering me. I could not write to you in my own hand because of an injury which, though slight, prevents me doing so.

Please do not forget to commend me to my sister.'

The Annonciades Célestes were founded in Genoa by RM Vittoria Fornari and Fr Bernardino Zannoni, SJ, and given papal approval in 1604. As R. says, their Constitutions included the vow of enclosure as here described. The Order came to Paris in 1623. The question of relaxing the strict vow of enclosure, in order to attract more recruits, came up several times in the century.

691227 RM PRIEURE [ANNONCIADES CÉLESTES, PARIS]   27 December 1669
Mug I/25

On maintenance of the grill and their fourth vow; even if their supply of recruits dries up, they must never sacrifice the integrity of their original institution by mitigations.

See above. The prioress was RM Marie-Christine Leprestre (1614–81), who entered the convent at the age of sixteen in 1630. She was prioress for fourteen years altogether and was one of a few nuns who took the optional fifth vow (which she observed for twenty years). As a result of this she never saw her brothers (her father died when she was 3) even at times normally permitted under the fourth vow, of which she was a fierce defender.

691230   RP PASQUIER QUESNEL, CONG. ORAT.   30 December 1669
U 1168 orig.; Tans,1

Guillaume, younger brother of Pasquier, is trying his vocation at la T.

An Oratorian like his brother, Guillaume had been teaching philosophy at le Mans.

70/1   RP VICAIRE, VAL-DIEU   [1670]
TD A

Sympathy on death of their prior.

Val-Dieu was a Carthusian house near la T. The vicaire *was the prior's deputy.*

*70/2   RM MARIE-LOUISE [BOUTHILLIER]   [? 1670]
TA aut

'The only signs we can give each other of the friendship which God wishes to exist between us, my dear sister, consists in helping each other by our prayers, and never ceasing to ask him to prepare us for his last judgement by entirely destroying ourselves. You tell me that I have completely left the world; I agree, but there is a world from which one separates oneself without much trouble and with little merit, and outward things are of such little consideration that one does not need great virtue to give them up. The main thing is to regret one's self, to live in sincere self-denial, to fill oneself with the spirit of Christ while genuinely renouncing that of the world, and never to resume what one once left by conceiving new affections which henceforth take the place of those destroyed and cause us the same cares, the same moods, and the same anxieties. That is a misery so common among persons specially consecrated to God's service, and so harmful to their peace of mind and salvation, that one cannot be too vigilant not to fall into such a dangerous trap, which devils lay in the strictest monasteries and the most regular observances. I pray God, my dear sister, to make you perfectly detached and so pure in his eyes that there is nothing in you to prevent him hearing you when you ask him, for me, for that holy frame of mind which I shall ask him for you all my life. Remember me and my miseries, I beg you again.

'I am sending the only cherry-wood cross I have left to Mother Prioress with a Camaldolese; I am her obedient servant, and beg her to pray God for me. Monsieur Pinette is my intimate friend and you [will find him ?] the same.'

700100 RELIGIEUSES, SAINT-ANTOINE, PARIS [January 1670]
TD C
Religious make their vows before an abbot as witness only; the Rule is their master and director.

R's aunt had been Abbess of the Cistercian house of Saint-Antoine until 1652, and was succeeded by two daughters of the powerful M. Molé, garde des sceaux. They refused to introduce, or even tolerate, reform and two or three of the nuns wrote to R. through their confessor, asking him to help.

700100a RP PRIEUR, TIRONNEAU January 1670
TD A
Criticises prior for causing dissension and lack of edification.

The commendatory abbot of this small house (diocese of Le Mans) was Erard de la Madeleine, Dean of Autun, R's friend; at least one former monk of la T. was there until he died in 1671, which may explain R's intervention in their affairs.

700101 RP ASSISTANT DU GÉNÉRAL [SAINT-MAUR] 1 January 1670
TC II/35
Did not know that X was going to come, but cannot send him back. R. had no part in making him give up post in RP's house and greatly esteems his congregation.

Almost certainly refers to Maur Aubert (cf. 700219). The two assistants in 1670 were Benoît Brachet and Claude Martin.

700105 CARDINAL JEAN BONA 5 January 1670
TD A
Congratulations on promotion to cardinal.

700115 RP PASQUIER QUESNEL, CONG. ORAT. 15 January 1670
U 1168, orig; Tans, 2
Report on Guillaume Quesnel: R. still thinks he has a vocation.

700124 JEAN FAVIER 24 January 1670
CF 344,f.47 aut.; A 2106,f.55; Gonod 26
M. de Tillemont spent a week seeing his brother [Le Nain] who was then a novice.[He was professed 21 November 1669] Came with Gérard. Only allowed to eat in the refectory on the last day. R. will write to Le Camus. Sad state of Bellérophon: 'all his fine human learning does not help him'.

Sébastien Le Nain de Tillemont (1637–98) was a renowned ecclesiastical historian, of strong Jansenist sympathies. The nature of Bellérophon's troubles is not known.

700216 BISHOP OF ALET [NICOLAS PAVILLON]   16 February 1670
TC I/17; TD A

Surprised to see Hardy at la T. but could not turn him away.

François Hardy, former theologal [canon theologian] of Alet, was professed as dom Paul in March 1671, aged about forty-six, and died in 1675. The bp was very displeased at losing him.

700216a RM LOUISE-HENRIETTE D'ALBON   16 February 1670
M 1214,92; A 2106,f.55 (partial); Mug I/28

Her father wants her to move, but she will find similar difficulties wherever she goes. If she expected religious life to satisfy her personal desires, she was mistaken. He will not try to adjudicate between her and her superior, but she must submit.

The superior was RM Louise Rogier. Later letters indicate that a clash of temperaments had provoked this trouble.

700219 RP GÉNÉRAL, CONG. DE SAINT-MAUR   19 February 1670
TC I/22

Refuses to return his religious.

The General was Bernard Audebert (1670–72), the religious Maur Aubert, professed in February 1671. This, and similar incidents, led to the Maurists appealing to Rome against such translations, and they were given a bull to prevent further clashes.

700224 RELIGIEUSES, SAINT-ANTOINE, PARIS   24 February 1670
TC I/53; TD C

Encourages them in seeking reform; does not sign the letter 'for considerable reasons'.

700224a RP PASQUIER QUESNEL, CONG. ORAT.   24 February 1670
U 1168 orig; Tans 3

Note on Guillaume Quesnel, who has taken the habit.

700405 BISHOP OF ALET [NICOLAS PAVILLON]   5 April 1670
U 848,? orig; TC I/18; Gonod 203

He only gave the habit to Paul Hardy after testing him for three weeks and on his refusal to return to Alet.

700615   RP PROVINCIAL, CELESTINES [FR FRANÇOIS GERVAISE]   15 June 1670
TC I/63

Arrival of more Celestine recruits causes R. both joy and sorrow. He never invited them and, while he would do what he could for Celestine order, finds it less flourishing than its Provincial does. Recent insulting letter should make him wary of attacking R's orthodoxy. Celestines now so decadent as to annul orginal bull against translation of its founder, Pope Celestine V [1294].

Seven Celestines arrived, and more were to follow. As the Order was in some domestic turmoil as well as troubled by Jansenism, there was a real risk that all its best members might contract out. Many Orders founded in the Middle Ages included in their original papal bulls of approval a stipulation against the translation of their members to prevent instability and poaching, but R. always maintained that such a prohibition lapsed if the Order in question fell into decadence.

700713   ABBOT OF CÎTEAUX [JEAN PETIT]   13 July 1670
TD A; Mug I/29

Respectful greetings on his election [20 June 1670].

700728   RM [MARIE-LOUISE] BOUTHILLIER   28 July 1670
Mug I/30

She wants to serve God. Hard to find suitable monasteries but the one in which she is is protected from all drawbacks. Confirms that rule of enclosure must be observed.

The address is simply 'his sister' but the final phrase seems to rule out Thérèse, the Cistercian, who never raised the question.

700805   RP PASQUIER QUESNEL, CONG. ORAT.   5 August 1670
U 1168, orig.; Tans 4

Asks for paper for MS book for use in choir.

700817   RP PASQUIER QUESNEL, CONG. ORAT.   17 August 1670
U 1168 orig.; Tans 5

Asks for MS paper for Abbot of Septfons also 'my intimate friend'.

700817a   RP PROVINCIAL, CELESTINES [FR. GERVAISE]   17 August 1670
Mug I/31

Concerning a Celestine monk now at la T.

700900 [RM LOUISE ROGIER] [September] 1670
M 1214,70; Mug I/27

Praises calm acceptance of the death of Abp of Tours on part of Louise-Henriette [R's niece and the Abp's great-niece].

Victor Bouthillier, Abp of Tours, died 12 September 1670.

700917   RP PASQUIER QUESNEL, CONG.ORAT. 17 September 1670
U 1168, orig.; Tans 6

Guillaume Quesnel has been ill but is now better. Further mention of paper for choir book.

700929 [RM LOUISE ROGIER] 29 September 1670
M 1214,91; A 2106,f.56 (partial)

R's only criticism is that she did not examine his niece's vocation carefully enough. Death of Abp of Tours unexpected: 'Two days to account to God for forty years as a bishop! What a terrible thing!'

The niece Louise-Henriette, had been brought up from an early age at the Visitation house in Tours, but only decided to take the veil there in about 1663. RM Rogier became superior again in 1667, until 1673, but as part of the trouble came from the Albon family, she could hardly be held responsible. Louise-Henriette was headstrong, favourable to Jansenist rigour, and in no way docile.

701000   RP PASQUIER QUESNEL, CONG.ORAT. [September/October] 1670
U 1168,orig.; Tans 7

Guillaume Quesnel has now left, for Limoges. R. rejects offer of payment.

701019   RP PASQUIER QUESNEL, CONG.ORAT. 19 October 1670
U 1168,orig.; Tans 8

Still kindly disposed towards Guillaume Quesnel.

701101   JEAN FAVIER 1 November 1670
CF 344,f.49 aut.; A 2106,f.58 vo.; Gonod 27

R. has been ill for eight or nine months with a slow fever, sometimes acute. Mme de la Barge at last reconciled with her parents, M. and Mme d'Albon.

Claude-Catherine, the eldest daughter, had married François de la Barge; the cause of the dispute is unknown.

701122   RP PASQUIER QUESNEL, CONG.ORAT. 22 November 1670
U 1168,orig.; Tans 9

Greetings.

701201 [RM LOUISE ROGIER]　　　　　　　　　　1 December 1670
M 1214,93; A 2106,f.58 (partial)

Denies rumours that he may now succeed his uncle as Abp. Sorry for the recently-deceased for being too little concerned with eternity.

71/1　RM ABBESSE, SAINT-ANTOINE, PARIS [MADELEINE MOLÉ]　　[1671]
TD A (fragment)

Purely formal.

710117　RP PASQUIER QUESNEL, CONG.ORAT.　　　17 January 1671
U 1168,orig.; Tans 10

Refers to Guillaume Quesnel, now happy.

710121　RP BERNARD [DU TEILLÉ],　　　　　　21 January 1671
　　　　　Collège des Bernardins, Paris
BN 23497, orig; Gonod 205

Disciplinary problems at college. Difficulty in finding worthy candidates for ordination.

710129　[RM LOUISE ROGIER]　　　　　　　　29 January 1671
M 1214,95; A 2106,f.59 (partial)

Trouble with one of the nuns [probably his niece]. Sorry for recently promoted Bp of Lombez, and for some very close friends similarly promoted, not one of whom he has congratulated. Episcopal office a heavy burden.

Roger Cosmas, a Feuillant, had just been made Bp of Lombez, and among the other four new bishops were R's close friends Harlay, Paris, and Le Camus, Grenoble.

710225　ABBOT OF CÎTEAUX [JEAN PETIT]　　　25 February 1671
TD A; Mug I/33

Respects and sympathy on his escape from attempted poisoning.

Georges Bourée, monk of Cîteaux, was convicted and executed after the abbot and others were taken ill following a poisoned meal on 6 February.

710226　RELIGIEUSES, SAINT-ANTOINE, PARIS　　26 February 1671
TD C

They are now allowed to practise the proper observance. They should ask permission of Abbot of Citeaux to keep abstinence, failing which they should firmly resolve to leave for a place 'where one is free to serve God and keep the Rule'.

710302   RP PASQUIER QUESNEL, CONG.ORAT.   2 March 1671
U 1168,orig.; Tans 11

The prior [Urbain Le Pannetier] is now writing to Quesnel direct on business matters.

710407   ABBOT OF CÎTEAUX [JEAN PETIT]   7 April 1671
Mug I/34; Dubois 1 p.395

State of the Order; speaks openly to him as to a good father.

710400   BISHOP   [April] 1671
TC I/21

Three Celestines were accepted as novices at Mass on Holy Thursday [26 March] and he cannot send them back to a decadent order in which it is impossible for them to work out their salvation.

710412   [RM LOUISE ROGIER]   12 April 1671
M 1214,96; A 2106,f.59 vo.

Avoids visitors as much as possible.

*710426   RM MARIE-LOUISE [BOUTHILLIER]   26 April 1671
TD/A

   'It is true, my dear sister that I was indisposed for five or six months last summer with a kind of slow fever, but my health is at present quite well restored. If a Christian only lives to die, it may be said that a religious, in whom the feelings of a Christian ought to be encountered in their perfection and purity, cannot have the least thought of preserving his life, except in so far as that seems to him to be according to God's order and will. I have already told you my views on the subject of your fourth vow and your separation from secular persons. It cannot be altered without attacking your observance in its most essential and holy feature. You are under an obligation to make every effort to prevent that happening. If that change should be made, take no part in it, endure it , but do not approve it, and whatever others do, never make use of that concession which, being contrary to the prescriptions of your rule, can only be considered as a most dangerous laxity. I pray God to give you all the strength and fidelity you need in a time of temptation. Remember me also before him, I beseech you. I am with every sincerity and affection, in Our Lord, yours' etc.

710521   TRP DE ST-PÉ,   21 May 1671
         PRIEST OF THE ORATORY, NOTRE-DAME DE VERTUS [AUBERVILLIERS, PARIS]
SS, Rec. Amelote, 219,aut.

   'The ecclesiastic who will give you this note, my dear Father, is my particular friend and will himself tell you the reason for his journey. I beseech you in Christ's name to give him your views and help him with your enlightenment, which he needs very much. I need say no more to a person of such ardent charity as you. I commend him to you with all my heart, I ask your blessing, very reverend and very dear Father, and please believe me in Christ yours' etc.

The tone of this letter, the only surviving evidence of contact with St-Pé, leaves no room for doubt about the warmth of Rancé's relations with a priest who was intimately linked with so many friends of Port-Royal, notably the Pascal family and that of Le Nain.

710607   BISHOP OF PAMIERS [ETIENNE CAULET]   7 June 1671
Carp p.174

Agrees that buildings for proposed monastery should be modest. R. would try to go and look for himself.

The bp had suggested that R. might start a small house in his diocese, and discussion on this went on for several months, but the King's refusal to approve any new monastic foundations (on economic grounds) prevented any result.

710618   M. L'ABBÉ, PARIS   18 June 1671
TC II/213

However much R. would like to help, M. must carefully examine his resolve. Always dangerous to leave a place where one has a cure of souls, but if he so decides, R. will welcome him.

The address simply indicates a secular priest, and this is what R. invariably said to such potential postulants.

710701   MME   1 July 1671
A 2106,f.60; Mug I/107

A religious who was validly professed can win no dispensation because her vocation was doubtful. She must stay where she is.

The reference may well be to his niece, and the letter to her mother, Mme d'Albon, since almost all the letters in this MS concern either Favier, the Visitation or the Albons. It also fits the known circumstances of parental interference and Louise-Henriette's doubtful vocation.

* 710705   MONSIEUR   5 July 1671
TC I/54

'Monsieur, I am duly grateful for the marks you give me of your esteem and friendship, and I should count myself fortunate if you had observed anything in me or in the discipline practised in this house which might oblige you to remember us and sometimes think of us before Our Lord. As regards your plan, Monsieur, I will say that however much I might like you to come and join us to serve Christ in penitence, I should not for anything in the world want to advise you to take the least step towards executing so holy a resolve, unless there are manifest signs of a true vocation, nor induce you to do anything either of us might regret. There must be no disguising the fact that the life we lead here is arduous and laborious, both in external austerity and in spiritual subjection, and what you have learned of it from ten days' experience is very little compared to what you would find in continuing it. The vigils, fasts, manual labour and the heat of the sun are arduous exercises, but the winter cold is much more so, and indeed it is only one's zeal for penitence which makes them tolerable, since the relief that can be granted to weaker brethren is very limited by the prescription of the Rule. What the prior told you about the ancient fasts is not without foundation, and I do not see how I can help allowing our brothers what they persist in asking on this point, since it is in conformity with the Rule and the examples of our first fathers, which we try to follow as closely as possible.

'As regards going bareheaded, it will be no more than you saw. I speak of these things, Monsieur, quite simply and I do not want to make them easier for you than they actually are, nor do I want to commit you in the hope of finding a facility which you would not subsequently encounter as it had been described to you. The life we lead here is ordinary, but still I do not consider that anyone should undertake it who is not firmly resolved to abandon his person and his health to all the hardships liable to be found in a life of penitence. That is certainly the first step that must be taken; the life of solitaries and monks must be considered as a martyrdom. They are men united together by God in holy conspiracy to deprive themselves slowly and imperceptibly, of a life which they are not allowed to destroy at a blow. You will reflect as necessary on your plan, Monsieur, you will examine it before God in all the detail it deserves, while on our side we shall pray him to give you light and make known to you what he asks of you. Whatever his divine providence ordains, I hope that your kindness towards me will be no less, and that you will not lose all memory of the friendship with which you promised to honour me. For me, Monsieur, I beg you to believe that I shall always have the same feelings for you, the same esteem and the same desire to show you that I am in Our Lord Jesus Christ' etc.

This is a particularly good example of R's extreme frankness in dealing with aspiring recruits, especially those attracted after a brief stay. There is no hint as to the addressee's identity.

710707   MONSIEUR   7 July 1671
A 2106,f.64 vo.

Thanks him for returning a letter written by R. during his novitiate, which he now totally disavows.

710708 [JEAN FAVIER]   8 July 1671
A 2106,f.62; TC I/115

R. has just had a letter from monks at Beauvais begging him to ask Favier to introduce reform; only five are left. Others have also commented on poor state of monastery. Reminds Favier of the duties of commendatory abbot; even almsgiving and performance of divine office are less important than piety and regularity of life in community. Advises him to call in Maurists.

The Maurists came to help in 1676, but refused to take over the abbey completely.

710715 RELIGIEUSE   15 July 1671
M 1214,66; Mug I/35

Monastic life should be a preparation for death.

710723 RELIGIEUX, SAINT-SYMPHORIEN, BEAUVAIS   23 July 1671
M 1214,84; Mug I/36

Instructions on the duties of religious life and comment on their proposal to join Maurist reform.

The letter was addressed to the whole community.

710803 JEAN FAVIER   3 August 1671
CF 344,f.51 aut.; A 2106,f.66; Gonod 28

The monks at Beauvais all ignore their rule and are not on the way to salvation. 'I assure you that fewer people are saved than you think; I mean fewer of those who do not neglect their salvation but work at it.'

710806 FRIEND   6 August 1671
Mug I/37

Against plurality of benefices.

710809 ERUDITE PERSON [? G. HERMANT]   9 August 1671
Mug I/38

Praises book on 'depths of our nothingness'.

710813 RELIGIEUSE, SAINT-ANTOINE, PARIS   13 August 1671
Carp, p. 318

She should leave, having done all she could.

According to Le Nain and others, she did leave, for a benedictine abbey, on the appointment of her brother as bishop. No obvious identification suggests itself.

710826 FRIEND 26 August 1671
Mug I/39
Illness of mutual friend.

710826a SUPERIOR [? ABBOT OF CÎTEAUX, JEAN PETIT] 26 August 1671
Mug I/40
Recognises abbot's difficulties, but only he can cure the ills in the Order.
The address is reasonably certain, but the date is doubtful.

710903 [RM LOUISE ROGIER] 3 September 1671
M 1214,100; A 2106,f.123 (2 last pages, wrongly dated 10 Dec. 1683)
Glad to know that his neice is now anxious to make amends for past misconduct. We must always prepare for death as if it were imminent.

710915 REGULAR ABBOT 15 September 1671
Mug I/41
Differences between ecclesiastics and religious, priests and solitaries.

710930 RM THÉRÈSE [BOUTHILLIER] 30 September 1671
TB 24
Condolences on death of abbess [Louise de Thou, abbess since 1640].

711004 RP, CELESTINE 4 October 1671
TC I/86; TD B
His former confrères doing well at la T. Willing to accept RP's brother, despite his deafness.
Probably to Joseph Ronat, prior of Sens.

711006 RP PASQUIER QUESNEL, CONG.ORAT. 6 October 1671
U 1168,orig.; Tans 12
François Quesnel, brother of Pasquier, has painted a picture of St Bernard for la T. Sends a book for binding.

711010 RP PASQUIER QUESNEL, CONG.ORAT. 10 October 1671
U 1168,orig.; Tans 13
Quesnel's disappointment [at not being nominated for the seminary at Langres].

711013 [ROBERT ARNAULD D'ANDILLY] 13 October 1671
Mug I/43
Congratulations on the promotion of his son [Pomponne].
Pomponne had just been appointed secretary for foreign affairs.

711013 RELIGIEUSES, SAINT-ANTOINE, PARIS   13 October 1671
TD C
They must persist.

711015 REGULAR ABBOT   15 October 1671
Mug I/42
R. still thinks the same [as in 710915].

711019 [JEAN FAVIER]   19 October 1671
A 2106,f.67
Fears he has too little influence to help Favier, but hopes to see him the next year.

*711026 BISHOP OF LUÇON [HENRI BARILLON]   26 October 1671
P f.599

'I had already learned, Monsieur, of your nomination to the bishopric of Luçon, and your letter found me with my pen in my hand. As I was about to give myself the honor of writing to you about it, Monsieur Duhamel arrived the day before yesterday and told me all the details. I must confess that my feelings on this occasion were very different from what they usually are in such circumstances, for instead of pitying you and sympathising with you in the task which you are beginning, my only thought was to praise God for making you by his divine providence what you have long been in my private intentions and desires. Go then with confidence where God's order calls you, as do the wishes and inclinations of all those who love his service. It should be a considerable comfort to you that at a time when cupidity and restlessness constitute the vocation of the majority of those who hold leading positions in the Church, yours should be so pure that everyone sees there the hand of God and regards it as his work. You know, Monsieur, what is needed to balance it; the holiest beginnings sometimes have quite dissimilar sequels, even those who have shown most zeal and vigour quite commonly slacken off, and unless one takes quite special care, it is easy to raise on solid foundations a building of earth and mud.

God, Monsieur, who has given you authentic motives, will surely be able to maintain them in a purity worthy of that of the ministry which you are only undertaking out of love of him and the fear of displeasing him. I beg you to believe that there will be no day in my life when I will not ask of him that you should have that grace as fervently as I ask for my own salvation. Sincerity does not allow us to flatter anyone, but truth presses me to open my heart and protest that the affection and esteem I have for your person is such that nothing could be added to it.

PS We shall await you impatiently and I look on the honour which you propose to do us by spending a few days in our desert as a blessing.

As regards the priory of Boulogne I completely agree with you, but as for choosing a successor, no one could do that better than you or with more discernment.'

Barillon was nominated to Luçon on 16 October, through Le Camus' influence. The final sentence shows that he lost no time in divesting himself of his existing benefice at Boulogne.

711103   RP PASQUIER QUESNEL, CONG.ORAT.   3 November 1671
U 1168,orig.; Tans 14

Refers to choir book and dom Charles Denis [a former Oratorian, to be professed at la T. in June 1672].

711104   RM LOUISE-HENRIETTE D'ALBON   4 November 1671
M 1214,99

Félibien is delivering the letter and will tell her to give up any idea of moving. She must now set a good example in a place where she has set such a bad one. Humiliation and self-denial are more important than outward austerity. She must publicly confess her 'disobedience, murmuring, restlessness and scorn of superior', and admit that she was wrong and the superior right. Her behaviour has been disgraceful and she must make up for it.

R's friend Félibien acted as go-between at Tours. The superior was still RM Louise Rogier.

711104a   [RM LOUISE ROGIER]   [4 November 1671]
M 1214,97

Félibien will deliver letter and further oral comments on behaviour of R's niece, who is now genuinely sorry for past misdeeds. Asks permission for Félibien to speak to her on R's behalf to veto any transfer. Regrets RM's suspicions of him, such an old friend.

711115   [MARQUIS DE POMPONNE]   15 November 1671
Mug I/44

Congratulations on promotion [see 711013]

* 711120   BISHOP OF LUÇON [HENRI BARILLON]   20 November 1671
L orig.; P f.600

'You could not have cast your eyes, Monsieur, on anyone more worthy than your brother, but divine providence has decreed that it should be without effect, for fear that the world, which always judges unjustly, should explain your action in a way contrary to your feelings. God, who presides over everything, will make you find a man according to his heart. I persist in my first thoughts on the subject of your appointment: it is entirely from God. Work with confidence, Monsieur; he has begun his work in you, and will complete it by giving the protection so necessary for those who bear charges of such great weight within the Church. My prayers are nothing, for God does not listen to sinners like us, but we shall all the same not break the promise we made. I beg you to believe that, and also that there is no one in the world who is dearer and will ever be more present to me than you. We shall have the honour of seeing you here when God wills. It is too kind of you to be willing to give us that consolation. Pray God for me, I beg you, and believe me with all possible respect and affection yours' etc.

The brother was Jean-Jacques, later prior of Gizy and canon of Laon.

711125   RP PASQUIER QUESNEL, CONG. ORAT.   25 November 1671
U 1168 orig.; Tans 15

Quesnel's recent *Abrégé de la morale de l'Evangile* warmly praised. RP de Monchy has been roughly treated while on a preaching mission at Grenoble for Le Camus.

Le Camus tried to persuade Monchy to join him permanently at Grenoble, but in vain. Monchy was accused of excessive rigour and physically assaulted.

711200   [RM LOUISE ROGIER]   [? December 1671]
M 1214,101; Mug I/1

Wrong to fear death.

711203   RM LOUISE-HENRIETTE D'ALBON   3 December 1671
M 1214,102

Idea of going to Port-Royal out of the question. Life as a Visitandine is no less sanctifying than that of Carmelite or Capuchin, though less austere. She must trust her superior, and only disobey if told to do something manifestly against God's orders.

This is the first and only time that this long crisis of revolt is explicitly linked with Port-Royal, but the problem is more likely to have been one of discipline than of doctrine.

711203a   RELIGIEUSE   3 December 1671
M 1214,65; Mug I/45

Love God wholly and solely. Obedience promotes humility, without which retreat may lead to pride. 'Better be distracted under obedience than in retreat by your own choice.'

711204 RP PRIEUR [CELESTINE]   4 December 1671
TC II/212; Du Suel, *Entretiens* p. 742

RP presses R. to take him, but his impulsive spirit and delicate constitution are obstacles. R. will risk it.
This may be Joseph Ronat of Sens again; see 711004.

711209 RP PASQUIER QUESNEL, CONG. ORAT.   9 December 1671
U 1168 orig.; Tans 16

Monchy is fortunate in being struck for God's sake (see 711125); M. Odouair has left for Beauvais via Rouen.

*711212 DOM ROBERT COUTURIER   12 December 1671
SS aut.

'I should have to see things, Reverend Father, more closely than I do, and be more specially informed about what goes on in your monastery and of your own feelings than I think I can be by letter to be able to speak to you as positively as you wish, and it seems to me that one can only say generalities about the things you write about. One must judge, Reverend Father, from your state in the post which you occupy whether it is necessary for you to change your residence and occupations. You know that if it is causing you considerable disturbance and putting obstacles in the way of your sanctification through the dissipations and enfeeblement which sometimes follow such exercises, you would be justified in wanting to give it up; but if it only causes you those difficulties which are almost inseparable from external occupations, and from which human wretchedness can never be exempt, the charity and obedience which you apply to it will make up in God's eyes for the losses of which you complain, and will replace the advantages which you might find in a less involved life and one more cut off from contacts with men. You must examine this before God with much care and attention, since there is nothing more dangerous than to change without legitimate cause, and move about when God's order fixes and halts us, especially for a person who wished, as his main impulse, to look at God throughout his life as would a victim and a sacrifice. Such a person is even more obliged than others to watch all his inclinations and motives, so as to do nothing which does not wholly depend on him.

Finally, when you have weighed up all these things, Reverend Father, if it seems to you that God wants you in a less divided life, and in greater calm than that of which you wrote and which you believe our house could afford you, we will receive you, as I have already told you, with joy and consolation. The way to do that is to ask permission; it will not be granted perhaps the first time, but I reply that it will not be refused if you persist in asking.

You tell me, Reverend Father, that you have been content to retain a seat of honour; allow me to point out in that connexion that you are saying something contrary to the ancient statutes of the Order, which forbade an abbot who had resigned to take any other rank save that of his profession; a General Chapter made a contrary ruling, which has been followed to the prejudice of the first, but there is no reason to suppose that one should prefer what human cupidity introduced into our Order in the corruption of the times to what was so holily established by our Fathers, who were saints and had the spirit of God; and then it seems to me that God asks something more of you than of those to whom he did not give the same inclination for this life of destruction and annihilation for which you sigh; I should not speak to you like that unless you had given me the cue yourself.

Concerning the distribution of your time, it is impossible to say anything in particular about it, but you know very well that any time remaining after you have discharged your duties should be employed in prayer, sacred reading and presence in choir, and I do not see why you dispense yourself entirely from that. St Thomas read Cassian's *Conferences* to cure any aridity that the study of theology might cause him. The Lives of the Desert Fathers, St Bernard, St John Climacus, Cassian, St Ephrem never fail to be of use to those who read them with the intention of sustaining the monastic spirit in themselves; it is so easily lost and the least external occupations are so liable to dissipate it that one can never, it seems to me, take too much care in preserving so rare and precious a treasure at this time, when people are contented with the surface of things and with being monks by their habits and a few similar observances.

I will say nothing to you of those so called *Constitutions of la Trappe*. We do not see that sort of thing in our monastery. From what I hear about these they seem to be some small regulations for the inside of the house to which someone has been pleased to give the name of constitutions, which they do not deserve. There may be something in them which is not in the *Usages* because they did not provide for everything, but I do not think there is anything hostile to their spirit. The main practices of our monastery are not expounded there. We took everything we could from the *Usages*, but we may easily have been mistaken, and so we are obliged to give opinions about it, and will receive any with joy. I have nothing, Reverend Father, to add to this note, except that everything passes away, our lives like everything else, and it often happens that God's moment finds us full of plans and projects; Man finds nothing more natural than to imagine and think, but it is quite rare to realise these plans and stay stable and constant, so that one has nothing to do but await God's eternity. I pray him to give you from this moment all the thoughts and feelings that you would wish to have at that time. Ask the same thing of him for me, dear Father. One grows older and does not think as one should of eternity, and we are always surprised to see that moment arrive. I am with all possible sincerity yours etc.

PS If I were in your place I should say nothing of what is happening at Bonnaigue, but would inform one of my friends so that he might give an account of it in case it should be discussed at the General Chapter.'

Dom Robert has been appointed prior of Preuilly by the Chapter of 1664, but from the context of this letter he seems to have gone back to his own house of Barbeaux by 1671, probably as cellarer, to judge from the description of his duties. 'The seat of honour' would be the precedence accorded to the former head of a monastery in command. *The unauthorised publication of the*

Constitutions caused R. great annoyance; as usual he appeals to the original Cistercian regulations, Usages, *to justify his own practice. Bonnaigue was a dilapidated abbey in the diocese of Limoges, being reformed with help from Septfons. The Chapter met in May 1672.*

711215 [JEAN FAVIER]   15 December 1671
A 2106,f.68 vo.

R's feelings about his own salvation quite irrelevant to that of Favier, who has behaved irreproachably. Accepts gifts of razors and grafting knife.

Thiers, Favier's home, was famous for its cutlery.

711227 ROBERT ARNAULD D'ANDILLY   27 December 1671
A 6037,f.415 aut.

Comments favorably on extract of letter from Pomponne sent by Andilly. R's friendship imperishable.

72/1 ALIPE   [1672]
Du Suel, *Entretiens*, p. 739

R. had warned him of hardships to be endured in winter.

This is probably the ex-Augustinian friar Alipe Audibert, who was professed as a laybrother in August 1673, and died 1681.

72/2 A YOUNG ECCLESIASTIC OF HIGH BIRTH   [? 1672]
Du Suel, *Entretiens*, p. 745

Unlike most people, Monsieur has long since banished worldly preoccupations.

72/3 MONSIEUR   [1672]
Du Suel, *Entretiens*, p. 735

Disavows authorship of so-called *Constitutions*, very different from regulations actually in force, though similar on certain points.

R. had been annoyed by the unauthorized publication in 1671 of Constitutions de la T.

72/4 RM SUPÉRIEURE   [? 1672]
Mug I/50

She fears to displease God in her new charge.

72/5 FRIEND [M. DE SACY]   [1672]
Mug I/86

Thanks him for work received, 'full of the doctrine of the saints'.

72/6   GUILLAUME LE ROY   [1672]
U 3069, p. 65 (extract); *Lettre de Tillemont*, 1705, p. 106.
M. Arnauld is the leading man of our age, and the most learned.'

72/7   RP 'FROM GERMANY' [? HEISTERBACH]   [1672]
BN 23497 f.32; Gonod 225
Long exposition of duties of religious; he has been to la T.

720104   [RM LOUISE ROGIER]   4 January 1672
M 1214,104
Delighted at good news of his niece. She should not take communion too often until her new conduct is confirmed.

720120   DOM SIMON GUÉRIN, CARTHUSIAN, BASSENVILLE   20 January 1672
TB 31; TC II/192
Guérin an old friend. R. quotes St Bernard on preference for siting monasteries in unhealthy places. Contrasts modern slackness and primitive fervour; the difference due to men and their greed.

720125   A DOCTOR [? PIERRE NICOLE]   25 January 1672
Mug I/46
Glad M. approves of la T. Thanks him for books sent.

720125a   ROBERT ARNAULD D'ANDILLY   25 January 1672
A 6038,f.3 orig.
Brief acknowledgement of Saint-Cyran's letters. Encloses letter to Nicole.

Jean Duvergier de Hauranne, abbé de Saint-Cyran (1581-1643) was, with Jansen, the founder of Jansenism. His letters were first published in 1645. It is quite likely that 72/5 refers to these letters, and certain that Nicole's letter is that of the preceding entry.

*720217   BISHOP OF LUÇON [HENRI BARILLON]   17 February 1672
L orig.; P f.601

'I did not doubt that God would give you the grace to find a successor for your priory of Boulogne according to his heart and yours. I have no personal acquaintance with Monsieur Picquet, but I have long known about his merit and virtue. I saw him some years ago in Champagne in an abbey of our Order, when he was conducting a mission in the diocese of Châlons, and I assure you that I would have chosen him from a thousand others. I praise Our Lord for inspiring you to give a great example by reducing yourself to a single benefice, and then sanctifying it in every detail. I do not fail to pray him every day of my life to bless in like manner all that your zeal makes you undertake for his service and glory. I will not say, Mgr, how much I respect you and how dear you are to me, that goes beyond all I could express. Please assure your friend of my honour and affection.'

R. had been at Châtillon in 1669, and also at Hautefountaine in Champagne.

720220   J-B BOSSUET [EX-BISHOP OF CONDOM]   20 February 1672
TB 40; Bossuet, *Correspondance*, I p. 233

Thanks him for book [*Exposition sur la doctrine catholique*].

720307   BISHOP OF PAMIERS [ETIENNE CAULET]   7 March 1672
U 3068; Dubois I p. 380 (dated 1670)

Has had to send away an ecclesiastic, unable for tempermental reasons to stand solitude and fasting at la T. Bp has written to Abbot of Prières, Vicar General of Reform, asking for a foundation in his diocese from la T. 'The place must be deserted, they need water, three or four acres of level ground, a little wood.'

See above 710607.

720401   [JEAN FAVIER]   1 April 1672
A 2106,f.68

Family financial troubles.

*720409   RP NICOLAS MALEBRANCHE, CONG. ORAT.   9 April 1672
Bibl. Mun. Orléans, MS 944-80, orig; *Revue des Questions historiques*, 1876; TB 48 (without PS)

'I kept delaying my reply to your two letters, and telling you that the importance of your resolution appalled me; however, after considering that God gives strength proportionate to the intentions he inspires in us, and that he can do anything in respect of our bodily as well as our spiritual dispositions, your perseverance and the firmness with which you seem determined to execute what you are convinced he wants of you causes me to have no more reasons for opposing you. So much so, Father, that if you are sincerely willing to abandon to divine providence the care of your person, your health, and your life, if you are entirely resolved to discharge yourself of all that concerns you so that he alone accepts that charge, if the horror of long winters, if the assaults of the seasons, if the deprivation of all human contact and consolation in which you would have to spend most of the years to come, if the requirement laid upon you of dividing your days between prayer and reading, finally if all the possible consequences of so great a renunciation as that which you would have to make do not share your heart, if the love of God, if your desire to belong solely to him and have no other occupation in the world but that of awaiting him, if the sight of eternity, always nearer than we think, makes you regard as a mere instant the length of your life, then come, Father, and follow the stirrings of grace. God, who alone can have inspired such feelings in you, will not fail to give you the protecttion you need, and sustain you in a life which you undertake only in order to please him.

For our part, there is nothing we would not do to contribute to your consolation. You know what we can do, which is very little; but a person taking so great a step must have complete trust in God, and expect nothing from human help. After all, Father, things look extraordinary because we look at them in the light of human conduct, which is usually very natural; but anyone considering them in the light of the examples left to us by the saints would think very differently about them. I pray Our Lord to enlighten you, to make you know his will and not to allow you to take a false gleam for a true light. I am in him with all my heart your etc.

PS I beg you in God's name to see that no one ever knows that you have spoken to me of your plan, because my job is to give advice to no one.

I think you should make a trip here, to see the place, before carrying out your plan, and if you were to adopt that resolution, it would have to be immediately after Easter, because I am obliged to go at the beginning of May to the General Chapter, and shall be away at least six weeks.'

Malebranche is known to have been in regular contact with Perseigne from 1674, and he wrote some of his philosophical work there, but this is the only evidence that he ever thought of visiting la T. It is not known whether he accepted the invitation. R. started off for the Chapter in May, but turned back on account of poor health.

* 720411   BISHOP OF LUÇON[HENRI BARILLON]   11 April 1672
P f.600

'I have just learned, Mgr, of the loss you have sustained in Monsieur de Morangis, and assure you that no one could be more touched by it than I. Among all the reasons I have for feeling this keenly, yours is that which specially comes to mind. I know how dear you were to him, and how grieved a soul like yours must be in so touching a circumstance. I am certain, Mgr, that you needed all the virtue you possess to moderate your distress. That is how the world is; nothing is stable, everything passes by with prodigious speed, we lose our friends, and those near to us, or they have to lose us. We should be very unfortunate if the moment of separation did not leave us with the hope of meeting again in God's eternity. I confess that my personal regreat at the death of poor Monsieur de Morangis will last a long time. You know better than anyone what my obligations are in this, since no one knows better than you all the kindness he showed me. In short, we must submit to God's orders and be always ready to leave everything when he desires that of us, however much and however properly we may be attached to them. I will not tell you, Mgr, how much all your interests concern me, it could not in truth go further than it does, and whatever you may think, you cannot possibly believe the full extent of my concern. I pray God to pile blessings and grace on you, and I am in Our Lord with all possible sincerity and respect yours' etc.

Antoine Barillon de Morangis, the Bp's uncle, died on 4 April 1672. He had been Duhamel's patron at Saint-Merri, and was deeply pious, as well as a respected lawyer.

720419 ANTOINE ARNAULD   19 April 1672
U 3068, p. 62 and 172 (extract); *Lettre de Tillemont*, 1705, p. 106
Very grateful for book just received [presumably part of *Perpétuité de la foi* . . . against Calvinists].

720419a RP ABBÉ[ORVAL, CHARLES DE BENZERADT]   19 April 1672
Mug I/47
'A monk ought much rather to weep over his sins than read theology.'

* 720501 MARÉCHAL DE BELLEFONDS   1 May 1672
BN na 12959f.1, orig.; TB 56; Mug I/48

'I do not think that I need to say very much to persuade you how deeply I feel about everything that concerns you, and I am sure that you are in no doubt that, since God has linked me with your interests in the most genuine and intimate way possible, I see you in the circumstances in which you are at present with very different feelings and views from those which others might have. For indeed, Mgr, if saints full of the spirit of truth, who are not mistaken, have believed that there were such insurmountable obstacles to salvation in the places from which divine providence has just withdrawn you that they have not hesitated to call those obstacles impossibilities, how, if one sees things like them, that is, with the eyes of faith, can one fail to revere God's conduct towards you, destroying so many obstacles in a moment and giving you so many opportunities to think about your sanctification? Truly, Mgr, one must agree that if from childhood our reason were not weakened by earthly affections, if all one sees and hears did not fill one's mind with preoccupations and false ideas, one would avoid with the greatest care what in fact one seeks so diligently and eagerly, and one would consider as real blessings and favourable events what one looks on as misfortunes and disgrace. I pray God that you make a holy use of the state in which his mercy has placed you, and that you will appreciate the uses and advantages of that state, as I am sure you recognize them. Everything passes away, Mgr, with frightening speed, and nothing deserves a place in the Christian's heart save God alone who is eternal. I humbly beseech you to believe that you will be more than ever present to us before him, that we shall commend to him with the greatest possible fervour everything that concerns you, and that nowhere in the world are you more honoured than here, nor is there anyone more faithfully, gratefully and respectfully yours in Christ than I, your most humble and obedient servant.'

Bellefonds had been disgraced and exiled to Bourgueil for refusing to serve under Maréchal de Turenne when Lous declared war on Holland in April 1672. Though Turenne was his senior, Bellefonds, as a marshal of France, objected to serving under anyone. There were rumours that he was thinking of withdrawing to la T. where he had spent Holy Week.

720505   ABBOT OF CÎTEAUX [JEAN PETIT]   5 May 1672
Dubois I p. 431

R. had set out for the General Chapter [opened that day] but was taken ill on the way. R. calls on abbot to take the Order in hand and cure the ills as only his authority can.

720514   DOM FRANÇOIS WEBER, HEISTERBACH   14 May 1672
TB 44 (Latin)

Usages and *Statutes* of Cîteaux strictly followed at la T. About fifty monks there. R. ready to accept him, but he should not delay.

720514a   DOM THÉODORE BOURLEZ AND   14 May 1672
          DOM RICHARD LAPP, HEISTERBACH
TB 67 (Latin)

They write from Cambron (Belgium), with a covering letter from the abbot of that monastery, deploring the state of Heisterbach; R. encourages them to come to la T. where they will be welcome.

The once great abbey of Heisterbach, near Cologne, was not necessarily as decadent as they said, but the Reform never spread to Germany and war had done much damage in the Rhineland.

720527   JEAN FAVIER   27 May 1672
CF 344,f.53 aut.; Gonod 29

Reform at Beauvais not urgent, and Maurists may not be willing to direct it. Problems over money with M. de Vernassal [R's brother-in-law].

720529   ABBOT OF CÎTEAUX [JEAN PETIT]   [29 May] 1672
M 1214,98 (wrongly dated 3 Sep 1671); Dubois I p. 435

R. appeals for a more understanding treatment of Reform. The new brief most damaging. For three hundred years the Order has been in decline, and the Reform is its only hope. Refuses charge of visitor as incompatible with true reform, and because Chapter was invalid.

On 22 April Petit has secured a brief from Rome, limiting the number of Reformed abbots on the definitorium, contrary to the provisions of In Suprema. *He did not disclose this until the opening session of 16 May, whereupon the ten Reformed abbots walked out after registering a solemn protest. Two days later the proto-abbots also walked out, and though the remaining abbots went on with the business until 27 May, the validity of the Chapter was widely challenged by the Reform and others. R. had been appointed visitor to fill a vacancy, but by accepting he would have seemed to recognise the Chapter's validity; it also seems wildly improbable that he would ever have accepted such an office. It is this letter which appeared in the* Examen du Chapitre Général, *published in 1673, without R's permission, as he claimed.*

720600   WIDOW [? MME DE SAINT-LOUP]   [? June 1672]
Mug I/49

She proposes to retire to the depths of a great forest; 'such plans are no longer appropriate to our times'.

Her husband had died in February 1672.

720600   RP JOSEPH RONAT, CELESTINE, SENS   June 1672
A 5098 orig.

Knowing poor state of Celestines, R. is willing to welcome Ronat at la T.

*720602   BISHOP OF LUÇON [HENRI BARILLON]   2 June 1672
L orig.; P f.762

'We shall not fail, Mgr, to do as you ask, and offer our prayers to God, helpless as they may be, at the present juncture, which you rightly regard as the most important in your life, but there can be no room for doubt that God has called you as he has, and since your election is his work, he will accompany it with every grace and blessing needed to make it successful in all that follows. He will give you the fullness of his spirit, which is so rare at this time, and without which the minister of life becomes a minister of death, for the ministers as for those committed to their charge and guidance. If the Bishop of Ephesus is not what he ought to be in God's eyes, and needs penitence to efface the stains from his life in an age full of fervour, what must one not fear in our age, when corruption is so great and universal that merely to escape it is to have in men's judgement exceptional virtue? I pray God to pour on you all the effects of his mercy, and make your heart in all things according to his own. That, Mgr, is what I shall ask him all my life as I promised you. I cannot say how much I respect you. After all the kindness you have shown me, you must now be kind enough to believe that my profound respect for you could not be greater. Fr Honde will be delighted to do as you order.'

Barillon was consecrated in Paris on 5 June. The Bp of Ephesus is Timothy (1 Tm 3).

720607   MONSIEUR   7 June 1672
Carp p. 318

Quotes St Bernard's letter to Adam.

Impossible to tell from the content whether this is Letter 5 or 7.

720608   JEAN FAVIER   8 June 1672
CF 344,f.55 aut.; Gonod 30

Thanks Favier for splendid gift of gardening tools. Wishes M. d'Albon would withdraw from court before he dies.

720700   [ANNE DE BOURBON, duchesse de longueville]   [? July] 1672
Mug I/106

Condolences on death of her son [comte de Saint-Paul, killed at the crossing of the Rhine, 12 June 1672].

*720706   G. LE ROY, hautefontaine   6 July 1672
U 767, aut.; TB 76

'I am impatiently waiting, Monsieur, for the religious from Heisterbach who have been at your house, to receive from their hands the evidence that you are sending of your interest in what concerns us. You must believe that we look on that in advance with such appreciation and esteem that we could hardly find anything there to which we would not fully subscribe. Allow me only to say one thing: it seems from the letter you did me the honour of writing that you think we thoroughly approve of the method of using fictions in order to find cause for criticism or humiliation; nothing we do could be further from such a practice. The Greeks used it, but as it is only permissible to those who are incapable of telling a lie, we do not take the liberty of imitating them in that. If you ask me then how we manage to find grounds for reproving persons of virtue, and who consequently fall very rarely into faults which can be corrected, I will say simply that every time I carefully consider the actions of our religious, that is, the best and most edifying actions, I see some defect, and as they are obliged by their status to strive constantly for perfection, that gives me occasion to reprove and humiliate them; that if it should ever happen that their actions were exempt from defects, there are always circumstances to which one can give an unfavourable explanation. You will perhaps say, Monsieur, that things must always be interpreted favourably; to that I will reply that what obliges us to act in that way is charity, and when it is the case that there is more charity in interpreting things against those who do them, and that such an interpretation tends to their advantage and the good of others, not only is there no objection to doing so, but such a practice is even more charitable. That such a useful effect is to be encountered everywhere cannot be doubted; the humiliation inflicted on the person criticised prevents him falling into the self-satisfaction which can arise from the best actions, and which destroy, or at least diminish, their value before God; it avoids the disadvantage charged to it, the brethren profit from the warning and from the virtuous way in which the criticism is endured, and are edified by their superior's care and strictness. There, Monsieur, you have a great number of good effects, and I do not think there is anything to be set against it, nor that anyone could find in the silence, which some would prefer to observe instead of reprove, anything to balance or remove these advantages.

It is easy to conclude from this that it is more charitable to reprove in the cases indicated than not; I am always supposing, Monsieur, that the persons humiliated profit by it, and that the good is seen to be successfully achieved. I must confess that I find it hard to understand how one can be, I do not say a monk, but truly a Christian, and not love, or at least suffer peaceably and patiently, what humiliates us. Let anyone define for me what it is to be Christ's disciple and bear that cross without which no one will share in his glory. In truth, Monsieur, unless one pays attention to it, one is only a Christian in theory and idea, and I have seen people, regarded as models of eminent virtue and masters of the spiritual life, who gave lessons on it, whose heads seemed full of all that is greatest and most sublime in mystical theology, and who went into convulsions when something occurred that displeased them or was in any way slighting to them. It does not cost much to talk like Christ, but to behave like him is something else. Yet, Monsieur, it is unfortunately those who do, and not those who talk, whom Christ will count as his own on that day when he will reward not the words and speeches, but the actions and works of men. I am quite sure that those are your views too, and that I am not telling you anything that you did not think more loftily than I could do, for, to speak frankly, I am one of those who speak and do not do, who load others with burdens which they would not want to bear or touch with the tip of their finger. Obtain for me the grace of doing better, I beseech you; I do not doubt that it will be so if you ask God for it as for something that you want him to grant, that is with ardour and perseverance. I expect that help from your charity, and am in Our Lord yours etc.

PS The good brother Martelot pays attention, he is small-minded and scrupulous, and has never had anything but bad upbringing, but he is beginning to change his ways and principles; he will never be anything very great.'

R. had first made contact with three monks of Heisterbach in May 1672 (720414). They seem to have been making a tour of reformed houses to see where they might settle down. This letter opened a virulent dispute over fictions. The affair had blown up after a visit paid by Le Roy to la T. in June 1671, when he had first seen an excellent monk (Paul Hardy) humiliated for a trivial (or even imaginary) fault and accept the rebuke serenely. Le Roy charged R. with inventing causes for reproof and as the quarrel became more bitter these so-called fictions soon bulked larger than the actual humiliations. R. was particularly upset by the implicit criticism of St John Climacus, his favourite monastic authority, from whom he derived his practice of humiliations.

720707   RP ABBÉ, LA FERTÉ [PIERRE BOUCHU]   7 July 1672
TB 80

Urges him to press cause of Reform more vigorously at Cîteaux; neutrality is not enough. He showed the right spirit at his last visit. Reformed abbots were wrong to break with him.

Bouchu, like the other proto-abbots, had briefly made common cause against Petit with the Reformed abbots at the Chapter.

*720718   G. LE ROY, HAUTEFONTAINE   18 July 1672
U 767 orig.   [answered 21 August]

'I do not have the honour, Monsieur, of writing to you with my own hand, because it becomes so bad and my characters so ill-formed that after a page of writing nothing is legible any more.

I have at last received your dissertation from the hands of those good German monks who arrived here only a few days ago. I have read it carefully; it is learned and scholarly, but allow me to say that it could not be less appropriate to anyone than those for whom you took the trouble to compose it. They fervently profess to be truthful and sincere, and I do not believe that anyone could feel more repugnance and aversion than they do for lies, fictions, and equivocations. They must have explained themselves badly, Monsieur, or you must have misunderstood them, or had unreliable accounts of what goes on in our monastery for you to have attributed to it conduct so contrary to morals, christian piety and the purity of its principles.

Regarding your views on the use of humiliations, if you had confined yourself to condemning insults, terms offensive to decency and honour, emotional disturbance, and fits of anger, we should share your views, Monsieur. Such manners have never been practised in our house, and we find them as repugnant as lies and fictions, but since you attack even those manners which are brisk and have the asperity deemed necessary to humiliate and confuse, let me tell you that after considering with all possible care your reasons for combating them, despite all the deference I should wish to have for anything coming from you, I have found nothing capable of persuading me, and I have not changed my mind. It is enough to remove any doubts that they come from God and that such a practice is very holy, to see that it accords with the rules of the Gospel, that it was established by so many great saints, who should be regarded as so many masters of monastic life, that it was ordered by our Fathers, St Benedict and St Bernard. It is to them, Monsieur, that we know God spoke; they had a special mission from him to explain his will to us, they have all the qualities needed to command our credence, and it is right that it should be their authority that determines our opinions. Besides I cannot believe that the way you treat the holy Fathers of the East on this point, especially St John Climacus whose authority is so weighty in the church that the most learned men of our day have called him the depository of ecclesiastical tradition, meets with approval from many. I can assure you at least that it will hardly win any here, in a place where his least words and thoughts are respected. I admit, Monsieur, that the way of humiliations and ignominy is a hard one, that few appreciate it or are capable of it, *durus est hic sermo, abnega temetipsum* [Jn 6:61], but the self-denial without which Christ declares that none can share in his glory has a wide scope and includes some strange things. What St John Chrysostom has told us of it (*Homily 56 on St Mark*) goes well beyond what can be endured in a monastery where things must be done with charity, discernment, and prudence, yet he is speaking to ordinary Christians and not to monks. Indeed those souls which love Christ and preserve the memory of the humiliations and sufferings of the cross what nothing so ardently as to humiliate themselves and suffer something for love of him; what grieves them is not to find enough chances and means of doing so, and they acquire them as much as they can at every moment of their lives. A monk is very unfortunate if he has any other views, being one who is no longer allowed to have a mediocre love for him by whose grace and for whose love he has ceased loving what he would have been permitted to love if he had remained in the world, *Non licet vobis parum amare propter quem non amastis quod liceret* (St Augustine) [*De virginitate* 55]. It is finally the sign with which Christ has marked the elect of the Father and which will distinguish his disciples from those who are not until he comes himself to separate them in the fullness of time. Though these words of St John Climacus are approved by few, they are no less true and holy, 'that whoever rejects just or unjust humiliations has renounced his salvation'. I accept to the fullest extent the humiliation God sends and embrace with all my heart the hand he has been pleased to use for that purpose. You attribute to us, Monsieur, odious principles and rules of conduct of which we have never thought, and you place at the head of your dissertation a title likely to frighten every man who bears the name of Christian. One must praise Christ for everything. We shall pray him with all possible ardour to give you in this world and the next as much honour and glory as we deserve opprobrium and ignominy. I am in him truly yours' etc.

66   The Letters of Armand-Jean de Rancé   720723

The date of reply on this and later letters was noted by G. Vuillart, Le Roy's secretary. R. does not exaggerate the illegibility of his writing. The title of Le Roy's Dissertation may vary from MS to MS, but always included the word 'fiction', which clearly offended R.

720723   BISHOP OF ALET [NICOLAS PAVILLON]   23 July 1672
U 848; TB 93; Gonod 204

Encloses with his letter one from dom Arsène Cordon.

Cordon, who was professed a month later, had been active in Jansenist circles at Sens, where he had succeeded Duhamel as curé of Saint-Maurice, but found peace at la T., where he became sub-prior and died in 1685.

720723a   BISHOP OF PAMIERS [ETIENNE CAULET]   23 July 1672
TB 92

Would be happy to set up a house in Bp's diocese.

This project had been mentioned before; see 710607 and 720307.

720807   RELIGIEUX   7 August 1672
Mug I/73

RP has been at la T. but cannot stay.

720817   RP PASQUIER QUESNEL, CONG. ORAT.   17 August 1672
U 1168,orig.; Tans 17

Death of RP J-F Senault, General of the Oratory. [3 August]

Elected General in 1662, Senault wrote an important treatise on the use of the passions.

*720825   MARÉCHAL DE BELLEFONDS   25 August 1672
BN na 12959 f.3, orig.; TB 103; Mug I/52

'Although M. de Tréville has kindly accepted the task of telling you how carefully we try to acquit ourselves before God of the debt we owe you, I could not prevent myself assuring you in person that you are always present with us before him, and that there is nothing we more insistently ask him for that the grace you need in order to find rest and peace in the state in which he has put you, in other words to find God himself, for there is none other who can be the peace and consolation of true Christians. The outside world will take as it may, and will reflect as it chooses on your retreat, but there is no room for doubt that it is a mercy that providence has granted you. God has opened for you a door to quit the court which you never expected; all the attendant circumstances are harsh and infinitely bitter. I am convinced,

Mgr, that however much you desired to think only of your salvation, you would never have chosen the ways by which he has led you. There is nothing more common than to see those who leave the world making agreeable plans for themselves, and looking for ways to enjoy their retreat; and the reason that one can withdraw without coming much closer to God is that one find the self again at the very time and in the very act which should lead to greater self-denial. God has preserved you from that misfortune by creating for you an unexpected event, and accompanying it with all possible unpleasantness. That is what truly marks those things that come from him, and he could not give you more visible signs of his goodness. You must be convinced of this if you are to make best use of the graces and advantages thus presented, and respond to his plans for you as faithfully as you should. The moment will come, and cannot be far off, since a thousand years are but an instant in God's sight, when you will see in a different light all that may now be causing you pain; you will know for certain that the events which seemed most intolerable were so many means willed by him, in his eternal dispositions, for achieving your sanctification. We shall continue, Mgr, to offer your person to Our Lord Jesus Christ to the utmost of our ability, having no other way to demonstrate the heartfelt respect with which I am yours etc.'

720829   [? JEAN FAVIER]   29 August 1672
A 2106,f.70 vo.
False rumours of R's death prompted by critics of austerity practised at la T.

720920   [ANNE DE BOURBON, duchesse de longueville]   20 September 1672
Mug I/51a
Renewed sympathy on death of her son [see 720200].

720922   [GODEFROI HERMANT]   22 September 1672
Mug I/52
Hermant must give up idea of retiring to la T. Public benefit to Church more important. St Basil to follow Athanasius.
Hermant was preparing editions of those writers, and sent copies to R.

721009   RP PASQUIER QUESNEL, cong. orat.   9 October 1672
U 1168,orig.; Tans 18
Election of new General [Abel de Sainte-Marthe, until 1696]. R. always sensitive to what happens to his friends.

721025 RP SUPÉRIEUR   25 October 1672
Mug I/74

Sorry for RP who has to lead religious who do not satisfy him. Willing to accept religious proposed.

*721025 BISHOP OF LUÇON [HENRI BARILLON]   25 October 1672
P f. 601

'I had indeed thought, Mgr, that you would have difficulty leaving Paris, and that it would not be as easy as you had thought to disengage yourself. Monsieur de La Brétèche [?], who was here a few days ago with Monsieur de Cendon [?], told me the details of your departure, and your separation from those with whom you had been so closely bound by God's order. I am not surprised at the difficulties and opposition encountered on every hand, and I can understand, Mgr, what souls formed according to God's heart can suffer on such occasions. Here you are at last in the place of which you must have said on arriving *haec requies mea in saeculum saeculi* [Ps 131:14]. God has led you there in an extraordinary way, but with such a manifest vocation that there is no more to do but live there worthy of God and respond to the purity of the election. I hope, Mgr, that he will give you that grace and will assure you of your vocation by the faithfulness of your works. That is what we ask Our Lord with all the care we should and which you desire of us. Continue, I beg you, to give me the honour of your friendship, and please believe that no one could with more affection and respect be yours' etc.

Barillon did not enter Luçon until 27 October. There were at least two distinguished brothers, both soldiers, called la Brétèche, one of whom became Governor of Poitou in 1678. Cendon is unknown, and is an uncertain reading.

721028 JEAN FAVIER   28 October 1672
CF 344,f.57 aut.; Gonod 31

Malicious rumours against la T. Favier sending a lad to try his vocation.

721100 RP PRIEUR   [? November 1672]
Mug I/75

R. wants him to know that they have gone back to the original rules for fasting laid down by the Rule and the *Usages* of Cîteaux.

721104 RP PRIEUR, CELESTINES, SENS [JOSEPH RONAT]   4 November 1672
TB 148

Encourages his thoughts of vocation at la T., but difficulties must not be underestimated: 'God does not call all kinds of persons to equally rigorous and penitent lives'.

721106 RELIGIEUX DE L'ORDRE   6 November 1672
Mug I/76
Let him come since his abbot agrees.

721121 BISHOP   21 November 1672
Mug I/53
'One must think of the end once one has passed a certain stage of the race.'

*721202 G. LE ROY, HAUTEFONTAINE   2 December 1672
U 767 aut.   [answered 5 January 1673]

'I had the honour of writing to you via the good brother Martelot, but as he told me when he left that he would not be going back to you, I did not send the letter; this poor brother, Monsieur, spent several months here, and I should have liked him to spend more. In fact it is only those to whom God gives a solid spirit and a humble heart who persevere in this monastery, and as these are rare qualities, a lot of people come to us, but we keep few. Our consolation is that it is written long ago, and it is the word of him who does not know what it is to be other than truthful, *nolite timere pusillus grex etc* [Lk 12:32]. Your prayers, Monsieur, will be of the greatest help to us in obtaining from Our Lord Jesus Christ that this prophecy should be fulfilled in ourselves. I ask them of you most urgently, together with the grace of believing me with all sincerity yours' etc.

On Martelot, see 720706.

721207 [JEAN FAVIER]   7 December 1672
A 2106,f.71 vo.
Favier should ignore rumours about R.

721223 BISHOP OF GRENOBLE [ETIENNE LE CAMUS]   23 December 1672
TB 113; Mug I/91

Rare for any Christian to live in penitence, most rare for prelates. Le Camus a worthy follower of St Charles Borromeo.

Charles Borromeo (1538–84), abp of Milan and a major figure in the Counter-Reformation. His disciplinary measures were most unpopular, but he vigorously reformed the clergy.

73/1 GODEFROI HERMANT   [? 1673]
TD A (fragment)
M. Le Nain has sent R. Hermant's life of Athanasius.

73/2   DOM JEAN-FRANÇOIS CORNUTY [? 1673]
MS *Chronique de Tamié*; Burnier, *Hist. de Tamié*, 5
Cornuty has been sent back to Foucarmont as novice-master.

73/3   DOM JEAN-FRANÇOIS CORNUTY [? 1673]
MS *Chronique de Tamié*; Burnier, *Hist. de Tamié*, 6
Glad that Cornuty accepts his situation. Offers advice on training novices.

73/4   BISHOP OF ANGERS [HENRI ARNAULD] [? 1673]
TB 301
Religious sent by bp had left his abbey irregularly, but R. will ask permission of the man's abbot to let him stay and atone for his faults.

73/5   BISHOP OF [? PAMIERS, ETIENNE CAULET] [? 1673]
Mug I/102
Question of making a foundation in his mountainous diocese. Refers also to resignation from his governorship of 'M' and the hope that his successor will follow Bp's advice.

'M' is almost certainly Tréville, governor of Foix, in Caulet's diocese, who resigned the post after his conversion. See 720723a.

73/6   CARDINAL [DE RETZ] [1673]
Mug II/11
Recalls their last meeting at Commercy [1669] and Retz's failure to implement resolution then expressed [of retreat to a monastery]. Asks Retz's support with Cardinal d'Estrées and commissioners appointed by the King.

Cardinal d'Estrées was French ambassador to Rome; the date is given by reference to commissioners, appointed to consider claims of the Reform in September 1673.

73/7   JEAN FLORIOT [1673]
Recueil concernant la morale chrétienne, 1745, vol. VI, p. 74, xix
R. disagrees with Floriot, whose work he otherwise admires, on permissibility of religious leaving cloister to help parents in need; 'natural law cannot make prescriptions against divine law'.

Sainteté, ch.XVI, deals at length with this point, which R. thought to be of major importance. See 730927 to Nicole. Earlier editions of Floriot's work do not include this letter, but it must have been written about the same time as that to Nicole.

*73/8 RM ABBESSE [LEYME, ANNE DE LA VIEUVILLE]   [second half of 1673]
Mug II/103

'Everything that you do me the honour of writing would finally have convinced me, if I had been less persuaded than I am, of the necessity of withdrawing yourself from the jurisdiction of the Order and putting yourself under that of the ordinary, as I already told you. In a word, you are obliged in conscience to employ all proper and licit ways for establishing strict regularity in your house and thus ensuring the salvation of the souls entrusted to you by God, and as experience has shown that it is precisely in all those given to you by your Major Superior, be they confessors or visitors, that you find views and behaviour quite contrary to what they should have in order to support your good intentions, and that they ruin what they should be building up, there is no room for doubt that you are obliged to seek under the Bishop's authority what you cannot find under that of the Order, especially as the complaints you addressed to Monsieur [the Abbot of Cîteaux] were not heeded. Even if what you do to that end is not as successful as you should expect, you will be cleared before God, who asks of you nothing more than that you should do what is in your power to promote his service in your house and secure the sanctification of your nuns. I think, therefore, Reverend Mother, that you should have a formal request presented to the King, in which you should explain that, having tried to restore good order in your house, which was not as regular as it should have been, you found in those from whom you should expect all manner of help in the execution of your plan such attitudes as destroyed in your nuns' minds all the good you tried to instill, that the religious given to you as confessors were men of licentious life, that the visitors sent to you were wholly ignorant of matters religious, full of lax opinions and principles, which in the course of their visits they impressed on the minds of your nuns, being quite contrary to the piety and regularity in which they ought to be living, that having complained to Monsieur [the Abbot of Cîteaux] of their incompetence, evil conduct, and the disorders caused by them in your community, he ignored your representations and made not the slightest effort to apply a remedy, and that you thus found yourself obliged to have resort to the Holy See to obtain permission to put yourself under the jurisdiction of the Bishop, since it was no longer possible for you to remain under that of the Order without seeing your community fall into all the worst misfortunes which bad direction can produce. That you beg His Majesty to give you his protection with the Holy See, and have instructions sent to his Ambassador to use his good offices with His Holiness so that you may be granted the exemption requested etc.

That is how I should act in your place, Reverend Mother, and if I did less I should not believe that I was acquitting myself of the duties imposed by my conscience.

As regards abstinence, I should not advise you to embrace it under the present circumstances; it is enough that you should retain the wish to do so when God opens the way to you.

What you must indispensably do in your present situation is to establish strict observance of the Brief [*In Suprema*] in your house, and once that is done, to apply yourself to raising your nuns to greater perfection, according to what God inspires you to do. You may surely believe that if you demanded greater perfection of them, people would not lose the opportunity of criticising your conduct and discrediting the rightness of your claims by accusing you of wishing them to adopt practices which are excessive and above their strength. Above all, Reverend Mother, do what you do with courage and trust in God's goodness. Your intentions are holy; all you think of is his glory and the salvation of your nuns. In a word you desire only what you are obliged to desire. What would you have to fear from human opposition, even if things did not succeed? To be opposed is the true sign of works which come from God, and the witness which your conscience will give on such an occasion should make up for all that might be lacking from the worldly side. I have nothing else to tell you, Reverend Mother, except that I pray God to support your good intentions, and to sustain you in all the fears you may have for the future. I am quite sure that you will meet with bad advice from those whose views are neither so pure or lofty as yours. I am in Our Lord Jesus Christ with all possible respect and sincerity yours' etc.

This letter seems to describe substantially the same situation as seen in that written in May 1673, and may be assumed to follow a few months later. The threat to appeal to be put under the ordinary proved effective, and rather than lose Leyme from the Order's jurisdiction the Abbot of Cîteaux eventually left her to her own reforming devices, but later letters show that harrassment continued.

730101   M. L'ABBÉ DE LA MADELEINE   1 January 1673
TB 119

At past fifty he should seek retreat.

730104   TRP ABBÉ, CLAIRVAUX [PIERRE HENRY]   4 January 1673
U 863

Deplores general state of the Order. General Chapters make things worse. That of 1667 caused 'scandalous confusion . . . temper and violence'. Proto-abbots do everything possible to stifle Reform. If, as head of a filiation, Clairvaux favoured introduction of general reform into France, foreigners would soon follow. R. only speaks so frankly because bidden to do so.

Henry had been Abbot since 1654, and resigned in 1676; he was not a man to take the initiative. It was widely held that foreign abbots would break away en masse if the French adopted general reform.

730104a   RM THÉRÈSE [BOUTHILLIER]   4 January 1673
TB 121

Greetings.

730109   VÉNÉRABLE MÈRE   9 January 1673
Mug I/55

'The extraordinary acts of the saints are not examples which ought to be followed' in modern monastic discipline.

She is apparently a superior who proposed some extravagant practice, from which R. strongly discouraged her.

730118   RP PASQUIER QUESNEL, CONG.ORAT.   18 January 1673
U 1168,orig.; Tans 19

Has sent respects to new General [Abel de Sainte-Marthe] but no reply called for.

730128   GODEFROI HERMANT   28 January 1673
Autographes Troussures, p. 234; TB 265 and 270

Thanks Hermant for translation of St Basil's treatises on asceticism.

730125   RP ABBÉ [ORVAL, CHARLES DE BENZERADT]   25 January 1673
Mug I/57

The number of 'anciens' (unreformed monks) staying on is an obstacle to reform. R. offers to accept postulants.

730130   DOCTEUR DE SORBONNE   30 January 1673
Mug I/58

Paris is a Babylon; 'instead of one idol, they are everywhere'.

730203   [JEAN FAVIER]   3 February 1673
A 2106,f.71

Eternity more important than men's malice.

730207   DOM JEAN-FRANÇOIS CORNUTY   7 February 1673
MS *Chronique de Tamié*; Burnier, *Hist. de Tamié*, 4

Has written to Abbot of Foucarmont asking him to send Cornuty back.

Cornuty, master of novices at Foucarmont, kept begging to be allowed back to la T. but spent seven years at Foucarmont.

* 730209   MARÉCHAL DE BELLEFONDS   9 February 1673
BN na 12959 f.6, orig.; Mug I/60

'You do me no more than justice when you do me the honour of believing that there is nothing in me more firmly established or more unshakable than my attachment to your interests and your person. I can assure you that your person is so present in my mind that no day passes but that I offer it to God with peculiar fervour. It is true that I have seen you very differently in the two states in which you have been for some time past; in the one I accounted you very happy, and in the other it seemed to me that you were much to be pitied. I think, Mgr, that you understand me very well, and that I do not need to go into this difference of views and feelings. Nevertheless, as the virtue of a Christian wholly consists in discerning the movements of God's will and letting himself be led by it, and since it is not impossible that he wishes you to be in the place and position in which you are at present, we shall not fail to ask him most earnestly to enlighten you, and meanwhile to preserve you in that integrity which is so rare and so little known, even by those who most profess to be his, and without which there is nothing genuine or solid in piety, since God's law has to be kept in every respect, and through breaking a single precept one loses all one might have acquired by exact observance of all the others. I pray God, Mgr, that your affairs will allow you a few days here in solitude and penitence, as you let us hope. I confess to you that whatever new resolutions I have taken to hide myself away more than ever and to try to pass the few remaining moments of my life in such a way as those to be succeeded only by God's eternity, I regard the honour of your visit as one of the most real consolations that I can have in this world. I beg you, Mgr, to believe me, and likewise the faithfulness and respect with which I am in Our Lord Jesus Christ,

Yours' etc.

Bellefonds' first disgrace did not last very long and he was now back at court (as he notes in his own hand on the letter).

730209a [JEAN FAVIER]   9 February 1673
A 2106,f.72 vo.

Favier's letter received after R's return from Paris, but would not have been able to do much against opposition from Maurists even if he had been in Paris.

The problem was still how to improve things at Beauvais.

730214 [M. DE SACY]   14 February 1673
TB 277

Discusses commentary on Ecclesiastes, Wisdom, and Proverbs.

730225 COMTE DE TRÉVILLE   25 February 1673
M 1214,103

Would have been glad to know that Tréville's detachment from worldly things had gone further. Only two or three persons will be excepted from R's rule of strict retreat, of whom Tréville and Bellefonds will be two. Hopes to see him in Lent.

Though Tréville was converted in 1670, he did not take up residence at the Institution de l'Oratoire *until 1674.*

730225a RELIGIEUSE [RM EUGÉNIE, BRUXELLES] 25 February 1673
Mug I/60; BN 19324 (extract, giving name of addressee)

She is quite right in thinking that she cannot achieve salvation by staying where she is; she should transfer to the Clarisses.

730225b RELIGIEUX 25 February 1673
Mug I/56

He may accept benefice so long as it does not entail cure of souls.

730301 RP PASQUIER QUESNEL, CONG.ORAT. 1 March 1673
U 1168,orig.; Tans 20

Thanks Quesnel for sending Bérulle's *Office de Jésus.*

Cardinal Pierre Bérulle (1575–1629) was the founder of the French Oratory and conspicuous for his devotion to Jesus as God Incarnate.

730405 RP PASQUIER QUESNEL, CONG.ORAT. 5 April 1673
U 1168,orig.; Tans 21

Has written to M. Feydeau. Quesnel will be welcome if he wants to visit, though greater seclusion is now the rule. Dom Arsène [Cordon] is well and his sight no worse.

M. Feydeau (1616–94), in 1673 at Vitry-le-François, was a fervent Jansenist and later criticised R. bitterly for his disavowal of Jansenist sympathies.

730409 CARDINAL JEAN BONA 9 April 1673
TB 289 (Latin)

Deplores state of the Reform and asks Bona's help in Rome.

730503 [JEAN FAVIER] 3 May 1673
A 2106,f.73 vo.

Glad to know Favier's health better.

730508 JEAN FAVIER 8 May 1673
CF 344,f.59 aut.; Gonod 32

The lad, fr Edmond, has had to be sent back; solitude did not suit him.

*730510   RM ABBESSE, LEYME [ANNE DE LA VIEUVILLE]   10 May 1673
TB 317

'It is a consolation for rightminded people, with our Order in an almost general state of decadence and desolation, to learn that God still preserves in it some souls who feel the gravity of its ills, are afflicted by them and yearn for its original sanctity, of which it may be said that no trace or vestige is anywhere to be found. You are one such, my RM, and your obligation to God for giving you such a holy attitude is all the greater because it is so rare; and few people at the present time have not abandoned truths and let themselves be carried away by the current of permissive and wrong customs. However, what you do me the honour of writing shows me that you are infinitely to be pitied for the fact that with such pure views and such pious intentions you can do so little for the reestablishment of good order in your house, that apart from the hostility you encounter in the spirits of those entrusted to your guidance, those who should persuade them to do what you so rightly desire dissuade them, and that the confessors and visitors instead of pointing out to them their obligations and their need to live according to the Rule in which they were professed, give them quite contrary principles and do not scruple to ruin all that you try to build up by your instruction and efforts. The ultimate evil, RM, and the clearest sign of God's wrath, is to see those who ought to act in his name and by his orders, and whose sole duty is to procure his glory to enlighten and sanctify souls, using their authority and ministry, either through ignorance or iniquity, to inspire in them conduct which dishonours his name and involves their consciences. It is specially on such occasions, RM, that a superior must employ all the understanding, strength, and vigilance given by God to resist the bad advice of these directors, and prevent its bad effects. He must speak, raise his voice, shout his complaints, and take them wherever he thinks they might be heeded. If those who have the chief authority in their hands looked more attentively at what the souls redeemed by Christ's blood are to him, and at the purity he demands of those whom he has withdrawn from the world and wanted to unite and consecrate to himself by the bonds and commitments of vows, if they thought of the account they will one day render him in their capacity as first fathers, they would use more discernment in choosing the people they employ to keep the holy flock of Christ, and we should not see, as we do every day, monks without piety, religion, or example in the place of true shepherds. Such disorders can only await a cure from God's hand, and will not be brought to an end by our complaints. Yet it is hard to be as moved by them as one should be and not give any sign of it, especially when the people with whom one discusses it have an interest and may derive edification from it.

As regards reform in the Common Observance, RM, there is no reason to hope for it, and those who, as you have been told, want it, do not really want it, or if they do want it, it is by illusory means and approaches, to which God will never give either blessing or success. They will talk of reform, as they have for so long, but licence will pursue its usual course, and these great plans, so vainly ostentatious, will be without effect and will come to nothing. The Order of Cîteaux, I say it with grief, is a vessel caught in a storm, leaking in every timber, without helmsman or helm; those who want to avoid shipwreck must think for themselves, in the ways offered to them by divine providence, of their own safety. That, RM, is what I think you should do, and since you want me to tell you what I think about it, I consider that you are in conscience obliged to see that the Brief issued under Alexander VII is observed in your monastery, that no life is permitted or authorised in the Common Observance except the one presented there, that anything practised apart from that is mere corruption, and that all who live failing to observe its rules are not on the path to salvation. If your confessors and visitors teach your sisters the contrary, they are seducing them; you should close the gates of your house to them, and interrupt the course of their functions and visits. If the first fathers supported them, and ordered you to follow their opinions and maxims in that respect, you would owe them no obedience. Although that Brief weakens the austerity of the Rule and relaxes its discipline in almost every detail, it would not be possible to say that one would not find salvation by following it, provided that one adds to it the spirit and piety essential to religious life, and from which no one has power of dispensation; the trouble is that it is hard to acquire and keep such inner perfection while living according to practices which are not perfect, and to rise to the saints' virtue, as one is bound to, by paths equally contrary to their teaching and example.

That, RM, is what obliges me to say that you must not stop at simply observing this Brief, and make that the limit of your perspective and intentions, but when you have established it in your community, you must try to give your sisters wider aspirations, and arouse in them the desire to conform their lives to the truth of their Rule, keep it exactly and in the way we have received it from God, through the ministry and hands of his saints.

As it is impossible that you will persuade all your sisters of that, it is difficult too to avoid some of them giving in and proving susceptible to such holy influences. But if they should all happen to show the same resistance, and all equally close their eyes to the lights of the truth, I am not afraid to say that you can do nothing nearer to God's heart, or better able to secure your eternity with him, than to submit yourself with courage to the blessed yoke they have rejected. Your dying consolation will be to have been faithful in the observance of your Rule, to have striven, by example and word, to have it embraced in all strictness by those whom it has pleased God to commit to your charge, and to have omitted nothing capable of raising them to the perfection of their state.

There will be no lack of arguments, RM, to oppose such a religious resolve, for the world is ingenious when it comes to contradicting God's wishes and ruining his plans. You will be told that you are doing something singular, that the difference between your life and that of your sisters will cause them not to trust you as much as they should, that since there is enough to achieve sanctification in the ordinary life established by the Brief, you have no grounds for wanting to aspire to more perfect things; but I am sure that you know as well as I that singularity is entirely holy and laudable when aimed only at making us more conformed to Christ's will, more submissive to his orders or advice, more like his saints, and to distinguish us from those who depart from their teaching and conduct. As for enjoying your sisters' trust less, it is much more natural to think that they will be touched by your example, and look respectfully in you on what they lack the resolve to embrace. You will even have the advantage of being better able to keep among them the regularity you have established, since it is hardly likely that they can refuse a lesser strictness to a superior who practises a much greater and more rigorous strictness. The third argument will not seem very solid, if you have once formed a conception of the degree of perfection required of souls given to Christ by the consecration of vows, and the difficulty of acquiring it. Far from neglecting anything which you know the saints have laid down for fulfilling the duties of so exalted a calling, you will be trying to observe its smallest rules, and be afraid to take risks by being too moderate in an affair as important as your salvation. Although one can work one's salvation in mitigations, it must be agreed that they remove many means, facilities, and advantages found in strict and literal observances, or the saints would have abused our credulity (which one would never dare think or say) by imposing on us a sterile and heavy yoke and giving us rules full of superstitious practices and useless observances. One may in truth dispense from corporal and tangible austerities, but one cannot diminish inner obligations; they subsist in their entirety, they are the same in every person and every time, and God demands no less perfection and sanctity in religious living under mitigations than in those keeping the rules in their original strictness. That is why there is always cause to fear in mitigated observances, for, to be exact, they leave all our debts to God unpaid; he is unwilling to remit what is legitimately his due, and they remove from us the means of discharging and satisfying them. We also see that the Church, like a charitable mother, impels us as much as she can to primitive practices, as being the most certain, and tolerates mitigations only out of compassion and the allowances she makes for her children's weaknesses.

You ask me, RM, if you can leave the jurisdiction of the Order to put yourself under that of the bishop. My answer to that is that we must not withdraw ourselves from God's order or change the dispositions of his divine providence, but as some of these are constant and immutable, so others are not; and when it happens that men's wickedness and the corruption of the times cause them to have an effect contrary to God's designs and destroy by inevitable consequences the good and the work they should strengthen, it is obvious that he does not wish them to continue, and one can change without scruples what is clearly opposed to the establishment of his glory and the execution of his wishes. God put you under the superiors of the Order for your sanctification, they should take the place of fathers, physicians, and shepherds; but if instead of giving you spiritual birth, curing your sickness, nourishing you with holy truths, they ruin the life and health of your souls, increase your ills and by themselves or by those to whom they entrust their authority, destroy in you, what they ought to be building up, then they cease to be your superiors, they lose as far as you are concerned the power of which they make such bad use; you should no longer render to them an obedience which cannot subsist with that which you owe to God, and you are entitled, and even obliged, to seek under some other authority the means of striving for your salvation, since it is not possible to do so under their guidance.

That is precisely the case in which you find yourself. Those who are given to you as confessors, from what you tell me, upset your sisters' spirits, fill them with wrong principles, stifle the good sentiments which you try to inspire in them; they are even religious living in scandal. The visitors who ought to prevent these disorders maintain them and in a three-day visit ruin more than you can establish by careful diligence and vigilance in several years. With evil thus reduced to such extremes, and capable of having even more distressing consequences, there can be no doubt that you have good reasons for removing yourself from the Order's jurisdiction and placing yourself under that of the ordinary. Such a plan will meet considerable difficuties in execution, but it may be well that they will not be insurmountable, and I am even sure that the man whom God has given you as bishop is too virtuous, zealous and charitable not to contribute as much as in him lies to make the plan succeed.

As regards your church, RM, I can give you no other advice than to construct and arrange it according to the spirit of our Order and the simplicity recommended by the saints. I know that such an opinion is contrary to the usage and habits of our time, but in truth I do not think that these should be preferred to the feelings of those who have received from God a manifest mission to speak to us of our duties, and give us rules of conduct. It seems to be enough for making up one's mind without difficulty between such opposite principles to know that the first originate in the concupiscence of men, the others have God's spirit for their principle.

In short, RM, whatever kind of life you may resolve to adopt, you should be convinced that your profession obliges you to nothing less than living according to evangelical perfection, to aspire ceaselessly towards it. That is for you and all your sisters a duty of necessity, which God will judge not from the false ideas which religious of lax and evil life have given you of your obligations, but on what they really are; and ignorance of essential truths which ought to be known, and trust in those with authority over us, who have distorted them, will be equally unable to protect us from the rigour of his justice. God, who has received you among the ranks of his brides, demands of you and all those to whom he has granted the same grace, a purity worthy of him. Men may well, out of proper and particular considerations, reduce the austerity of your lives, but not the sanctity of your behaviour. You may well, as I have already said, be discharged from some corporal aspects of the rule, and some practices of outward penitence, but as for those which concern direction and progress in piety, the ordering of your souls, that is a duty for which there is no dispensation, that is the right of God alone, and on that no human power has the right to lay its hand. You are therefore obliged, RM, by your profession to practise, as far as you can all that is spiritual in your rule, all the instructions it proposes in the chapter on good works and degrees of humility, regarded by most monks as mere pious speculations and not as constant rules of conduct. I am not afraid to say that you will only be genuinely religious inasmuch as you are faithful in the observance of these holy practices, after a great saint has declared that any assembly which does not offer to God spiritual hosts and the sacrifice of a contrite heart is abominable in his eyes.

What concerns you personally, RM, is to instruct your sisters more by your practice than by your words, to be as superior to them by the regularity of your life as by the rank and authority which God has given you over them, so to behave that they live and learn from all your acts, as from a living book, what they should avoid and what they should embrace. Above all, RM, erase from your heart and your memory all the advantages which your birth may have given you in the world. You cannot retain any external signs of it without offending the simplicity of your calling and him whose spirit, as he says himself, rests only on the humble. Remember on every occasion that the only glory and greatness you should recognise on earth is that of belonging to Christ and serving him.

I see that I am far exceeding the limits of a normal letter, but you obliged me to do so by the one you did me the honour of writing to me, by the trust you showed in me and by the necessity in which you placed me of telling you what I felt. I should not have replied as I ought, and as God seemed to ask of me, if I had expressed myself at less length and with more reserve. I pray him to bless your plans, to give you light and discernment to know the way in which he wishes you to walk and not to let you listen to the bad advice of those who would like to stop you allowing yourself to be led by the movements of his spirit. I am in him with all respect yours' etc.

Apparently the abbess had woken up very late to the fact that the provisions of In Suprema *might apply to her house, and the situation here described arose from her efforts to implement the Brief against opposition from above as well as from below. From 1662–1672 the visitor for the province to which Leyme belonged was Pierre Capolade, prior of Bonnecombe, but he was reported absent through sickness at the General Chapter of 1672 and in his place was nominated François Lonjon, provisor of the rundown college of St Bernard at Toulouse. For some reason Leyme is not listed in the records of the Chapter of 1667, though three daughter houses appear, and it is only in 1683 that Leyme and the fourth daughter house are listed, so that it is not clear when, or by whom, the abbey had been visited before then. The Vicar-General of Cahors went there in 1668, as to all the other feminine houses of the diocese, and left valuable details. The Bishop since 1660 was Nic. Sevin, an active and pious man who died in 1678. The abbess had undertaken major building work in the church, to which she eventually added two chapels.*

730515 RP ABBÉ [? SEPTFONS] 15 May 1673
TB 293

Always glad to hear from him.

*730518   G. LE ROY, HAUTEFONTAINE   18 May 1673
U 767 aut.

'I am sending you, Monsieur, my answer to the letter I had from this good Benedictine. I admire his zeal and resolve, I hope that Our Lord will give his blessing and that he will find no difficulty in executing his plan. I am telling him that we shall receive him with joy whenever he come to us. I am not surprised that the two others did not persevere; it is quite hard to resist arguments, when most of the time good and bad arguments look so much alike. I have nothing to add to this note except to assure you of the respect with which I am in Christ yours' etc.

730600   TRP ABBÉ   [? June 1673]
Mug I/79

A small injury to his hand prevents him from writing. Refers to letter to Cîteaux published despite him.

This seems to be the letter 720529, declining charge of visitor, and published in 1673 in Examen du Chapitre de 1672. *His correspondent could either be Jouaud (who died in June 1673) or perhaps Pierre Gaultier, Abbot of le Pin, who succeeded Jouaud as leader of the Reform.*

730607   RM MARIE-LOUISE [BOUTHILLIER]   7 June 1673
TD/A

'You can only cause me much joy every time you let me have news of you and show me that you remember me. We shall commend to Our Lord the person you indicate, and pray him to give her grace to be able to consecrate herself to his service in so holy an observance and community as yours. I did not deserve the honour M. de la Taignan, her father, did me in thinking of me, still less his kindness in taking up and supporting our interests, as he told you, in the Parlement. Please tell him, my dear sister, that I deeply appreciate so special a favour, and that I shall try to show my gratitude before God which is all I can do in my situation. Remember me before Our Lord, my dear sister, and believe me in him with all possible affection and appreciation yours' etc.

The person in question seems to be Sister Marie-Ange-Alexis de la Taignant, who died on 5 May 1677, presumably having been professed in 1673 or 1674.

730607a   ROBERT ARNAULD D'ANDILLY   7 June 1673
A 6038,f.73 orig.

Glad to know that Andilly is now quietly back in his retreat. Mme du Plessis-Guénégaud has visited and talked of Andilly.

She was Elisabeth de Choiseul, cousin of Gilbert, bp of Comminges and then Tournai. Her salon had been a rendezvous for Jansenists and R. attended it before his conversion.

730607b   [RM LOUISE-HENRIETTE D'ALBON]   7 May 1673
A 2106,f.73 vo.

Glad to know that she now lives in peace and harmony. Essential that she should be truly obedient to her superior.

730607c   RP ABBÉ [? DE LA COLOMBE, PIERRE DE LA SALLE]   7 June 1673
Mug I/63

Problem of a disobedient monk; if he submits treat him like a kind father; if not seek a dispensation to send him away.

730611   JEAN FAVIER   11 June 1673
CF 344,f.61 aut.; Gonod 33

Edmond 'a good lad, very pious . . . Once servants reach a certain degree of piety they are no longer any use'. Does not think Order of Grandmont will suit him: 'this reform, from what I have heard, is very insecure; it is so much in the hands of the General that he can upset it when he likes.'

The small Order of Grandmont, to which R's priory at Boulogne belonged, was gradually reformed from 1642, and Thiers, Favier's home, became the centre for the reformed movement. With the death in 1689 of the General, Charles Frémont, the impetus died away. Favier was in correspondence with several Grandmontine houses, and it was natural for him to send Edmond to one after he had failed at la T.

730611a   MME [DE SAINT-LOUP]   11 June 1673
Mug I/64; BN 19324 (extract, with name of addressee)

She must learn to accept losses; 'penitence does not consist only in weeping, but in weeping over what God wishes us to weep over.'

730619   ROBERT ARNAULD D'ANDILLY   19 June 1673
A 6038,f.81 orig.

Sad at death of Mme Bouthillier [R's aunt]; it was through her that he first knew Andilly.

She died on 26 May 1673.

730624   RP PASQUIER QUESNEL, CONG.ORAT.   24 June 1673
U 1168,orig.; Tans 22

RP Payen had been at la T. for six days.

730700   RP   [? July 1673]
Mug II/72
Regrets unexpected recent death. *Requêtes au Roi* give cause for hope. News from Rome not surprising.

As well as a request drawn up in the name of all the members of the Reform, one, signed by R alone, was also presented to the King, begging intervention in the protracted dispute following In Suprema (see 730807). Jouaud had died suddenly on 2 June, and the Requêtes were presented to the King by the Abbot of Châtillon on 22 August, so that this undated letter could be July or August, probably August. In Rome it looked as though the Common Observance was about to prevail, but the tide appeared to turn in September, clearly after this letter was written.

730701   MONSIEUR   1 July 1673
Mug I/65
Would like to see M. and worries about his health.

730702   ROBERT ARNAULD D'ANDILLY   2 July 1673
A 6038,f.90 orig.
Had told Mme Duplessis-Guénégaud that M. de la Vernète had behaved badly.

*730712   G. LE ROY, HAUTEFONTAINE   12 July 1673
U 767 aut.   [answered 2 August]

'I am very sorry, Monsieur, that we are to be deprived of the consolation for which we had hoped, for since there is no way of removing the difficulty put in the way of the good religious whose letter you were kind enough to send me, his plan must remain unfulfilled. In truth, his superiors are demanding something quite unjust and against all the rules. God alone knows vocations, and our inner hearts are always uncovered before his eyes, but as regards men, especially those who are as unenlightened as I, they need time and long trial to be able to make sure, and even then without certainty, of the secret dispositions of individuals. I have nothing, Monsieur, to add to this note except that I am most obliged for your interest in our affairs, and it is with all possible respect and gratitude that I am in Christ yours etc.

PS Dom Rigobert is not failing to do as you order. It is his chief concern before Our Lord; he does not deem himself worthy of the honour you are doing him and is duly grateful.'

Rigobert had been prior of Hautefontaine before coming to la T. and had much offended Le Roy by politely refusing to return there as regular abbot.

*730719   BISHOP OF LUÇON [HENRI BARILLON]   19 July 1673
L orig.; P f.762

'I cannot let your Theologal [Canon Theologian] leave here, Mgr, without taking the opportunity to remember myself to you, and express my consolation at hearing from him in detail how God is blessing your solicitude and labours. I had hoped for nothing less for you from his mercy, and I never doubted for a moment that having called you as he did he would take care to lead you. I praise him with all my heart for the ease which he causes you to find in the functions of your ministry and the docility he puts into the hearts of your people, but above all for the faithfulness with which you devote yourself entirely to their sanctification and service. I use the word service because your chief glory is to be a servant in the house of him who came into the world, not to demand or receive service from men, but to give it to them. I am sure, Mgr, that one of the main feelings God has given you is that of service, as it is the most important, and that you looked on yourself as the servant of all those souls in your charge from the moment when you saw yourself their father and shepherd. It is a great thing for a prelate to work diligently at governing a diocese and to make it his sole occupation, imitating the Son of God in his pastoral vigilance, but to follow him in his humiliations and abasements, that is extremely rare in these days and something few even think of. Yet, you know as well as I do, if that wish does not fill his heart, animate his movements, motivate his words, nothing is less worthy of a bishop's calling and the perfection to which God's order commits him than the life he leads, whatever the apparent regularity it may have. For the rest, Mgr, no one could be more edified and pleased than I have been with your Theologal. His views seemed to me so pious and strict, his zeal for good, his love and respect for your person so great that one could not wish for more. I confess that though our resolutions about solitude are stricter than ever, we were unable to keep them as far as he was concerned. Everything which bears your name and confesses it carries too much weight and recommendation not to dispense us from that resolve. Always be my friend, Mgr, as much as I honour and respect you; though that is going very far, I expect nothing less from your goodness.'

*730723   RP ABBÉ [CHÂTILLON, CLAUDE LE MAÎTRE]   23 July 1673
Mug I/66

'You will learn our news, my very dear Father, from fr N. who passed this way, and you will know from him what thoughts have occurred to us on the subject of our Observance and how to preserve it. I cannot help hoping that God will not permit its ruin, and will not abandon us into the hands of those who would not like us any better than they do if they knew us better, as long as in all this we aspire solely to his glory and the renewal of the true spirit which he inspired in our fathers.

'I hope that your journey will be successful; but if you want Our Lord to bless it, remember that you must go in a spirit of penitence, banishing from your heart all desire for things of vanity and mere curiosity. Judge for yourself, my dear Father, whether, going to Rome for the reasons which make you go there in the desolate state of our Observance and with such clear signs of God's anger against us, you could possibly have any other feelings than to try and appease him by sincere penitence and humility; and if such an attitude would be compatible with the pleasure you might take in a journey which offers in abundance, and even under the most innocent pretexts, all kinds of delight and satisfaction. If you fall into such unseemly behaviour, you will have to account for it fully to God, and that alone is more than is necessary to make all your negotiations of no avail. By God's mercy I committed no great excesses when I was sent to Rome, yet I did not live as withdrawn and penitent a life as I should have, and I assure you that if my health permitted, I would have made a second journey there to repair the errors of the first. It takes very little to lose God's protection for ever. Since that of men has failed us, we must do everything to dispel the wickedness of the age by our own good lives; in the name of God, remember that. The advice I give you is not the fancy of someone wrapped in meditation; I speak to you, my dear Father, after solid reflection. The trust which you surely recall having had in me gives me the right to speak to you freely. God will ask you to justify the smallest of your actions, and no unnecessary ones are permitted to men of our profession, particularly in the present situation, when tears should be our normal diet. If I could do anything to help you while you are away, there is nothing possible which I would not be willing to do to show you, my very dear Father, that no one could honour you with more affection than I. I am yours' etc.

It is by no means clear whether or not Abbot Le Maître did go to Rome, and it seems that the mission of 1677 of Abbot Fleur de Montagne of Foucarmont was the next, and last, Reformed initiative in Rome.

730725   RP PASQUIER QUESNEL, CONG.ORAT.   25 July 1673
U 1168,orig.; Tans 23

Forwards a letter from Payen, who has come back after two months. R. advises him against a vocation at la T.

Payen appears to be an Oratorian.

730725a   DOCTEUR DE SORBONNE   25 July 1673
Mug I/67

M. has been ill, but now better and could allow himself time off his pastoral duties for a visit to la T.

730729   RP PASQUIER QUESNEL, CONG.ORAT.   29 July 1673
U 1168,orig.; Tans 24

Sends an answer to RP Hubert, an Oratorian: 'It is rare that ecclesiastics are destined for la T. I confess that unless I find in them twice the vocation I require in seculars, I find it hard to decide to accept them.' Cistercian recruits also have to go through the novitiate at la T. because 'they are so grossly ignorant of everything concerning their rule . . . I have not yet met one who found cause to complain of our conduct.'

Hubert (1640–1717) was presumably one of R's many recruiting agents.

730802   JEAN FAVIER   2 August 1673
CF 344,f.63 aut.

Edmond has failed to find a community to accept him and would do better staying with a parish-priest. Death of M. de Vernassal [15 April].

Vernassal left a daughter and two sons orphaned, and a lot of financial wrangling with R's brother Henri.

730807   LOUIS XIV   7 August 1673
Dub I/459

Respectful covering letter for *Requête au Roi.*

730808   MINISTRE ET SECRÉTAIRE D'ETAT [? POMPONNE]   8 August 1673
Mug I/69

Sends him *Requête au Roi* and begs his help in the cause of the Reform.

730817   DOCTEUR DE SORBONNE   17 August 1673
Mug I/70

Three ecclesiastics accepted as postulants in past three days, but R. would never accept any who were capable of serving the Church elsewhere unless they had a clear vocation.

*730819   G. LE ROY, HAUTEFONTAINE   19 August 1673
U 767 aut.   [answered 15 September]

'I beg you to believe, Monsieur, that there was no intention of offending or annoying you in the paper which you saw in the hands of the Bishop of Châlons. It was composed only from considerations of christian charity, and apart from the fact that you most urgently requested it of me, I did not think that I could with conscience fail to defend, according to my lights, men and holy truths which, it seemed to me, you were attacking with no grounds or justice.

There was no need, Monsieur, for you to trouble to make observations on it, and allow me to say that it is most unlikely that the Bishop of Châlons would become any more involved in discussion of this affair. There is no moment of his life without its special purpose. It would not be showing proper respect for his occupations, and it seems to me much more suitable to leave in his hands the dissertation, answer, and remarks without ever talking about them. For my part, Monsieur, although on this occasion I have dispensed myself from one of my chief duties, that of keeping quiet and remaining silent, there would be many grounds for criticism if I were to carry things further and become engaged in endless disputes and replies. Please therefore allow me, Monsieur, to leave it at that, to assure you that I cease to remember all that was said and exchanged, that I forget all grounds for complaint, even the title of your dissertation, baseless though it is, and that I protest that there is no service or mark of respect I should not be willing to pay you to show that I am yours' etc.

Vialart de Herse, Bp of Châlons was a friend of both parties and unsuccessfully tried to heal the breach. The paper in question is R's reply to Le Roy, as always widely disseminated under a supposed seal of secrecy.

730827 FRÈRE 27 August 1673
Mug I/71

Obliged to seek a less austere life than that of la T. R. will pray for him as 'for the rest of our brethren, among whom I will always number you in my heart'.

730900 MONSIEUR [September 1673]
Mug I/93

The commissioners have been granted but not named.

They were named on 27 September, to adjudicate on claims of Reform.

730900a RP, COLLÈGE DES BERNARDINS [? September 1673]
Mug I/80

On RP's dispute with superior.

The letter is almost certainly to Bernard du Teillé, provisor of the college, who had been appointed visitor of Reformed houses on Jouaud's death, but because the Abbot of Cîteaux made the appointment, it was rejected by the abbots of the Reform, not on personal grounds, but constitutionally.

730907 MADAME [? D'ALBON] 7 September 1673
Mug I/72

On blows caused to family by successive deaths.

M. de Vernassal had died in April, Mme Bouthillier in May, and it is probably to his sister that R. writes.

730914   [JEAN FAVIER]   14 September. 1673
A 2106,f.74 vo.

Recently spent three days on business of the order at *Institution de l'Oratoire* in Paris, received numerous visits, but said mass in private chapel. Denies rumours about him.

730916   [? RM LOUISE ROGIER]   16 September 1673
A 2106,f.75 vo.

Saw RP X for two days only. Asks for prayers.

This unaddressed letter is probably to the Visitation at Tours, either to RM Rogier or his niece, simply on the grounds that the series is mainly to these correspondents.

*730920   MARÉCHAL DE BELLEFONDS   20 September 1673
BN na 12959 f.8, orig.; Mug I/181

'Convinced as I am, Mgr, of your zeal for the glory of God and the kindness with which you honour us, I can only believe, regarding the matter on which we had the honour to write to you, that you have not found the opportunity or the means to do what you have not done in this respect. I would not have been bold enough to make a recommendation to you unless I had believed that you would receive it quite freely and without embarrassment. The thing we ask, Mgr, is, as it seems to us, perfectly just; and it seems to me that nothing could be more appropriate to the life we lead than to seek the means to live in peace, and to prevent anyone troubling the calm of our solitude. However, as it is possible that others will have different views about this than ours, and that what we have regarded as just and reasonable will not be so considered by those who have our destiny in their hands, we are prepared to accept whatever may befall in a spirit of equal submission; and in that we are much more concerned with God's order and the obligation to follow it than with our desire to succeed in these matters. I confess to you, Mgr, that once one is as convinced as one should be that everything falls under divine providence, from which nothing is exempt, one finds God's will written everywhere, in ill as in good fortune, and one submits to it without great difficulty. It is a real misfortune to attach what is most precious in this world, I mean peace and quiet, to uncertain adventures and make one's state of mind depend on that of human affairs, which almost never turn out as we wish. If they sometimes appear to succeed, they are always accompanied by vexatious circumstances which prevent us from finding in these affairs pure joy and satisfaction. God permits this and in his mercy spreads bitterness over all the events of life, in order to disabuse us about creatures and make us understand that we seek from them vain consolations which they are not capable of bestowing. That is a truth which you have long experienced, Mgr, and I am even sure that you have gone further, that your experience has not been fruitless, and has produced in you all the consequences and effects that it should. But, with all that, one needs constantly to bring this truth before one's eyes, for it is easy to forget it, or at least we usually behave as though all memory of it had been effaced. All this, Mgr, is a language scarcely spoken or heard in the world in which you are. But God, who gave you to understand it, will not allow you to lose that understanding, and I am convinced that he will often say to your innermost heart what you do not hear from the mouth of men. There is no necessity, Mgr, for me to say very much to make you believe how dear to me is all that concerns your person and particularly your sanctification. I assure you that no day goes past but that I ask it of God and this is one of my chief obligations until I breathe my last. I am with more faithfulness and respect than I can express yours etc.

PS I do not know how to thank you, Mgr, for the tokens you have given us of your remembrance and charity combined. You have raised us from our poverty without intending or thinking to do so, for what has been sent to us on your behalf is too magnificent for persons like us, who profess to be the contrary. Thus we have destined the object for use on special days, and not for daily use.'

*730927 PIERRE NICOLE 27 September 1673
T 2240,13 orig.

'We are sending you, Monsieur, the justification for our remark on the passage in the *Morale* permitting religious to leave their monasteries in order to help their parents in extreme need. St Thomas decides exactly the opposite in his *Summa* q. 101 of the 2.2 art. 4, in the answer to the fifth objection; he says that a religious who has been professed must be deemed to be a man dead to the world and may no longer leave his cloister, in which he is, as it were, buried with Christ, and is no longer allowed to involve himself with concern for secular matters. St Basil says roughly the same thing, also St Bernard. In fact, one can only imagine two normal ways whereby a religious can subvent his parents' poverty, one being manual labour, the other employment in some benefice or the celebration of masses. As regards the former it is hardly likely that a religious, weakened already by the austerity of his life, can work sufficiently to provide subsistence for both his parent and himself together; as regards the two other ways, I leave you to judge, Monsieur; for my part I do not believe that the poverty of parents is a legitimate sign of vocation for ecclesiastical functions.

The author you were told about who testifies that the religious of Cîteaux said mass only on feast days and their vigils is quoted under the name of Pierre de Reims, Bishop of Paris, in the preface to the book *De la tradition de l'église*, p. 16 of the fourth edition. If this author means by feasts Sundays and reserved feasts, his account has as its basis the Usages of Cîteaux, which states that if a religious who is a priest has not said mass on Sunday, he can say it on some other day of the week. But note that in each monastery there was said every day a conventual mass, one of the Virgin, and one of the dead with proper colours, and for the days of Easter, Christmas, and Pentecost they applied the mass of the feasts themselves to satisfy the intention and the two later masses at which they made special commemoration. It is further certain that religious are not absolutely obliged to say mass on feast days and Sundays, and that they abstained from doing so for quite slight reasons. Priests who did not want to say mass were even permitted to receive the lay communion with the brothers. There, Monsieur, are our observations, to which you will pay whatever attention you see fit. I profit again from this occasion, Monsieur, to tell you how much we appreciate the honour you did us, and the consolation remaining to us from it, and I can assure you that whatever you may think of our gratitude, you could never believe it to be as great and as deep as it is. It is with all my heart and all the esteem of which I am capable that I am yours etc.

PS You will oblige me by assuring Monsieur Arnauld of my profound respect for him.'

The Morale *refers to the book by Floriot, usually known as* Morale ... du Pater, *published in 1672, in which Floriot maintains that duty to needy parents takes precedence over religious vows. R. was still arguing the contrary more than ten years later. Nicole had just paid a visit to la T. and Arnauld was about to. Pierre de Reims, better known as Peter the Chanter (Pierre le Chantre, Petrus Cantor) never became Bp of Paris, although his name was proposed, and after a distinguished teaching career in Paris died as Dean of Reims in 1197. His principal work was published in 1639 under the title, taken from the opening words,* Verbum abbreviatum. *In chapter 29 (PL 205:104) there is some discussion about saying Mass, but neither the exact passage nor the book on church tradition mentioned here (almost certainly not its proper title) can be identified.*

*731002   GUILLAUME LE ROY   2 October 1673
U 767 aut.

'I have just this moment learned with great sorrow of the loss you have sustained of your nephew. As I know how dear he was to you, and for how many reasons you must have loved him, no one could be more keenly touched than I. Please believe therefore that I share all your feelings on this subject to the fullest extent, and that there is nothing I would not do to show you this. Meanwhile, all I can say is that God does not seek our advice when he decides about our lives and those of the persons we most love, that he acts as master and sovereign of that which is his alone, and whatever he does, we have no right to complain, but on the contrary have the indispensable obligation to submit to all his wishes. That much you know better than I, Monsieur, and that is what cannot too often be repeated on such occasions, when nature, dead as it may be, still returns fully to life and often causes us pain. I pray God, Monsieur, that he may himself be your consolation and that he may grant you all the grace you may need, to use as he requires it of you in a situation as grievous as this. I am beyond all I can say yours etc.

PS Forgive me for writing so badly; I did not want to let the brief opportunity go by.'

Le Roy had four married brothers; it is not known to which nephew this letter refers. Even by R's standards this letter is abominably written, with many erasures.

731004   DOCTEUR DE SORBONNE   4 October 1673
TD E

Criticises 'a good father' who has ruined the Order by working for twenty years in the name of general reform. Sends his *Requête au Roi* [composed in August]. The King has appointed commissioners. More than fifty brethren at la T. 'who care very little for this world and are ready like Maccabees to die in defence of the faith'.

731025   MGR [? BISHOP OF ANGERS, HENRI ARNAULD]   25 October 1673
A 2106,f.75

Only respect prevents him from writing more often. Mgr's brother visited recently and was much impressed.

Antoine Arnauld visited at the end of September.

731027   RM   27 October 1673
A 2106,f.76 vo.

Greater importance of interior dispositions than external practice in religious life. Refers to SS Bernard and Benedict.

731100   M. L'ABBÉ   [October/November 1673]
Mug II/23

R. has just spent two days in Paris; is sending Abbot of Châtillon to see him for the good of the Reform.

Both the date and addressee of this letter are problematic.

731029   LOUIS DE MARILLAC   29 October 1673
Mug I/100; BN 19324 (extract with name); Le Nain, *Vie* 1719, I p. 157 (with date)

Marillac prevented by bad health from instructing people in general, but concerns himself with training ecclesiastics. R. invites him to la T.

*731113   MARÉCHAL DE BELLEFONDS   13 November 1673
BN na 12959 f.10, orig.; Mug II/2

'I marvel, Mgr, at the conduct of God who involves you more than ever in worldly occupations, when he inspires you with more desire to be his and attach yourself to his service. As you have taken no step nor made any effort to procure such employment, which results entirely from the choice and goodness of the Master, there is every reason to believe that God will not refuse you the protection which he normally gives to those who follow the promptings of his providence and look at things with christian eyes, as coming from his hand, although they are transmitted by the hand of men. Although the situation in which you are, Mgr, does not appear very suitable for preserving the sentiments and desires which you have been receiving for some time from God's mercy, yet it is not so contrary to that as one might think. It is hard for you to think often that there is no quality which God more claims than that of Lord and God of hosts, that he does indeed control all their movements, that battles are only engaged and won by his orders, if you do not at the same time have continual cause to be occupied with him, be elevated to him, and even to be united with him amid all the occasions which a man less christian would have for being separated and distracted from him. As you know, Mgr, nothing could more effectively put you and keep you in such necessary dispositions than to hold before your eyes as much as you can the exact reckoning that you will one day make to God of the charge imposed upon you, and of the means you have taken to acquit yourself as worthily and deservingly as you should of so great and difficult a command, believing that there is none so effective as to look at God in all things, to undertake nothing without consulting him and to expect much more from his assistance than from all the strength and might of men. As for us, Mgr, we shall not cease raising our hands and our hearts to heaven to commend to him all that concerns you. This has long been one of our principal obligations, which we discharge with all the more care and fervour as we know your needs to be greater and your person more exposed. Do me the honour of believing that I am with all possible respect and faithfulness in Our Lord Jesus Christ yours etc.

PS We will not fail, Mgr, to pray God for the persons you commend to us. He has chosen souls everywhere, which he can preserve when it pleases him from the world's corruption, but that is very rare.

Our affair, Mgr, has had the success we desired. You say nothing about it, but I am sure that it is to you that we are chiefly obliged.'

Bellefonds annotated this letter 'on my service in Flanders'. He had been recalled to command, and fought at Maastricht and Tournai. R's affair presumably refers to attempts to enlist royal favour on the side of the Reform.

731123   MME [? DE SAINT-LOUP]   23 November 1673
U 863 orig.

Thanks Princess Palatine for her kindness and Mme for looking after their interests.

The Princess was Anne de Gonzague (1618–84), whose conversion by Bossuet in 1672 (with support from R.) had caused universal wonder.

*731129   G. LE ROY, HAUTEFONTAINE   29 November 1673
U 767 orig.

'The first I knew of your illness, Monsieur, was when I received news of your recovery. God spared us the anxiety it would have caused. It only remains for us to praise him for restoring your health, and that we shall not fail to do, concerned as we are with it. The weather is so bad at present that it will be some time, and not without difficulty, that your strength will come back. Although I am sure, Monsieur, that my respect and consideration for you need no guarantor, I am none the less delighted that you should have been assured on that score by persons in a position to know my innermost heart, and whose testimony you cannot regard as suspect. I humbly beg you to believe that my feelings in this respect have at all times been what they should be, and that you do me justice in thinking of it as you tell me you always have. There is nothing, Monsieur, that I would not do to merit that opinion and show you how sincerely I intend to retain it, but being unable to do anything about it, all I can do is to form wishes. Do me then the honour of believing that it is with all the fullness and sincerity of my heart that I accept the assurances that you offer me of the goodness with which you honour me, and that I could not possibly be more grateful, nor more respectfully yours etc.

PS I have received, Monsieur, the two copies you did me the honour of sending, and I had many reasons for regarding them with esteem and emotion. First the content of the work, which is most edifying, second what you contributed to it, finally my consideration for the author. For two years the poor man pressed me insistently to receive him into this monastery, and his age was the only reason preventing me from admitting him, yet, far from being put off by refusals, two days before dying he wrote to one of his friends to say that the time had come for him to make his retreat here, that he was ready to leave, and that if there were any difficulties about accepting him here he was resolved to die at the door.

Dom Prior and dom Rigobert are most obliged to you, Monsieur, for doing them the honour of remembering them, and assure you of their humble respects.'

731229   JEAN FAVIER   29 December 1673
CF 344,f.65 aut.; Gonod 35

Very sorry for Edmond, but life at la T. has not changed, nor has Edmond's basic nature, and he will never fit in there. Sends *Requête au Roi.*

74/1   RM, GIF [ANNE DE MONGLAT]   [? 1674]
TB 278

Importance of decision regarding her recent appointment as abbess.

She did not actually take over until May 1676.

74/2   RM [AGNÈS DE BELLEFONDS]   [1674]
Mug II/83
Monsieur [Bellefonds] has left court and 'you did not consider his retreat a disgrace'.

74/3   M. L'ABBÉ   [1674]
Mug II/78
Hopes to see M. one day; he is in charge of some nuns. Refers to *Requête au Roi* and *Eclaircissement* [*sur l'état présent de l'Ordre de Cîteaux*, published 1674].

74/4   BISHOP   [January ? 1674]
Mug II/77
New year greetings. Sorry to hear of bp's poor health.

* 740123 RM MARIE-LOUISE [BOUTHILLIER]   23 January 1674
TD/A
'My dear sister, I am extremely obliged for the signs you give me of your charity and thought for me. My life is not as useful to the world as you think. The place I occupy is of such small consideration that when it pleases God to remove me and deprive me of life, I cannot see that anyone will be the loser. Ask him, my dear sister, to give me grace to die well rather than to live a long time. We shall not fail to commend to him my niece's vocation with particular care. Please remember us before Our Lord and offer him my person and needs, which are infinitely greater than I can say. In exchange we shall continue to present to him everything that concerns you and pray him to make you holy in this life and the next. I am in him and with all my heart yours' etc.

The niece in question is probably Mlle de Vernassal, whose vocation is discussed again in 1679, but she was only about ten in 1674, and the reference may be to R's other niece, Louise-Henriette d'Albon, who had been going through a very difficult time at Tours.

*740206   G. LE ROY, HAUTEFONTAINE   6 February 1674
U 767 orig.
'I am most deeply obliged to you, Monsieur for giving me such proof of the honour of being in your mind, and I do not doubt that this will be a fortunate year for me if you address yourself to God with the prayer that it should be for me as you desire. True Christians who seek God alone and who are engaged solely in studying his will in order to follow it cannot have bad ones, for since they make following his will their sole form of happiness, they are always content, and are equally consoled by the bad as by the good things that happen to them. I do not belong to that

number, Monsieur, by my conduct, though I am obliged to belong by the duties of my profession. You cause us great joy by letting us hope that we may have the honour of seeing you. I humbly beg you to believe that I feel too strongly about it not to look forward to that moment most impatiently. I pray God, Monsieur, to heap blessings on your head, and protest that it is with all possible respect and sincerity that I am yours etc.

PS Dom Prior and dom Rigobert thank you profusely for being kind enough to think of them, and are not failing, either of them, to offer you to Our Lord. The latter has been ill for six weeks with very bad rheumatism, which made us fear something worse. He is beginning to get better and come into choir.'

740302   [RM LOUISE ROGIER] 2 March 1674
M 1214,94

Religious life demands submission to providence. His niece was right to resist a move.

740319   SR LOUISE [DE LA VALLIÈRE] 19 March 1674
TD A (fragment); BN 19324 (extract with name)

'Living in outward penitence only to be lost in the end are not incompatibles.'

*740328   MARÉCHAL DE BELLEFONDS 28 March 1674
BN na 12959 f.12, orig.; Mug II/16

'I have just learned, Mgr, that you have withdrawn from court, and this news has reached me with no details of the circumstances. I can assure you that no one, without exception, could feel more keenly than I do everything that concerns you, but I should not be speaking to you sincerely if I said that the news grieves me, being convinced as I am that God is neither known nor served in the world you are leaving, and that to be occupied and employed in it constitutes as many obstacles and impediments to your salvation as a life of retreat offers means and facilities for achieving it. Those very people, Mgr, who live in the world with the greatest number of rules are often as exposed as those who profess to keep none; for as it is almost impossible for them not to consider themselves in the light of their disorders and excesses, so they rarely fail to find the means of justifying themselves in their works, and it very frequently happens that they do not scruple to be content with the sort of life which is anything but what it should be to be looked at by God and bring before his eyes the marks of a christian life. So it is, Mgr, that those accidents which worldly people call disgrace are not in fact such. One would need to have no principles or knowledge but theirs, or rather to be as deprived as they are of moral rules and discernment, to judge as they do, since in truth these are not strokes of ill fortune, but the design and conduct of God's mercy, using unexpected events to pull those who enjoy his special protection from the midst of the court, as from the midst of a shipwreck. I do not doubt, Mgr, that these are your thoughts and feelings in the present situation, and I venture to say that you would not be responding to the grace that God has shown you if you did not recognise his hand, through all that might hide it if you had been less enlightened by him. We shall ask him from the bottom of our hearts that while he speaks to you, he will grant you understanding of his word and the faithfulness to execute it in every respect. God does not always speak to men with the same strength, and he usually remains silent towards them when, having explained himself through some important events, his word has not been as successful and effective as it should have been. More attention should be paid to God's seasons than is generally realised, and the chief object of a true Christian's study is to husband every moment. We offer you, Mgr, ourselves, our house and our prayers; that is all we have to offer in our helpless state. We are bound to you by so many bonds of affection, gratitude and respect that we can find no words to express it.'

Bellefonds annotated this letter 'on my second disgrace'. He had fallen out with Condé and been once more dismissed, this time to l'Ile-Marie, near Valognes.

740424   JEAN FAVIER   24 April 1674
CF 344,f.67 aut; Gonod 36

R. is fond of Edmond, but there can be no question of receiving him at la T. M. Albon is in Paris on business, but there is no sign that he will pay his debts.

740500   MME COMPAGNON   [May 1674]
TD C

Profession of her son [Etienne, professed May 1674, died 1716]

740521   RP PASQUIER QUESNEL, CONG. ORAT.   21 May 1674
U 1168, orig.; Tans 25

Death of Maréchal de Laigues [1614–74], 'a solid and trusted friend'.

*740702   MARÉCHAL DE BELLEFONDS   2 July 1674
BN na 12959 f.14, orig.; Mug II/185

'Allow us, Mgr, the honour of assuring you that we follow you into your retreat and remember you before God as is our duty and as we promised. The more I think of the way he has disposed your heart and made you free, the more you seem to me obliged to recognise such great goodness with great fidelity. Since there is no sign that God has removed you from the court for ever, and no one could advise you to remain in retreat once his providence opens the door to you to leave it, so none of those who have your true interests at heart can fail to tell you that you must be careful to make of your present state what God wants you to make of it, and profit from such a happy occasion to strengthen yourself to despise those things which you know it is not in your hands to preserve, and to gather new strength to resist those which experience has shown you attracted you most. It is beyond dispute that it is not possible to recover full health in those places where one has contracted sickness, when the cause has been unhealthy air; similarly there are certain spiritual disorders which could never be cured in the outside world and which persist despite all efforts to find a remedy. In fact, the reason that efforts meet with so little success is that their roots go down deep in us, that the world is like a field in which they find abundant nourishment, and we only tackle them very feebly. What is worse, their progress, like their origin, is imperceptible, and we only discover them once they have caused extreme damage and ravages in us.

You can judge from that, Mgr, how much you owe to God's mercy, how evident it is that is watching over you, and thinking of your salvation with paternal care, when he takes you away from the places, people, occupations and dealings of your ordinary life, and you can see that you could not have a more binding obligation than to make good use of these blessed intervals, so that being strengthened while you are away from the world, you may return to it with less danger when his order recalls you. I say his order, because I suppose that a Christian would never become involved in the world again of his own volition, and being convinced that he must consult God at every step, and in every act, he will be still more convinced when it is a question of putting himself in a dangerous situation, and one in which without powerful protection from above one could never maintain oneself for a moment. Only those who hate the world can live in it with any kind of security. Every time we find ourselves in the world from our own inclination and the attraction it has for us, we expose ourselves to all the harm it is capable of doing us, and it is only too true that it poisons and delivers the fatal blow to those weak enough to love it. I tell you, Mgr, what you know as well as I. But it is a truth of such importance, which so easily escapes us, that it is always useful to set it once more before one's eyes, and I even think that there is no other which it is more necessary for you to consider and observe, as much to avoid future misfortune as to console you now. I pray God, Mgr, to fill you with his grace more and more. Do me the justice of believing that I ask him for nothing more earnestly, and that no one could be more faithfully and respectfully than I yours etc.

PS A few hours after you left here I received a letter from the Bishop of Séez in which he indicated to me how eagerly he wanted to come and see you. The letter was handed to me four days after its date; I send it on to you, Mgr, so that you should know how warmly he is disposed in all that concerns you.'

*740704   MARÉCHAL DE BELLEFONDS   4 July 1674
BN na 12959 f.17, orig.

'I had the honour of writing to you, Mgr, only four days ago, and I should no doubt have spaced out my letters more if the Bishop of Séez had not charged me with ensuring that you received the letter you will find in this packet, and at the same time telling you everything possible so that you should know how much he honours you and is alive to all that concerns you. He was certainly much mortified to have been deprived of the consolation of coming to see you, and I should find it hard to safisfy him and tell you all the annoyance he felt on this matter. He is writing to you himself and so, Mgr, I have nothing to add to this note but my most sincere assurance that no one could be more faithfully and respectfully yours' etc.

740707   [JEAN FAVIER]   7 July 1674
A 2106,f.77

Had written in April with copy of his defence of the Reform. Suffering continual fever, increased by any unusual effort, but not prevented from keeping vigils and fasts.

The April letter may well have been 74/3.

740722   [JEAN FAVIER]   22 July 1674
A 2106,f.78 vo.

Still alive despite rumours, but sadly short of his obligations to God.

740730   RELIGIEUSES, SAINT-ANTOINE, PARIS   30 July 1674
TD C

They can, and should, leave the monastery with a good conscience. Tells them not to address him as 'Monsieur'.

By June 1676 they had all left.

740805   RM LOUISE-HENRIETTE D'ALBON   5 August 1674
A 2106,f.79 vo.; Mug II/8

He does not write often but prays continually for her. She should stay where she is and regard the place of her profession as her tomb.

740800   [RM LOUISE ROGIER]   [? August 1674]
Mug II/97a

'My niece was quite right to withhold consent to what was desired for her.'

Presumably her transfer, in letter above.

740800a ARCHBISHOP [OF PARIS, FRANÇOIS DE HARLAY] [August 1674]
Mug II/27

Condolences on the death of Abp's nephew [killed at battle of Seneffe] and the death of one of brethren [Benoît Deschamps].

740815 [? RM LOUISE ROGIER] 15 August 1674
A 2106,f.79; Mug II/97

R. finds burden of being superior crushing. A priest of rich family should prepare for death in retreat, not in worldly pursuits.

*740825 MARÉCHAL DE BELLEFONDS 25 August 1674
BN na 12959 f.19, orig.; Mug II/79

'The peace and tranquility, Mgr, which you are enjoying in your retreat, far from offering you any reasonable cause for suspicion, is a clear sign of God's hand, and to tell the truth your soul would be neither peaceful nor content amidst so many reasons for being otherwise, looking at things with human eyes, if God were not involving himself and giving you powerful protection. You have received his order, Mgr, and considered his will in your disgrace with such complete detachment, your heart has remained so free from all the different passions which upset worldly people in such situations, that it could hardly have occurred that this initial grace which he granted you was not accompanied by very many more, and that he should fail to grant you subsequently the necessary fidelity to persevere in such christian dispositions. Things, Mgr, are at rest when they are in their natural place and situation; in the case of our heart that means God, and when we are in his hand and our will is submissive to his, it must necessarily follow that our heart ceases to be anxious, its agitation is stilled and it enters into total peace and perfect tranquility. Thus, Mgr, so long as you remain in this state of dependence towards God in which you have been hitherto, so long as you listen to his voice in order to follow it once it is known to you, so long as you conceive no plans contrary to his providence, do not try to anticipate it, and observe its very prompting as rules of your conduct, the whole world conspiring together cannot prevent you from living in contentment.

However, Mgr, God, who knows that it is not expedient for us that our souls should remain always in calmness, will no doubt permit some kind of storm to rise in yours, but the emotions will be slight, and if they ruffle the surface of the water a little, the depths will not move from their normal fixed and stable state. Virtue is like those great trees which put forth their deepest roots and stand their firmest when they are buffeted by the violence of the winds. I am quite sure, Mgr, that whatever befalls, when you compare your present condition with that which you would have if you were in the world, not only will it appear tolerable to you, but you will even find it a happy one, if you merely cast your eye on the countless reefs and dangers which almost always bring misfortune to those who sail those waters and have caused saints to say, seeing things as they really are, that those who come out safely are, as it were, escaping from' the midst of shipwreck. It is by no means my thought that you should never return to the world, but I do not hesitate to say that it must be God who recalls you; his will must come first and yours simply follow.

We lost one of our brothers four or five days ago, if one can speak of loss in referring to a death which bore all the visible signs of being happy. He had spent seven years in this monastery, so punctilious in his duty and so faithful in everything, that it was scarcely possible to find anything to criticise in his conduct. I asked him shortly before he left us in what state of mind he was going to appear before the judgement of Jesus Christ. He answered me textually that he regarded the day of his death as a feast and a wedding-day, and he could find no better way to express his detachment from all mortal things than to compare himself to a leaf blown away by the wind; he was dying in deep peace and tranquility, yet in all he had done he could see nothing on which he could rely before God's judgement, but he put all his trust in God's mercy and could not understand how a man who had rendered such wretched service could have received from him such grace. If a religious, Mgr, whose life had appeared above reproach, saw nothing good in all his works, what shall I find in mine, I who live in dissipation compared to him, and take on myself to tell others truths I do not practise? But what are we to think of those whom God leaves in the corruption of the world and who spend their lives ignoring and scorning his holy law? Blessed are those whom he has withdrawn into his refuges and who await beneath the wings of his protection the end of these days of misfortune and iniquity. This personal observation slipped out, and I mean it only for your ears.

The care you are taking to put your house in order is not only worthy of a Christian, but absolutely necessary, since the Apostle declares that anyone failing to do so should be counted among the faithless. Few people reflect on this duty, and even those who profess to lead a life of piety apply themselves to it so superficially, and thus to no purpose. They are content, as they put it, to order their own lives, without considering that this is not possible, and they will do nothing basically pleasing to God, as long as they fail in this primary obligation. Charity, according to God's word, is what brings order and regularity to our lives. One cannot wound charity in anything essential without falling into disorder and confusion. You were quite right not to cut down on your household so far; that would no doubt have been regarded as a kind of declaration which, it seems to me, would have been untimely.

Regarding the opinion for which you ask me, Mgr, I can tell you that Sr Anne-Marie de Jésus' ideas seem to me very correct and enlightened, and I can only agree with them. God's order must be respected in all things, and we must leave things as he has arranged them; it is a very subtle, but very real, sort of presumption to move people and change the way he had disposed them without genuine necessity. A monk must be in his solitude, a religious in his community, ecclesiastics in the world to help and teach christian families and people. It is not enough justification for moving them from that state to say that it is to achieve some good, for good must be achieved by good and right means, and when those which have to be adopted are not entirely so, then that good should no longer be esteemed as such, and we can no longer say that God desires it of us. In a word, Mgr, anyone who does behave in that way is violating God's order, is exposing the person whom he is committing to a life not meant for him to the weaknesses that are inevitable when one leaves the bounds of one's profession, is setting an example with dangerous consequences and, what is more, is making himself responsible before God for all the mishaps and results of the change he has brought about. I pray Our Lord to complete in you what he had begun with so many blessings, and so to destroy in your heart all affection for the things which are not eternal that he may alone possess it, and that there be nothing with him that does not serve his glory and promote your sanctification. I am with inviolable respect and faithfulness yours' etc.

The monk who had died was Benoît Deschamps, on 20 August. Anne-Marie de Jésus is the former Mlle d'Epernon, a Carmelite with Bellefonds' aunt.

740903   GODEFROI HERMANT   3 September 1674
Autographes Troussures, p.235
Has just received *Lives* of St Basil and Gregory Nazianzen.

*740909   MARÉCHAL DE BELLEFONDS   9 September 1674
BN na 12959 f.22, orig.; Mug II/86

'I am sending you, Mgr, a second letter from [the Bishop of Séez] in which the poor man opens his heart to you, and speaks to you of his difficulties and worries. They really are very great, and what is worse, he feels them very keenly. He tells me he could not stop himself writing to you again, however much he respects your privacy. I am quite sure that a consoling word from you will do him more good than all that everyone else together might say. It is a strange thing, Mgr, which no one would have imagined, that someone like him, coming from the court and taking up a position which gives him wealth, dignity, and honour (to adopt the values of worldly people) should fail to count himself fortunate and enjoy his good fortune in perfect peace, yet by a turn he never expected his elevation has not only failed to make him happier than he was, but has truly become for him a subject of affliction, filling his life with weariness and grief. So it is, Mgr, with all human affairs, their outward appearance is attractive and striking from afar, but at close quarters and when one experiences them they are anything but what one hoped for. It is a consequence of God's mercy so to have disposed all transitory assets that not one is without some element of bitterness, for if any should happen to be exempt, we should become so attached to them that we should need extraordinary grace to give them up, since despite all the experiences and reasons we have for setting no store by them, one finds so few people judging them rightly and with contempt.

I have just learned of the death of M. de Villandri. That is certainly an event worthy of compassion, since, as you know, his occupations were not those of a man preparing to die, although the world no longer had any pleasure to offer him, and his fortune and the state of his affairs must have given him thoughts which do not usually come to those who are enjoying prosperity. He finished his life as frivolously and uselessly as he had always spent it. He was struck down as if by a thunderbolt, and the moment he least expected decided his eternal fate. These are great lessons that God gives us from time to time. Nowhere does he speak to us more powerfully than in such accidents. Those who are in the world and follow its rules become no better for it, because besides their hardness of heart, which is great, they see nothing to efface those rules from their mind and from their heart; but those to whom God has given more christian feelings and dispositions are most unfortunate if such examples make only a passing impression on them, whereas the loss of those whom God carries off in such terrible and tragic circumstances should urgently move them to work more carefully and earnestly at their salvation. It was written that one man should die for the good of the people [Jn 18:4], but we may say that God every day sacrifices a large number for the sanctification of his elect, and what represents great harshness for some is a great mercy for others. In short, since there is no moment when God may not stand at the door, as Scripture says, so there is none when we should not be ready to open to him and the true piety of a Christian should be accompanied by continual vigilance, without which, Mgr, we remain miserably bound to earthly things and heavenly things have in our hearts anything but the place and importance due to them.

I have nothing to add to this note, Mgr, except that I am as usual, that is with all the respect and faithfulness of which I am capable, yours' etc.

Villandri was Balthasar le Breton, sieur de Villandri, a notorious gourmet and libertine (see Boileau, Satire 3, v. 24) who was found dead a moment after retiring. Mme de Maintenon, in a letter of 6 September, seems to be the first to comment on his death, and not long after R's comment Sr Louise de la Miséricorde (de la Vallière) wrote to Bellefonds in similar terms. To die unprepared after a life of conspicuous self-indulgence was a fate that genuinely horrified even the most ordinarily religious people at the time.

740919   RELIGIEUSE   19 September 1674
A 2106,f.80

Pleased at her attitude. 'He who suffers is most fortunate.'

741000   RP ABBÉ   [? October 1674]
         [? FOUCARMONT, JACQUES FLEUR DE MONTAGNE]
Mug II/100

R. has been asked to go back to Paris about mid-November. Glad abbot is pleased with Fr M[? aître = novice master, Cornuty]

741000a MARQUIS DE POMPONNE   [October 1674]
TB 457

Condolences on death of Pomponne's father, Arnauld d'Andilly [died 27 September 1674], an old friend who in recent years had renewed warmth of friendship.

741000b BISHOP [OF SÉEZ, JEAN DE FORCOAL]   [October 1674]
Mug II/4

Expressions of obedience, but reluctant to go to Paris on affairs of Reform because of his own ill health and imminent death of one of monks.

*741008   RM MARIE-LOUISE [BOUTHILLIER]   8 October 1674
TA orig; TD/A

'I beg you to believe, my dearest sister, that it is because I am lacking neither in the affection I owe you nor in the genuine desire to contribute to your consolation that I have not answered the letters you took the trouble to write to me. But, to tell the truth, I avoid as far as possible giving advice to anyone, especially when it does not seem likely to be of any use; which always happens, when one makes general statements, or even particular ones, without being fully informed of details concerning persons, which can scarcely be expressed in letters. For, my dearest sister, when I tell you that we must unreservedly abandon ourselves to the dispositions of divine providence, bear with resignation every situation into which he [God] allows us to be put, that he is equally Father at all times, whether he treats us gently or severely, that all his orders deserve our respect, that the path of aridity and dereliction, if we use it as we should, is more profitable than that of consolations; that our souls are purified by temptations as the sea by storms; that it is enough for our sanctification to know God's will and follow it; that our rules are the guardians and preservers of our innocence; and that no evil can come to us in this world provided that we observe them as faithfully and strictly as he requires, then I am telling you important truths, but truths which you know as well as I do, which you will find in all the books and all the authors who have spoken of these matters, more clearly, profoundly and amply than I could in a letter of a few lines; and as for the application, it is almost impossible for it to be either appropriate or useful when it comes from so far away, and when one does not have thorough knowledge of the persons' feelings. Therefore, my dearest sister, I can only say to you in general that, having embraced a holy profession in a monastery where the rules are in force, you have only to follow the paths that they indicate; they are sure, and provided that you do not stray from them, you cannot go wrong.

Your joy, my dear sister, should come from the evidence of your conscience that you love God, want to serve him, and have received from him all necessary help and assistance. And if you consider as much as you are obliged from how many perils and misfortunes he has delivered you by withdrawing you from this wretched world, there will be no moment of your life which you will not spend acknowledging the bounty of his mercies. I pray God, my dear sister, to engrave these feelings so deeply in your heart that they never leave it, and that you find them whenever they are attacked by all those thoughts which trouble you, since nothing is more likely to dissipate them and establish you in profound peace. I wish that, my dearest sister, as I wish it for myself, and I will take no less care in commending all your needs to Our Lord in our prayers and sacrifices than my own. Your peace of mind is too dear to me for me to fail in this. I ask the same charity of you, for although I do not complain, yet I am full of my wretchedness, and God alone, in his goodness, in which I put all my trust, prevents its weight from crushing me. Pray him for me, I beg you once again, and do not doubt that it is with all my heart that I am yours etc.

PS Please assure the Very Reverend Mother Superior of my deep respect for her. I am most grateful to my sister for remembering me, and ask her particularly before God to do so, and in the hope that he will grant me to die more religiously than I have lived up till now.'

741023   ANTOINE ARNAULD   23 October 1674
T 2183,f.28 vo.; *Lettre de Tillemont*, 1705, p. 107

Regrets that he cannot take young man proposed, but the lay brothers' dormitory is full and they will have to stop recruiting.

*741029   BISHOP OF LUÇON [HENRI BARILLON]   29 October 1674
P f.764; Mug II/73

'I have received your honoured letter, Mgr, through the Dean of la Rochelle, and do not need to tell you that although we increase each day our plans and resolutions for observing stricter retreat, yet I cannot help making special exceptions for anything coming from you and bearing your recommendation. For the rest, Mgr, what I learn about you does not surprise me; I am most consoled, for I never doubted that you would contribute the necessary fidelity to match the purity of your vocation, as it came wholly from God, and you know that those he calls cannot be sure of remaining in his hand and under his guidance as much as they should. I am convinced that your chief occupation and care is to make yourself worthy of a calling which has been successful in every detail. I do not fail, Mgr, to keep my promise to you, and although we do not deserve to be heard by God, there is no day when we do not present your person to him several times. It is too dear to us for us not to look on that as one of our principal obligations. But, Mgr, I need you much more to be good enough to remember me and all our community before Our Lord Jesus Christ. We have so far made such poor use of the great mercies he has shown us, that what we must most fear is to be weighed down by the quantity and number of his acts of goodness. Indeed, apart from some good intentions, I see nothing but misery and cause for confusion in my life for when I have to appear before him who is not satisfied with mere acts of will, but demands works, and works which are full and according to his measure. That is the feeling in which I beg you to grant me your assistance before him, and particularly when you offer him the sacred mysteries. Do me the honour and justice of believing that no one in the world could be with more affection and respect than I yours etc.

PS I found in the Dean of la Rochelle all the good you had told me. He is full of God, and seeks him with as much humility as if he had not yet made a single step in his service.'

The Dean of la Rochelle was Philippe de la Brosse (d.1695).

741200 SR ANNE-MARIE [D'EPERNON] [December 1674]
TB 485

Advice on confessions and keeping Advent and Lent.

741227 GODEFROI HERMANT 27 December 1674
Autographes Troussures p. 236

Pities religious whose letter Hermant has sent. Neither Carthusians nor Benedictines allow a monk to go his own way, and after fourteen years of profession he should stay where he is.

75/1 RM, GIF [ANNE DE MONGLAT] [1674 or 1675]
TB 481

She should accept charge of abbess and practise Rule integrally. 'I do not say that it is absolutely impossible to find salvation in mitigations, since the Church tolerates them.'

75/2 RP ABBÉ [ORVAL, CHARLES DE BENZERADT] [1674 or 1675]
Mug II/20

Reform at Orval has begun. R. discourages him from excessive fasts, tried at la T. on request of monks but abandoned after two years. 'Discretion, when free of all laxity and carnal indulgence, is a greater virtue than penitence; there can even be some humility in leaving some distance between your outward practices and those of our Fathers, who were saints.'

75/3   CANON REGULAR   [1674 or 1675]
TD C

Correspondent has seen R's letter to a German monk. If he wants to join fr Etienne [Compagnon, professed May 1674] he will be welcome.

In 1672 R. wrote a long letter on the religious life to an unnamed German monk, possibly one of his Heisterbach correspondents, and this was often copied. See 7217.

750200   BISHOP OF TOURNAI [GILBERT DE CHOISEUL]   [February] 1675
TB 477

On a recent visit to Paris R. saw the commissioners.

*750227   MARÉCHAL DE BELLEFONDS   27 February 1675
BN na 12959 f.24, orig.; TC II/229

'I thought I should have the honour of writing to you from Paris, where I have been obliged to go on the business of our Observance, and I even believe that M. de Tréville told you that he was sending you a letter from me, but I found myself so overwhelmed by the demands of people and affairs that I was not able to do so. I will admit, Mgr, that all I saw seemed to me fit to excite compassion. Some agree, at least according to what they say, that nothing we can do in this world is better than working for our salvation, yet their every step and their every act takes them further from it. Others think about it seriously and apply themselves, but they are equally to be pitied, being constrained to live in the midst of a world where all principles are so false, pleasures so corrupt, and occupations so dissolute. I do not yet know if my journey will prove to have been of any use to our Reform, but I know that for myself it has been most useful. It made me resolve afresh to live a life of stricter solitude than hitherto. It confirmed me more than ever in the opinion I already held, that one must turn one's back on men if one is truly to belong to God, and that if those whom he calls to a life of retreat knew its blessings and advantages, nothing on earth could ever remove them from it. These are truths, Mgr, which no more strike the reason than the senses of worldly people. They maintain that a man is unhappy when he is away from court, and that restlessness and boredom are the necessary effects of retreat; but I am convinced that your thoughts are quite different, that you now know from experience what was already familiar to you from your own insights, and that when you compare your present situation with that which you had when you were in the world, you find an almost infinite distance between them. For in the end all the zeal and vigilance of the most virtuous people who live in that climate can barely do more than ensure their survival and support them against the torrent; even so it is almost impossible to resist so faithfully and steadily that one is not often compelled to let oneself go and give in to its violence, whereas retreat gives incredible facilities for walking in God's ways, and the life led in retreat may be considered as one of continual progress.

These, and similar, considerations, Mgr, will make you appreciate the happiness of your present state, will make you sincerely oppose anything which might end it, will fill you with holy inclinations and fortify you against the world's temptations if ever providence involves you once more with it. However that may be, Mgr, what you must study and chiefly aim to do is to confirm in yourself what Our Lord has been so long effecting by his grace, and to see to it that this seed of benediction that he has planted grows deep roots, so that his work subsists and stands firm against all movement and agitation. You can be sure that what you have not obtained from God in peace, you will never acquire in tumult, and if you have not made the necessary provisions and preparations in time of plenty, you will find yourself without help and protection in time of need. The hands of his mercy are never closed so tightly as on those to whom they were most widely opened, and God acts with perfect justice in being invariably sparing of his gifts once his generosity has proved fruitless, and we have not profited from his liberality as much as we should.

We hope, Mgr, to have the honour and consolation of seeing you in our desert at the end of Lent. I do not need to tell you how impatiently we look forward to it, any more than I need to assure you how warmly, respectfully and faithfully I am yours' etc.

R. had had to go to Paris in January/February in a last desperate attempt to save the cause of the Reform.

750303   COMTE DE TRÉVILLE   3 March 1675
TB 507

R. has written to Pinette about a definite resolve he has made, and should have started observing total silence long ago.

From the context this seems to refer to controversies over Jansenism and the like.

750319   RP PASQUIER QUESNEL, CONG.ORAT.   19 March 1675
U 1168, orig.; Tans 26

The reform is going well at la T.

*750410   MARÉCHAL DE BELLEFONDS   10 April 1675
BN na 19259 f.26, orig.; TB 513

'I must once more express to you, Mgr, my great regret at being obliged to go away from la Trappe and leave you there; it was what you wanted, and your opinion alone decided me. My journey had as much success as I expected, that is to say, none at all. I found things in the state in which, as you know, I had been told they were.

My presence did not change them. I saw the person in whom I had some reason to pin my hopes, but all I got from that quarter were many assurances and protestations that everything possible had been done in the matter, and that they were totally unable to give us any help. I was easily convinced that this was true, for it is not very difficult to persuade a man whose chief rule is that one should never think ill of anyone unless there are evident and certain grounds. Thus, Mgr, I spent less than four days in Paris. I have returned to my solitude, never again in my life to leave it, and never to listen to any arguments which may be contrary to the resolution I have made. All this is a great lesson teaching us not to count on the friendship and judgements of men, that one is usually mistaken in looking for consolation in the success of affairs, even when undertaken in the sight of God for his glory and the edification of his church, and that the only way of attaining peace in this world is to want nothing but the will of God and to remain in a state of suspension such that one can easily turn and incline to whichever side one sees the movements of providence bringing one. I confess, Mgr, at the present moment my heart would be full of bitterness and my spirit cast down if I were not sustained by such feelings, and I would not be able without deep grief to see before my eyes the dissipation of a work which is assuredly of God, which would have done more to contribute to his glory than any other, and which could so easily have been preserved. May God be blessed in all things; his conduct demands our respect and submission no less in the ills which he allows to afflict us than in the good things with which he consoles us. I am telling you nothing, Mgr, but what I know you practise. I pray God to increase the feelings he has given you in this regard, and to continue to strengthen your heart against all the temptations which could possibly weaken them. Do me the honour and justice of believing that there is nothing that I more fervently ask him for, that your person is more dear to me than I could express, and that it would be impossible to add anything to the respect with which I am yours etc.

PS We left you, Mgr, some rather rough drafts of an account of some of the details of the deaths of two of our brothers. You will readily understand, and I do not need to tell you, how important it is that these should be seen by no eyes but yours.

Despite all my haste to arrive in time to find poor dom Paul alive, he died on the 5 April, at 6 in the morning, six or seven hours before I arrived. He still had the courage to go into the church the day before and receive Our Lord, although he was in an amazingly weak state. He died without agony, and seemed simply to have fallen asleep. He was conscious to the last. I recommend him to your prayers.'

The person R. saw in Paris may have been an ecclesiastic or a minister, perhaps Abp Harlay. This was indeed his last visit to Paris, and he never again left la T. except for his visits to les Clairets in 1690–92. The drafts mentioned in the PS were the first of the long series of Relations *and concerned Benoît Deschamps and Jacques Puiperrou. Paul Hardy was the subject of a third.*

*750410a RM MARIE-LOUISE [BOUTHILLIER]   10 April 1675
TA orig.

'I found, my dear sister, on returning from a journey to Paris, one of your letters, advising me that you were so indisposed that you could not write yourself. I beg you to believe that I am most sorry about that, and will not fail to have the novena you desire started on Easter Monday. God is trying you, my dearest sister; that is a good sign, because, according to Scripture, he chastises in time those whom he most loves and is preparing for eternity. There is no suffering which such a thought will not console, when it is at all keen. I pray Our Lord to give you the disposition you need to make holy use of your infirmities, and I am in him, I beg you, my dearest sister, not to doubt it, with all due affection yours, etc.

PS I am most obliged to the RM Prioress for doing me the honour of remembering me, I beg you to assure her. Please also express to the person whose hand you employed my warm thanks for her kindness in thinking of me. Tell my sister too that I commend myself to her prayers and am wholly hers in Our Lord.'

750415   BISHOP OF ALET [NICOLAS PAVILLON]   15 April 1675
U 863; TC I/19

Account of the death of dom Paul Hardy [died 5 April].

750420   BISHOP OF GRENOBLE [ETIENNE LE CAMUS]   20 April 1675
U 863

Back from third and last visit to Paris, where cause of Reform has been lost. Four monks, all known to Bp, have died in past six months. Bellefonds was there two weeks ago. Le Camus should relax his austerities as incompatible with his duties. The Augustinian who brought his letter needs a dispensation from Rome to be admitted.

On 19 April the Conseil d'Etat *pronounced in favour of the Common Observance, thus putting an end to any hopes that what had failed in Rome could be achieved in France. Four more monks were to die before the year was out.*

750500   SR ANNE-MARIE [D'EPERNON]   [? May] 1675
TB 553

She should not stay away from sacraments beyond what appropriate lenten preparation requires, otherwise she will suffer 'a spiritual languor which we almost always experience when our communions are rarer than they should be'.

750500a   BISHOP OF TOURNAI [GILBERT DE CHOISEUL]   [May] 1675
TB 503

Defeat of Reform not surprising. Refuses to send back religious of other congregations.

*750604 RM AGNÈS DE BELLEFONDS   4 June 1675
TD C

'Very Reverend Mother,
   I share as much as I ought in your consolation at the commitment of Sister Louise de la Miséricorde [Mme de la Vallière]. From what I have been told, to-day is the day of her profession. We shall not fail to recommend her to Our Lord and pray him to accompany this quite extraordinary action with the fullness of his grace and spirit. I have no need to tell you, Reverend Mother, how much I honour and respect you, for I am sure you are quite convinced.
   It is a long time since I had news of M. le Maréchal de Bellefonds. I do not doubt that he is following his accustomed ways, and advancing with great strides. I confess that his dispositions when he did us the honour of visiting us at the end of Lent filled me with consolation. I was most sorry to have been unable to speak to you about him on my last journey to Paris. He had even charged me with telling you about an affair on which he had written to you. But my stay in Paris was so ill-starred that I was obliged to end it as soon as I possibly could.
   I will say nothing of my affairs. The state in which you know they are could not be more pitiful. Some people believe that Rome will order something against our monastery under the impression that we are quite without any protection. It will turn out as God wills. I shall try to know his will, and do it with so much regularity and measure that there is neither weakness nor presumption in my conduct.
   I very much need your prayers, Reverend Mother, and I am sure you do not forget me before Our Lord. I recommend to you five of our religious who have died in the past six or seven months and two others who are ready to follow them. I will tell you, from whom I hide nothing, that their spirits are so great that, although we need them very much for the edification of our house and the preservation of the little good that God has established there, I none the less see them leave for eternity with joy and with no regret.
   I do not know if you have been given a letter I wrote to M. le Maréchal de Bellefonds six weeks ago. Allow me to ask you to assure Sister Anne-Marie de Jésus [d'Epernon] of my most humble service.'

Mme de la Vallière was indeed professed on 3 June and Bossuet preached. R's trip to Paris was so rushed that he had to leave Bellefonds behind at la T. and for some time afterwards the defeat of the Reform's long campaign filled him with despair.

*750700 MONSIEUR HAMON   [July 1675]
TD/A

'It is true, Monsieur, that all my thinking leads me to believe that God will soon withdraw us from this world, and in truth we ask for nothing from God more insistently, but I confess that on this point I am a little more restrained than my brethren, as I do not find myself as ready as they are for this great journey, and every time I compare my life with theirs, it seems monstrous. We are, however, not prophets, and we may well be wrong. Regarding my health, about which you are kind enough to show concern, it is quite good, as is that of dom Le Nain. It is good enough for neither of us to fail to do any of our duties, but as there is more vigour than strength in that, it could be said that it is only a spark glowing live while it lasts, and will not last long. So it is with the lives of all men, but especially ours, for it must not be doubted that our life of regularity, although little enough, weakens its principles and shortens its course. What does it matter, Monsieur, whether it is long, provided it is good, and what difference can one make between a life of normal span and one which ends in the middle of the duration it might have had at the moment when one as much as the other has to finish? We have long been dead to the world, and should not be counted among the living. I say nothing to you of my appreciation of your concern for our interests, but I can assure you that it is far beyond all my words. It is a favour which I ask you to continue, and I sincerely assert that it is one of the most real consolations I can have in this world. It is true that six of our best religious have died over the past six or seven months, and a seventh is ready to follow them.'

Between December 1674 and July 1675 six monks died, with a seventh in October. The only comparable rate of mortality was between November 1680 and June 1681, when eight died, and this letter could just possibly be dated April/May 1681.

750700a RELIGIEUSE, PARIS [July] 1675
TC I/72

Affairs of Reform in a bad state. R. left his solitude to no purpose and will not do so again. Missed her on his visit [in April] but had seen her on previous occasion.

In April R. had paid a visit to the Carmelites, so this letter is most likely to his sister at the Annonciades.

750704 RP PASQUIER QUESNEL, CONG. ORAT. 4 July 1675
U 1168 orig.; TB 545 (wrongly dated 10 July); Tans 27

Has received Quesnel's editions of St Leo. R. compares himself to St Hilary and Savonarola, both frustrated in their attempts at reform.

The allusion is presumably to Hilary of Arles (403–449), disgraced by Leo, as documents in Quesnel's book explain. The book was put on the Index in 1676 for its strong Gallican line. The Dominican Savonarola (1452–98) was hardly a happier comparison; he supported Charles VIII of France against the rulers of his native Florence, fell foul of the Pope and was executed as a heretic.

750715   RP PASQUIER QUESNEL, CONG. ORAT.   15 July 1675
U 1168 orig.; Tans 28

R. is going to read the story of Savonarola. Dom Charles Denis [former Oratorian] died an edifying death the day before.

750800   RM [EMILIE] DE BOUILLON   [August] 1675
TD C

Death of her uncle, maréchal Turenne [27 July]. All his great distinction gone before God's judgement.

750805   MADAME DE SABLÉ   5 August 1675
TB 551

She has been gravely ill. Put her trust in God and do not worry about health.

*750900   BISHOP OF CONDOM [J.B. BOSSUET]   [September 1675]
TB 559

'I would not have wanted, Mgr, to give the habit to Monsieur J., knowing the interest you take in him, without first writing to you. His brother, who has thoroughly discussed things with him, and with whom he has been entirely frank, will be better able than anyone to give you an account of his disposition, and for my part I shall only say that I have never seen in him the slightest sign of caprice or frivolity. He has conceived his plan according to the proper rules, from his desire to think solely of God and his salvation, and from his recognition of the fact that those who are concerned with worldly affairs are less interested in that than anything else. He talked to me about it, Mgr, with such piety and firmness that I was both surprised and pleased. As for the austerities of this house, he has not experienced any great difficulties; he has begun by becoming used to the diet, the vigils, and the work, but what I would be more afraid of is that the obedience, constant silence, and solitude may cause him trouble and become a burden, but we can only find that out with time. I beg you to believe, Mgr, that I follow his reactions with the utmost attention, that I will take all possible care of him and try according to my modest lights to do only what is according to God's will and for his sanctification. I do not need to tell you how highly I value all that comes to me from you, and for those you recommend, since I am sure that you have no doubts on that score. He is indeed fortunate if God calls him to a life of retreat; the world is nothing, less even than those who set no store by it think.

My last visit to Paris, and the way our business there was decided, has more than confirmed my feelings about it, and I can say as St Bernard once did: "I bless God for taking from me before my death certain consolations in which I no doubt took too much pleasure, so that I should learn from my own experience to put no more trust in men and the world".

I pray God entirely to destroy in you the world's spirit and teachings, and that nothing should keep you in the world but the sight of his glory and the fear of quitting the place in which you find yourself committed by his orders. May he accept the good you do there by working so successfully for the sanctification of the people.'

This letter bears no date, but the reference to R's trip to Paris (April 1675) and its place in a reliably dated series put it almost certainly in September 1675. Though Bossuet resigned as Bp of Condom in 1671, his correspondents (including the King) continued to address him by that title until he was appointed to Meaux in 1681. The letter has apparently not been published before. The postulant may be identified with virtual certainty as André Jannel, a cousin of Bossuet's from Montpellier, who stayed only a short time before transferring to the benedictine house of Saint-Faron at Meaux, where he was professed on 7 May 1677. He died at Saint-Denis in 1726 (Bossuet, Correspondance, XIV, p. 452) R. remained in touch with him; see 901203.

*750922   MARÉCHAL DE BELLEFONDS   22 September 1675
BN na 12959 f.29, orig.; TB 562

'I learned only two or three days ago that your son had been extremely ill; I do not doubt, Mgr, that you regarded this misfortune in your usual spirit of resignation, nor that God has given you on this occasion the same protection that you have received from him in so many others. He has done no more than raise his hand, without wishing to strike the blow, so as to make you realise that you must always be ready to give back to him what he may ask for at any moment. There is only one way to be happy in this world, and that is to desire simply and solely what is pleasing to him. For, as his will is always accomplished, ours cannot fail to have its effect when it does not differ from his, and thus one finds reason for satisfaction in all kinds of events.

Many considerable events have taken place since I had the honour of seeing you, and I am sure, Mgr, that you will have reflected deeply and usefully upon them. I mean the conversion of the Cardinal de Retz, and the death of Monsieur de Turenne. The one strips himself and loses by voluntary abdication all that had animated his life, condemns by an action almost without parallel fifty years of behaviour and teaches men what they do not want to understand, namely that the only true happiness is for those who belong to Jesus Christ and serve him. The other ends by a grievous misfortune a career full of glory, to use worldly terms. All that he took such pains and trouble to acquire is now of no use to him, since whatever of it remains in the memory and opinion of men, he is now no more than what he is before the eyes of God who has judged him. One must admit, Mgr, that the ways of God are impenetrable. The Cardinal gives himself entirely to God and devotes the last years of his life to penitence, after resolving to do so more than ten years ago, and his delay in executing God's will has not exhausted God's patience. And Monsieur de Turenne, who had only just conceived the intention of retiring, as you may have known, and only awaited the end of the war to execute it, is struck down by a bolt from the blue, and denied the grace of effecting what he had been inspired to plan. Although his death was preceded by a number of circumstances which indicate that he was thinking seriously of his salvation, yet the hopes which he leaves on that subject are very uncertain. If Christians had faith, and really believed what they should about this life and the next, the places that these two men have just left would remain empty, and scarely anyone would be found who wanted to replace them. If all human greatness and dignity is an obstacle to salvation, and if one goes further away from God as one rises in the world, can one at one and the same time stop at fortunes that are only apparent and transitory, and desire solid and constant felicity? Or is it not rather clearly and publicly to declare that one is renouncing eternal blessings when one attaches oneself to temporal ones? Although I am quite sure, Mgr, that the holy dispositions that God has given you are increasing more and more, and that you faithfully use the special grace you receive from him, I confess that, feeling as keenly as I do on everything concerning you, I should be enormously comforted to hear something of this directly from you. Do me the honour, Mgr, of believing that no one could respect you more than I nor be more fully and sincerely yours etc.

PS I am sending you a letter from the Bishop of Séez. He has so much respect and consideration for you that he deserves a little in return. If you think to write to him, Mgr, and do us the honour of sending his letter, we will not fail to see that he gets it.'

The death of Turenne (born 1611) at Sassbach on 27 July was a grievous blow to French arms. He had been converted from Protestantism by Bossuet, presumably an indication in R's eyes that he was at least thinking seriously of salvation. Retz's conversion, so long awaited and often proclaimed, took the tangible form of retreat to the benedictine abbey of St-Mihiel, near his home at Commercy, but he stayed there only from June to October, since the Pope expressed strong disapproval of such behaviour from a cardinal.

Bellefonds had a son, name untraced, who died at the age of eight or nine, and it is probably he who is here referred to. The elder son, Louis-Christophe, was then thirteen or fourteen, and died in battle in 1692.

751000   RB ABBÉ [? CHÂTILLON, CLAUDE LE MAÎTRE]   October 1675
U 3069, p. 92 (extract)

Has learned news from religious sent to Chaloché. Abbot may see Abp of Paris but without making any proposals.

Chaloché, near Angers, had joined the Reform in 1673 with only three professed monks, and R. may have lent one.

751003   JEAN FAVIER   3 October 1675
CF 344,f.69 aut.; Gonod 37

Du Suel's *Entretiens*; R. had had four or five conversations with him when Du Suel tried his vocation at la T. Disastrous state of Cistercian Order. Denies seeing only

Jansenists in Paris; paid no visits, but at the *Institution de l'Oratoire* saw Mme de Guise, duchesse d'Orléans, Cardinal de Retz, Cardinal de Bouillon, the Premier Président.
Du Suel's somewhat fanciful version of conversations with R. had come out in 1674. The roll-call of distinguished visitors vividly illustrates R's value to the Reform; the duchesse d'Orléans was Elisabeth of Bavaria, second wife of the King's brother, the Premier Président was Guillaume Lamoignon. See index for others.

751005   RP PASQUIER QUESNEL, CONG. ORAT.   5 October 1675
U 1168 orig.; Tans 29

Would like to have seen Quesnel with M. Pinette when latter came. Acknowledges letter from Bp of Alet transmitted by Quesnel.

751010   BISHOP   10 October 1675
TB 574

Bp's recent visit. R. will be more careful about guests in future, as some are shocked rather than edified.

*751018   RP [BERNARD DU TEILLÉ] AT THE COLLÈGE DES BERNARDINS   18 October 1675
T 2240,13 orig.; TB 576

'My Reverend Father,

'I am not surprised that you encountered very wretched things in the course of your visit, and that those who ought to have given you a hand and supported the good you were trying to do should have opposed it. It would certainly be difficult for things to be in a worse state than they are, and it will not be long before we see in all the monasteries of both observances complete uniformity. Regarding your proposal, Reverend Father, God knows how much I wish that he were honoured and served in our observance, and how delighted I should be if that were achieved by the efforts and under the authority of the Abbot of Cîteaux, whom I have always distinguished from the other Fathers, not only because of his rank, but also for his personal qualities. However, I will tell you sincerely that when I addressed the King for the preservation of our observance, I resolved that in the event that my undertaking was not fully as blessed as I had reason to promise myself, I should look on its lack of success as evidence of God's will, and remain for the rest of my life in our monastery, with the sole occupation of strengthening our brothers in well doing, thinking of my sins, and preparing for death in retreat and penitence. All those ideas have been fortified since our affairs were decided, and I may say, without wishing to appear more committed than I am, that they are the only ones occupying me at present. Such feelings are scarcely relevant to those I should need to have if I were to engage myself in wider cares, and strive to find means and expedients for reestablishing our observance.

Thus, Reverend Father, all I can do in my present state, and according to the disposition given me by God, is to pray, as for my own salvation, for the sanctification of all those whom he has called to it. In truth if one is not careful, one can pass one's life in dissipation under the cloak of specious pretexts and appearances. We live amid violent agitations, although the profession in which we are engaged demands profound peace and complete separation from everything likely to disturb that peace, and we find ourselves, as it were, dragged off to the gates of death, without noticing, by the impetus of business and passions. I confess that if that were to happen to me both the error and the misfortune would be great, since I had no other motive in leaving the world than to await God's moments in silence and repose. If you do us the honour of coming to see us, my Reverend Father, we will say more about it, and I am sure that you would not advise me to withdraw from the divine order and embark on commitments and occupations so contrary to his designs, and his conduct towards me. Time, and all that passes with it, is nothing, and eternity alone merits a place in the mind and heart of a Christian. Keep for me the honour of your friendship, and believe me that it is not possible to be more sincerely yours' etc.

Bernard du Teillé, then joint head of the college, was about to become Abbot of l'Etoile. On the sudden death of Jouaud, leader of the Reform, on 2 June 1673, the Abbot of Cîteaux had appointed him visitor of reformed houses in the Ile de France, but the reformed abbots refused to recognise the appointment (on constitutional, not personal, grounds, for he was widely respected). In 1676, as Abbot of l'Etoile, his appointment as visitor was repeated, and this time accepted. R. refers to his Requête au Roi of 1673. He himself had eloquently refused the post of visitor conferred on him in his absence by the Chapter of 1672.

*751100   MLLE DE GOELLO   November 1675
TB/584

'It is a most extraordinary thing, Mlle, that I should have lost all memory and recollection of a hand I have known so well, and for such a long time, so that I attributed to you a letter which did not come from you, and then took the occasion of saying things and giving advice which would suit you. The letter which you have kindly written made me very glad, Mlle, for I confess that among all the complaints you make against yourself and for all your heartfelt remarks about your needs and miseries, I see too clearly to have any doubts that God looks on you with mercy, that he is effecting your salvation, and that you sincerely wish to be only his, although you have not yet achieved as much as you want, and as much as you ought to. It is a lot for someone who is just beginning and who comes to him after straying as far and as long as you have, to desire him, to seek him with understanding and discernment, and to reject as you do wrong paths and to take, and stay on, the right ones.

It is true, as you rightly say, and in that I am struck at the way God has enlightened you, everything is self-love, we seek out ourselves in everything, and in even the best of our resolves, we usually act from wrong motives. We leave the world because the world no longer pleases us, or we fear that we no longer please the world. We imagine that with such dispositions we shall more easily achieve our aim of belonging to God; but wanting it in a manner so imperfect and so unworthy of him is no better than not wanting it at all. That is why there are so many pious men and women, and so few genuine conversions, why so many people profess to be pious, while so few really are. Piety is merely apparent, a mask, unless it is solid, and for it to be so we must have nothing before our eyes but God, his glory, and our sanctification; we must purify our hearts from every attachment, so that God becomes master there, we must destroy all affection for creatures and put ourselves solely in his hand, depending on him alone. What I am saying should not cause you any trouble; it is a disposition which will come from God. It appears from your letter that you have already made all the preparations, and God who has provided them will finish the task so long as you keep faith with him as much as you can, force yourself on those occasions which most tempt your self-love and resolve to value God's approval more than men's esteem. In truth, Mlle, when you come to think about it, the kindness with which God stretches out his arms to you, the steps he has taken to bring you back to him, the trouble he has taken to draw you out of the deadly torpor in which you were languishing, the paternal tenderness with which he leads you by the hand, is all so attractive and inviting that you will find it is not enough to be his in an ordinary way and so rare a grace demands understanding out of the ordinary.

I am not surprised that people say you are a Jansenist. It is a kind of bogey that worldly folk, and the fashionably devout, who wish at any price to reconcile their own affairs, interests, and pleasures with the cross of Christ, set up against those who deviate from their views and follow strict principles. Let them say what they like, your consolation lies in the evidence of your conscience, and you adhere to no other party but that of Christ and his Church. Walk in simplicity, leave disputes to those who enjoy them, and for your part avoid them completely; you would be ill advised if, striving, as you should, to punish you own passions, you were to share those of others.

I am delighted that you are pleased with your confessor. He is a good man, charitable and enlightened on matters of faith. His principles are pure and strict, and I believe him to be quite incapable of using those purely human rules and slack concessions employed by most directors who merely soothe spiritual ills and consciences and do not know what it is to cure them. I pray that God will continue to take care of you, Mlle, and if I do not often write to you, I can assure you that you are none the less very present before him in my eyes, and that no day passes but that I speak to him of you and your needs as much as I am able. Above all do not let the sight of the great truths dismay you; the path which frightens us when we look at it suddenly and all at once becomes subsequently smoother, and God will see that you accomplish gradually and almost imperceptibly what might at first have appeared to you to be beyond your powers.

Perform faithfully the exercises you have prescribed for yourself. Enjoy reading about holy things. Although prayer is the channel through which God communicates his grace, do not force yourself to begin with. Pray according to the inclination and facility that God gives and I hope that he will bring his work to a happy conclusion. I do not need to tell you how deeply I am concerned about it, nor how much I am in Our Lord Jesus Christ' etc.

Mlle de Goello, then about fifty, was living in her nephew's home, the Hôtel de Soubise, (now part of the Archives Nationales.)

751100a   RM AGNÈS DE BELLEFONDS   November 1675
U 3069, p. 108 (extract)

Refutes rumours of his alleged Jansenism. Bellefonds admirable in disgrace; had spent some days with Abbot of Val-Richer, 'a most ignorant and prejudiced man, small-minded, banal and crude, but still a kindly man of good conduct. One might even say he is more an ecclesiastic in spirit than a solitary . . . There is one good thing about the Jansenists; if you do not speak ill of them, they speak well of you, . . . but as for the others [Molinists] unless you share their passions . . . they consider you their enemy.' Bellefonds would do well not to go too often to Val-Richer, but rather to local Benedictines.

The Abbot of Val-Richer, Dominique Georges, had indeed a long ecclesiastical background before becoming a Cistercian, and maintained close relations especially with Jesuits. R's criticism of his fellow delegate to Rome is exceptionally strong, even by his standards.

751100b   [GUILLAUME LE ROY]   November 1675
U 3069, p. 124 (extract)

On a wretch who passed by la T. some eight or ten months earlier, recommended by the Bp of Autun, took the habit and left after fifteen days.

This was Hippolyte Beauchâteau, ordained in 1666 to the Cong. de la Doctrine Chrétienne, then left to go to Hautefontaine, then la T. and in July 1675 to England, where he abjured, and pretended to be Antoine Arnauld's brother, Luzancy. He took his MA at Oxford, became a deacon in the Church of England and held various benefices. He was so notorious a trickster that as late as 1695 James II refers to him in a letter to R.

751100c   MADAME   November 1675
U 3069, p. 125 (extract)

Glad she has kept to her pious resolutions throughout her journey.

751100d MADAME [? DE SAINT-LOUP]   November 1675

From a material point of view she is to be pitied, but 'what can God give you in this world that is better for you than persecution and patience'? The Princess Palatine should withdraw from the world.

751100e [? DUC DE MAZARIN]   November 1675
U 3069, p. 131 (extract)

Hopes for reconciliation between M. and his wife.

The only person with whom R. seems to have discussed marital problems was Mazarin, whose wife left him in 1671 to go and live in England (and died there in 1699). Otherwise there is no clue to identification.

751100f RP   November 1675
U 3069, p. 120 (extract)

'The Abbot of [Foucarmont] may say what he likes, the best course is to remain in peace.'

Fleur de Montagne, abbot since 1672, was to lead an abortive mission to Rome in 1677, in the course of which he died, and was one of those who did not accept the settlement imposed in 1675.

751100g MONSIEUR   November 1675
U 3069, p. 106 (extract)

Asks him to take Association to Annonciades himself and greet his sisters.

Letters of Association were often sent by religious communities to other communities or to individuals, promising to include them in prayers and intentions. The practice still exists at la T.

751100h [RM MARIE-LOUISE BOUTHILLIER]   November 1675
U 3069, p. 100 (extract)

Sends Association. Respects to RM Superior.

751100i MADAME   November 1675
U 3069, p. 103 (extract)

Willing to direct her by letter, or help in any way, but cannot leave enclosure. She is thinking of a religious life, but would do better to look after the poor.

751100j BISHOP OF CHÂLONS [FÉLIX VIALART DE HERSE]   November 1675
U 3069, p. 95 (extract)

Bellefonds annoyed that Bp of Coutances is preventing teaching of theology at Valognes, where Luthumière is suspected of Jansenism. Asks Bp's help.

Luthumière was a friend and neighbour of Bellefonds, and whatever his personal views (probably quite orthodox), beyond doubt employed and protected, perhaps unwittingly, Jansenist teachers at the seminary he had founded. The diocesan, Loménie de Brienne, at Coutances in any case ran his own seminary.

This odd series of extracts, all from letters written in the same month, was compiled by dom Le Nain for inclusion in his Vie of R., *and while some are clearly selected with a view to refuting the charge of Jansenism, others seem quite random.*

751100k   DUCHESSE DE LONGUEVILLE   [? November] 1675
TB 557

R. has seen the priest she sent.

751200   COMTE DE TRÉVILLE   December 1675
TB 588

Comments on Tréville's journey to Alet.

Tréville had gone there not only to see the Bp but also because his official post at Foix was not far away.

751200a   DUCHESSE DE LONGUEVILLE   [December] 1675
TB 579

Visit of priest she sent. Tréville's visit to Bp of Alet.

751200b   BISHOP OF ALET [NICHOLAS PAVILLON]   December 1675
TB 616

Tréville's journey. Reform threatened.

751200c   RELIGIEUSE   December 1675
TB 594

Her pitiful state causes him deep grief; she must renounce her passions.

*751202   PIERRE NICOLE   2 December 1675
T 2240,13 orig.

'I have read, Monsieur, the third volume of the *Essais de Morale* sent to me on your behalf with inexpressible pleasure and edification. It contains such pure and lively truths, and you make them so apparent and palpable, that if our corruption were not what it is and our souls less weighed down by the weight of our cupidity and old habits, you would cause us to make a lot of progress in a short time. Yet if the heart is not carried away, the mind is convinced, and has no means, it seems to me, with which to combat such constant principles and such solid and manifest proofs. Self-love, as you make us put our finger on it, is to be met in almost all our actions, and in their every detail. One cannot take a step without catching one's foot in one of the traps it sets for us, and the only way to avoid them would be to walk in the same simplicity as the saints, which results from a most extraordinary protection by God. I confess, Monsieur, that in view of the way in which you use your health, the public has every interest in seeing God preserve it. I can assure you that I have even more interest in it than anyone, not only from the fact that I profess to honour you and esteem you, as you know, but also because I see myself everywhere in your works on moral direction, because all the sicknesses you treat in them are mine and everything you say makes the most profound impression on me. I am infinitely obliged, Monsieur, at your kindness in remembering me. Pray believe that I am duly grateful, and that no one could be more sincerely and devotedly yours' etc.

R. had had the previous volumes in 1671 and 1673; there was a fourth.

*76/1   RM AGNÈS DE BELLEFONDS   [1675/6]
TD C

'I cannot tell you how consoled I am when I think that you remember me, and that sharing in your friendship I cannot but share in your prayers; as I value them highly, I most urgently ask you to continue them.
   I am sure that you are speaking sincerely when you complain about yourself, but I am sure too that you do not have the reason that you believe to do so. With all the charity you have, you can hardly fail to be keenly touched by what goes on in the world, yet you bring to it so much moderation that you certainly do not fall into excesses. There is indeed nothing more intolerable than to see people not scrupling to impute anything they like to the most blameless persons according to their own passions and interests, and no innocence is shielded from the envy and malice of men. Those who are no longer of the world are fortunate, but those who do not know what is done there and do not hear the least news of it, are still more so, for detached as one may be from goods and affairs, one is not detached from truth and justice, and those whose heart is upright cannot but suffer when they see these things attacked. The main thing is to look at God in all things and consider the various acts of men as dispositions of his providence. Nothing is more just than to endure patiently what he endures himself and does not punish in those who commit it. The time will finally come when he has promised to justify innocence and punish calumnies, and give unto each according to his works. When one lives in that faith and hope, as one is

obliged to do, there is no injustice for which one cannot find consolation, be it personal or concerning our friends. I tell you, Reverend Mother, what you know as well as I. Father de Monchy will tell you our news. We should very much have liked to keep him longer, but that was not in our power. Keep your accustomed goodness towards me, and please believe, I beg you, that it is not possible to be with more sincerity and respect than I yours' etc.

76/2   RM ABBESSE [? ESSAI]   [? 1676]
TC II/225

She has solid christian reasons for wanting to resign, and her niece has all the qualities required to succeed her. 'Allow me to say that you must take care in giving up the title of superior not to retain the authority.'

Marie-Françoise Trotti de la Chétardie resigned on 4 February 1676 in favour of her niece, Françoise, coadjutrix since 1662, hence the date and identification proposed.

76/3   RM ABBESSE, PORT-ROYAL DES CHAMPS [MARIE DE FARGIS]   1676
U 3069, p. 71 (extract)

'Your views are so reasonable and fair that one would have to be otherwise not to agree with you.'

760100   RELIGIEUX   January 1676
TB 596

Distressed by RP's letter; he must not leave his monastery.

760100a   MONSIEUR [? PELLISSON]   January 1676
TB 611

Has read the brief but penetrating *Méditations*.

760100b   NICOLAS PINETTE   January 1676
TB 613

Regrets that Pinette has divulged confidential accounts [apparently *Relations* of recent deaths at la T.]

*760100c   RM ABBESSE, LEYME [ANNE DE LA VIEUVILLE]   January 1676
TB 624

'I am extremely sorry about the trouble and vexation stirred up against you, but in fact you could not have escaped them or helped doing what you have done without failing in your most essential duty, and abandoning the care of the souls committed to your charge by Our Lord. Your consolation must come from the testimony of your conscience; and as you looked to God alone without doubt when you exposed yourself to all these drawbacks, nothing could be less proper than to take note of the judgement passed on your conduct by men of either little understanding or much prejudice. Yet, RM, since you ask my opinion, I will only say that I think you should write to the Abbot of Cîteaux and urgently request him to appoint someone to give you absolution from the alleged excommunication. Although you are basically quite safe, because all competent persons have assured you that it is null and void, nevertheless for the public edification and the reputation of your monastery, you ought not to stay much longer in that situation. You should also beg him to nominate another visitor, since your conscience does not allow you to open the gates of your house to someone whom you should exclude for so many solid and important considerations, and unless he grants you what you ask, you will be constrained without further delay to address yourself to the secular powers. If the Abbot of Cîteaux does not heed as he should so right and reasonable a request, you must present a request to the King, explaining the whole affair and the extremities to which you have been reduced against every rule of piety and justice. Should the matter fail to meet with the success which, according to all appearances, it should have, the firmness with which you undertook it must be reduced to suffering in patience and resignation such an extraordinary event; humble yourself in God's hand, who often permits those who are nearest to his heart to remain in tribulation, groan in violent temptation, and see their best plans meeting unsurmountable difficulties on the part of men. If the Abbot of Cîteaux absolutely insisted that this visitor should, once only and as a pure formality, come into your house and chapter under such circumstances as you indicate in your letter, then you must point out to him that you are not allowed by the rules of the Church to admit him except for a real and effective visit, and since this one is a mere charade, you cannot consent to it without acting against the Church's intentions and violating its ordinances. If he were none the less to stand firm, and reconciliation depended on that condition, it seems to me that you should once more ask the Bishop of Cahors for his advice, and follow it, while making all necessary declarations and taking all necessary precautions and safety measures. It seems to me that your conscience may go that far, and God will be willing for the sake of establishing peace to relax some of the firmness he has inspired in you.

What you are kind enough to tell me about the Abbott of Septfons surprises me more than I can say. Ever since I have known him I have sought every opportunity of serving him, and eagerly; I have given him every possible sign of friendship, there is no good office I have not rendered him in temporal affairs or the conduct of his house; I have comforted him in his afflictions, and have felt them as though they were my own. I have given him advice in the difficulties he has met, I have supported him against our Fathers who wanted to expel him from our Observance, I have kept monks of his, whom he sent to me, for years at a time, and have taken as much care of them as of our own brothers, I have written to them many times at his request to fortify them in temptations and difficulties which made them want to leave him, and they stayed with him only out of deference for my views. Nearly a year ago he came to Paris intending to take advice from me on one of the most important circumstances of his life; I had gone there on the business of the Reform; we saw each other several times, and parted in complete accord; it is the strangest thing in the world that with no preceding event, without writing to me, without explaining himself to me, he should suddenly speak of my person and conduct as he could not have done if I had been his greatest enemy.

Although I believe that I am fully justified in your eyes, RM, and it is quite clear that he has persuaded you of nothing to my disadvantage, it seems however that there is some need to enlighten you on the main subjects for complaint which he alleges.

1. Not only is it not true that I spent a week at Port-Royal, but I can assure you that I have never stepped inside there since I became a monk, although as I have come and gone to and from Paris on the business of the Reform I have half a dozen times passed within a mile or two of that house. This is not because of any estrangement, for I think it to be a most holy and religious community, but because every time I have been obliged to leave our house I have always resolved to take no steps that were not necessary.

2. As regards the Celestines, it is true that he went further against my opinion than he should, and as those fathers wanted to take advantage of the fact that I wrote to him about it, he replied that I should not worry about it and that he would declare whenever I wished and judged the moment ripe that what he had told them had been of his own accord and without my participation.

What he says of attrition is equally groundless; it is pure imagination and I assure you that nothing of the kind ever entered my head.

As regards the religious we gave to him, the truth is that when they left our hands they were full of most religious dispositions, but these they soon lost when they were in his hands. They found no regularity of any kind in his house, he left them to their own devices, without guidance, they talked together as freely as they wished, they learned in no time what they should never have known in their lives, they had contacts with strange monks, he ruined their health by making them sing matins and High Mass when there were only four or five of them, and he did all that was needed to extinguish in them all spirit of their calling and fill them with distaste and dislike for it. There was one whom he took from us in the seventh month of his noviciate and then received for profession; he was only sixteen, very promising, but he had hardly taken his vows when, against all wisdom and all rules, he made him cellarer, and charged him with a task of which he was not capable. He stifled in his heart the piety that was still weak, and only newborn, and cast him into dissipation and disorder. He later asked me for other religious, but I could not bring myself to give them to him, as much because I had none willing to leave me and it was not right to force them as because I could not in conscience entrust them to a superior in whom I saw neither ability, diligence, nor strictness.

As for reproaching me for lack of mortification, I have nothing to reply; it is even greater than he thinks and spreads abroad. I confess that all my passions are very much alive, and I have so far done anything but apply myself as I should to destroying them. However, it is certain that every time rightminded people have risen forcibly against great abuses and great injustices, men of the world have not failed to look on them as fanatical and arrogant, and to attribute to motives of rancour, violence and bitterness what resulted solely from their charity and zeal.

That is already too much, RM, to let you judge the rest, which to tell the truth is just a mass of gross fantasies which he should never have uttered in front of people who were well-informed and able to answer. With all that I believe that he means well, but he is wrong in his methods because he is insufficiently enlightened and too credulous. I pray God to disabuse him and give him all the sanctity, glory, and merit of his profession, and I assure you that however offensive the way in which he treats me, I shall never lose a single opportunity of serving him. One is lucky to find such opportunities in the course of one's life; the injustices of men are always justice on the part of God, who in his mercy, and to punish the secret faults of which we are guilty, allows men to impute to us those of which we are innocent. It can happen that calumniators acting with a corrupt heart and inspired by their passions are still the executors of God's vengeance; that is what makes calumnies useful, and lets God allow the reputation of his saints to be attacked. As for us, who should live in love of abasement and scorn, and whose faith should be more lively and vigorous than that of ordinary men, it is not enough to suffer calumnies with patience and without protest; we are obliged to go as far as feeling joy at them. What difficulty can we have in doing so, RM, if we are really convinced that those who do not like us justify us when they condemn us, and the more they try to abase us in the eyes of men, the more they exalt us in the judgement of God and his angels? After all, that is an attitude which he asks of us above all; it is the main one, and without it the greatest of all misfortunes is that we bear the name and habit of a profession whose truth we do not hold.

What you have been told about our diminishing the austerity of our life is not true, and far from it being the fact that those of our brothers who have been taken away by God have caused us any weakening, their deaths were so happy, and God was good enough to link them with so many visible signs of his mercy, that all it produced in us was an ardent desire for a similar fate, with the result that our brothers have committed themselves afresh before God to persevere steadfastly to their dying breath in a style of life which we cannot doubt is according to his heart, since he has deigned to favour it with his grace and special blessing. We have even added two considerable practices; the first to sleep in our cowls, and the other to glaze our cloisters, and do our reading there as our fathers did five hundred years ago, so that we use our cells only for sleeping at night. I have written you a long account, and it would have been still more extensive if I had tried to answer in detail all that was in your letter, but as I did not think that was necessary, I also thought that I should at least throw some light on the main causes of dissatisfaction felt by the Abbot of Septfons, and that charity obliged me to do so as much as truth.

As for his accusation that I am a J[ansenist], I will say only that I have never belonged to any party but that of Christ and his Church, that during all the disputes of the past as of the present I have held myself entirely aloof from every one, and that no one in the world could be further than I from espousing any partiality. Such indifference does not please people who want others to share their passions and enthusiasms. We must praise God for all things and make our rest and peace consist in the blessing of being his and the sincere desire to serve and please him; such a consistent and invariable attitude cannot be taken from us by the envy or the malice of men. I am much obliged to you for your interest in my affairs, and it would give me great pleasure to be able to be successful in showing you convincingly that the gratitude I feel could not be greater than it is, any more than the esteem and sincerity with which I am yours' etc.

The General Chapter did not meet between 1672 and 1683, so the offending visitor was probably still Fr Lonjon. Beaufort's problem in 1675 no doubt concerned the leadership of the Reform, following the death of Jouaud in 1673. R's account of relations with Septfons can in part be supported from documents; for at least two years Septfons' novices did come to la T., until proper buildings were ready for them at home. Beaufort's connexion with the abbess is probably through the Noailles family, whom his father had served and with whom she was closely connected by family and other ties.

The reference to Celestines looks like another episode in the struggle of that Order's superiors to prevent their monks defecting to stricter Orders, and in particular to la T. Note yet again R's extreme sensitivity to any suggestion that he had Jansenist sympathies.

* 760106   MARÉCHAL DE BELLEFONDS   6 January 1676
BN na 12959 f.32, orig.

'I received the day before yesterday a letter from M. [the Bishop of Châlons] in which he told me that he has been ill, dangerously so, for two months, and asked me to tell you that as soon as his health is a little better and he is able to see to it, he will not fail to answer you and write what he thinks and feels. I can hardly believe that this is any different from what you think, but I am very sorry that his indisposition obliges him to delay explaining himself, since it could happen that matters would no longer be such that his opinions could be as effective and useful as you had hoped.

Permit me, Mgr, to profit from this occasion to renew the assurance that I remain your faithful servant at the beginning of this year, and to protest that I ask nothing more fervently of God than that he should give you the grace to spend it in the way closest to his heart and most useful for your sanctification. I am sure, Mgr, that that is what you have principally before your eyes, and convinced as you are of the vanity of all perishable things, you turn all your thoughts as far as possible towards those which are fixed and permanent and undergo neither change nor vicissitude. A Christian's sole occupation in this world must be to await and desire the eternity of Jesus Christ, and the saints claim that he lacks faith and is a Christian only in name if he lacks such a holy disposition. Keep me in the honour of your friendship, Mgr, and believe that no one could be more sincerely and deeply respectful than I, yours' etc.

The Bp of Châlons was R's old friend Vialart de Herse.

760130   RP PASQUIER QUESNEL, CONG. ORAT.   30 January 1676
U 1168 orig; Tans 30

R. has received three-volume *Life of Savonarola*, and will arrange payment.

This was the Latin life by G-F. Pico della Mirandola, republished in Paris, 1674.

760200   SR EMILIE DE BOUILLON   February 1676
TB 636; TC II/338; BN 19324 (extract giving name)

She was right to abstain from communion in expiation of her fault, but should now resume her usual practice and accept God's forgiveness.

760200a MADAME DE SAINT-LOUP   February 1676
TB 639

As her health is no better she should spend Lent as she did the year before.

760217   MADEMOISELLE [? DE VERTUS]   17 February 1676
U 863 orig.

R. had forgotten to answer her question about RP de Monmouton. If he wants to come to la T. he must seek permission of the proto-abbot [la Ferté], but such people easily take offence.

Internal evidence suggests Mlle de Vertus as the addressee, but the rest of the correspondence is missing and no more is known of Monmouton.

760309   JEAN DESLIONS, DEAN OF SENLIS   9 March 1676
Le Nain, *Vie* (1719), II/602

Surprised that the world finds extraordinary the quite common life led at la T. Thanks him for details of Carthusian primitive observance.

*760314   MARÉCHAL DE BELLEFONDS   14 March 1676
BN na 12959 f.36,orig.; TB 663

'I am sending you, Mgr, the reply from M. [de Châlons ?] which I received only yesterday. You will see that he agrees neither with you nor with me. It is quite remarkable that people having the same intention, that of procuring the glory of God and the good of souls, should treat the same things in such different ways and attitudes. M. [...] claims to be fully informed about the affair. He bases his opinion on particular information which he imagines you did not have, and thinks that what is needed is firmness and resistance, where you, and I too, were convinced that it would be much better to acquiesce and compromise. I have read the letter he writes you, and he sent it to me open. When I think, Mgr, what diverse opinions and contrary feelings men have concerning every matter, I assure you that I count myself happy indeed to have no other rule to follow in this world but to love God, keep out of sight, and be silent. It is very hard amid perpetual disputes to hold to so right a course that one does not incline to either side, but remains always in a state of balance and indifference. So far God has preserved me from any partiality, and I hope more than ever to remain in this state of suspension, although it is agreeable to no one, for you know, Mgr, that men do not like neutrality when their interests are at stake, and what they want are partisans and sectaries. God takes such care to inspire us with contempt and aversion from all disputed matters, and gives us such ample opportunity to live in complete detachment from all persons and affairs, that we can quite easily acquire and retain the dispositions so necessary to those who want nothing but peace. Death, which we always have before our eyes, and which is incessantly present in that of our brothers, is the most powerful of all motives for this. I confess that it is difficult for us to consider ourselves otherwise than as men who are no longer of this world. It is only a month since we lost one of our brothers; our Prior died two days ago and we have several others who will not be long in following them. Not only is the way in which it pleases God to remove them from us consoling for the signs we see therein of his mercy, but it is infinitely useful, because it makes that terrible event so familiar that there is at present nothing which takes precedence in our brothers' hearts over the desire to die. That should not be reckoned of much account, for St Augustine says that that sentiment should be found in all Christians. He wants them to be no less impatient for Jesus Christ's second coming than were the patriarchs and fathers of old for the first, and he could not understand how one could love Christ and fear his presence. That is a truth which does not have general currency, but it is none the less constant, and the reason it is so little recognised is that there are very few true Christians. We must agree that if we were as vigorously persuaded as we should be that this world is our place of banishment and that our bodies are our prisons, we should look on the moment of our death as one of consolation, since nothing else can end our exile and captivity. But far from that people try to find eternity in time and to create fixed and permanent enjoyment of things whose use is granted only for a few instants. One must know the wretchedness of men, feel it, pity them, and, if possible, not belong to the number of the wretched.

    I pray God, Mgr, to continue to strengthen you with blessings and grace, that dying in this holy period with Christ in a death which is no less real and effective than that we have just mentioned, though it is different, you may receive on the day of his resurrection a completely new spirit, birth and life. Do me the honour of believing that no one could be more faithfully and respectfully than I yours' etc.

The reading 'Châlons' is almost certain. The affair in which R., Bellefonds and the bp were involved was that of the seminary of Valognes, founded by the abbé Luthumière, and for long under suspicion of Jansenism. The Bp of Coutances, Loménie de Brienne, tried to take action to restrain Jansenist teachers at the seminary, but Luthumière used his very noble connexions to denounce the bp at court in 1675. In the event the bp was justified, but it is by no means clear that Luthumière himself was a convinced Jansenist, even if some of his close collaborators were. R. and others had tried to win support for him, especially from such prelates as the Bp of Châlons, friendly with many Jansenists if not himself at all unorthodox. See 751100j.

Euthyme Verrolles died in January, the prior, Urbain le Pannetier, on 12 March.

760317   BISHOP OF GRENOBLE [ETIENNE LE CAMUS]   17 March 1676
TC I/41; (date given in note to TB 1752)

Bp has worried about future of la T. after R's death, but R. accepts the workings of providence. Not surprised at Bp's wish to end his days in retreat.

760400   MADAME DUPLESSIS-GUÉNÉGAUD   [March/April] 1676
TB 660

Condolences on the death of husband [16 March].

760400a   BISHOP OF GRENOBLE [ETIENNE LE CAMUS]   [?April] 1676
TC I/11

R. not intending to reduce austerity despite many recent deaths. He has had a chest infection for six months and been bled five or six times.

Six monks died in 1675, and four more in 1676, very likely of some tubercular infection.

*760415   MARÉCHAL DE BELLEFONDS   15 April 1676
BN na 12959 f.38,orig.

'I have nothing new to tell you, Mgr. We continue to praise God for the success he has given to your affairs and to pray him to pour his grace and benediction on your plans and facilitate their execution. The main thing is, Mgr, that you are building on solid foundations, I mean sincere renunciation of the world, with all its vanities and glories. I do not doubt that in preserving the fidelity you owe to God and having no other thought than that of belonging to him you will go a long way in a short time. When God's moment has come, nothing is more important than not to neglect it. I remain with more respect and fidelity than I can express yours etc.

PS We have found here a bound New Testament, and *Imitation of Christ* and some other works. I wonder if it might be yours. Be good enough, Mgr, to let us know so that we can send it to Mother Agnès to pass on to you.'

760425   MADEMOISELLE [? DE VERTUS]   25 April 1676
U 863 orig.

Has only just discovered that the letters he writes to Leyme go via Mlle. Monmouton must wait for the right moment.

*760500   RM ABBESSE, LEYME [ANNE DE LA VIEUVILLE]   May 1676
TB 670

'This note, RM, is just to assure you of my delight at learning from your last letter that your alleged excommunication has at last been lifted. You were right to hold fast, for your interest was that of God, and if you had given up you would also have abandoned his cause and that of your sisters. As regards your visitor, I am very sorry for you, and you can hardly avoid falling into bad hands, since all the religious of the Common Observance, even those with the best intentions, have no real lights, and there are barely any who have not found reasons for authorising laxity of life. The worst of it is that those who are considered decent, because their conduct is not vicious, are to be feared more than the others, since people who are denounced are less able to do harm than those who enjoy some kind of good opinion. Apart from the fact that the latter are more easily trusted, they themselves have no doubts, they boldly make up their minds and imagine that they cannot be mistaken because they do not live in corruption with many others. What you have to do, RM, is to try and win the hearts of your nuns, or at least the majority, and show them that they will damn themselves wretchedly if they follow ways which do not conform to their rule and adhere to the evil principles of those advising them. If you were strengthened by the majority, your firmness for the cause of right and your regularity together would astound your visitors and none would dare resist you.

I will not say any more on the subject of the Abbot of Septfons, except that you are not the only one to whom he has spoken about me in the terms you mention; I have heard from many quarters similar things. I forgive him with all my heart; I should serve him if I could, but that does not stop me regarding his conduct as I do. God, who desires us to give pleasure to our enemies and love them, does not for all that want us to tear our eyes out, approve what deserves to be condemned, and speak well about those who are unworthy. Charity is quite holy, and does not know what it is to offend either truth or justice. Among the great number of persons whom he has received of late in his house, there are some whom we have rejected from ours, and I find it hard to believe that he will make of all that motley collection an exemplary community. God bless him, and I hope that he will be served at Septfons as at la Trappe. I ask you to remember me before God, and please believe that no one could take more interest in all that concerns you, or be with more respect and gratitude yours' etc.

* 760507   MARÉCHAL DE BELLEFONDS   7 May 1676
BN na 12959 f.40,orig.; TB 672

'We have every reason to bless God, Mgr, for the fact that your affairs have been as successful as you do me the honour of informing me, and that matters have been concluded with greater ease and felicity than one could have dared to hope. These are quite extraordinary effects of God's goodness, and you feel this so keenly, as it seems to me, that I have no doubt that you accept as you should the plans he has for you, and will apply yourself henceforth solely to regulating the whole conduct of your life on what he desires. Your views on this are so christian and so right that all one can wish for you is fidelity in execution and perseverance in following it up. After all, Mgr, if you were to find yourself once more in the places and employment in which you have been, what would you see there but what you have already seen? And what did you see but what should be erased from the heart and often even from the memory of those who desire to walk in the ways of Jesus Christ, not those of the world, and who know that one aspires in vain to eternal things if one does not live in oblivion and scorn of those things which are not eternal? I assure you, Mgr, that anyone who hopes as much as he is obliged to for the rewards and fortune which God prepares in the land of the living for those who serve him, is not only hardly concerned to occupy the chief places in this region of death, but even avoids as much as he can any advantageous situation, since there is not one such but is a trap, a real reef, full of a malignity from which the most faithful and scrupulous vigilance can barely offer protection.

My indisposition, which returned two days after you left here, prevents me saying more to you, but will not prevent me from recommending you to Our Lord, and praying him until I breathe my last to complete your sanctification. I am, Mgr, with deep respect yours etc.

PS The Marquis de Saint-Pierre does us some justice in wishing us well, for I can assure you that he left us full of esteem and regard for his person, his wisdom and his virtue. I am very glad to enjoy the good graces of a man of his merit. I told you recently that we have found a book here which I think belongs to you. It is a New Testament bound in with the Psalms and some works of piety. Be good enough to let us know about it.'

The Marquis de Saint-Pierre was Charles Castel, who had married Bellefonds' aunt Madeleine. The couple built a remarkable boat-shaped church at Saint-Pierre-Eglise, near Cherbourg, still today decorated with rigorist injunctions on fasting and similar preparation for the sacrament.

760522   MADEMOISELLE [? DE VERTUS]   22 May 1676
U 863 orig.

Very sorry to hear how unwell she has been; time for fear to give way to confidence. Monmouton must wait until his abbot has his bulls from Clairvaux and say nothing about letter from R.

Pierre Bouchu, Abbot of la Ferté since 1655, had been elected to Clairvaux in February 1676 but did not actually go there until May 1677.

*760522a BISHOP OF LUÇON [HENRI BARILLON]   22 May 1676
P f.764

'I am extremely sorry, Mgr, not to have been able to receive the ecclesiastic on whose behalf you wrote, for apart from the fact that you have complete power over me, I very much wanted to extend my hand to him and help him to leave the situation in which he has been for so long, but in fact I was prevented by reasons I cannot tell you in a letter, and which you would approve if I had told you. Although we do not often have the consolation of writing to you, Mgr, we are still informed of your news, and know from different quarters how God continues to bless your labours and care. More than a year ago, when I was in Paris on the affairs of our Observance, the Bishop of la Rochelle was kind enough to come and see me. He spoke to me about you in detail and at length and told me what no one else could have said as well as he did. I praise God that your hopes have not been deceived, and will pray him with my last breath to give you that persevering fidelity without which you know that what you have so far done in his service would be of no avail. Allow me, Mgr, to ask you for the succour of your prayers and to say, that although God does not cease to protect and sustain us in the resolutions he inspired in us to serve him, yet we have been deeply pained by the number of our brothers whom he has taken from this world in the past fourteen or fifteen months. We have lost ten, including our prior. My health amid all that is not too good; I was not at all well at the end of this Lent, and my present state cannot yet be called a real recovery. We must adore God's ways and submit wholeheartedly to all his wishes. That, Mgr, is the grace which I beg you to ask on my behalf, for as regards what little good he has procured in this monastery, as it is his work, it is right to abandon the care of it to him and leave him to dispose of it. Keep for me the share you have given me in your friendship, unworthy as I am, and please believe, Mgr, that no one in the world honours you more than I, or is with more affection and respect yours' etc.

The Bp of la Rochelle was Henri-Marie de Laval (1661–93), son of Mme de Sablé.

*760611 MARÉCHAL DE BELLEFONDS   11 June 1676
BN na 12959 f.43, orig.; TB 674

'I am very sorry, Mgr, that your affairs are not being carried out with the promptness and ease which you found in dealing with them. However that should not come as a surprise to you. St Augustine says that God in his mercy mingles bitter things with those in which we might find some sweetness to prevent disorders in our heart, which always becomes more attached than it should to the things that please it. Indeed those who serve God meet difficulties almost everywhere, as God takes particular care to purify through inconvenient happenings and disagreeable circumstances their designs and intentions, however good and holy these may be. Yours, Mgr, are so christian and so right, and what you desire is so exactly what you ought to desire, that I cannot believe that he will fail to give it his blessing. The main thing is to await his chosen moment and to submit one's will to his, not only in the substance of things, but in their timing. You know that everything is regulated and that nothing escapes his providence, and by desiring something too ardently one risks desiring against God's order. You must not be surprised, Mgr, if the world is too much with you. The world is too wicked and man too weak for him to lose altogether its opinions, memory, and ideas. It is even very useful that these things should be preserved and should present themselves with importunity. Otherwise one would be lulled into a sense of false security, without noticing that there are within oneself secret faults and that one conceals inclinations which oblige us to mistrust everything, to be vigilant and ceaselessly on our guard. You could not do better, Mgr, than settle down, and nothing could contribute more to your peace of mind and purity of heart. Every step that is not necessary is always harmful, and those who desire to belong to God as much as you do, and as much as he wants it of you, could not go too far in cutting out those things that are not capable of leading them to him. All the same I confess that I should be very distressed if that were to deprive me of the honour and consolation of seeing you, and I do not claim by any means that you should include among things that are useless a journey to la Trappe. However that may be, Mgr, I beg you to believe that there is no place in the world which is more yours and where you are more respected than here.

PS I am sending back your book; you would have had it long ago if I had been sure it was yours.'

760611a   RP PASQUIER QUESNEL, CONG. ORAT.   11 June 1676
U 1168 orig.; Tans 31

Death of RP Séguenot. R's own health slowly recovering.

On Séguenot, see 58/1.

760726   MADAME   26 July 1676
TB 676

She is thinking of leaving the world, but prudence is required before leaving family for cloister. She should leave court, live in the country and read the Bible.

760806   JEAN FAVIER   6 August 1676
CF 344,f.73 aut.; Gonod 38

Edmond has told Favier untrue stories about R's health.

*760812   MARÉCHAL DE BELLEFONDS   12 August 1676
BN na 12959 f.45,orig.

'As I learned some days ago that some of the letters I had written to Mother Agnès had been lost, I thought, Mgr, that it was possible that my answer to the last letter you did me the honour of writing might have had the same fate. There was nothing important in it, nor anything to make me apprehensive about someone seeing it, but none the less I should be upset to know that it had fallen into the hands of anyone but you. I spoke to you, Mgr, if my memory serves me, of the consolation which, I am convinced, you have found in your retreat. I said that you should not be surprised if sometimes the world came back to you, and that it would be very difficult for you so to lose the memory of things past as to efface them from your heart. The world, and the impressions it makes upon us, are too wicked, and we are too drawn to it by all our inclinations to be able to destroy it entirely within us without much pain and effort. It is even useful for us to be persuaded by our own experience so that we should be more careful to shun and avoid everything that might bring us closer to it, and that we should realise more fully what we owe to God, when he withdraws us from it and in his mercy breaks the things that tied us to it. I also said, Mgr, concerning what you told me about your resolve to stay at home, that nothing could contribute more towards the peace and quiet you sought, that all unnecessary steps are always harmful, and that those who wish as much as you to belong to God, who manifests that this is what he asks of you by all the grace he has already shown you, could not go too far in cutting out those things which are not capable of leading them to him. In short, Mgr, there should be nothing useless in the life of a Christian, and when one thinks that one will have to render an account at Jesus Christ's last judgement of one's least word, one will no doubt be reserved in one's actions and demands. I confess, however, that I should be upset if that were to deprive us of the honour and consolation of seeing you, and I should find it hard to agree that you should include among things of no utility a journey to la Trappe. I beg you to believe, Mgr, that there is no place in the world which is more yours nor where you are more desired and respected than here.

PS It is now more than two months since I sent back your book to Mother Agnès to pass on to you. It is true that she received it without knowing for whom it was intended, and the letter in which I told her it should be sent to you never reached her.'

The letter presumed lost seems to be 760611.

760813   COMTE DE BRANCAS   13 August 1676
SS orig. (pp 6 and 7 only); TD (dated 1678); Gonod 207

Danger of judging heresy in others. R. simply signed and would do it again.

This long letter is reproduced in all the lives of R., but comparison with the two extant pages of the original casts doubt on the accuracy of all copies. R. took his usual line about the signature against Jansenism (See 59/1); he had merely obeyed his superiors. He never discussed the doctrines themselves.

760824   SR ANNE-MARIE [D'EPERNON]   24 August 1676
TB 694

His health is better. She lives in a good community and should simply persevere.

*760827   RM ABBESSE, LEYME [ANNE DE LA VIEUVILLE]   27 August 1676
TB 696

'We shall not fail, RM, since you wish it, to have the *Usages* of our order translated for you; but although we have already had the translation started, you will not have it as soon as I should like, because I shall have to go over the whole thing, and since my health is not completely restored I cannot devote myself to it as I should wish. Even if the *Original Spirit of Cîteaux* was condemned by a general chapter, which I have never heard, reading them would be no less holy, useful, or permissible; that would be the result of passion and not of justice, and should not keep you from reading them. I will say no more about the Abbot of [Septfons]; I was told some days ago that he was in Paris. What you wrote about him, and what I know of him from elsewhere, means that it is well worth taking special care to pray for him. Please believe once again, RM, that all he has said about me is pure fantasy.

As regards the religious of whom you speak, you would do well to be rid of her. If the Rule allows one to expel a religious who is incorrigible, lest the others fall into disorder through his bad example, there can be no doubt that you cannot in conscience allow this creature to be transferred to another monastery, rightly fearing as you may that the corruption in her heart spreads and is transmitted. As for returning her dowry, I do not think that anyone would be unreasonable enought to suggest it; as for the pension, if her parents gave one when she became a nun, I should prefer to give it back rather than fail to get rid of the nun, in case she could not be put elsewhere without that condition, and it will be greatly to your advantage to have got rid of such a bad person.

You no doubt owe much respect and deference to Monsieur de [?], but you might have told him that, as in your Order there are statutes and punishments laid down for those who apostasize, you were not free not to use them, and perhaps he would have yielded to your representations; but after considering all you tell me, I see that you could do nothing better than concede what he asked of you. It is most important in your present situation to behave in such a way as always to enjoy his favour. You did well to oppose as much as you could the confessor's easy ways; you were quite right to speak to him as you did, and if he had known his job he would have anticipated the advice you gave him by acting more strictly and in a more ecclesiastical manner. Do me the honour, RM, of always believing that no one could be more concerned than I in your interests, and that I am moved by your troubles and the persecution you suffer more than I can say. I pray Our Lord to be your comfort and strength, and am in him with all esteem and truth yours' etc.

Le Premier Esprit de Cîteaux (Original Spirit), *by Julien Paris, Abbot of Foucarmont, was first published in 1653, and revised in 1664 and 1670. Together with his* Nomasticon *(1664) this was the major source book for the Reform. The Chapter of 1672 (whose validity was widely contested) implicitly condemned diffusion of these works, though not by name (see Canivez,* Statuta Capitulorum, *7, pp 435ff, at Stat. 66).*

The immediate cause of Beaufort's mischief making was R's letter to Le Roy about fictions, but personal rivalry played a part. The unnamed 'M' sounds like the Bp of Cahors.

760829   [JEAN FAVIER]   29 August 1676
A 2106,f. 81

Continuing rumours of his death. Hopes Mme X will actually carry out her resolution and that Mlle X continues on the right road.

The cryptic references are almost certainly to members of the Albon family, perhaps his sister and one of his nieces.

760900   RELIGIEUSE   [? September] 1676
M 1214,105; A 2106,f.122 (partial; dated 5 November 1683)

She regrets her lack of progress in virtue. Discusses his letter to B., which is causing controversy, and a copy of which she has seen.

In the heading the copyist has spelled out the name of Bellefonds, though the body of the letter refers only to 'M. de B.' It seems much more likely that this is Brancas, to whom R. had written on 13 August.

760917   DUCHESSE DE MONTPENSIER   17 September 1676
TB 702

She has asked about a possible successor to Abbot of Foucarmont; R. knows no one suitable.

Jacques Fleur de Montagne did not die until 1678, and it remains unexplained why Mme de Montpensier ever raised the question, since she had no power of appointment.

*760928   MARÉCHAL DE BELLEFONDS   28 September 1676
BN na 12959 f.47, orig.; TB 707

'I cannot resist telling you, Mgr, that Monsieur de Brancas has at last been to see us, as you have desired for so long, and that his visit has produced exactly the effect that you had predicted. All the impressions that people had managed to give him against our house have been completely effaced. He was both pleased and touched by what he saw, and he seemed to me entirely satisfied as regards the things which, as you know, caused him pain. Reasonable as he is, he is at pains to express no disapproval of the fact that, remaining in a spirit of obedience and submission as I have always done, I refrain from judging anyone and consider as my brothers those whom the church numbers among her children. Most people would be unable to understand that the charity of Jesus Christ does not know what it is to form judgements and suspicions, and that the most reliable course for those holding no authority and having no right of inspecting others, is to do what they ought and remain silent. As this is the true way for those who are disinterested, it is not surprising that it is followed by so few. It is hard to find people who go to God by ways that are straight and pure, who have him solely before their eyes, and who do not seek to gratify their own passions on the pretext of their zeal for his glory and service. I confess, Mgr, that in M. de Brancas I found such extraordinary goodness and devotion to God, so genuine a desire to be his and serve him, that I am quite amazed that anyone should acquire such christian dispositions in such an un-christian world. For all that he is infinitely to be pitied. Although one can in fact steer a ship through tempests, one is always exposed to extreme perils and makes little headway, and that with much difficulty, and nothing is more rare than to see such voyages end safely. This is a truth known perfectly only to those who are in harbour, and I am sure, Mgr, that since you have been there, when you go over in your mind the different tides and turbulences of the sea of the world, and the dispositions even of those who profess to find their salvation in it, they seem to you proper objects of compassion for being so little distrustful of the situation in which they find themselves and fearing nothing, living as if they were in safety when dangers beset and surround them on every side. That reflection is no doubt a great consolation to you in your retreat, for what must be your gratitude for the grace you have received from God, drawing you by the hand from the midst of this world, where there are almost as many obstacles to serving him as there are men, occupations, and affairs, and how must you view the situation in which he has now put you, when you think that not only have these difficulties been destroyed, but that he gives you countless means and facilities for working at your sanctification. Nothing, it seems to me, could make you more faithful or more aware of his mercies to you, and prevent you ever becoming ungrateful or forgetful, than comparing these two states. We pray him every day, Mgr, as much as we can to complete his work and by multiplying his favours to increase your fidelity and gratitude. I am with all due respect, do me the honour of believing me, yours etc.

PS I must say once more, Mgr, that M. de Brancas showed me so much kindness, confidence, and frankness that I could not appreciate it more. I beg you to oblige me by telling him something to that effect, because he will certainly write at length to you of his journey to la Trappe.'

This visit of Bellefonds' kinsman by marriage had far-reaching effects on R's public relations with Jansenists and anti-Jansenists.

761007 MADEMOISELLE [? DE VERTUS]   7 October 1676
U 863 orig.

A miracle that she has recovered. When in Paris [1675] R. had recommended a good, but not well-known, Oratorian to Mlle's sister, who had spent her life in 'prodigious negligence and futility'. Encloses letter to Leyme. Respects to Prioress.

If the identification is correct, the sister would be Mlle de Goello, and the Prioress that of Port-Royal, where Mlle de Vertus lived.

761014 ANTOINE ARNAULD   14 October 1676
T 2183, p. 28; *Lettre de Tillemont*, 1705, p. 108

R. has had so much trouble with Mendicants that he will only take them on express papal instructions. Another young man has been put in novitiate, but is so thin that nobody expects him to last. Generally opposed to accepting weaklings, as they can be a source of relaxed discipline.

*761028 COMTE DE BRANCAS   28 October 1676
SS orig.

'I would not dare, Monsieur, to say any more about the many kindnesses you heap on me; they must be endured without reply and we must content ourselves with remaining grateful before God and in our innermost heart. What we are doing is so slight a thing that it should be buried in profound oblivion as far as the world is concerned and it would be enough for us that God, who has promised to heed the desires and wishes of those who fear him and want nothing more than to please him, should be the witness; he, I say, who puts up with the weak and does not judge the wretchedness of his servants with strict justice.

You believed, Monsieur, what you chose and spoke about us and our monastery according to what your charity caused you to find of edification there. Rest assured that it is no small mortification to know that things are being said about us of which we feel ourselves to be unworthy. I confess, Monsieur, that given the difference of opinions and variety of minds in men, one would be fortunate indeed not to know what they are saying, but that is not possible, and so the best one can do for one's peace of mind is to have God alone before one's eyes, to look to him in the whole conduct of one's life and do exactly what he seems to demand of us, without being remotely concerned with pleasing men. Apart from the fact that they can never be satisfied, it is wrong to try and even worse to succeed; and indeed one always exposes those whom one approves and praises to great temptations. A normal virtue resists calumnies, but a very purified virtue is needed to defend oneself against praise.

I will say nothing new to you about what you tell me, and my submission has been at all times so simple and free from any restrictions that no one can doubt what I am, although I have abstained from speaking of matters which do not concern me.

It is so hard to be fair in one's words and keep within strict limits, and it so often happens that in treating the most [holy] matters one becomes inflamed with a far from [holy] zeal, that it is a great fortune to have nothing to do in this world but live and keep quiet. That is why I am more determined than ever to do that, unless God opens our lips by some extraordinary event and manifest need.

I fear, Monsieur, that after I have cleansed myself of suspicions of Jansenism, a second problem remains; that is to prevent people thinking that I favour the opposite party. For I confess that the moral teaching of most of its members is so corrupt, their principles so contrary to the holiness of the gospel and all the rules and instructions given to us by Christ, either in his words or in the ministry of his saints, that there is scarcely anything less tolerable to me than to see my name used to give authority to opinions which I condemn with all my heart. What surprises me—I say it, Monsieur, with grief—is that on that score everyone is dumb, and even those who profess zeal and piety keep profound silence, as if there were anything more important in the Church of God than to keep purity and faith in the conduct of souls and the direction of morals.

For my part, never having become heated against anyone because I have always kept myself aloof from all kinds of connexions, when I look at things with the disinterestedness of a man who wants to have only God and the truth before his eyes and try to discern the reason why people become so excited about certain matters and so cold and indifferent about others, no explanation seems more natural than that what motivates most men is self-interest, that on one side is pleasing and winning, and on the other just losing (I speak of those who are theologians and cannot be unaware of the sense and consequences of things). As in this world there is nothing to be lost or won, and I have reduced to eternity alone all my aspirations and hopes, these are modifications and restraints which I can neither appreciate nor approve. In truth, if God does not take pity on the world and does not remove the effect of men's constant effort to destroy true principles and substitute others which are not true, the evils will multiply and we shall see almost total desolation before long. As you can see, Monsieur, the position I adopt is that most likely to make everyone oppose me and content no one.

Your daughter has done me the honour of writing to me. I find her fidelity towards God admirable; there appears to be such sincerity and ardour in her desire to belong wholly to him that I cannot believe that you fail to be consoled at seeing her as you wish her to be. We do not fail to commend her to Our Lord. This will be henceforth one of our principal obligations and the trust with which she honours us puts no limits to our debt.

It is Madame de Guise's piety which has made her find some sort of edification here and remember what she saw, and I can see, Monsieur, that you have taken great care to recall her ideas of us, and that there are no good offices you do not render us.

As regards the friend of whom you speak, you know that he is a fiery person and always expresses himself vigorously on things affecting him; but apart from piety, of which he has a lot, he has also qualities of intelligence, honour, and probity which win him friendship and esteem.

I much value being remembered by the Abbess of Lys. I have long honoured her merit and person, and unknown to her I have held in high esteem the regularity and discipline of the monastery she leads with such success and blessings.

As I was about to close this letter, Monsieur, I received a second one which you did me the honour of writing, full of evidence of a fidelity worthy of you. I am not surprised at its contents, not only because the person to whom you gave the first news about it had already given me the [gist?], but because there is no ill turn I would not expect from someone who did this to me. The deed is so black that I would not dare to call it by the name it deserves. It is a question of a letter I wrote five or six years ago to someone who condemned certain mortifying exercises in use among us, and which were established by the saints and practised in all regular observances and almost throughout the ages. Nothing was further from my mind than making the letter public, and I gave a copy to only two or three of my friends, of whom he was one, in strictest confidence; he promised to keep it secret, and you can see how he did so. Basically the paper is quite exact, and contains nothing anyone could condemn, except out of gross ignorance or violent passion, and I am sure it would have edified you if you had read it. However, if one sees and examines things with the intention of finding something to criticise, I do not know what would be exempt from censure. The passage about which you and Monsieur de Tréville write is perfectly orthodox, and there are many passages in Scripture which say the same thing. It would take too long to discuss that here, but on that point, Monsieur, you can reply in general by saying that I may have erred through imprudence and ignorance, because I have much of both, but that whenever my errors are pointed out to me I will recognise them without difficulty. I do not make it a point of honour to maintain them, but I am still persuaded that the paper is entirely truthful and correct.

If I had known what objection is being made against the passage, and what Monsieur de Tréville, writing to me about it, asked me more distinctly, I would have enlightened you. The way people treat me, Monsieur, is more odious, more violent and more contrary to the rules of charity than if they had set up an ambush in a wood to kill me; according to the terms of Scripture that is called *Sedet in insidio in occulto ut interficiat innocentem* [Ps 10:8] I have never done anything but good to the person who has given rise to this whole fine business, and I have never done harm to the person who is so vigorously stirring it up. I leave you to judge, Monsieur, full of piety and honour as you are, what such conduct is. God will give me grace to preserve on this occasion, painful as it is to me, all the charitable feelings he commands me to have, and I would gladly give the last drop of my blood to serve him, as I would for the salvation of those who do not scruple to mix up the faith with human opinion.

As the good monk is neither very clever nor very scrupulous, as you can see, he may easily have changed the paper, for, if I remember right, he copied it himself in a great hurry.

I see, Monsieur, that this is a very long letter, and I recall too late that St Bernard said the rule of silence is broken just as much by letters as by speaking, and he wanted people to be as brief and strict in one as in the other. Keep for me, I humbly beseech you, the honour of your friendship, and do me the honour of believing that I am most keenly aware of all for which I am obliged to you and that it is not possible to be more respectfully yours etc.

PS I forgot to say, Monsieur, that the thought that occurred to me concerning this whole affair, before it broke, was clearly to inform the Archbishop of Paris and send him the paper, asking him to act as he saw fit, so that I should not be obliged to make my own defence or to maintain my belief and faith against those who attack it so unjustly. But as we can only know through you the state of affairs, you must be kind enough, Monsieur, to let Mother Agnès know, if it should lapse or the rumour continue, so that in this matter people should act as we agreed was suitable, There are certain steps to be taken, which cost something, as you may believe, to a man who fears nothing in the world more than to be talked about.'

Brancas had two daughters. This reference is most probably to Françoise, who married the prince d'Harcourt in 1667 and was a known correspondent of R's. Le Lys was a cistercian abbey near Melun.

The latter part of the letter refers to Beaufort's perfidy in divulging R's reply to Le Roy's Dissertation on humiliations, and the consequent charges of Jansenism made against R. 'The good monk' is Beaufort, the other person Le Roy.

* 761102   RM AGNÈS DE BELLEFONDS   2 November 1676
TD C

'Very Reverend Mother,
You must have much charity to endure all the trouble we give you, and I confess that I should be extremely troubled at importuning you as often as I do if I did not have complete confidence in your goodness towards me. As I heard nothing by the last regular post, I thought the rumour had ceased and, being without foundation, could not be sustained. In truth I cannot understand that malice and envy can go to such excesses as to attempt to find errors in the most proper and holy expressions imaginable. For assuredly all I said was in the sense and according to the expressions of Scripture and, short of condemning Scripture, it is not possible to condemn what I put forward. If I had been told positively in writing the basis for these gentlemen's intended censure, I should have explained my thoughts precisely and cleared up the alleged difficulty, but since what was said was said so confusedly, I only replied in general terms. By Our Lord's grace that causes me no anxiety, and I can assure you, Reverend Mother, that I am not in the least disturbed. When I think that the saints were attacked by men's envy on similar subjects, that their sanctity, innocence, and great reputation did not shield them from this kind of assault, and that St Teresa was brought before the Inquisition and charged with crimes for the holiest actions and practices, I have good reason for consolation, and I confess that the greatest of my

troubles, what confounds and afflicts me, is that, being a great sinner, I see myself treated as though I were not one. Today is All Saints' day; it is very right to forget everything and think only of them and the means whereby they were sanctified. We could do no better to become worthy of having them as intercessors before God than to imitate them and regard their lives and acts as the rule and model of our own. After all the only harm men can do to us by their injustice is to trouble our hearts and give us dispositions contrary to those needed to become like them. I have great need of the help of your prayers to obtain from God the grace of suffering in peace all that it may please him should happen to me. Do me the honour of believing that no one could be with more gratitude and veneration than I yours etc.

PS I should very much like to know if M. de Brancas was content with the last letter I wrote him. In it I allowed something to slip out which is fundamentally only good, but which he might apply to himself against my intentions. I am deeply obliged to him, and surprised at the kindness and warmth with which he interests himself in all that concerns us. I beg you, Reverend Mother, to tell him on that score anything you can to show him how grateful I am.'

R. had written to Brancas on 28 September.

*761106   MARÉCHAL DE BELLEFONDS   6 November 1676
BN na 12959 f.49,orig.; TC II/1

'The letter that you do me the honour of writing to me, Mgr, tells me in a few words what I ought to be, but at the same time it puts before my eyes all that I am not. It is true that if I had lived since I consecrated myself to the service of Jesus Christ as your charity and opinion of me leads you to believe, my death would be entirely enviable, and it could very properly be said of me *Nolite flere super mortuum* [Lk 23:28], but far from keeping the faith and completing the work entrusted to me by Our Lord, as you think, I have made such poor use of all the grace which he has showered on me and responded so badly to his designs for me that I find myself overwhelmed by the weight of his mercies as well as that of my sins, and I can only consider myself, unless he gives me time to repair my past infidelities, as a man leaving this world with empty hands. That does not prevent me, Mgr, keeping my trust alive and seeing, it seems to me, in God's goodness what I do not find in any part of my conduct. For as he penetrates the depths of our consciences, he knows that my will has been superior to my actions and that fundamentally I would have wished to serve him in a manner more in keeping with his orders and the sanctity of my condition. I expect him to judge me according to these hidden and inner dispositions and take some account of the preparation of my heart, since it is he who gave it according to his word *praeparationem cordis eorum audivit auris tua.* [Ps 10:17]

The rumour circulating about my death has been baseless, for although I have been indisposed for nearly five months with inflammation in the chest accompanied by some fever, I was not sufficiently ill for anyone to believe I was in the state in which

I was said to be. Wretched as my life is, it causes distress to enough people for news of my death to be easily accepted and published abroad. That, Mgr, does not make me change my opinions or feelings. I hold that it is indeed fortunate to be pleasing to so few, that the majority is always worth the least, and that the word Christ uttered for the consolation of his servants, *Nolite timere pusillus grex* [Lk 12:32], applies to even fewer persons than is generally thought.

I share as much as I should your joy in putting the last touches to the Lord's house. I do not doubt that this action took place with all the spirit and piety you could hope for, and that God will bless all its consequences. I pray him, Mgr, to send to you workers worthy of your zeal and the purity of your principles. Times are inauspicious and men have never worked with such diligence, and perhaps even such success, as now to destroy the holy rules by which each Christian is obliged to conduct himself. If God does not take pity on the world, evil will win almost everywhere, and there will scarcely be anywhere or anyone left unaffected. Men do not want to shake off the yoke of the faith, nor do they want to be devoured by continual pangs of conscience. No one can bring himself to change his way of life, so complaisant directors must be found to flatter conscience instead of curing it; they apply themselves solely to seeking for expedients and means to soothe the unquiet conscience and stifle its remorse. As for you, Mgr, the life you propose in your retreat is scrupulous and holy. It is modelled on that led by Christians in the early times of the Church. They were incessantly occupied with God, and the desire to please him. Their only concern in this world was to advance his glory and service. His will alone was their rule in all things, and as they wanted nothing but that and his will is always fulfilled, they were always content and enjoyed profound peace. Souls, just like bodies, turn and turn again looking for a comfortable position that suits them, but whatever they do there is only one in which they can find rest, and that is the one God has destined for them. In a word, we must be exactly what God wants us to be, and unless we are entirely in his hand, dependent on him and in a manner pleasing to him, life is a mere succession of troubles, annoyance, and anxiety. And the best that men without these feelings and views can do is to deceive themselves for a time, satisfy themselves with their illusions, live wretchedly and hide their wretchedness from themselves. The prudence of the worldly can go no further, and what is most deplorable about it is that the clever ones are those who are most skilful at deceiving themselves. God, who has not only drawn you from their midst, but put you on the road on which you must serve him, will bring you to find there that holy joy which is the gift of his Holy Spirit, which he puts into the hearts of all those who live in the love of justice and of peace. You will discover that being subjected to the yoke of Jesus Christ is a freedom of infinite sweetness, and nothing is more true than what the prophet meant to tell us in these words *Melior est dies una in atriis tuis super milia* [Ps 83:11]. And if God allows clouds to rise over your retreat, and its serenity to be sometimes darkened, it will only be so that you realise more fully that here on earth there is no perfect and constant serenity, and to make you desire more ardently that unchanging tranquility that suffers neither variation nor vicissitude. I am not surprised that Our Lord sometimes sends you people who talk to you of him and edify you since he so often sent his holy angels into the most remote solitudes for the consolation of those who belonged to him, he took care of their persons and their life, and was pleased to extend his paternal providence to the least of their needs. As you know, Mgr, nothing escapes him and his eyes are constantly upon those who fear him. We shall continue to offer you to him in our prayers until our dying breath, and there is nothing I personally can do with more fidelity, since nothing in my heart comes before the gratitude and respect I have for you.

PS I must tell you, Mgr, that someone has tried to get me into trouble. Some five or six years ago a certain person sent me a paper against some practices preserved in this monastery, which have been established and observed by all the holy monks of the church, and throughout all ages. I was obliged to reply, and at some length, in a letter I wrote him. I gave a copy of it to [Beaufort ?], who, as you know, gives me no cause for pride. At that time he was my friend and gave me his word that he would show it to nobody. A few days ago he had the idea of giving it to [Sister Thérèse of the Carmelites of the rue du Boulais] who put it into the hands of some theologians she knows, in order to find in it at any price something that could be censured. The letter contains nothing that is not perfectly catholic as regards the faith, as well as what concerns morals. However, as passion reveals what charity and justice do not see, these gentlemen began by thinking that there were some passages that could be condemned. I was even told that they had begun to spread rumours about, and then I heard that it was not thought that this would have any consequences and the thing would collapse of its own accord. You see, Mgr, that to avoid criticism it is enough to do nothing worthy of criticism. So the prophet asked God that, having kept all the laws of equity and justice, he would not abandon him to the evil designs of his calumniators, *judicium et justitiam non trades me calumniantibus me.* [Ps 118:121]

The gentleman you recommended passed by here some seven or eight days ago. His manners are so innocent and his intentions so pure that we could not fail to be much edified. However, he is undecided as to the sort of life he will choose to give himself to God and serve him. As he has not studied, and is even opposed to doing so, he will find it hard to become a religious, because at present there is no observance in the Church which does not demand some ability. If God had given him a vocation for la Trappe that would have shortened his road considerably. He seems to me very anxious to go to war. A lot of virtue is necessary to keep any in such a career.'

The PS refers to Le Roy, and the paper and reply are documents in the quarrel over humiliations. The indiscreet friend is known to be Beaufort, but the name has been heavily erased. The Carmelite (partly erased but legible) was a former court lady and correspondent of R's friend Mme d'Huxelles. The convent in question was very different from that in which RM Agnès was. R's sensitivity to any charges of Jansenism was by no means unreasonable, since the fate of la T. depended on his reputation for avoiding partisan entanglements.

The reference to the Lord's house is to a retreat house constructed by Bellefonds for clergy and laymen of the area round l'Ile-Marie. He also set up a small hospital (opened in 1687 by the Bp of Coutances). At first he had help from three Eudist priests from Coutances, but they eventually found the place so damp and unhealthy that they left. The chapel designed by Mansart received ornaments from the Dauphin among others, and like the hospital, originally intended for twenty wounded soldiers but subsequently enlarged, was still to be seen until destroyed in the bombardments following D-day in 1944. Only the very elegant façade and some of the walls remain. Throughout this correspondence concerning Bellefonds' retreat, R. is clearly thinking of the very active role his friend was playing in local religion, but there are few explicit references like this one.

761115   M. L'ABBÉ DU VAL, CAEN   15 November 1676
TB 740

R's successor as commendatory abbot [Nicolas Druel] has decided to enter the novitiate and become a Canon Regular. R. sends *Constitutions* of Saint-Victor as a guide and exhorts him to follow observance.

*761121   COMTE DE BRANCAS   21 November 1676
SS orig.

'I see, Monsieur, from what you do me the honour of writing that the rumour which had been stirred up against me is dying down of its own accord and will not go as far as one might have supposed. As affairs in the world are usually motivated much more by the passions than by reason, this one, although lacking all foundation, could easily have had regrettable effects and consequences. However, Monsieur, one must admit that the injustices done to us by men are always just from God's angle, and he often allows to be imputed to us imaginary faults of which we are innocent to punish us for real faults of which we are guilty. Thus the first thing one must do in the face of ill treatment is to humiliate and condemn oneself, and to regard those who are the instruments and causes of that treatment as ministers of God's vengeance. Calumnies are in fact the surest signs we can have of God's concern for our sanctification and the true means he uses to accomplish upon his elect his designs and eternal will. It is not enough to suffer in patience, we must receive them with joy, and we must never be drawn into justifying our reputation when attacked, unless we are convinced that God's glory and order requires it. It is shameful for a Christian, who should seek only the approval of Christ and his saints, to worry whether he has or has not that of men.

As for the Abbot of S[eptfons], I will serve him all my life as though I had every reason in the world to be satisfied with him. But God, who commands us to love our enemies, does not bid us trust in them, and charity is no longer a virtue when prudence and wisdom do not guide it. As the things said about me are all positive and based on particular details of what took place between him and me, it is hardly possible that explanations will be any use; an absolute denial is needed, but the trouble is that the persons from whom I have learned these things are ready to maintain them. It must be admitted that fidelity among men is rarer than people think, and one cannot be too circumspect in the discernment and choice of friends.

I am not worthy of the kindness and confidence with which your daughter honours me, but it is true that I wish more than I can say that God should follow such great beginnings with real progress, and that desires which appear to me so pure and so Christian should have all the effect and consequence to be hoped of them. The ways by which God is leading her are the true ones, she must be convinced of that, must prefer them to all others and try to make holy use of them. We do not fail to offer our prayers for this to God, and if we were more righteous than we are, she would realise it more.

I am most distressed at what you tell me of Father de Monchy's condition, but after all he is fortunate in being on the point of completing a holy career with an end full of blessing. He has kept the faith, fulfilled his work, and it only remains for him to receive his reward. For all that we shall still ask God to keep him on in this world for the edification of his church and consolation of his friends.

I am most obliged to Father Amelot for expressing himself in our favour as he did. It is easy, Monsieur, to find in the approval of a man of his learning and piety some consolation for the injustice attempted against us.

There is nothing that could be added to all my gratitude for the proof you give me of the honour of your friendship. Do me the honour of believing that no one will ever be more sincerely and respectfully yours etc.

PS I forgot to say, Monsieur, that I never showed or gave the paper in question to anyone except in strict confidence, that I do not know how the Abbot of Septfons could imagine the contrary and that I should be extremely vexed if it were ever to become public.'

Brancas' daughter was the princess d'Harcourt.

761129   SR ANNE-MARIE [D'EPERNON]   29 November 1676
TB 745

Deplores continued gossip about himself, but short of breaking off all external contacts, there is no way to avoid it.

7611206   MADAME DE SAINT-LOUP   6 December 1676
TB 752

She has brought up again an affair twenty years old [signature of formulary against Jansenism]. He will remain faithful to his friends, but even friendship has limits. He stands by his original decision [to sign unconditionally]. 'In your place I should prefer prayer to conversations.'

761220 RP PASQUIER QUESNEL, CONG. ORAT.   20 December 1676
U 1168 orig.; Tans 32
Has written to Le Camus, whom he greatly admires.

*77/1 RM AGNÈS DE BELLEFONDS   [1677]
TD C.
'Very Reverend Mother,
   I am sending you a letter from the Bishop of Séez for M. le Maréchal de Bellefonds, and as I know that in it he speaks of me in connexion with a rumour that is abroad, I must tell you what it is, but on condition that you let no one know that I wrote anything about it to you.
   The Bishop of Evreux saw fit to publish everywhere that the Abbot of Val-Richer had told him that M. le Maréchal de Bellefonds had broken off his friendship and contact with me because he had recognised that our opinions and conduct were dangerous, and that he, the Abbot of Val-Richer, had entirely disabused him of any good opinion he might have of me. Although I regarded that as a delusion and the effect of the ill-will of that good abbot and many others like him, this story still gained currency and found people who heard it with pleasure. The poor Bishop of Séez, who is extremely sensitive in anything that concerns me, and to whom the Bishop of Evreux spoke of it, was so upset on his return from Paris that he had the greatest difficulty in getting over it, and felt obliged to advise M. le Maréchal de Bellefonds of it. I considered that I should give you this small explanation so that if you were by chance to hear of the matter, you should know its basis and origin. You cannot imagine, Reverend Mother, how furiously the devout in Normandy rage against me and how annoyed they are that everyone does not speak ill of me, my person, and my house. You can judge that it would never occur to me that M. le Maréchal de Bellefonds could be taken in by so ill-founded an idea as that, and I have too much confidence in the solidity of his discernment and the goodness with which he honours me to have worried about the slightest cloud in this matter.
   I hope that his return will not cause prejudice to his piety, and that he will remain as much attached to God in the world as possible.'

The Bp of Evreux was Henri de Maupas du Tour; Dominique Georges was still Abbot of Val-Richer. After Bellefonds had paid a visit to Val-Richer in November 1675, R. had strongly criticised his former friend, the abbot. This letter refers to the same events. See also 771223 to Bellefonds.

*770104 CURÉ OF SAINT-JACQUES-DU-HAUT-PAS   4 January 1677
      [LOUIS MARCEL]
TD/D; BN 25080

   'I have remembered, my dear Monsieur, that I have not replied to the main question in your last letter. I am most grieved by the rumours that are abroad, and what is more annoying is that I am afraid that, if I have to explain myself, I shall not be able to do so in such a way as to satisfy the persons you know, whatever esteem and consideration I have for them. I do not know what is being attributed to me, nor what words are being put into my mouth, but here is exactly what I have been able to say when obliged to give some explanations on the matters in question. If it is not verbally the same, at least it is the same sense. I have never defended Jansenius, I condemned the censured Propositions, I submitted to the papal Constitutions, simply and without restrictions and just as the bishops desired of me, according to the prompting of my conscience, which told me only that such was the best and most sure way to behave. Those who acted in contrary fashion had their reasons, but I never approved those reasons and still do not. However, I have always been careful not to condemn them, not only because it would be out of character for me, and God forbids me to judge anyone, especially those who, being in the bosom and communion of the Church, and among her children, should be regarded as our brothers, but also because I have not been willing to charge myself at Christ's judgment with having decided on an affair of this kind and importance.

When the Peace of the Church was declared, I thought that all memory of past disputes should be effaced, and that no distinction could be made between persons whom the Pope had accepted without lacking in the respect due to him and insulting his conduct. I should very much like, my dear Monsieur, to say more, but that is the limit of my conscience; in an affair of this nature it must be neither indiscretions or human considerations, but one's innermost conscience, that is consulted. I have avoided as far as possible declaring myself on such questions, but every time I find myself obliged to speak about them, I can say only what I feel and what I think; and in truth, after all my reflections, I have been unable to adopt any feelings or thoughts but these. I confess, Monsieur, that as the end of my life approaches and my health grows weaker, my submission increases, and I am sure that if I should happen to be mistaken in following the opinion of those given to me by God as pastors and guides, my error will not be imputed to me, and I shall say with confidence *Non sum turbatus te pastorem sequens, et diem hominis non desideravi* [Jr 17:16], since it is he alone at whom I look in those who represent him and take his place for me. As in all this he knows the disinterestedness of my conduct and the purity of my motives, he will judge me in his compassion, and men will have no legitimate cause to complain about me, when I have put nothing above their friendship than that of Christ. The ultimate perplexity is to find oneself between one's friends and one's conscience. Pray for me, my dear Monsieur, I beg you, and please believe that no one could be more sincerely yours' etc.

    Compare R's letters of 1676 to Brancas. The opening references to Jansenius go back to the situation first mentioned in 59/1. In 1653 the Five Propositions, *allegedly drawn from Jansenius' book* Augustinus, *were condemned by Rome. Successive papal decrees, backed by the French bishops, demanded submission to the condemnation and, later, to the allegation that the* Propositions *were genuinely to be found in the book, which the Jansenists always*

770207a   The Letters of Armand-Jean de Rancé   149

denied. *In 1669 a truce was declared, known as the Peace of the Church, and active persecution of Jansenists ceased until controversy broke out again in 1679, when renewed persecution drove Arnauld and others into exile. During the Peace, R. received many visits from Jansenists, but remained scrupulously neutral at all times.*

770114   MONSIEUR   14 January 1677
TB 778
New year greetings.

770114a   COMTESSE DE B[ELIN]   14 January 1677
TB 780; TC II/134
She should be converted without delay. 'Whatever people may say, you can be sure that almost no last-minute conversions are genuine.'

770120   MADAME DE SAINT-LOUP   20 January 1677
TB 785
He has burned her letter, and she must burn his on the subject about which he has thought more in three months than in fourteen years. Only the Church's authority can make him change his mind, not that of M. N. 'I consider him a great saint, but God does not give complete enlightenment to all his saints.' R. wants to remain submissive to the Pope and not be obliged like some to make submission on his deathbed.

Apart from the fact that N. is clearly a Jansenist, there is no clue to his identity.

770122   DUC DE CHEVREUSE   22 January 1677
TB 788
Respects.

770207   RP PASQUIER QUESNEL, CONG. ORAT.   7 February 1677
U 1168 orig.; Tans 33
RP de Chevigny recommends someone, but it is not clear whether as lay-brother or choir-monk. 'Lay-brothers must have more physical strength than choir-monks.' An Oratorian sent from Aix three months earlier is doing well as a lay-brother.

Nicolas Chevigny (1622–98) had been a soldier before joining the Oratory in 1664. He conducted missions in rural areas.

770207a   RP PASQUIER QUESNEL, CONG. ORAT.   7 February 1677
U 1168 orig.; Tans 34   [probably wrong date]
After some hesitation will give habit to young man sent by Quesnel and put him in

the novitiate. Would be delighted to see Quesnel at la T. 'but for ever, that is another matter, and I would feel many scruples about taking you from a Congregation which needs men and workers, and depriving the public of the aid you render'.

The young man must be Théodore Faverolles.

*770208   RM MARIE-LOUISE [BOUTHILLIER]   8 February 1677
TD/A

'I did not write to Madame V[alant] as you asked, and what stopped me was that I do not write to anyone unless it is absolutely necessary. What we could do was to be sorry for her and pray God for her. As she is in the world, and shares its opinions and principles, what you told me came as no surprise, but I confess that I was most surprised to see you feeling and thinking in a quite unexpected way. What more could God do to reassure you against the fear of death than call you to a state which should above all fill you with aversion and contempt for life and engage you under a most holy rule in a monastery where it is observed most strictly, in exemplary and edifying fashion? The first step to be taken by those who are consecrated to Christ by religious vows, according to what the saints tell us, is that of freeing themselves from all apprehension about death. Indeed a person who renounces everything, strips himself of everything and puts his own self first in the number of things from which he parts, in order to give himself with a whole heart to Christ and take him for his only lot, as you have done, should regard and desire the end of his life as the beginning of happiness. For he must cease to live in order to be wholly bound to Christ in a way which prevents any separation. If I were not convinced that you have been completely faithful in the observation of your rule and that you have lived as punctiliously as God requires, I should look on your terror at the thought of death as an effect of infidelity. But as I do not doubt that you have responded by your every action to the sanctity of your state, and your conduct has been worthy of your promises made to God, I am willing to believe that it is a temptation, and that the devil, who has not up to the present been able to take away your fidelity, is trying to make you lose confidence. He is an enemy who wages cruel war on us, and when he has been unable to prevent us serving God with the piety and religion demanded of souls united to God by the bonds of the most holy profession, there is no effort he does not make, no trick he does not use, to prevent us from reaping the fruits and rewards. Even if he cannot bring us to think well of ourselves and have a high opinion of our works so that we fall into pride, he decries them, persuades us that there is no good in them and that they deserve only punishment, so as to make us fall into despair. However, my dear sister, no matter how good my opinion of you, I will still give you a piece of advice, and take it myself as well. If I were in your place, I should examine myself carefully, penetrate as far as possible into my innermost heart, I should study myself before God and make a particular effort at knowing the depths of my conscience, I should apply my rule in its fullest extent to the state and all the consequences of my life, and because we are usually bad judges of ourselves, I should consult the person whom God had given me for a superior, and if, according to her enlightenment as well as your knowledge, your conduct seems to be correct, you find nothing in it to give you just cause for reproaching yourself, you seem to have been faithful to Christ and to have kept the faith, then you must banish all fears, remain at peace and hope from his mercy that he will complete in you what he has begun. But if after that discussion you judge that your life has been less regular than it should have been, your conversation less holy, your works less full; if you notice that you have not observed the rule on every point; if you have neglected some of them and, using that unfortunate distinction which overturns all the piety and discipline of the cloister, you have omitted those passages of the rule or your constitutions which you judged of minor importance, contenting yourself with the main ones, without calling to mind that things done deliberately and voluntarily, or even from imprudence, when caused by habitual neglect of the least articles in rules, should be regarded as criminal transgressions; finally, if you have dispensed yourself in any way from what is laid down by your rule to advance you in God's service, and you have been lacking in care and vigilance to execute it in every detail, then you can be sure, my dear sister, that your fear of death has no other cause than the conviction and secret remorse of your conscience. You must take it as a warning given you by God to change your ways, to make your conduct more regular and thus obtain from him that holy confidence which he never refuses to souls which are faithful and serve him religiously, which extend their zeal to the smallest as to the greatest things, and fear nothing in the world so much as displeasing him. The saints say that we fear to die because our souls are not pure enough to appear before the eyes of the one who is to judge them, and that it is normally our unworthiness which is the real cause of our terrors. I tell you all that, my dear sister, because, by an error which is all too common in cloisters, people imagine that they are doing enough to satisfy the duties of their profession when they observe some strictness in what seems most essential in the vows, while they transgress the rules they imagine to be less important and do not scruple to dispense themselves from practices which they do not think necessary. Blindness is so great that they do not notice that transgressions, however slight they may be, if neglected, attract greater ones, that people who are ready to commit minor wrongs fall into great ones, that everything done against rules with knowledge and deliberate will is a grave fault, because it implies contempt. One cannot omit a regulation made by legitimate and holy authority on the pretext that it is either not necessary or useful, without putting one's own judgement above that of that authority and following one's own opinion at the expense of the preference one should have for the enlightenment of authority, or more precisely, without rejecting God's order and doing injury to his goodness and wisdom, because the laws established for the direction of religious congregations are not of human invention, but pure effects of his mercy, using the ministry of men and the intermediaries of his saints to declare his will to us as through his interpreters and prescribe for us the ways and means by which he has resolved to sanctify us.

Thus, my dear sister, it is past understanding how far we excite against us the anger of God's majesty when we make distinctions between precept and precept, law and law, when we reject his and submit to others by our discernment, according to our personal views and, in a word, to favour our selfish desires and natural inclinations, which move us to take back a liberty which no longer belongs to us, and which we have renounced by our profession so as to subject ourselves to Christ's yoke. What happens is that those who live in such evil attitudes, such irreligious principles, spend an unhappy life and finish it still more deplorably. Make no mistake about it, there is no peace in this world except for those who remain in God's order, who regard his will as their rule, who are not only strict in their observance of his commandments, but follow and embrace the least of his intentions. Apart from that, my dear sister, there is nothing but anxiety, confusion, and spiritual afflictions, and God will never give peace except to those who desire him above all and prefer him to all things. As I believe that these are your genuine views, and that you are very far from having others, I ascribe, as I have already said, this strange fear of death to an attempt by the devil to throw you into mistrust and trouble the peace and serenity of your heart. That is a temptation which you will destroy through your trust and by the strictness of your life, and provided that you keep yourself beside Christ and serve him with the love and fidelity required of the close, tender and holy union you have with him, he will calm the agitation of your heart and banish all its fears, and you will regard with joy, as a blessed transition, that final separation of which the mere thought, from what you tell me, shakes your constancy. I beg you to believe, my dearest sister, that no one could be more concerned than I by all that affects you, that I feel your pains and ills as I do my own, and that my affection for you could not be greater. I pray Our Lord to fill you with grace and the spirit of your profession.'

770214   SR ANNE-MARIE [D'EPERNON]   14 February 1677
TB 797

R's health is poor. Reform is crumbling.

770218   RP PASQUIER QUESNEL, CONG. ORAT.   18 February 1677
U 1168 orig.; Tans 35

Ready to receive lad sent by Chevigny. 'Principal quality demanded of our religious is absolute docility.'

770223   JEAN FAVIER   23 February 1677
CF 344,f.75 orig.; Gonod 39

Winter so harsh that R. wonders if spring will ever come. Sorry that Grandmontines have been disappointed by the novice [? Edmond] who failed at la T.

770308 MARQUISE DE TOUROUVRE   8 March 1677
TB 603; TC I/28

She must not teach her children to sing, play cards, gamble or allow them to go to the theatre, only permissible if one is obliged to go and has totally killed one's passions.

770321 RP PASQUIER QUESNEL, CONG. ORAT.   21 March 1677
U 1168 orig.; Tans 36

R. thanks Quesnel for sending book, which he warmly praises.

This is L'Idée du sacerdoce et du sacrifice de Jésus-Christ donnée par le RP de Condren, *dedicated to Le Camus. The book, based on lecture notes of Condren, was the joint work of Saint-Pé, Desmares, and Quesnel, and has been reedited several times, up to 1901. Charles de Condren (1588-1641) in 1629 succeeded Bérulle as General of the Oratory. He published nothing himself, but his disciples published his letters and this book.*

* 770324 RP BRUSCOLY, CONG. ORAT.   24 March 1677
U 483 orig.

'I was very glad that the mother approved her son's plan, for the consent of so christian a mother as Mme Faverolles always brings a blessing. Her son is absolutely decided, and I may say that the things which cause others difficulty cause him none. I hope that God, who inspired him, will not leave his work unfinished and will give him the grace to consummate his sacrifice. His mother has nothing to worry about, all he needs is prayer. Once he has made his profession she can do what she likes, and whatever God puts into her heart.

'I wish, my very dear Father, that the hearts of those who are acquiring the Jubilee in Paris, as you tell me, were as changed as their faces. The outside does not cost much, and it is not very hard to put on an appearance for God for four days. Paris is a second Nineveh; would to God that sackcloth and ashes were as common there as they were in that great city. But it is the misfortune of our times that penitence is much decried, and nothing is more difficult to persuade men of than the necessity for penitence. You know better than I, being involved in the conduct of souls, how rare are true conversions. Pray God for mine, I beg you, Reverend Father, and do me the justice of believing that I am with all my heart yours etc.

'Be good enough, please, to pass on to Mme Faverolles the letter I am writing her.'

Nicolas Faverolles, aged 22, had just come to la T. and was professed a year later with the name Théodore. 1675 was a Jubilee, or Holy, Year, in Rome, and the privileges were extended to other places for a period thereafter.

770328 PRINCE DE SOUBISE   28 March 1677
TB 819; TC II/23

Answers letter sent from camp at Valenciennes. Prays for prince's conversion, but he must try too. He may lose his life for the King, but will be giving it to God.

770400 RM [EMILIE] DE BOUILLON   April 1677
TD C

She was right to make a general confession. She has a good director; respects to prioress and community.

*770404 RM ABBESSE, LEYME [ANNE DE LA VIEUVILLE]   4 April 1677
TB 828

'You care too much about my health, RM, and your opinion of me is so far from that which you ought to have that I cannot think of it without confusion. I assure you that I am very far from being, as you believe, imbued with such an austere, rigid spirit of penitence, and I have much more need of stimulation than restraint. I regard all your views on the subject as resulting from your charity. I agree with you that without diverging from the rule, or the conduct of our Fathers, I may use the means of relief that you indicate, and although I find it hard to bring myself to do so out of personal inclination, I should have no objection to yielding to the opinions of people who feel kindly towards me and take more interest than I deserve in what concerns me. You are one of those, RM, and I do not know how to show my gratitude sufficiently.

What I wanted to write to you about the Abbot of [Septfons] is that I shall in truth show him in the future all the charity I ever did, but when it comes to trust, I shall have none. I have told him so positively, so that he shall not be mistaken and take the signs of simple friendship for the effects of true trust. I tell you that for yourself alone, for I have resolved, and even written to tell him, that I shall never say anything to make it known that there has been any chill between us, seeing that nothing in the world is so unedifying as to see such misunderstandings between people who profess piety. Having examined all things before God, I thought that charity and christian prudence demanded only that of me, and that without failing in one or other I could do no more and no less.

You are the first, RM, to tell me what I did not know about his conduct, but you have not been the only one. I find it hard to believe that he will ask my opinion or advice, things no longer being fundamentally what they were and the ways in which he walks being so far removed from mine. Nothing could be less true than what he maintains concerning the proclamation of faults; the Rule lays them down for all kinds of exterior faults; it requires the accusation to be made either before the superior or the whole assembly. It does not impose the same obligations for secret and interior faults, and is content to prescribe that one should accuse oneself of them in secret to the superior, or those put in his place. Apart from that we must observe the Rule of St Benedict, not in accordance with our individual ideas, but as our Fathers understood it and taught us. Nothing is more firmly established in the *Usages* of Cîteaux, which are the original constitutions of the Order, than the proclamations to be made every day in chapter for all kinds of exterior faults committed against the Rule and regulations of the monastery, and anyone disagreeing must lack all knowledge of the ancient practices of the order.

Regarding the doubt you put to me, RM, I would say that there is no reason for you to receive novices unless you have persons capable of guiding them or are able to devote yourself to doing so. For certainly, however good their attitudes, they would soon lose them in contact with those of bad attitude, so that you would increase your ills instead of diminishing them.

You cannot in conscience give the religious habit to someone whom you do not consider worthy, and in whom you do not see signs of vocation, whatever recommendations she may have.

Nor can you in conscience appoint to a benefice anyone lacking the qualities necessary to acquit himself of his obligations. It is better to lose your right of filling it than to keep it by ways which are not God's. That is a rule which must be observed on such occasions, and from which one must never depart. Perhaps that will cause you trouble, but no matter; it was written long ago that those who want to live in strict piety will be exposed to many objections. It is scarcely possible to suit God and men at the same time.

I have nothing more to tell you, RM, I beg you only to pray God for me, and ask him to subject my heart entirely to his will, whether it pleases him to withdraw me from this miserable world which I love only too much, unworthy though I believe it to be of all love and esteem, or wishes to leave me in it still to punish my sins, for as far as the benefit of others is concerned, I consider myself wholly unable to contribute anything, and I am fully aware that I can only ever occupy in the Lord's house the place of a useless servant. I am with too much respect and sincerity to be able to express it yours' etc.

Beaufort's reported views on proclamations clearly fall within the disputed context of fictions and humiliations, where, as always, R. appeals to ancient precedent.
A number of benefices in the area round Leyme were in the Abbess' appointment.

*770414   G. LE ROY, HAUTEFONTAINE   14 April 1677
U 767 orig.

'It is not your Dissertation, Monsieur, but the answer, which, I learn, has been printed, that causes me *extreme distress*. The fault I committed was to communicate it to someone who made a copy, and did not preserve the secrecy and fidelity he owed me. Your Dissertation can hardly fail to have a similar fate any day, since it is at present in the hands of so many people. I can offer no remedy, except to be patient and suffer in peace the mortification that has come upon me. The Abbot of Châtillon has doubtless told you, Monsieur, how this came about, and the just cause I have for complaint against the person who divulged the paper. It would do no good to recount the story to you. I will only protest that my *grief* at this vexatious event could not be more intense, and that had it been in my power to suppress the paper and all the copies, no word of it would ever have been heard. I humbly beg you to believe this, and that I am yours' etc.

For Le Roy's Dissertation, see 720718. Claude Le Maître, Abbot of Châtillon, was Le Roy's neighbour and trusted friend of both R. and Le Roy. R's reply was published, against his wishes, in 1677 as 'Lettre d'un abbé sur le sujet des humiliation... 'The leak came apparently through R's old friend A. Félibien. The underlinings are in the original.

*770420   MARÉCHAL DE BELLEFONDS   20 April 1677
BN na 12959 f.55,orig.; TC I/25

'God who knew that my opinions were not very necessary did not permit the letter you did me the honour of writing to reach me before the eve of the Resurrection of Our Lord, and I do not doubt that he gave you all the grace and enlightenment you needed to prepare you for this great festival, which must be considered above all others as the source of our sanctification. The passion and death of Jesus Christ, powerful as it was in itself, would not have had effects and consequences for the redemption of the world if he had not won for us by his resurrection from the dead the hope and right to enjoy a new life, of which since the Fall we had to endure such hard and unhappy deprivation.

If the situation and state in which you are in the world does not allow you to live so exact and austere a life as those who are there no longer, I see Mgr, that it does not remove your desire to do so, and your will goes far beyond your external works. That is an advantage which one has in dealing with God. As he penetrates our innermost heart, and sees its movements and inclinations, or rather effects them himself by his grace when they are holy, he also does not fail to regard and accept them as real and effective, and it often happens that one enjoys abundance of riches in his eyes although one appears extremely indigent in the eyes of men.

If you have difficulty finding people capable of giving you useful advice in the world in which you are, you must believe that Jesus Christ, who is the shepherd of shepherds, will himself tell you what he tells others through the ministry or intermediary of men. It is he, strictly speaking, who has charge of you, and from whom God his father will demand an account. Provided that you listen to his voice in silence and removed from all that you know might prevent him speaking to you, and genuinely desire to follow him, then he will be faithful to explain himself and let you know what he desires of you.

You are fortunate, Mgr, to enjoy solitude, or rather to find God there and enjoy his presence. Many are those who are led there by his spirit but to whom, nevertheless, he does not give the same grace. For although they have gone out from among men, although the single desire to serve him and strive for their salvation has been the true motive for their retreat and they are unable even to turn their heads towards the world they have left, yet God with perfect justice allows that they should not be exempt from agitation and anxiety and should not encounter that profound peace they sought. It pleases him to exercise their patience and their faith and he only grants to their fidelity and perseverance what he refused at the beginning of their conversion. It is something so great to find appreciable consolations from seeing and considering God's goodness, that it is no matter for surprise if it rarely happens, and occurs in few people.

You say, Mgr, that the days seem short to you despite the solitude in which you have spent the winter. That is a sign that they are well filled and have no empty spaces. As your occupations are regular and you have established a certain order to which I am sure you submit yourself as much as possible, time can only pass quickly, and you are bound to come to the end of each day pleasantly and imperceptibly. That is a blessing that God attaches to the conduct of those who serve him with love and pleasure, *videbantur dies pauci pro amoris magnitudine.* [Gn 29:20]

As for people in the world, as they live in disorder and confusion and only act from alien motives, as their whole life, is strictly speaking, a mere circle, the different passions which drive them perpetually revolving and returning, *in circuitu impii ambulant* [Ps 11:9], if sometimes they go as far as to stop for a moment and look where they are going, all they discover at every turn is the effects and works of their own covetousness. All their life is full of boredom, tedium, and bitterness, and inevitably days seem like years to them.

It is true, Mgr, that most of the people who give themselves to God and think of their conversion put all their piety in certain spiritual exercises, regard austerity and penitence as worth nothing, as if it were neither necessary or useful, and fall without realising it from a life of pleasure into one of ease and comfort. For my part, as I see that Christ recommended nothing to us more than penitence, that there is nothing which the saints his disciples, who had the fullness of his spirit, have taught more by their examples and their words, I consider that incapacity alone can dispense us from it, for apart from the fact that the body, having played its part in our depravity and disorder, should justly also bear part of the penalty, it seems to me that not enough is made of subjugating the senses, of bodily purity, of deadening desire, and so many other advantages which are the effects and fruits of penitence when people neglect it, being as it is the true means of acquiring these things. And then can one honour as one is obliged to the sufferings of Jesus Christ when one does what one can to exempt oneself from suffering? However, Mgr, all that is done in the spirit of God must be done with rule and measure, and I do not claim that in the state you are in you should overburden yourself, nor that your desire to destroy your self should make you undertake things beyond your strength.

The care that God takes to cause occasions to arise, from what you say, to humiliate you is a sign that you are present in his mind and that his providence is watching over you. But the tranquility which you preserve amid temptations is the result of a far from ordinary mercy. God did much for you when he gave you the resolution and firmness necessary for breaking with the world, but he did incomparably more when he gave you the courage to break with yourself. That is what you are doing every time you accept peaceably and unconcernedly the humiliations which come your way. Not only will you suffer them in patience, but you will love them, if you are really convinced that breathing, as the saints say, is no more necessary for maintaining natural life than humiliations for preserving the life of grace. I pray God, Mgr, to increase it in you and strengthen it more and more. I am sure that everything that comes back to you from the world gives you regret at quitting it, and that you are daily confirmed in the great truth that says that it is to use time against God's order, and against that for which he destined it, to spend it otherwise than in loving and obeying him. *Deum time et mandata ejus observa, hoc est enim omnis homo.* [Qo 12:13] You belong too much to God, Mgr, for me not to ask the assistance of your prayers; grant them to me I beg you. I expect that grace from your goodness, as well as that of believing that I respect and honour no one in the world more than you.

PS I care too much about your satisfaction not to ask you whether you have found any ecclesiastics such as you wanted.'

Easter Eve was 17 April. Bellefonds was looking for clergy to help him run the retreat house he was setting up at l'Ile-Marie.

*770625   G. LE ROY, HAUTEFONTAINE   25 June 1677
U 767 orig.

'I will not answer in detail your explanation or the letter you did me the honour of writing, Monsieur, but I am most distressed that the letter which causes you such pain should have been printed. I can assure you that had it been in my power I would have suppressed all the copies, and that it would never have seen the light, at least in my lifetime. As regards your Dissertation, Monsieur, think about it as I may, I can only conclude that my explanation is entirely natural, and that I judged it most equitably. However, if other views and enlightenment should come to me, I would make them public with pleasure, not only for my own humiliation, on which you give me such charitable opinions, but also for your personal satisfaction. I beg you to believe, Monsieur, that I will never come to prefer my own satisfaction at any time more than truth, and nothing will prevent me from being in Our Lord yours' etc.

*770702   MARÉCHAL DE BELLEFONDS   2 July 1677
BN na 12959 f.59,orig.

'The gentleman through whom you did me the honour of writing came rather late this afternoon, wanted to leave early to-morrow morning and found me indisposed, so that I have time only to express my gratitude for your kindness in remembering me. I praise Our Lord for the blessings he showers on your person and on what you have undertaken for his service and the edification of the places to which his providence has led you, and I do not doubt that the faithfulness with which you recognize so much grace will make him bestow still more on you. No prayers are so effective and powerful before God than the holy use we make of his mercies.

I received only two or three days ago your last letter through the Carmelites. I will not answer it, Mgr, except to say that if it were true that one has insights and perceptions regarding the interests of the persons one regards and respects in proportion to the sympathy one feels for them, then no one could be more far-sighted and perceptive than I concerning your interests, since there is no one who is more closely attached to everything that affects you. I do not need to say much to persuade you of this, for I am sure that you do me the justice of believing that no one could be more fervently and faithfully than I yours etc.

PS The Bishop of Séez has just left here. We spoke a lot about you and he pressed me hard to assure you, when I next had occasion to write to you, that no one in the world feels more respect for you than he. This is something he has frequently asked of me, and I must confess that I have not complied as fully as I should.'

770703   MADAME DE SABLÉ   3 July 1677
TB 840

She talks of retreat; more important for her to abandon worldly values than to take religious vows.

770704   MADAME DE SAINT-LOUP   4 July 1677
TB 843

Has refused to admit the doctor [Hamon] to refectory. 'A major rule of our house is never to call in a doctor, whatever illness occurs in the religious, and be satisfied with a surgeon.' He himself seeks death, not health.

770720   [JEAN FAVIER]   20 July 1677
A 2106, f.82

Favier's difficulties in finding a worthy priest. Advises him to consult Bp of G[renoble].

770801   DUCHESSE DE [? LUYNES]   1 August 1677
TB 847

Humility is good, but should not be pushed as far as dejection and depression.

770815 BISHOP OF TOURNAI [GILBERT DE CHOISEUL]   15 August 1677
TB 855

R. refuses public reconciliation with Le Roy, whose dissertation on humiliations has violated all R. cherishes. Acknowledges precious help of M. de la Houssaye [died 1674] in writing his reply. 'My crime is that I supported the sanctity of the desert and the humiliation of the Cross.'

M. de la Houssaye was nephew of the Bp of Châlons, Vialart, and a maître des requêtes *in close touch with Antoine Arnauld.*

770819 MONSIEUR   19 August 1677
TB 865

R's health poor.

*770823 MADAME DE SAINT-LOUP   23 August 1677
TD/A

'I quite believe, Madame, that the Bishop of Tournai did not write to me in concert with the Abbot of Hautefontaine's friends, but he certainly is too quick to condemn me to a kind of reparation to which I am not obliged. He says first that I followed and indulged my passion. That may be, but how does he know, and how can the impulses and feelings of my heart, which are known to God alone, be so plain to him? He has not seen the *Dissertation*, he knows nothing of what has occured between the abbé Le Roy and me, yet he judges and blames me at once. There are friends with whom I am less closely linked, of the same dignity as he, who defend me highly and who, after receiving this fine explanation, have told him their views and advised him to stay quiet. It seems to me that I should expect as much from the Bishop of Tournai. None the less I am convinced of his fundamental friendship and goodness of heart, and these circumstances, unpleasant though they are, will never prevent me from doing him justice, or giving him the love and honour of which he is worthy, that is to say as much as I am able and with all the force and extent of my feelings. I have already written to tell you how the Bishop of Tournai and I remained well satisfied with each other.

As for Monsieur Di[rois?], I do not know what he may have said, but I do know that I told him nothing on this subject. He has been my friend for twenty-five years, and I could have spoken to him with some confidence, yet I said nothing to him, provided it is reported in my terms and my manner, which could cause anyone pain. Indeed I think the simplest thing is to see no one and speak to no one, for so long as I am talking, everyone will make me say what suits them best.

I have long realized that upright people are unwilling to tell crude lies, but they still help themselves and give things an appearance and bias which make them no longer what they were, when that serves their points of view and fits in with their designs.

For the rest, Madame, this is the last time that I shall write to you on these matters. It is embarrassing for me to hear such long discussion of an affair which I do not care about, and in God's name I beg you to tell me no more about it. I have necessary affairs, with which God has charged me, to weigh me down every day. I can hardly find time to do them and acquit myself of the smallest part. It would really be a mistake to concern myself with these affairs, convinced as I am that nothing could be more useless, because men are never satisfied. Take what I tell you on this quite literally, Madame, and no less my assurance that I honour you and will pray God for you to the last moment of my life.'

Gilbert de Choiseul was Bp of Tournai; G. Le Roy Abbot of Hautefontaine. The bp, like many of R's friends, had been trying to patch up the quarrel over fictions. François Dirois was a theologian who had gone to Rome in 1672 with Cardinal d'Estrées. He had close ties with Bossuet and Le Camus, but since 1664 had moved away from Port-Royal.

*770829   MARÉCHAL DE BELLEFONDS   29 August 1677
BN na 12959 f.61,orig.

'I cannot let slip the opportunity of Monsieur de [Tourouvre ?] or the bare moment he gives me without assuring you, Mgr, of my very humble service, and remembering myself to you. I do not need to tell you, Mgr, how present you are in our memory, nor how much care we take to present you to Our Lord. I beg you to believe that none of my obligations takes precedence over that, or is more scrupulously discharged. Mother Agnès' illness had alarmed us, and among several reasons which made us apprehensive as to the outcome, those which concern you were the chief ones, for I am sure that a loss of that kind would have affected you deeply and strongly. God has preserved her so far, and I learn from Paris that there are grounds for hope and that the expected attack did not return. I am sure that she is so useful in the world that whenever God withdraws her she will leave the deepest regrets in all those who are fortunate enough to know her. Yet the life of man is in God's hand, and when it pleases him to dispose of it he does not consult either our needs or our inclinations. Keep for me, Mgr, the place with which you honour me in your friendship, unworthy as I am, and do me the justice of believing that no one is more faithfully and respectfully than I your' etc.

The name, only partly legible under erasure, is probably that of R's neighbour the marquis de Tourouvre.

770903   RM [EMILIE] DE BOUILLON   3 September 1677
TD C

Hopes Prioress [RM Agnès de Bellefonds] will be spared.

*770912   RM AGNÈS DE BELLEFONDS   12 September 1677
TD C

'Very Reverend Mother,

As my anxiety and fear at your illness were extreme, I could not but feel real joy in learning that the fever had left you, and that Our Lord leaves you still in this life for the consolation of so many persons to whom you are necessary, as also for the continuation of what his grace has effected in you with such success and blessing for so long. Your soul, Reverend Mother, was, as it were, in your hands and you were quite ready to hand it over to his, but it pleased him to give it back to you, to prolong your exile and to delay further the moment of your deliverance, although I do not doubt that you make most holy use of his behaviour towards you and look upon all the dispositions of his providence with perfect equanimity and submission. We will not fail, Reverend Mother, to ask him always to increase such feelings in you, and bring about by his mercy that you may say with the holy apostle, death would be favourable to me, but Jesus Christ is all my life. I am in him with more respect than I can express.'

*770914   RM AGNÈS DE BELLEFONDS   14 September 1677
TD C

'Very Reverend Mother,

It is most charitable of you to have taken so much care over the request I made of you. The best way I can mark my gratitude is to forsake my opinion and follow those of yourself and Sister Anne-Marie, as you will see in the letter which I have the honour to write to her; there would be no point in repeating to you my own thoughts on this same subject.

I fully realise the loss you have suffered, and it will be very hard for whoever succeeds M. de Saint-Nicolas to possess enough qualities to make up for it. He had at one and the same time holiness of life, wisdom, charity, experience, and particular concern for the conduct of your house. We must pray God to fill the heart and mind of the person who will take his place. Indeed, things being what they are, it seems to me that you cannot make a better choice. Never will times be more trying and men more rare. Ever since I first knew M. Pirot I have esteemed him highly, and I hope you will be pleased with him. I never cease to be amazed at the prejudice, or rather the malice, of the world. The ease with which suspicion is cast on decent people is incomprehensible, and I learn from daily experience, as you do, Reverend Mother, that unless one gives oneself up completely to the passions of the Molinists, they observe no restraint and do not scruple to condemn innocent people incapable of becoming involved in any affair or any party, and publishing against them anything which they think might bring on them public hatred and aversion. For my part, my opinion has always been, and I guess that yours is the same, that it is much better to be the object of their passions, violent though they may be, than to be the partisan and slave of those passions.

I do not need to tell you, Reverend Mother, how keenly I feel everything that affects your community and your person. I do not doubt that in that respect you do me complete justice and believe me to be, with all the respect due to you, yours' etc.

M. de Saint-Nicolas was Hippolyte Féret, born at Pontoise, curé of Saint-Nicolas du Chardonnet and superior of the Carmelites from 1662–77. Edmé Pirot (1631–1713) was a close friend of Bossuet, a canon and chancellor of Notre-Dame, and had preached at Mme de la Vallière's clothing in 1674. R's relations with the Molinists (Jesuits and their allies) were never good, and became rapidly worse as he continued good personal, but never partisan, relations with Jansenists. The letter to Sr Anne-Marie cannot be identified.

770914a DOM JEAN-FRANÇOIS CORNUTY   14 September 1677
MS *Chronique de Tamié*; Burnier, *Hist. de Tamié*, 1

Abbot of Tamié has been to see R. Abbot of Foucarmont will release Cornuty.

Abbot Somont of Tamié had just been at la T. where, in an emotional scene, he begged R's forgiveness for past hostility and signed an undertaking to introduce the Reform at Tamié. This completely unexpected event brought into play Cornuty's special vow of ten years earlier to return to Tamié should that house ever be reformed.

770915   DUCHESSE DE LUYNES   15 September 1677
TB 874

'The supposed insensibility is merely the dryness and aridity of those who . . . come back to God.'

770918   RM [EMILIE] DE BOUILLON   18 September 1677
TD C

Prioress cured.

770920   COMTE DE BRANCAS   20 September 1677
TB 875

R's health poor, but unimportant. Praises RM Agnès de Bellefonds and Bp of Grenoble. Wishes to stand aloof from disputes within the Church.

770920a   DUCHESSE DE LONGUEVILLE   20 September 1677
TB 878

She is on right path. 'It is not enough to serve God unless in his way, by his lights, and in exact conformity with his designs.'

770925 RM [EMILIE] DE BOUILLON   25 September 1677
TD C

Sending a letter to her brother, the Cardinal. Prioress better.

771000 DOM JEAN-FRANÇOIS CORNUTY   October 1677
MS *Chronique de Tamié*; Burnier, *Hist. de Tamié*, 2

The monks are at last on their way to Tamié to start the Reform.

Alain, Antoine, and Albéric were sent, and joined by Cornuty.

*771001 CARDINAL DE RETZ   1 October 1677
TB 882

'Mgr, I can no longer help myself or delay further, I must send a man expressly to have news of your Eminence, and it is impossible for me to rely on what I can learn from public and uncertain rumours. I have had the honour of writing several times without receiving a word in reply. If I considered that in the light of my own unworthiness, I would take no notice of your silence, but when I think of the kindness and trust with which you have always honoured me, I can only feel deeply grieved. I therefore beseech your Eminence to put an end to the pain I have so long felt, and tell me something of your affairs, since there can be no one who is more concerned about them than I. If my health were better than it is, and I were still capable of travelling, it is I rather than this letter that your Eminence would have seen, despite the dangers and difficulties of the roads.

I recently wrote to your Eminence asking for letters of recommendation to be sent to Cardinal Cibo in favour of the Reform, and now I ask them for myself. His Holiness has granted me a brief allowing our religious to elect a prior after my death in the event that this abbey should once again fall *in commendam*. My brother, who is in Sicily, was in Rome at the time, and when he went to pay his respects to His Holiness, the Pope spoke of me in terms of a kindness which I did not deserve. That gave me cause, Mgr, to write to the Pope and thank him for the favour he had shown me, and also to ask for another, namely, to protect our monastery, to authorise what is practised there, and to forbid anyone to vex us in the exercise and observance of our rule. As we keep it just as our Fathers did and in accordance with the first constitutions of our Order, I am hoping that His Holiness will heed us, so long as he receives evidence to show him that what goes on here gives edification to the Church. I am sure, Mgr, that if your Eminence does me the honour of expressing himself in our favour on that point, as I humbly beseech him to do, his words will be credited and will be as authoritative and effective as we could wish. As that is the only way open to me, which nothing but the guidance of God, and not my own, has established in this house, it seemed to me that I was obliged to take it, and my conscience compelled me to omit nothing which might contribute to the preservation of God's work. It is the greatest possible obligation that I could have towards your Eminence, for although you have already shown me abundant favours, this, as you can see, is of such a nature as to surpass all the rest. I am however, Mgr, linked to your Eminence by so many bonds and obligations, that I can assure you that my devotion to your service could not be greater, and that nothing could add to the loyalty and profound respect which I have for your Eminence.'

The first brief referred to was issued in August 1677; the second, here requested, in May 1678. R's letter to the Pope is given below, 10 October 1677. R's brother was constantly on active naval service in the Mediterranean. The letter to Cibo was in connexion with the mission to Rome of the Abbot of Foucarmont, Jacques Fleur de Montagne, who had just gone there.

771010   POPE INNOCENT XI   10 October 1677
TD C; Carp, p.592 (Latin)

Reports origin and progress of his work of reform. Asks that work may be preserved by renewal of right to elect a prior should la T. return to commend.

A first brief was granted on 2 August, and a second on 23 May 1678, conferring right as requested.

771202   COMTESSE DE B[ELIN]   2 December 1677
TB 891

She must act before it is too late. 'When God tires of speaking to men he keeps eternal silence with them.'

771202a   MARQUISE D'HUXELLES   2 December 1677
BN na 12959,f.191,orig; TB 893

Never suggested that she should give up everything at once and retire to a desert, but whatever directors may say, the easy ways do not lead to salvation.

771222   BISHOP OF GRENOBLE [ETIENNE LE CAMUS]   22 December 1677
TB 901

Thanks him for kindness shown to the monks on the way to Tamié. Praises the Abbot of Tamié's dedication to regular life 'but it is a long way from the head to the heart, and from the mind to the will.' Comments on recent deaths of Premier Président [G. Lamoignon] and Chancellor [E. d'Aligre], a pious man.

*771223   MARÉCHAL DE BELLEFONDS   23 December 1677
BN na 12959 f.63,orig.

'I do not need to tell you with how much joy we learned your news, for I am sure that you do not doubt it and believe that I feel nothing more keenly than what comes to me from you. I did not know you had been indisposed, and I praise God that you are now better. He visits those who serve him, and men who look only superficially at his ways are alarmed and imagine that all is lost when in visiting us he shows that he is mindful of us and is treating us like persons whom he loves and who are dear to him. When those who live in some degree of penitence and regularity are affected by indisposition, they are infallibly advised to adopt changes without rule or measure. I am convinced, Mgr, that someone who is indisposed should live differently from someone who is not, but those who profess to belong to God must also behave in their infirmities in such a way as to demonstrate that they differ from those who profess to belong to the world. It is right, as it seems to me, that those whom God distinguishes by his grace and mercy take care to distinguish themselves by the austerity of their lives and the purity of their morals. Let men say what they like about it, penitence is a mark which God has imprinted on almost all his saints, and they have had it not only in the feelings of their hearts, but it has always been observed in their works and their conduct. It is the wisdom and love of Jesus Christ which should be your rule, Mgr; as you should not reject all the advice given you about your health, so you should not accept it all indiscriminately, and I am sure that much of it will be neither as effective nor as useful as people think. If you were a solitary without ties or dependants, one would not hesitate to tell you that life is only worth losing, that we must punish our senses for the excesses they have made us commit, and the best use we can make of our bodies is to destroy them for the salvation of our souls; but realising your situation, one has other thoughts, and although one certainly agrees that you should concede to penitence what is owed by a Christian who has led a worldly life, yet one cannot help saying that this should be done with moderation, and charity is against your burdening with anxiety and fear those to whom you find yourself bound by the orders of divine providence.

You have a great obligation to God, Mgr, in the fact that you find such comfort in reading Holy Scripture, for although it contains an infinity of charms and beauties, you would not appreciate it as you do unless enabled to do so by a quite special grace. That is what St Augustine asked of God in the ardour of his prayers, *sint scripturae tuae castae deliciae meae [Ennar. in Ps 38.2].* Go on loving and reading the Bible, it will constantly give you fresh strength. It will strengthen more and more your will in the love of Jesus Christ and contempt for the world, it will purify your heart, enlighten your spirit and fill it with the truths it needs so badly as a protection against the loose principles which attack and enfeeble piety if God does not protect it and if one is not continually on one's guard. The greatest happiness that a Christian can enjoy in this world, if he cannot particpate as much as he would like in the body and blood of Christ, is to participate in his word, and converse with him in a holy familiarity while awaiting the moment when he will come himself to bring him complete happiness by his presence, particularly when the divine instructions are not reduced to mere intentions but are translated and expressed in action. For you know, Mgr, that reading would do more harm than good if it were not followed by scrupulous observance. St Gregory says that he who truly believes the word is he who takes care to practise what it teaches. I am sure that is the object of all your study, and your peace of mind would not be as it is unless your conscience bore witness to your works.

We never cease, Mgr, to offer our prayers to God and ask him to grant you perseverance. That is a duty which we shall discharge until our dying breath, since that is the only way to demonstrate our faithfulness to you, together with the attachment and profound respect we have for you.

PS It is true that the Bishop of Evreux did me the honour of coming to see me, and having been enlightened on a number of matters of which he had heard reports with no reasonable basis, he was as satisfied with all my views and convinced of the injustice done to me as you may be.

Besides, Mgr, I must tell you some news which will delight you; the Pope has sent me a brief giving the right and power to our religious to elect a prior after my death to govern them should the abbey return into commend. The King received the brief with incredible kindness, reported it to the Council himself, and paid out of his own pocket for the letters patent to register it, which was done in three or four days in the most favourable circumstances possible. This is an extraordinary act of providence, ensuring as far as possible the small good that it has pleased God to establish in this monastery. If I find a chance to do what you bid me with M. le T. I shall not fail to do so. He is a man of much merit, recognised by all.'

A letter of 1677 to RM Agnès refers to the part played by the Bp of Evreux, Henri Cauchon de Maupas du Tour, in spreading rumours of a supposed estrangement between R. and Bellefonds.

78/1   COMTE DE TRÉVILLE [? January 1678]
TD C (fragment)
Death of Bp of Alet [December 1677].

78/2   [RM MARIE-LOUISE BOUTHILLIER] [?1678]
Mug I/95
Question of vow of enclosure; refers her back to letter of 1669.

78/3   RP ABBÉ [TAMIÉ, ANTOINE DE SOMONT] [1678]
Mug II/94; BN 19324 (extract with name)
In establishing Reform in his house abbot should closely follow Constitutions and *Usages* of Cîteaux. Should belong wholly to his monks, 'be the first in the most base and humiliating tasks'. Wine permitted, but no recreation.

78/4   RP PRIEUR, SAINT-VICTOR [NICOLAS TACONNET]   1678
TB 908; TC I/66

Prior should resign if really incapable of guiding souls in his care. 'A religious does not have to fall into gross excesses to become an enemy of God . . . since an ordinary life is enough to condemn those who are obliged to lead a more perfect one.'

* 78/5   RM AGNÈS DE BELLEFONDS   [1678]
TD C

'Very Reverend Mother,

Everything that M. de B[rancas] writes to me confirms what you tell me, which is that he is full of friendship for me and is never tired of showing it. God knows how much I should like to be on good terms with everyone and to give no one cause to complain about me, but what can I do about the Abbot of Septfons after what has happened, other than being for him what I am? The charity I owe him is complete, but as regards trust, that is another matter. God, who enjoins the one on us, forbids us the other. It is with wisdom as with charity; I am no more permitted to be lacking in one of those virtues than in the other. Yet it is to act against all christian prudence to have confidence in a man whom one knows to have no fidelity. Thus, Reverend Mother, I can do nothing else about him than sound him out, when opportunity arises, and assure him [of my charity?], but to indicate that I once again give him my friendship as it was in the past, and that all my impressions of his behaviour are so effaced that he can come back with me and live as if nothing had ever come between us, there is no way in which I can do that, for if I did so in good faith, I should be lacking in all the rules of prudence and good sense, or else I should not be sincere in giving him cause to think so when it was not the case. I see all the possible consequences of such a line of conduct, but I none the less do not feel in any way embarrassed, and providing that my conduct has nothing in it displeasing to God, I do not care about incurring the disapproval of men. It is true that I wrote him a strong and humiliating letter, and I did so because I thought that God's order . . .' [the rest is missing].

The letter is undated, but relations with Beaufort began to improve in 1678.

* 780113   BISHOP OF LUÇON [HENRI BARILLON]   13 January 1678
L orig.; P f.705

'It is too kind of you, Mgr, to take as much interest as you do in the favour we have received from the Pope and the King or, to be more exact, from God's goodness, who holds in his hands the hearts of both of them. It is certain that I could wish for nothing better for the maintenance of what little good Our Lord has been pleased to establish in this monastery than the power given by His Holiness to our brethren to elect a prior to rule over them in the event that the abbey were to go back into commend after my death. I look on that as an act of God's mercy, who never abandons those who put their hope in him. We have good cause to humble ourselves, Mgr, and to work at becoming better than we have been up to now, in order to acknowledge before God a favour of which we were not worthy. I confess that it was a real consolation to have received at the same time this double mark of the goodness and favour of Pope and King at a time when the envy of men was spreading abroad unpleasant rumours against us, for which we had given no cause by our conduct. To tell the truth, although we preserved great equanimity amid all the injustices which the world did us, we still felt genuine joy at seeing ourselves justified in a way which should shut the mouths of those who did not scruple to consider and decry us as people who led a fantasy life, without the permission or approval of the legitimate authorities. For the rest, Mgr, if I do not have the honour of writing to you more often, it is because I respect your occupations and know that they are so continual that one ought not, except in case of necessity, rob a single moment from them. I still know your news and am fully informed of the fidelity with which you discharge your ministry and the success which God gives to your solicitude. I thank him for it every day of my life, and can assure you that not one passes but that I present you to him in my prayers with special diligence. There is no obligation which I feel more strictly binding, and which I discharge more conscientiously. Love me always, Mgr, I beg you, and do me the justice of believing that no one in the world honours you more tenderly than I, and that nothing could be added to the respect with which I am yours etc.

PS For the rest, Mgr, just think that your brother is our Intendant and that he and we maintain that you cannot dispense yourself from making a trip to these parts; that is one non-residence for which I am sure God will not call you to account. I admit that it would be an unspeakable delight for me to see you once again in our desert before I die.'

R. had wasted no time in applying to the new Pope, Innocent XI, (1676–89), for this concession. Barillon's brother, Antoine, became Intendant at Alençon in April 1677.

780123   CARDINAL AGOSTINO FAVORITI   23 January 1678
Le Nain, *Vie* (1719) II/712

Thanks him for Brief on electing prior.

*780206   RP ABBÉ, TAMIÉ [ANTOINE DE SOMONT]   6 February 1678
TB 923

Congratulates him on good start, will give him all possible help, but he must be careful in his admissions. Strongly advises him against allowing monks to study philosophy: 'You will dry up their hearts, through study you will take away the spirit of prayer, you will put them off manual work'.

*780206a RM ABBESSE, LEYME [ANNE DE LA VIEUVILLE] 6 February 1678
TC I/57

'I pray God, RM, to give you not just one year, but a long life full of blessings; I mean that he should give you more and more the means to serve him, for I am sure that you neither know nor wish any other happiness than that. I am amazed at N's blindness. It is true that religion is a contract made with God, but one ought not and could not promise him in a commitment as binding as that of vows to violate his laws and transgress his holy will. Yet is it not just such a fine declaration solemnly to promise him to convert one's ways, and shape the whole conduct of one's life according to St Benedict's Rule, while making the mental reservation to live as others live, that is to violate that rule in almost every particular and to live without scruple or remorse in manifest prevarication? It is strictly speaking to mock God when one promises to destroy his law. And there is no way to remedy such a disorder once one has been unfortunate enough to fall into it, except by rectifying one's ways, giving up abuses and embracing the truth one had ignored. It is true that when one has entered upon a commitment that is holy and lives in it with religion and piety, although not keeping the integral Rule, one is still able to achieve one's salvation. But when, on the contrary, the commitment amounts to a real reversal of the Rule, abolishing its discipline, principles, regularity, and practices, it can only be considered a state of death and malediction. It must even be noted that ignorance in a case of this kind provides no excuse, because one cannot without sin not know the things one is obliged to know, and there is nothing a religious is more strictly and indispensably obliged to know than what his profession is. As the Rule of St Benedict is in the hands of each, and each committed himself according to that Rule, he must have known what it contained, and he cannot have failed to be informed that what it prescribed was wholly contrary to the life he proposed to lead. So it cannot be disputed that all who have embraced that mitigation are guilty, and God regards them as people whose profession is nothing but continual transgression and contempt for his commandments. The sin is no less for having become public; neither custom nor consideration for the persons who commit and approve it can authorise it, and the criminals are no more excusable for having numerous accomplices in their illusion.

As for anyone telling you that one is not obliged to go beyond what one has promised to God, you can reply precisely that that is true when the promise is wholly good, right, and holy, but when it is unreasonable, and contrary to his will and precepts, it is an illicit commitment in which one cannot abide or be with a clear conscience.

When people adduce as a strong argument that all who are in the Common Observance only left the world on condition that they should live according to the usages they found established, tell them that they would have done better to remain in the world, for the public edification as for their own salvation, that they would not be scandalising the Church, profaning holy places, bringing abomination into the sanctuary, and dishonouring the habit and profession of the saints as they do every day by their dissolute and excessive conduct.

Such principles and opinions are, RM, most assured, and the good father cannot be much of a person, or his blindness must be extreme, for him to challenge so clear and constant a truth. In a word, whatever he may say, stay firm in the observance of Alexander VII's Brief for your nuns, and as regards you personally, attach yourself to the Strict Observance, since you have adopted it, and rest assured that you cannot fail to do either without offending your conscience.

My health, RM, since you want to know, is always the same, it varies according to the weather, and I feel more or less indisposed by the fever which constitutes my sickness in proportion to the greater or lesser moderation of the atmosphere. Ask God, I beg you, to detach me entirely, not only from all desire to live, but from any feeling for the things of this world. It is shameful for a religious, obliged to nothing less than to live for God alone, to have and retain a single thought of which God is not the beginning and the end. If those good fathers who support and authorise mitigations followed the obligations of a religious, they would not have enough leisure or enough tears for weeping over their aberrations and misdeeds. But sinners, after despising God for a long time by their consistent opposition to all that he wants of them, end by losing all understanding, and the final ill to which God abandons them is hardness of heart and blindness of spirit.

I cannot express my appreciation for all the kindness you show me. God, who alone causes it, must show you himself. I must however assure you, RM, that no one will ever be more than I yours etc.

PS As regards your nuns who want to leave, if, as I do not doubt, you have done all you could to correct them, make them better than they are, and give them the spirit of religion which they have never had, then you can let them go as incorrigible, since the Rule allows them to be expelled, for they would inevitably by their bad example prevent all the good which you are trying to do.'

N. is presumably the visitor, still opposed to reform.

*780213   RP BRUSCOLY, CONG. ORAT.   13 February 1678
U 483 orig.

'It gives me enormous joy, my very dear Father, that the person you directed to us has received from God the attitudes necessary for enabling him to embrace the kind of life we lead here, which, wretched as it is, still requires a strong and vigorous nature. But God did not wish this good man to have enough to execute the desire, which he believed Our Lord had inspired, to withdraw among us. He no doubt wants him elsewhere, and it is hardly possible that, wishing to serve him as much as he does, he will not find the means to do so. What I can say, Reverend Father, is that no one could be more pleased than I by his integrity and piety.

As for brother Théodore, he has been indisposed for some days with a bad cold and some fever. His illness will, however, not amount to much. It seems that God allowed it to test his vocation, and to make us recognise in him the firmness and resignation of someone who had spent fifty years in religion. If he perseveres as he has begun, it can be said that he will be entirely according to God's heart, and I confess that I have every possible reason to be pleased with him. I have nothing to add to this note, my very dear Father, except that I am duly grateful to you for all your kindness, I have absolute confidence in your prayers, and it is with all my heart and all the esteem you deserve that I am yours' etc.

References like that to the first, unidentified, recruit in letters to Bruscoly and others give a good idea of how people came to try their vocation at la T., usually without success.

780215   RP PRIEUR, SAINT-VICTOR [NICOLAS TACONNET]   15 February 1678
TB 926

Prior should resign since he lacks the 'superhuman strength, wisdom and virtue' to reform his house.

He did so soon afterwards.

780222   RP PRIEUR, BARBEAUX   22 February 1678
Autographes Troussures, p. 537

R. reluctant to admit monks for brief visits, but as the Visitor (Abbot of Prières) and Prior wish it, he will. There will be less austerity after Easter, but R. leaves timing to man's discretion.

*780224   RP BRUSCOLY,   24 February 1678
'PRIEST OF THE ORATORY, AT SAINT-HONORÉ'
U 483 orig.

'The person who will give you this letter, my very dear Father, is one of my close friends. As he is going to spend some time in Paris, and has for long sincerely wanted to serve God and belong to him, I thought I could not do better for his consolation than direct him to you, and I beg you to be good enough to give him occasionally a moment of your time and leisure. I hope for this grace from your charity, and ask it for him with all my heart. Continue always to keep for me the honour of your friendship and the help of your prayers before God, and believe, my very dear Father, that no one in the world honours you and is more yours etc.

PS Brother Théodore is not yet cured, but I still hope that his illness will come to nothing. It has only strengthened his resolve, and I should be extremely sorry if his indisposition prevented us from accepting him, for it is true that I have never seen a better heart and will than his. I beg you, my very dear Father, to take the trouble to go and see Mme Faverolles his mother so that she knows about his illness, but she is not to be alarmed by it.'

780229 FR JEAN-PHILIPPE LOUME,   29 February 1678
        GRANDSELVE
TB 931; TD F

He should leave his dissolute monastery as soon as possible.

780303 DUCHESSE DE LUYNES   3 March 1678
TB 933

She should instruct her daughter while still young.

780305 JEAN FAVIER   5 March 1678
CF 344,f.77 orig.; Gonod 40

A conscientious commendatory abbot is more excusable than a regular abbot who is not conscientious. If Favier can find a good man for Beauvais he should hand over, otherwise not. Trouble with Le Roy over humiliations.

*780307 RM ABBESSE, LEYME [ANNE DE LA VIEUVILLE]   7 March 1678
TB 939

'I will say no more, RM about how much I appreciate all your kindness, for I am sure that you do me full justice in that respect and believe me so genuinely to be what I should be as regards you, that any fresh assurances I could offer would be vain.

It is a constant misfortune to have a visitor like yours; but God has given you much grace to have filled your heart with such revulsion from his lax principles. What religious of some ability of the Common Observance have over those who are ignorant is that they are more interested, blinder, and fuller of bad arguments to support and justify the wickedness of their lives and conduct. They do not even fail to use the example and writings of St Bernard to make the simple believe that their ways are straight, and that they walk in the paths of truth. Yet they are mistaken in everything, they abuse the saints' authority, and make them say out of context what they never said or thought. It is not true, as this good father assures you, that murmuring was common at Clairvaux while St Bernard ruled there. It was a monastery full of saints, they lived there in such perfect mortification of body and spirit and were so submissive to all the views of that great man that there was nothing of which they were less capable than the slightest opposition to any of his wishes. I must remind you of some evidence which permits of no reply.

The first comes from William, Abbot of Saint-Thierry, author of the first book of the *Life of St Bernard*; this is what he says in chapter 9:

"Those men who were truly religious, and whose prudence was equal to their piety, revered in his [St Bernard's] sermons and addresses even those things they were unable to accomplish, and although in their confessions they were amazed at conduct which seemed new to them, because it appeared to give some cause for the feeble to despair, they believed however, according to the words of Job, that it was not permissible for them to contradict the saint's words, and so they did not excuse themselves, but in the presence of the man of God accused themselves of those weaknesses of which no man in this life can be justified before God." [Jb 4:17]

In chapter 10: "Although they were so numerous, they did not cease to be solitary, and the order by which charity was regulated there meant that though they were many in that valley, they were still, as it were, alone, because whereas a man in dissipation and disorder acts towards himself as a troop and multitude of men, even when alone, here on the contrary the unity of spirit and regularity of silence among so many meant that each individual was, as it were, alone, the order of the discipline governing their words and actions preserved solitude in their hearts among so numerous a company . . . . For the care of their spiritual father, aided by grace, had produced in them the result that they endured not only steadfastly and without a murmur, but with great satisfaction, all that the body is able to bear, and many things which previously seemed impossible to men subjected to the flesh."

Such sentiments were not passing, but established on such firm and unshakable foundations that the saint's long journeys and absences did not weaken them in the least.

That is what we see in the second book of the *Life*, written by Bernard [sic], Abbot of Bonneval, chapter 7:

"During so long an absence of the saint, the devil could not disturb the peace of Clairvaux by his wiles, he could not sully the purity of these holy souls, and this house of God, which was founded on rock, could not be shaken in any of its parts. The servant of God, absent in body but present in spirit, had so cemented and fortified his work by his fervent prayers, that there was no crack nor opening to be seen in so great a building, he found on his arrival no differences to reconcile, no hatred broke out, or was nourished and maintained by his absence and submitted to his judgement, the young made no complaints against their seniors concerning any dissolute or lax behaviour, they were all in a firm and irreproachable state, in a perfect society, consummate union, all animated with the same spirit in this house of God."

All that account hardly corresponds with your visitor's words, and he must be lacking either in sincerity or memory, or he must have read anything but what he should. I am not surprised that these honest monks do not like reading that sort of book, for they would surely find everywhere in them nothing but severe condemnation of their life and conduct. They are like the serpents in Scripture who stuff their ears so as not to hear the words of their charmer [Ps 57:5-6].

It is however true that a kind of murmur did arise in St Bernard's monastery, but of a kind into which neither the good father nor any like him are likely to fall; *Life of St Bernard*, book I, chapter 10:

"The ardour of these holy solitaries for penitence went so far and their thirst for it was so insatiable, that the great austerity in which they lived seemed to them a life of ease and delight." I must tell you what more we learn. "This satisfaction had caused them another reason for murmuring, which was all the more dangerous because they thought it more spiritual and less human; for if they had convinced themselves and had the thought firmly engraved in their minds as by the witness of their own conscience that every sensual pleasure was the enemy of the soul, and believed that we must flee all that the body uses for food with some feeling of pleasure, because the sweetness of the divine love animating them made them find the most bitter things sweet and delightful, they imagined that they lived with more delights in the desert than they had done before in the world, and that they were thus being brought back by a different path to the sensual life they had led."

After all that, I agree that among so great a number of saints there were some warped spirits who had none of that eminent virtue which shone on their brethren, since it has always been God's way to mingle the evil with the good; but there could be nothing more absurd than to infer from that that this congregation was not very holy, and to say that Clairvaux was a house of murmuring because some individuals fell into that fault, or to claim that such a disorder occurring among some bad monks in a monastery ruled by a great saint should make us tolerate and fail to punish it in less perfect communities; on the contrary there can be no doubt that St Bernard criticised it, punished those who were guilty, and arrested its course by his care, vigilance, and firmness, so that the contagion was not passed on. He was too full of the spirit of St Benedict, too much a lover of the rule to neglect what it bids him to do on such occasions, that is to warn, reprove, punish, excommunicate, chastise rigorously, employ prayers to God to restore to duty anyone unfortunate enough to have failed it, and finally to cut him off from the congregation if he persisted in his aberration, lest the sickness infect the whole flock. Consequently, RM, a superior who wants to follow the example of St Bernard must make every effort to prevent murmuring entering his monastery or to banish it if it has entered, and there is nothing possible or legitimate which he is not obliged to do, according to the precept of the Rule, to oppose those who try either to introduce or maintain it.

That seems to me enough, RM, to show you that your visitor is not very correct in the advice he gives you; as he has spent his life among people who live without regularity or discipline, in monasteries where it is as common to murmur as to breathe, one should not be surprised if he treats it as of no account and regards it as a necessary evil. For my part, having been in more disciplined places and by God's mercy not judging things by the customs and opinions of men, I make little distinction between homicide and murmuring. They are crimes which will equally deprive those who commit them of the kingdom of Christ, and I am not afraid to say that God's spirit cannot live in a monastery where people do not scruple to murmur, and that it can only be considered a ladder of iniquity and assembly of malediction.

There is nothing less evident, from the fact that St Bernard reproved monks in his exhortations for sloth and negligence, than to conclude that it is useless now to reprove those who fall into the same faults, and the answer to those who use such bad arguments to leave religious unpunished must be: 1. since St Bernard reproved such vices and God has set him before us as a perfect model of the true superior, we must imitate him and do as he did; 2. that his reproof was either successful or not. If successful, we must hope that God will give his blessing to the same conduct; if in vain, we must believe that if, despite the sanctity and reproofs of St Bernard, negligence and lack of fervour were to be seen in his monastery, then we shall now see simply horrors in the cloister, if superiors who lack St Bernard's sanctity fail to watch for and punish the faults committed there.

It is also to be noted that we learn again of St Bernard that he reproved his religious as idle and negligent for acts which might make worldly people consider them saints (*Sermon* 4 on the psalm *Qui habitat*). So we must believe, as he showed himself, that there were few religious reproved in this way because of their fault, and such reproof was often used to humiliate them, take from them any idea of their virtue and anticipate the faults into which, being human, they might fall (*Sermon* 3 on the Dedication).

To conclude, RM, you must be convinced that those who tell you that faults, however slight they seem, must not be corrected, are wrong. There has never been true regularity where there has not been punishment. All the saints have laid down penalties according to the degree of fault in the rules they have given us, because they knew that these were necessary not only to punish those who committed them, but to prevent others being committed. Fear is one of the means which God wants superiors to employ to contain those put under their charge, impunity is an infallible source of every kind of disorder and vice, and it is a constant principle, since it is the truth itself which has taught us, that if less considerable faults are neglected, other greater ones cannot fail to occur. If one wanted to go back to the origin of the ills in undisciplined observances, one would find that the lack of diligence of superiors and their failure to chastise those who strayed from their duty was the original cause. After all, it is enough that you have a rule which teaches you that a superior will only be discharged at God's judgement of the souls entrusted to his guidance if he has used all possible means to keep them in the observance of their rule, and as punishment is one of the chief means, it is not to be doubted that God will judge him guilty and an accomplice of the excesses he has neglected to punish.

I think that is enough to resolve your difficulties, or rather to confirm you in the views you already held, for I am sure that you have too much understanding and knowledge of the obligations of your calling to have been taken unawares by such gross and baseless fantasies. We shall not fail to commend to God the person who desires it. I wish she could be inspired to join you in her idea of doing more than she has done so far; it would provide you with important assistance in backing up the resolve given you by God. I pray him to keep it alive in you, and let you find all necessary facilities for executing it.'

R. is paraphrasing rather than translating from the Vita prima *of St Bernard, edited by Mabillon in 1667; modern chapter numbers are different. The passages cited are based re-*

spectively on *PL 185:243D, 248B, 284B*, and *244A*. *The Abbot of Bonneval who contributed to the* Vita *was Arnauld, not Bernard.*

780315   MONSIEUR DU SUEL, ARRAS   15 March 1678
TB 948

Has given the habit to a lay-brother sent by Du Suel. Understands his desire for solitude.

This was probably Siméon Lambert, professed March 1679, aged 25; died 1681.

780315a   [? PIERRE NICOLE]   15 March 1678
TB 950

Thanks him for his last work, the best of all [probably *Essais de morale*, vol. IV and last, 1678].

*780324   RP BRUSCOLY,   24 March 1678
           'PRIEST OF THE ORATORY AT SAINT-HONORÉ'
U 483 orig.

'I have just this minute received your letter, my very dear Father, and I did not want to delay giving you a piece of news that will not displease you, namely, that we received last Saturday the profession of brother Théodore. He made it in so vigorous and edifying a manner that it would have consoled you had you been there to witness it. I confess that there is no room for doubting that he has done God's will, and that it is God who brought him to our monastery for his sanctification. I was convinced of that by his fidelity during the whole course of his novitiate, but especially since his illness, so much so that I should have thought I was resisting the impulses of the Holy Spirit if I had not granted him the consolation he insistently demanded of me, come what may. His mother should be pleased to have brought into the world a son according to God's heart, and who by his prayers and his piety can draw God's blessings on her and all her family. She can be sure that we shall take every possible care of him. I am most obliged, my very dear Father, for your kindness towards the young ecclesiastic I recommended to you. If anything occurs to me about the Archdeacon's nephew I will let you know. Farewell, my very dear Father, pray Our Lord Jesus Christ for me, and rest assured that it is with all my heart that I am yours etc.

Brother Théodore's illness does not grow less, but his courage increases. I commend him to your prayers.'

The Archdeacon of Paris was Claude Ameline, a former Oratorian; his nephew is unidentified.

780324a   DUCHESSE DE LUYNES   24 March 1678
TB 851

RP de Monchy's return providential for her.

780406 MADEMOISELLE DE VERTUS   6 April 1678
TB 953

'You have received enough from God to give back something to men.'

*780410   RP BRUSCOLY, CONG. ORAT.   10 April 1678
U 483 orig.

'Finally, my very dear and reverend Father, poor brother Théodore has gone to God, sooner than we thought he would. I can say that he has gone to God because only those called by Our Lord Jesus Christ die so blessedly and with so many marks of his mercy. We found nothing in him from the moment he took the habit and entered upon the religious life which did not edify us, and I must confess that the insistence with which he asked me to be allowed to consecrate himself entirely to Christ by vows, together with the holy frame of mind in which I saw him, made me resolve to grant him what should have been from all appearances, and was in fact, his happiness and consolation. This poor brother bore all his illness not only patiently, but joyfully, and every time he spoke to me of his desire and hope of dying soon, one could see serenity on his face, and indeed his greatest fear during the whole course of his illness was not to die from it. He made his communion on Palm Sunday; on Maundy Thursday he received his Easter communion and viaticum together; at four in the morning we gave him extreme unction, and shortly after eight I closed his eyes and he gave up the ghost with such keen piety, such deep peace, and such complete consciousness that he retained it until his dying gasp. That, my dear Father is the destiny of our poor brother, which will no doubt appear to you as it does to me worthy of envy. Have the charity to give the first news of it to his mother, for no one is better able than you to show her that as her son was born mortal like other men and left the hand of God only to return to it, she should be appreciably consoled to know that he returned there so happily. Life is a mere vapour. One would need never to have known, or to have forgotten, that it is bounded by eternity in order to find it of any importance. I do not need to recommend him to your prayers, for I know very well what he owed to you and your charity towards him. Love me always, I beseech you, my very dear Father, do me the grace of remembering me before God and being convinced that no one could be more sincerely than I yours etc.

PS I beg you not to delay seeing Mme Faverolles so that you are the one to tell her of brother Théodore's death.'

Théodore died on 7 April, from 'inflammation of the chest'.

*780501   RP BRUSCOLY,   1 May 1678
          'PRIEST OF THE ORATORY, RUE SAINT-HONORÉ, PARIS'
U 483 orig.

'Your letter, Reverend Father, consoles me absolutely when I see in what a pure and holy manner you have taken the death of our poor brother Théodore. If you had witnessed it you would have observed things which would have filled you with inspiration. I have written to Mme Faverolles, who wanted to give something to our monastery, that she was not to think of it, that we received her son purely for God's sake, and that we were resolved to maintain that view, but that I thought she should put the poor in place of us and share her charity with them, according to her son's intention. He did not in fact make a will as he could have done, because I told him that he should leave everything to be disposed of by his mother, being sure that she would take into account, as she had advised me, of the letter he had written her concerning his dispositions.

The Feuillant of whom you speak is still here, and I believe that he will persevere. You can assure Mme Fournier, his mother, that we shall take every care of him.

As regards the canon of Séez, my very dear Father, you judged quite correctly. He is as you say, he is undecided, but basically what he wants is good; he does not want to offend God, and your thoughts and mine are exactly the same. He must stay in the state in which God has put him, and I cannot see anything to prevent him doing so, or to distract him from what seems to be his true vocation. I will write to him in that sense, and I do not doubt that he will follow your advice. Farewell, my very dear Father, pray Our Lord for me, I beg you, and believe that no one in the world is more truly yours than I.'

The Feuillant is Jean-François Fournier, a Parisian, aged 36, who was professed in 1679 and lived on until 1711. Note that neither in his case nor in that of Théodore is any mention made of a father. The canon of Séez with whom R. had most to do was M. le Chevalier, who tried in vain to persuade R. to take him at la T. and by 1678 was director of the diocesan seminary. Bruscoly died on 9 December 1678.

780522   RELIGIEUSE   22 May 1678
A 2106,f.85 vo.

Reassures her about his health. Praises her own conduct in adversity.

780611   RM [EMILIE] DE BOUILLON   11 June 1678
TD C (fragment)

Has written to Cardinal de Bouillon.

780615   PAUL BARILLON   15 June 1678
TB 960

Encouragement.

780705   [JEAN FAVIER]   5 July 16 [7] 8
A 2106,f.10 vo. (wrongly dated 1658)

Sends a letter on humiliations recently printed which Favier had seen some years before.

*780711   [RP BRUNO FERRAND]   11 July 1678
TD/C

'To let you know how I am thinking, my very dear Father, I have taken a firm resolve to withdraw into solitude more than I have done hitherto, to separate myself even from the small number of persons I was accustomed to see, so that I should no longer have any other occupation than that of asking Christ to have mercy on me. As I prepare myself for a death worthy of a man on whom he has heaped so many gifts of grace, awaiting the time when I can give up the charge and guidance of others so as to die in obedience as a simple monk, having done before men everything which depended on me for the preservation of what little good God was pleased to establish in this house, it is very right that I should address myself to God and spend what time I have still to live in praying him to fulfil his work and take pity on those who have come together solely in his name and in the sole desire and intention of pleasing him. However, my dear Father, no matter how great is my retreat, you may believe that it will not exclude you, or Father de Monchy or Monsieur Pinette. Like you I feel that there is not a moment to be lost. God be blessed in all things, he knows that it is his glory alone which I have before my eyes. We await your news, my very dear Father, pray for us, I beseech you, and believe that I am yours etc.

PS I beg you to tell Mother Agnès how our affair is progressing, asking her to keep it secret. Her prudence, her charity, and her friendship for us allow us to hope for every help from her.'

Identification of this letter, of 780717, 781011, 781126, which succeed one another in the same series as copied, together with at least one preceding them, now surviving only as a fragment, depends on the last of the series, 801116, in which the address is spelled out in full. At the time he entered la T., in 1684, aged 63, Ferrand was prior of the Premonstratensian house of Genlis, near Dijon. According to the Relation *of his death, R. knew him 'in the world.'*

*780717   [RP BRUNO FERRAND]   17 July 1678
TD/C

'I will pay all the attention I should to the reflections of Father de Monchy and yourself on my proposed resignation. Ultimately all I want to think about is preparing myself for death in peace and completely separated from anything which could in any way dissipate or weaken that thought. I have nothing more to tell you, my very dear Father, except that I am entirely yours through such pressing commitments and reasons that they could not be stronger.

Just as I was sealing this letter, my very dear Father, I received your last one, in reply to which I will just say that I shall be delighted if you come to see us and that there is no one who looks on you with more honour and affection. Farewell, my very dear Father, love me always and do not forget me before God.'

See 780711. He did visit, and came a second time before deciding to end his days at la T.

780803 COMTE DE TRÉVILLE 3 August 1678
TD/C

Brief received from Rome on future regime at la T. Cardinal Cibo wrote on Pope's behalf. No trouble expected from Clairvaux.

This must refer to the second brief, of May 1678.

*780804 MARÉCHAL DE BELLEFONDS 4 August 1678
BN na 12959 f.65,orig.; TC II 120

'It is very just of you, Mgr, to believe that you are very much present to me before God and that there is no one whom we commend to him more diligently and conscientiously, but your opinion of us goes beyond what we deserve when your charity persuades you that our prayers can render you a service which you should only expect of persons of consummate piety and virtue, not of those who have so far had only the desire and wish to be so. The life you lead, Mgr, is so disciplined, and you have arranged everything with such good order and wisdom, that there is doubtless nothing that cannot be approved, and you cannot fail, seeking God with entirely pure intentions and desiring him only, as you do, for love of him, to find him and receive from him enlightenment and direction. However, men who are not always in agreement with God and usually form judgements very different from his have observed in your conduct things which do not please them. You are very right to feel little concern about this, knowing as you do that good can never be established without encountering opposition and censure, and that anyone wishing to embrace the service of Jesus Christ must resolve to stand firm against the opposition which the world always arouses against him. God, Mgr, is the only one we have to please, and when we have him on our side and find in the witness of our conscience nothing but what meets the obligations of fidelity which we owe him, then we must remain completely calm, and nothing would be more inappropriate than to waver in our resolutions and plans according to the different impulses which almost always arise from the envy and passions of men. God wishes those who serve him to pay a price, and it must be admitted that one would be rewarded already in this world if what one does for his service met with general approval. God himself did not have that, although infinitely worthy of it. It is written that he was, as it were, the object of scorn and denial. The happiness and consolation of his servants comes from being treated like their Master, and if there were a choice between condemnation and applause, I assure you that one should not hesitate to opt for humiliation in preference to glory. There is nothing more common, Mgr, than to find people who wish to serve God, according to what they say, but who would be very upset not to have the esteem of men. In a word, it was not for love of men that you began the work, and so it will not be for their love that you will abandon it. The charity you practise towards the poor is most sanctifying and exemplary; it is to serve Jesus Christ himself, since he claims them for his own and counted any help given to them as given to him. I am not surprised that this has caused you some difficulty, nor to learn that you have overcome it. It is a struggle that had to take place between grace and nature, the spirit of the world and that of Jesus Christ. The main thing is that the latter has won, and I am sure, Mgr, that that did not happen without bringing you much comfort.

God is most merciful to you in making your wife support you so well in your plans, and share so piously in all your projects. One must wish you both faithful perseverance, and the only way to obtain it from the only one who can give it is to humble yourself greatly in his eyes, even in those acts which seem best to you, and however conscientious and regular your life, to consider yourself a useless servant in the house of the Lord. I do not doubt that these are your feelings, and that God, who wants you to be entirely his and does not want you to be satisfied with serving him in any ordinary way, has founded in you the house he is to build on solid rock, that is, a genuine humility without which there can be no true piety. I will continue to pray him to complete what he has begun with so many blessings and edification. I do not need to tell you, Mgr, how interested I am in all that concerns you, for I am sure you do not doubt it, persuaded as you are of the respect and fidelity with which I am yours etc.

PS I recently had the honour to inform you that I had received a brief from Rome, giving our religious the power to elect a prior to govern them after my death, should the abbey return into commend. I asked the Pope for another to confirm the first and regulate a number of points regarding the conduct of this monastery. His Holiness granted it with a goodness I did not deserve, after being informed of all that goes on in this house. The King received it with the same approval as the first. I do not know, Mgr, whether God wishes the small good which he has established amongst us to have any duration, or whether he wished to console us, before our lives draw to a close, by giving us the means publicly to destroy the calumnies of those who have not scrupled to attack me personally, as well as the conduct of this house, to make our views suspect and condemn us as people following their illusions and acting on their own inspiration, without being authorised by the power of the church.'

780807   [JEAN FAVIER]   7 August 1678
A 2106,f.86

An ecclesiastic may help his parents out of church funds provided he regards them as poor, but not to maintain their social standing. Denies consulting Bp of Alet about it.

780827   RP PASQUIER QUESNEL, CONG. ORAT.   27 August 1678
U 1168 orig.; Tans 37

Troubles of M. Jarghillen and his benefice at Tours. Guillaume Quesnel has been in Grenoble. Hopes Oratory survives present difficulties, and has such obligations that he would do all in his power to help.

The alleged Jansenist sympathies of the Congregation were causing acute trouble. Guillaume was superior of the seminary at Grenoble 1678-84.

*780922   BISHOP OF LUÇON [HENRI BARILLON]   22 September 1678
P f.766

'I do not need to tell you, Mgr, how inpatiently we await the honour you propose to do us, for I am sure that, persuaded as you are of the way I honour you and of my feelings towards you, you cannot doubt that our impatience is as great as it should be, that is to say, as great as is possible. Monsieur de Morangis, your brother, had already told me that he had obliged you to put off your journey for a time, and I confess that I all but resented the fact that he was delaying one of the keenest joys which I could have in this world. I regard the pleasure of seeing you in our desert, I assure you, as a special blessing for me and for our house. I will tell you more, Mgr, when we have the pleasure of having you here. Meanwhile do me the justice of believing that nothing will ever equal the respect and affection with which I am yours' etc.

The brother is Antoine de Morangis, Intendant at Alençon.

*781006   MARÉCHAL DE BELLEFONDS   6 October 1678
BN na 12959 f.69,orig.; TB 973

'Although I am quite convinced that you are no less convinced of the deep sympathy I feel for all that concerns you, and although I do not need to declare this afresh, I will not refrain from telling you that no one could have felt more keenly than I the news that you had been ordered to return to court. I considered this change, Mgr, in the sight of God, and as his providence rules all things and especially what concerns those who serve him and particularly profess to belong to him, I did not doubt that he had inspired the King to recall you and, since on your side you merely follow his dispositions, that he would subsequently give you all the necessary protection to enable you to live in the midst of the world with all the fidelity you have maintained throughout your retreat. Fundamentally he is the master everywhere, and although the court is a realm in which he gives fewer signs of his sovereign presence, which seems to be less apparent there, yet he reigns there absolutely over whomsoever he pleases and in the manner in which he pleases. There are souls who heed him, who glory in his service, and whom the world cannot influence to the prejudice of the obedience they owe him. You must, Mgr, be among that number, be it never so small. What you have declared by the life you have been seen to lead for some years now gives you much strength against all that might shake your resolve, and no one will find it strange that you should maintain a commitment as holy and public as that which you are known to have made. As you came nearer to God by withdrawing from men, and as in him one fully recognises their vanity and wretchedness, I am sure they will make you pity rather than envy them, but that should not stop you treading most warily and being everywhere most vigilant, for the evil in the human heart is so great that nothing is more common than for it to act against what it sees and feels and to love what it knows to be unworthy of love. It can be said that in order to enjoy true security, as far as that is possible here on earth, one must go in fear in those very actions and places where one is convinced one has least to fear. We will not fail to recommend you to Our Lord all the more carefully and diligently for knowing that you are going to be more exposed than you were in your solitude. Do me the honour and justice of believing, Mgr, that nothing can equal the respect and fidelity with which I am yours etc.

PS I must say a word to you, Mgr, since I have occasion to do so, of the affair stirred up against the Bishop of Séez in these parts. Monsieur d'Angennes, who is his neighbour a quarter of a league from Séez, took it into his head seven or eight months ago to be governor of Séez. He pointed out to the King that the post was vacant. He did not find it hard, being supported by M. le duc de Montausier, to obtain the appointment. However, from time immemorial the bishops of Séez have been governors of the town, there have never been any others, and its possession is as old as their see. Whenever anyone has tried to disturb them there the kings have never failed to maintain them. When the King first heard of the right of the Bishop of Séez, His Majesty ordered withdrawal of the appointment which M. d'Angennes had won by surprise, but as the King then left for the country, M. de Montausier prevented execution of the order, and on His Majesty's return asked him for commissioners to examine the substance of the affair, which was granted, to such effect that it is at present in the hands of M. le maréchal de Villeroy and M. Colbert. I am sure from my knowledge of the matter that the bishop's right will appear absolutely obvious to them, and that they will be surprised that anyone tried to cheat him so. What I can tell you, Mgr, is that if the Bishop of Séez were to be worsted in this affair, he would thenceforth lose all credit in his diocese, and the least of his priests would be more respected than he. I am giving you all these details because you might happen to hear of the affair. I forgot to tell you a most remarkable circumstance, namely that M. d'Angennes, in order to persuade M. de Montausier to ask on his behalf for the appointment to the governorship, told him as a matter of fact that he was doing so with the cooperation and approval of the Bishop, as I have seen with my own eyes in a letter written by M. de Montausier to the Bishop. I am sending you a letter he has written to you which I have just received.'

The marquis d'Angennes was the son of Mme de Rambouillet who founded the first salon in Paris. His sister Julie married the duc de Montausier (1610–90) who was successively Governor of Normandy and tutor to the Dauphin (until 1679). Villeroy (1598–1685) had been tutor to Louis XIV and Colbert was chief minister, so the affair, which dragged on acrimoniously, was evidently of some consequence.

*781011   A PRIOR [RP BRUNO FERRAND]   11 October 1678
TC/C

'Whatever one does, there is little to be gained in worldly contacts for the men one sees and to whom one believes oneself to be of use, but there is much to be lost for oneself. People like you and me, who once led a wholly worldly life, could never spend too much time in retreat making up in solitude and secrecy for what they so unhappily destroyed in dissipation, and I assure you, my very dear Father, that a true penitent can never go too far in hiding himself and refusing himself to men, especially when God's order has engaged him in a way of life which itself leads to separation, as may that in which you and I find ourselves through his mercy shown to us. Farewell, my dear Father, love me always and do not tire of commending me to Our Lord.'

See *780711*

781022   COMTE D'ALBON   22 October 1678
A 2106,f.83 (dated 1677, but corrected by a list in Favier's hand which is more reliable)

Strange that he and R. have so little contact, since he is a man of piety. Briefs ensuring continuation of la T. after R's death, libels against him. R. simply follows a rule corrupted by others, even St Teresa had to suffer calumny. *Relations* have edified some and depressed others. Sorry never to have seen him at la T.

This, the only identifiable letter surviving to his brother-in-law, is strangely formal. The Relations *began to come out in 1677. R. frequently quoted St Teresa's example to justify his own conduct.*

781105   RP ABBÉ, TAMIÉ [ANTOINE DE SOMONT]   5 November 1678
TB 977

Abbot of Foucarmont [Jacques Fleur de Montagne] died in Rome after securing a judgement favourable to the Reform. Prior at Tamié [Alain Morony] very depressed, and R. offers to take him back. Unlikely that authorities will hinder life at Tamié or la T.

Fleur de Montagne died on 27 September, and Varese, the Nuncio in Paris, on 4 November, so that the progress of the negotiations, which had indeed been favourable to the Reform, was halted and eventually reversed. Dom Alain, who had been prior of Perseigne before migrating to la T., had been appointed prior on arrival at Tamié, but was replaced by Cornuty and came back briefly to la T. before being sent as chaplain to Maubuisson 1682.

781105a   BISHOP OF GRENOBLE [ETIENNE LE CAMUS]   5 November 1678
TB 981

Praise of a new bishop, their mutual friend. [Louis Lascaris d'Urfé, Bp of Limoges].

*781105b G. LE ROY, HAUTEFONTAINE   5 November 1678
U 767 orig.   (in answer to one of 29 Oct.)

'As I have always had', Monsieur, all the consideration due to your merit and your person, I could not fail to be extremely glad to learn, from the Abbot of l'Etoile and by the letter you did me the honour of writing, the place that I enjoy in your good graces and your charitable feelings towards me. I humbly beg you to believe that there is nothing I would not do to deserve them, and I hope, Monsieur, that you will grant me continued favour, desiring as I do to convince you by real services, if I were able, that I am with perfect sincerity and esteem yours' etc.

The Abbot of l'Etoile was Bernard du Teillé, trusted by both R. and Le Roy, as is evident from several extant letters written to the latter. He had just paid a brief visit to la T. and always tried to act as peacemaker.

781112   RM ABBESSE   12 November 1678
TB 984

Warns against doctors, concerned with the body to detriment of the soul.

*781112a RM ABBESSE, LEYME [ANNE DE LA VIEUVILLE]   12 November 1678
TB 986

'I have read the letter you sent to me RM, and after much consideration I do not see anything in it to which one could not subscribe. It is certain that charity must lie in every part of a superior's conduct, and gentleness in many, but I do not think that one should or should wish to remove all severity and asperity in direction, for if that were the case, there would not be in a religious community firmness, vigour, or strict discipline; everything would go by the easy ways, by paths of indulgence and slackness, and there would be anything but the good example and edification to be seen which should be there. Severity is like salt, and so long as it has all necessary moderation and is accompanied by prudence, there can be no doubt that considerable profit and fruit can be derived from it. St Bernard did not think otherwise, such are the rules and principles he gave us, and I have too good an opinion of your correspondent to believe that he does not share such right and reasonable ideas. I would add that a superior must find the secret of making severity appreciated and desired, and persuade those to whom he is severe that charity alone makes him so, and he is acting not from personal inclination but with a view to their progress and their own benefit.

As for your doubt regarding the excommunication discussed in the chapter of the Rule, I must say that opinions differ, but for my part I consider that St Benedict is speaking of major excommunication, and not only is this apparent from the horror he attaches to it, but from the terms he uses, which are the very ones used by St Paul when he speaks of the excommunication he inflicted on the incestuous Corinthian;

that has always seemed to me the correct opinion, and I have never been able to accept the reasons for which it is opposed.

Since it was your intention when you took up abstinence to maintain it, and it was not just a trial, you can no longer give it up except in the cases mentioned in the Rule and to the extent that your infirmities oblige you. Our rule is so wise that instead of demanding what is beyond our strength, it dispenses us in case of real necessity from a part of the things we have promised.

I pray God, RM, to give you the health and strength to accomplish what you promised him; we can be faithful to him at all times, since the rules apply to the infirm as much as to those who are not, and dispense the former from the rigours which they require the latter to observe. Please believe always, I beg you, that no one in the world could feel more sympathy and interest than I at all that concerns you, and I am in perfect sincerity yours' etc.

*781126   [RP BRUNO FERRAND]   26 November 1678
TD/C

'Happy is he, my dear Father, who is in the place where God wants him to be and has no other thoughts than those of serving him. There are no others besides those which are not forbidden to persons who belong to him as much as you and I should, and there is nothing so great and so holy that he does not demand it of those whom he has pulled out, as the prophet says, *a fornace ferrea AEgypti ut faceret sibi populum haereditarium* [Dt 4:20]. We are so much the portion of Christ and we belong to him through such pressing commitments that we cannot, without behaving most unjustly towards him, give anything of ourselves to the world, and it is certain that those places which irrevocably separate us from it and make our solitude perfect are preferable to those which still leave us some kind of pretext and reason for meddling in its affairs. The prayer which we should most usually make to God is to efface the world, if possible, from our memory as much as from our heart. You are in mine, my very dear Father, in the way you should be, I beseech you not to doubt it, and I will consider you there, if God pleases, until my dying breath.'

See *780711.*

*781130   MARÉCHAL DE BELLEFONDS   30 November 1678
BN na 12959 f.73, orig.

'There is much to thank God for in the grace you receive from him. For my part I am not surprised, for I always hoped that his hand would sustain you wherever his providence permitted you to be, and as your return resulted neither from your impatience nor your restlessness, I do not doubt that God will show in the midst of the world the same protection he gave you in the place of your retreat. However, if it is not impossible to sing the Lord's songs in a strange land, one must believe, and one needs to tell oneself often, that it is very difficult to keep his ways faithfully when one is surrounded by affairs, pleasures, cares, opportunities, and examples which constantly propose quite different ways.

God has not commanded all men to leave the world, and it is to his mercy, greatness, and glory to have in all kinds of places and situations persons who serve him and are according to his heart, but there are none whom he has not forbidden to love the world, or any of the things belonging to it. That is an obligation from which he dispenses no one at all; it is a universal precept, and nothing better demonstrates how difficult it is to fulfil than the rarity of those who observe it.

In short, Mgr, if anyone wishes to belong to Jesus Christ and abide in him, according to the apostle's phrase, that is, live by his spirit and be united with him by bonds of his charity and grace, he must necessarily walk as Christ himself has walked, *qui dicit se in ipso manere, debet sicut ille ambulavit, et ipse ambulare* [1 Jn 2:6], must live as he lived on earth, act like him, think like him, in a word, share all his likes and dislikes, and on every occasion do what he considers Christ would do in his place.

It is an illusion to suppose that the life of a true disciple is anything but a retracing of that of the Master, and we should quite vainly aspire to being like Christ in eternity (which is the expectation and ambition of all Christians) if we did not work in time to conform our conduct in all things to his. This is a truth that seems hard to those who love the world and have made a pact with it, but that does not make it any less constant a truth, since truth itself taught it to us, but instead of affecting us with gloom and dashing our hopes, it must animate our faith, excite our zeal, our vigilance, and our piety, for he who imposed this obligation on us gives us the means and facilities to fulfil it. God does not lay traps for men, he gives the power to execute his commandments, and he does not know what it is to prevent those from finding him who seek him with pure and sincere intentions.

I am sure, Mgr, that the society in which you are is not so devoid of people that you meet none who think like me, and who do more, for they live according to what they think. I fully expect their number to be small, and, if that were not so, Jesus Christ would not have told us as he did that the way of life is narrow and the gate so strait that even among those who seek there are few who find.

All that, Mgr, shows the necessity of being ceaselessly watchful, carefully looking at all one's ways and having as much as possible before one's eyes him who should be the rule and soul of all our actions. That is something to which you can easily make yourself faithful, since God made you feel in your retreat that the world can only be displeasing to those who are Christ's, and nothing can compare with the pleasure of serving and pleasing him.

For the rest, Mgr, I cannot forbear to open my heart to you regarding the rumours ceaselessly spread abroad about me, and to which, by God's grace, I have never given any legitimate foundation by my conduct. I do not mention this for your enlightenment, because I know that you have no doubts concerning the purity of my views, and are wholly just towards me, but so that you may on occasion, if you deem it appropriate to give me such proof of your goodness, say that I have always been what I am still on the matters of the moment.

I will then say, Mgr, that since I ceased to be of the world, I have never belonged to any party save that of Jesus Christ and his Church (for I confess that before my retreat I belonged only too much to that of his enemies, that is, the world, the flesh, and the devil). I have seen the disputes in the Church with real pain, and I have taken no other part in them than that of a man afflicted before God, groaning at the foot of his altar, as he watches the bosom and womb of his mother rent by her own children. I have always believed that I should submit to those whom God had given me as superiors and fathers, I mean the Pope and my bishop. I have done what they desired of me, and I simply signed the formulary concerning the Propositions of Jansenius, without restriction or reservation. I have exercised such restraint in all these disputes that I have not only refrained from talking about them, but I have even prevented any report of them reaching this community or anyone opening their mouth about the questions or the persons involved. The more I knew that people's minds were being drawn into the dispute and that the two parties were becoming more heated, the more I held aloof, for fear of getting into anything contrary to my profession or likely to disturb the calm of my solitude and interrupt the peace I had sought there, remaining however firmly and consistently resolved to embrace with perfect submission the orders of the Pope and the decisions of the Church, and it can indeed be said that while almost everyone was in a state of agitation, we have enjoyed profound peace and quiet.

As regards the substance of these matters, I have always held that it was not my business to become involved, that God did not ask of me that I should query the dogmas of the faith, but try to practise the truth it teaches, and that instead of arguing about the grace of Christ, I should think rather of attracting it to myself and those whom it had pleased him to entrust to my charge and direction, persevering in prayer, silence, humiliation and other like dispositions, and that without a manifest order from God I should not leave a situation so suitable and seemly to my state. However, if anyone wanted to know my opinions on these things, I have never had any private views and have always followed those of the Church.

As to my opinions on christian morality, I publicly profess to adhere solely to those taught by Christ in his gospel, and in the way that the holy fathers, his interpreters who have received his spirit and his mission, have explained them. It is there, at the true source, that I think Christians should draw the rules of their conduct, and I can neither approve nor understand how anyone should weaken holy truths in order to strengthen the inclinations of nature and favour its concupiscence. Jesus Christ declared that he did not come into the world to establish a false peace, but to bring the sword, that is to cut and separate us from it, to destroy the law of the flesh and establish the rule of the spirit.

I am quite convinced that one should avoid extreme opinions, and not take things to a point one cannot reach, but I am equally convinced that it is no less dangerous to enlarge the paths beyond the limits prescribed by Christ, to call evil good, to make lax concessions, to flatter sinners in their iniquities and put, as the prophet says, cushions under their elbows [Ezk 13:18] instead of covering their heads with sackcloth and ashes. By that I mean that one must never fail to tell them truths, make them recognise their obligations and the gravity of their wounds, and inspire in them the feelings of a deep and genuine conversion.

That, Mgr, is a statement of my thoughts and my conduct. I pray God that men will be content with it, for I should be most distressed to be an object of scandal or stumbling-block to anyone, but if I am not sufficiently fortunate for my wishes to be granted, God, who forbids me to have any aim or intention of pleasing men, and who teaches me that a Christian must not seek comfort or peace other than in the witness of his conscience, will preserve me in that which he has given me hitherto, and I hope that he will not allow any response in me regarding those who treat me so unfairly which would make me deserve to be deprived of it and abandoned to trouble and confusion.

What pains me most in all this is that Christians should incur heedlessly a certain loss when they attempt, without scruple and without cause, to cast suspicion on the faith and religion of a perfectly Catholic man, to discredit him personally and attribute to him principles and opinions he has never had.

Nothing is stranger than to see those who would not wish to touch on their neighbor's most trivial behaviour, quite easily attack his faith, and say that his belief is not sound, which is to accuse him of the greatest of all crimes, yet they must know that their zeal and their intention, whatever it may be, will not be justified at the moment when God shows false justice for what it is and punishes the malicious and calumniators as severely as blasphemers, murderers, and adulterers.

It is an established fact, Mgr, that one cannot in conscience publish evil reports of someone unless one knows with certainty that he is guilty and is obliged to declare it, and I should like to ask those who so easily give themselves the right and freedom to decide on the doctrine of a man living in obscurity, perfectly submissive, interfering in nothing, who has never said or written a word capable of awkward explanation, what necessity drives them to it, what certainty they can have about his principles and conduct, never perhaps having seen him and knowing nothing of him except what they have learned from vague and unreliable reports, and how they reconcile that with the precept of Christ forbidding them so strictly to pass judgement, and with such rigorous penalties.

Do they maintain that having aroused unjust suspicions and circulated deflamatory rumours against an innocent person, they will be absolved just for saying "I was wrongly informed; I was not thinking", and that God will dispense them from redressing by public satisfaction the wrong and injury they have done to him?

In short, Mgr, I should be ashamed to complain if it were a question of a less considerable and damaging charge, and if the saints did not teach me that a Christian should give witness that he is sensitive when anyone touches his faith and belief. Besides, I know that my profession requires me to look on myself as a broken vessel, fit only to be trampled underfoot and reduced to dust. In truth if men attack me from aspects in which I am not what they believe me to be, there are in me evils and iniquities almost without number known to no one, and about which no one says a word, so that I cannot believe that the obvious iniquities which come to me from the world are not secret and true judgements from God, nor fail to consider men in this respect as the ministers of his orders and executors of his vengeance.

This is the disposition in which I am and which I must preserve all the more as, with the end of my life drawing near and the gates of eternity before me, there is no more powerful motive for God to judge us with clemency and goodness than being judged by men without compassion or justice, so long as we remain in charity and peace, and pray him to grant mercy to those who refuse it to us.

Here, Mgr, is a long letter for a man who professes to live in silence. I went further than I intended, but I am sure that I could not have done so to anyone who took more interest than you in what concerns me, honoured me with more particular kindness, or bore with me more charitably than you, and then it is the last time I shall speak of such matters. The retreat in which I have resolved to end the rest of my life will be, God willing, so strict and rigorous that the rumours from the world will not penetrate our solitude, and will not reach us. There is not a moment to lose, and although at all times one must husband them, that is particularly the case when there are few left, when one is ready to go and give an account of them and is as convinced as I am that one will have to repent of all those which did not serve either Christ's glory or our own sanctification.

I pray God, Mgr, to heap on you every blessing and prosperity. I would not venture to wish you those of the world if I were not so hopeful that you are in a position to make holy use of them, and that they would help you become even better than you are. I am with unequalled respect and fidelity yours' etc.

Innumerable copies of this letter circulated, and it was printed at Grenoble in 1679, and thereafter very often, either separately or with others. The so-called Peace of the Church effected a ceasefire, rather than an armistice, and was to end in April 1679; but note that R. publicly declared his obedience to the hierarchy's ruling before the final assault on Jansenism had begun. R. is telling the full and plain truth in claiming to have signed the Formulary in a spirit of unquestioning obedience, and above all in asserting that no discussion of the Jansenist question was ever permitted at la T., despite the presence of many monks with Jansenist pasts. R's implicit condemnation of Molinist moral theology did not save him from attracting fire from both sides. He was certainly right thus to proclaim his obedience and neutrality in controversy, and it is remarkable how he continued to enjoy the friendship and respect of many Jansenists who could never have hoped after this to win him to their cause.

*781130a MARÉCHAL DE BELLEFONDS 30 November 1678
BN na 12959 f.79, orig.

'I received your honoured letter only three days ago, Mgr. I hope that the one I am sending you will be what you want. In it I express all my thoughts with the utmost sincerity; it is from the heart, and I confess that I am very glad that those who attribute to me views and opinions I do not have should know that I feel the injustice they do me, that I am convinced that they cannot do it with good conscience, but that I still profit by it and keep all the charity towards them that God bids me have. Fundamentally, Mgr, those who first spread those rumours have no other target than the life I lead, and so long as it remains strict and distinguishes me from the great number of people who walk in broader and easier ways, someone will always find some reason to impute to me whatever they like, and I will never satisfy men. The truth is that having done all I should to disabuse them when I had occasion to do so, and feeling no reproach from my conscience regarding those things of which they accuse me, their evil intentions will not trouble my peace, and will not make me take one step beyond what God asks of me. As long as the world lasts, being ready as I am to leave it, it will seem to me but a moment, and I count the judgements of men only for what God wants me to count them.

I am quite delighted, Mgr, with the way things have turned out on your return, but do not think that my joy is human; in all that I look at the dispositions of providence. I am convinced that it takes quite particular care of you, and that while giving to men what you should not refuse them, you will do nothing unworthy of the grace that God has given you and the life you led in your retreat. Remember whence his hand drew you, think often about it, so that you never lose the memory and his kindnesses live eternally in your heart.

The passage from scripture and the reflections made upon them are entirely christian. We shall not fail to put them in the guests' room, and we shall be careful to leave on them some indication of their provenance; it is a matter of too great edification that people should know that these are the thoughts and topics of someone of your quality and rank. It is true, Mgr, that no one could be more obliged than I to M. de Condom [Bossuet]; things have happened which it would take too long to relate, in which he has shown me kindness I did not deserve. I beg you to be kind enough yourself to let him know that I remain sincerely and perfectly grateful to him. You tell me nothing about your health, yet I learn that it is not very good. You should take care, and neglect no means of restoring it. It is time for me to realise, Mgr, that I am being a burden to you, and that you have something else to do than read letters as long as this. I hope you will forgive me the ease with which I ran on. Do me the grace of believing that it is the result of the confidence I have in your kindness, and that no one could add to the attachment and fidelity with which I am yours etc.

PS I forgot to tell you that the strongest evidence used against me is M. de Tréville's friendship; people will not accept that he can be one of my friends unless I agree with his view in everything. Yet we never talk of those questions with which people like to imagine I am preoccupied, and M. de Tréville is too wise and circumspect to talk to me of things in which he knows I do not wish to be involved.

As it may happen that you hear of the affair of the Bishop of Séez about which I have already had the honour of writing to you, I cannot refrain from telling you again that it is a real persecution on the part of those who stirred it up, and that if it should happen that he succumbed, he would henceforth be without any respect in his diocese and incapable of doing any good there. If you could see your way to rendering him any service in this, it is a matter worthy of your piety and your care; although I have the greatest regard for him, in this connexion I am looking rather at the good of his diocese than of his person. The poor man has been ill since you visited him with a bad quartain fever, but I hope it will come to nothing.'

This personal letter makes it clear, as the one intended for wider diffusion does not, that the latter was written at Bellefonds' request. [Tréville] was regarded by many as someone whose friendship implied Jansenist sympathies. The Bp of Séez and his problems are first discussed in 781006.

781208   DOM FRANÇOIS D'ORIVAL, LUXUEIL   8 December 1678
TB 1008

If he accepts the rigours of la T., prays a lot, asks his superiors for permission, R. will take him as sent by providence, whatever displeasure this may cause.

He was professed in 1665 in the Congregation of Saint-Vanne, but died stabilised at Cluny, so if he did come to la T. he did not stay.

*781217   BISHOP OF LUÇON [HENRI BARILLON]   17 December 1678
P f.767

'I am quite delighted, Mgr, that your business has been at last concluded to your satisfaction. I had hoped both from the rightness of your cause and the piety of the King that things would turn out happily and successfully, and I praise God that I was not mistaken. The people who support the Church's cause, and take up its protection in disputes, are so rare that we could not too earnestly pray God for their preservation. You are more obliged to them than anyone, and the evidence which you have just received of their friendship pressingly commits you not to fail in so essential a duty. As for me, Mgr, who am infinitely more concerned than I can say in anything that affects you, I will wholeheartedly join you in the gratitude which I am sure you feel, and in any thanksgiving you may offer to the Lord who inspires men and who, holding their hearts in his hands, creates in them whatever impressions he chooses. I do not know, Mgr, when it will please God that we shall have the pleasure of seeing you, but I find it hard to believe that your residence, strict as it is, and my attachment to my monastery which closes every door to me and does not allow me out, will enable me to hope for it. My health is still poor and my life is just a continual wasting away. I wish you all prosperity and pray God to bless your conduct and let you find in your solicitude fruits which already in this world reward your cares and labours. Keep your friendship for me always, I beg you, and believe that no one could be more affectionately and respectfully than I yours etc.

I will not fail to send you a map of our Thebaid.'

Barillon had been in Paris since July 1678 dealing, successfully, with the fate of two monasteries in the diocese (Jard and St-Michel-en-l'Herm) and a mission to Beaulieu, a strongly Protestant area.

79/1 RP ABBÉ [CHÂTILLON, CLAUDE LE MAÎTRE]   [1679]
Mug II/96; BN 19293 (extract with name)

R. is too unwell to go to Paris as requested. No question of allowing a religious to take waters at Bourbon, and R. had even refused to approve of his sister [Thérèse] doing so.

79/2 RP ABBÉ [SEPTFONS, EUSTACHE DE BEAUFORT]   [?1679]
TC II/133; Mug I/103

Wishes him well in Paris, approves his decision to stay firm in Reform. Neutrality impossible. Silence at la T. stricter than ever. R. would like to resign, but must do God's will.

79/3 RP TACONNET, SAINT-VICTOR   1679
TD C

He cannot break his commitment to retreat.

79/4 RP ABBÉ   [? January 1679]
TB 1029

Abbot of l'Etoile left two days ago, and thinks affairs of Reform going very badly and compromise with Cîteaux will be necessary. Proposes putting three names to Chapter, to choose one as Visitor for each province.

Abbot du Teillé of l'Etoile passed briefly at la T. at least twice at the end of 1678. Reference to the Chapter is probably to be explained by the fact that, though one was not held until 1683, restoration of peace (at Nijmegen in 1678) removed the excuse for further delay.

*790104   RP HENRI DE FOUCHIÈRES OSB, CONG.   4 January 1679
         DE ST-VANNE (SENT BY M. ARNAULD)
TD/C

   'Reverend Father, I have read with care the letter you did me the honour of writing to me, I have attentively considered it before God, and I confess that after considering your past feelings and present state, all I can say to you is that there is every reason to believe that God wants you to be henceforth in a less distracted and divided life than that in which you have been up till now, and that it is his spirit which inspires in you the desire to leave your original observance to embrace one in which, without being singular or conspicuous, you can spend the rest of your days in penitence, retreat, and silence. It is with those sentiments, Reverend Father, that I delay no longer in telling you that it will not depend on us if you do not execute what Our Lord is inspiring you to do, and that we shall receive you with joy and pleasure when divine providence gives you the means of coming to seek us, either with your fathers' consent or without, provided only that you have asked their permission. God knows that in this I have no wish to displease or wound them, and it is only for fear of opposing a holy vocation and preventing its effect that I address you so candidly. You doubtless know what are the practices of this monastery, the strictness observed here, and the profession one makes of living not only in mortification of the senses, but especially of the spirit, I mean in perfect renunciation of self, one's own judgement and all one's thoughts, abandoning oneself entirely to the hands of those whom it has pleased Christ to put in charge. I pray him, Reverend Father, to fortify your heart, and help you find the necessary ways and facilities for fulfilling his will. I shall count myself fortunate to be able to contribute to it and show you subsequently by my care and service that I am in all sincerity yours' etc.

   He had been professed at Luxueil in 1651, and died at Saint-Vincent de Besançon in 1702. Cf 790110 to Arnauld. He proved unsuitable, and R's Jansenist critics were most annoyed.

790104a   RP PASQUIER QUESNEL, CONG. ORAT.   4 January 1679
U 1168 orig.; Tans 38

Agrees to send Association to Quesnel. The former Oratorian, marquis de Nocey, is 'alone in the depths of a great forest'.

   Nocey had just begun his hermit's life, first in the forest near Perseigne, then at la T., where he died in 1692.

790110   ANTOINE ARNAULD   10 January 1679
U 913

R. has already told monk of St-Vanne [Fouchières] to come when he likes, but asks Arnauld to explain that R. does not agree with all his views and he might do better to stay where he is if he lacks confidence in R.

790115 MME DE GUISE   15 January 1679
Maupeou, *Vie* I/414; Dubois I/605

Justifies his letter to Bellefonds.

790119 RP PASQUIER QUESNEL, CONG.ORAT.   19 January 1679
U 1168 orig.; Tans 39

Sends Association, but asks Quesnel to keep it quiet, because 'our fathers are very chary of granting such things for fear of becoming overburdened with duties and obligations'.

790121 MME DE GUISE   21 January 1679
Maupeon, *Vie* I/420; Dubois I606

Reaffirms position of letter to Bellefonds.

790124 DUC DE LUYNES   24 January 1679
TB 1039

Discusses directors.

*790124a MARÉCHAL DE BELLEFONDS   24 January 1679
BN na 12959 f.,83, autograph.

'I had already heard, Mgr, that God had given his blessing to the letter I had the honour of writing to you, but at the same time I learned that it had not pleased everybody. That did not surprise me, for I did not expect it to please those who were prejudiced or partisan. Most men want supporters of their views, and cannot bear anyone who has reservations or criticisms when it concerns their passions and opinions. Those who do not want to be disabused must be left with their beliefs, and for my part I am fully resolved to remain in peace and not to trouble myself with the judgements and fantasies of the world. If you spend Lent here, Mgr, as you allow us to hope, I shall tell you particular things on that subject that I cannot write. You have good cause to thank Our Lord for the protection he has given you. One must agree that without the aid of a hand as mighty as his one could not keep one's footing in places which are so dangerous and slippery. However faithful to him you have been able to be, you will doubtless find much value in the short time that you are going to give to a stricter and more withdrawn life, for anyone who spends his life in outward functions, even the most holy, finds it hard not to collect dust and stains in affairs and contacts which are not holy. I pray Our Lord Jesus Christ to renew his blessings and grace upon you in this new year, and add many others. I am with deep respect yours etc.

PS Since the person whose hand I usually use is ill I have been obliged to write to you with my own, and as I do so very badly and with difficulty, I fear you will find it hard to read my letter and I beg your pardon.'

The letter referred to is 781130. Dom Rigobert was R's usual secretary at this time. R's hand is barely legible, as he admits.

790200   RM ABBESSE, ESSAI   [? January/February 1679]
         [FRANÇOISE TROTTI DE LA CHÉTARDIE]
TB 1052 (undated); TC II/318 (end) and II/328 (beginning) with separate dates of 14 and 21 January 1683

She is giving up her silver crozier.

She had succeeded her aunt in 1676, until 1687. The date 1683 is most unlikely for such a change from silver (to wood).

790201   MONSIEUR [? D'ALBON]   1 February 1679
CF 344, f.79 aut.; A 2106, f.8 vo. (dated wrongly 1649); Gonod 41

Now that God has miraculously put an end to his youthful disorders, M. must spend the rest of his life making amends.

*790202   RM ABBESSE, LEYME [ANNE DE LA VIEUVILLE]   2 February 1679
TB 1017

'I am extremely sorry to hear of the state you have been in, RM, and if we had known of it earlier we should not have failed to double our prayers asking God for your preservation, but I can see that he has anticipated them by his mercy and that there is cause to change them into thanksgiving. Although you tell me that your health is better, I shall not stop worrying about it until I am assured of your complete recovery. God's secrets are impenetrable, he allows countless persons who contribute nothing to his glory or the edification of the Church to enjoy the health of an athlete, while those whose intentions are good and who sanctify others by sanctifying themselves through fervent piety and strict life, he allows to be weighed down with infirmities and ills and consequently rendered unable to do what they so ardently desire. We must bless Our Lord for everything; he knows better than we do what is to our advantage, and what should console us is that he is in our innermost souls, he knows what goes on there, and in judging us will look at our hearts rather than our hands. I hope, and I may say that I do not doubt, that he will be content with the zeal and fidelity of yours.

For the rest, RM, I see that you would like everyone to think of me as you do, but apart from the fact that that would not be right, it is useful to me that people should speak ill of me, and it would be a very bad sign if, being as much of a miserable sinner as I am, I enjoyed the sort of approval you wish for me. God is too good to allow that to happen; he knows that blame is much better for me than praise. I am yours' etc.

790203   COMTESSE D'ALBON   3 February 1679
CF 344,f.81 aut.; A 2106, f.7 (wrongly dated 1648); Gonod 42

Would like to hear from her own mouth that she wants to serve Christ and make up for all the years given to the world.

From the date and tone of this letter it seems quite likely that the one written two days before was to the comte d'Albon; Favier's collection of autograph letters is almost exclusively concerned with himself and the Albons.

*790300   RM ABBESSE, LEYME [ANNE DE LA VIEUVILLE]   [March] 1679
TB 1026 (possibly dated May, which is wrong)

'I am very glad, RM, to see that you do not doubt the esteem and consideration I have for you; it is God who has given me such feelings, and nothing in the world can alter them, although they are quite useless to you and I can do nothing for your service. I find it very hard to decide what I should say to you on the matter on which you ask my opinion, and on your idea of appealing to Rome in case you should be subjected to such treatment as I have told you was being planned for you; for I know that affairs there go on for ever, and only finish after extreme delays. You would have to present a supplication, have someone to advise on the basis of your rights and the injustice done to you. Such dispositions can only be taken with the greatest trouble, and such a commitment has inevitably considerable consequences, and unless there is someone to take care of it and advance your arguments diligently, it is unlikely that they will be heeded or have the success for which you hope. You can easily see, RM, whether you have anyone through whom you can take such measures at Rome, for otherwise I do not think there is any reason to think of it. I will not advise you to do anything contrary to your duty, but there are occasions and times when the strictness and rigour of discipline have to be relaxed if one cannot see that it is observed in its integrity by those in one's charge. As there are points on which one must stand firm, there are also others which demand some adjustment; that depends on the nature of the thing, the quality of the persons, and the circumstances. It is very hard for a man who only sees the difficulties from far away to tell you anything specific which is precise and accurate enough for you to take note. It is easy enough to give general rules and principles, the difficulty lies in applying them. I am even virtually certain that what I am saying to you now does not give you either the enlightenment or opening to act. I pray God to enlighten you, and to show you himself what you should do to follow his will and stay within the terms of your duty, from which you should on no account deviate. The chief of our arguments, and indeed the only one we must heed, is that of conscience, and nothing shoud prevail over what we cannot grant without offending it. That is your rule, to which you must be inviolably attached; the main thing is not to go wrong in discerning it. I shall take the keenest interest all my life in what concerns you, I beg you not to doubt that, and to believe me in perfect sincerity yours etc.

PS I forgot to tell you that the Abbot of [Septfons] has been to see me, and we met as though we retained no memory of things past. I have a rule which I follow as much as possible, which is that Christians, especially religious, must on many occasions fail to remember. He spoke to me of you most moderately, and did not seem to feel about you as you think.'

790306   RM LOUISE-HENRIETTE D'ALBON   6 March 1679
A 2106, f.87 vo.

'What sanctifies men is not so much carrying the Cross as loving it', and she should not complain of her easy road.

790400   RP   [? April] 1679
TB 1023

The ecclesiastic recommended two months ago has received the habit, and is luckier than another, found unsuitable for la T., who was killed by a falling tree on his way to the Grande Chartreuse.

*790511   RM ABBESSE, LEYME [ANNE DE LA VIEUVILLE]   11 May 1679
TB 1059

'It is true that an indisposition which lasted almost throughout Lent, as well as that of the monk whose hand I use to write to you, has prevented me from giving you news, and you would be doing me a great injustice if you inferred from my silence anything inconsistent with my esteem for you and the sincerity with which I honour you. I do not think that you would wish to judge it from outward signs which do not, as you know, affect at all the essential feelings of the heart. I beg you to believe that mine are inviolable, and that neither time nor the cessation of contact could destroy or weaken them.

I am very glad that you have resumed abstinence, for that shows that your health is restored, and the state in which it seemed to be from your last letter made me fear that your infirmities were becoming persistent and that you would have difficulty throwing them off; I praise God that things are better than I thought.

For the rest, RM, I must tell you that I have learned that one of your nuns has written to M. l'abbé [?] to complain about your person and conduct; she claims that for very small faults you discipline her harshly, that you put her in prison, and for trifles deprive her of participation in the sacraments. I am sure that she is not telling the truth, and that you have too much wisdom and moderation to treat her like that however she is still believed and M. [?] feels himself obliged to rescue her from the oppression in which she claims to be. Among many things which he proposes to do to that end, he intends to deprive you of your jurisdiction and authority over your nuns. It would be most vexing if he tried such extreme measures, and for my part I would advise you, as it seems most unlikely that you will raise your religious to a state higher than that in which they have long been, however much you correct them, or that you will do them much good by such ways, to be less strict and severe in punishing their faults, to the extent that your conscience and duty allow you. There are some faults which one cannot help punishing, others to which one can turn a blind eye, when punishments, instead of making people better only embitter them and make them worse than they are. It is a great principle that evils must be endured when they cannot be cured by punishing. I take too much interest in all that concerns you not to say what I think on such an occasion as this. Do me the honour of believing that I keep for you personally all due respect and consideration, and I beg you never to allow yourself to entertain any other idea on that than what you should have. I will add nothing to this note, except that I am with perfect sincerity yours' etc.

R's opening reference to his indisposition during Lent shows that his previous letter to Leyme must be dated March rather than May. M. l'abbé is probably Beaufort.

790518   [JEAN FAVIER]   18 May 1679
A 2106,f.87

Excuses long silence, but has a fever every night.

790527   RP ABBÉ, ORVAL [CHARLES DE BENZERADT]   27 May 1679
TB 1062; Mug II/69

Reform at Orval progressing, with fewer unreformed (*anciens*) and many true monks. R. thinks conferences at Orval too frequent, not enough separation of religious from outside world, and regulations concerning the sick are inadequate.

790526 TRP ABBÉ, CLAIRVAUX [PIERRE BOUCHU]   26 May 1679
TB 1068; Mug II/50

Strongly disapproves of his sister, Thérèse, taking waters at Vichy. Nuns 'should look on their cells as their graves . . . and not love health more than salvation'.

Cf 79/1

790600 RM ABBESSE, GIF [ANNE DE MONGLAT]   June 1679
TB 1082
Encouragement in her weariness.

790607 MONSIEUR LE NAIN, MAÎTRE DES REQUÊTES.   7 June 1679
TB 1073; Mug II/57
Death of RP de Saint-Pé, M.'s former director, a holy man of continuing influence.

R. had been on close terms with this Oratorian, who had once directed the family of Pascal at Rouen.

790610 RP PRIEUR, PERSEIGNE [ROBIN COUTURIER]   10 June 1679
TB 1076
Abbot [commendatory] of Perseigne ill; dom Claude [Brachet de la Miltière] would be welcome for a few days. No money should be demanded of novices, and one who shows 'levity and little piety' should be excluded. 'As regards silence, we made our brothers love it before fixing it as strictly as it is now.'

*790710 RP ABBÉ, CHÂTILLON [CLAUDE LE MAÎTRE]   10 July 1679
TB 1086

'My very dear Father, I have not received the letter which you say you wrote, and can assure you that if it had reached me, I should not have failed to answer. I am delighted that you saw the good Father F; it was doubtless a pleasure, for he is one of the best of men, and devoted to his friends. I am sure he includes me in that number, and that I do not have the last place there. I still hesitate to accept him among us, anxious as he is to come, for his age and our austerity frighten me, and I would not wish for anything in the world that he should embark on a course which he could not sustain.

I am very pleased at what you tell me about the abbey of Orval, but would have liked you to go into rather more detail; for, to speak frankly, it seems to me that there is so little retreat and so little of that strict silence in which they should live, and I see so little attention paid to that, that I find it hard to believe that those good monks will go very far or hold out for very long. May God grant them blessing and increase. I wish he would give you the means of beginning what you have wanted for so long, but there are in fact fewer men than ever capable of such a strict and penitential life. Enough come forward, but almost none persevere. Two of our brothers are preparing for death, and I do not think they have another two weeks to live. They are Brother Palémon and dom Bernard, two religious who render great service and edification to the monastery, and in losing them I am losing what amounts to twelve men. Yet what consoles me is that they are both awaiting death with gay and tranquil faces, and consider themselves as coming to the end of their desires and their career. How fortunate they are, my dear father, and would to God I were in the state and spirit in which they are. It comes no doubt from their great fidelity and life of retreat. That is what I lack, for however much I try to withdraw into retreat, I never do it as much as I should, and as for fidelity, you know how hard it is to find it anywhere but in complete separation.

Farewell, my very dear father, I beg you to pray God for me with all possible diligence, as for one who has extreme need for prayer and is more than anyone yours' etc.

As a neighbour of Orval, the abbot saw it more often than most; R. was always sceptical about their reform. Palémon des Essarts died on 11 August; Bernard Vingtain, a former Celestine, on 16 July, having been professed in 1673 and 1676 respectively.

790722   BISHOP OF CHÂLONS [FÉLIX VIALART DE HERSE]   22 July 1679
TB 1104

Bp gravely ill.

*790723   BISHOP OF LUÇON [HENRI BARILLON]   23 July 1679
P f. 768

'I was quite delighted, Mgr, to hear your news and talk to Monsieur Louis of the things which concern you, since I take more interst in them than I can say. I would have a lot to say to you if he were going to give you my letter, but as that is not so and he will send it through the usual channels, I am obliged to be more reserved. It is certain that if the people you mention had been more restrained and had given themselves up less than they did to their desire to see each other and be together, they would have avoided the storm that fell upon them, but events have [brought out?] their obstinacy, they want to go their own way, and so it is not surprising if they bring down on themselves troubles and strife. I will impatiently await, Mgr, the time of the rendezvous you have given your brother in this desert, for I can have no greater joy than to see here the two persons in the world whom I most affectionately honour and who hold first place in my heart. I beg you to keep for me the place you have given me in yours, and to be sure that nothing can equal the respect and fidelity with which I am, Mgr, yours etc.

PS I say nothing of the care with which we commend you to God; that is a duty which I do not fail in.'

M. Louis was a canon of Luçon and a trusted colleague of the Bp. The people who want to be together were Protestants pressing for the right of assembly to worship.

790729   [JEAN FAVIER]   29 July 1679
TB 1106; A 2106,f.87 vo.

R's health still poor, but he can follow community exercises.

790803   RP ABBÉ, ORVAL, [CHARLES DE BENZERADT]   3 August 1679
TB 1108

R. has received Orval's constitutions. Discusses the sick, separation from outside world, conferences, different practices of French and Germans (only two French at Orval). Abbot not obliged to attend as deputy to States (Imperial Diet).

Orval, in Luxembourg, was, except during a period of French occupation, in Imperial territory, and near the linguistic frontier, but the language of the monks seems to have been French.

790810   MADEMOISELLE DE [? LUYNES]   10 August 1679
TB 1112

She and 'duc' are pleased with R.P.M[?onchy]

Cf 790124

*790817   RP ABBÉ, CHÂTILLON [CLAUDE LE MAÎTRE]   17 August 1679
TB 1119

'My very dear father, your letter confirms what I had thought about the reform at Orval; it is a lot for a beginning, but if they do not take care to tighten things up, to make their silence and solitude stricter, and maintain the brothers in great humility, the work will not go far and will be anything but what it should be. When you have seen it at closer hand and spent some time there, I am sure that your judgement will be the same as mine, and you will recognize many things there which have nothing to do with the idea we have of the perfection of our calling. I do not say that in order to disparage, for I am struck with admiration at the change in the monastery and the superior's courage in undertaking it despite all the difficulty and hostility he has encountered. I pray God to strengthen him, and give him all the understanding and enlightenment he needs.

As for you, my very dear father, do not lose heart; God's good time comes when one least expects it, and I cannot believe that he will not grant anything to your intentions of seeing that he is served in the place which he has entrusted to you. But you are barely in a position to accept people before you are worrying about not having any.

Tamié does not have as many religious as you think; the number has not increased, according to the latest letters I have had from there. It is true that Septfons has considerably increased, and that their observance has become strict and regular, but he has been working at it for twelve years. Besides I can tell you that the abbot has been to see me twice since Lent, and the memory of things past no longer remains in my heart. I saw him as I used to before any of those things had happened which, as you know, gave me cause to complain about him. Charity alone must be eternal; it begins in this world and goes on into the next, uninterruptedly maintained. Everything else has to end, and those who have had some estrangement must be impatient to resume relations. I think you feel as I do; in truth it is very difficult to be estranged from men, whatever reason one may have, without being estranged from God, and as I see it, nothing is more impossible than to keep the necessary reserve and moderation towards those who have treated us unjustly and done us harm, so that one remains within the rules prescribed by charity. Of all the precepts given to men by Christ, there is surely none which is harder to observe than that to love one's enemies. Yet anyone who does not keep it, and is content merely to love his friends, has kept only half the law, and God will look on him with no less indignation than if he had broken it entirely.

I am not surprised at your idea of retiring, for I should certainly have the same idea, and even more strongly, if I were in your place; however I do not think you will find anyone to advise you to follow it out, until God enlightens you and opens doors which at present you find closed, not only because of the awkwardness of an election, but also because of the danger there is in leaving the place in which God put you. So it is most likely that your desires will always remain as they are, I mean dry and sterile, and will produce nothing of what you believe would console you. I hope you will find consolation in some other way, and even if it is not in the establishment of that strict observance for which you have so long been yearning, it will at least be in your submission to God's orders and in your fidelity in conforming yourself to his will. There alone you will find serenity, and you will be deceiving yourself every time you seek it anywhere else. I will add nothing more to this note, my dear father, except to pray Christ to heap blessings on you. Pray him for me, I beg you; I am not well, the end of my life is near, and I do not know what I should do to make myself worthy of a happy death. Your prayers will help secure one for me from God, so long as you are careful to offer them to him out of the kindness of your heart. Farewell my dear Father. I am yours' etc.

Tamié had begun reform little more than a year before, and only two of the original monks, together with the four sent from la Trappe, the abbot and three novices constituted the community. The reconciliation with Beaufort is confirmed by letters to others and was clearly genuine, after all the bitterness engendered in 1676. The main difficulty at Châtillon came from the extensive damage to buildings and revenue caused by war; the monks seem to have been quite a good community in themselves.

*790817a   RM ABBESSE, LEYME [ANNE DE LA VIEUVILLE]   17 August 1679
TB 1117

'I have no answer to the facts you adduce in your last letter, but I wish that the conduct of the Abbot of S[eptfons] towards you were such that you not only had no cause for complaint, but even were enabled to lose all memory of things past. Your intentions for good and for the regularity of your monastery are, in my view, so right and reasonable that I wish that there was no one who did not approve them and do you justice; but usually things do not happen like that, as God, to try us and humiliate us, allows our best plans to be challenged and we meet more opposition from men when we have him most before our eyes and act most for his glory. In such a case the witness of our conscience must be our comfort and repose, and I may say that if we stand firm in that feeling we endure the most hostile events in great peace of mind and our constancy is never shaken. I am sure, RM, that that is your situation, and I have not contributed to it as much as you think and are kind enough to tell me; all I have told you are mere commonplaces, which you would have encountered just as well through your own reflections as through me. Besides I should count myself most fortunate if I had been able to do you any good, and indeed I take such interest, as I have often declared, in all that concerns you, that I shall never lose a single opportunity of showing it. Do me the honour not to doubt that and to believe that it is with perfect sincerity and esteem that I am yours' etc.

790822   RP PASQUIER QUESNEL, CONG.ORAT.   22 August 1679
U 1168,orig.; Tans 40

'As I have imposed perpetual silence on myself on the subject on which you wrote, I will not answer your letter, except to say that I am much obliged to you that our differing opinions do not prevent me from retaining some part in your friendship.'

The subject in question is Jansenism, and R's signature of the formulary, discussed at length in 781130 letter to Bellefonds. Disagreement over the latter in fact brought cordial relations between R. and Quesnel to an effective end.

790825 DUCHESSE DE LUYNES   25 August 1679
TB 1126; Mug II/108

Condolences on death of daughter.

790800   RP [? DE MONCHY]   [? August 1679]
Mug 11/109

On death of the duchesse de Luynes' daughter.

790903   MONSIEUR   3 September 1679
TB 1129

'At last poor Cardinal de Retz has finished his course; he died with much piety and resignation to God's will, showing his obligation to God for not taking him amid his disorders, but waiting until he came to repent.' Had paid off 40,000 livres just before his death.

Retz died on 24 August 1679.

790904 RP PRIEUR, PERSEIGNE [ROBIN COUTURIER]   4 September 1679
Autographes Troussures, p. 538

Never wanted to accept Benedictine, fearing that he was just restless. R. has no time to check prior's translation. Condemns two bad religious who should not be allowed out. Dom Julien presses R. to let him go back.

Julien Kerviche was professed at Perseigne in 1663; his elder brother was sub-prior there.

790906 RP PRIEUR PERSEIGNE [ROBIN COUTURIER]   6 September 1679
Arch. de l'Orne, Alençon, orig.

If everyone did what they could, the Reform would be assured, but R. does not have enough authority to persuade those who disagree. Dom Paul is bringing back the memoranda. R. wrote only day before.

Dom Paul seems to be the Barbeaux monk referred to as trying his vocation at la T. in February 1678.

790909 MONSIEUR DE NOCEY   9 September 1679
TB 1134; TC II/8

Would like to visit him in his solitude, but cannot leave la T. Disapproves idea of another ecclesiastic coming to share the hermitage. Six outings a year too many, three or four about right.

This letter suggests that Nocey had not yet moved from Perseigne to the woods near la T. He was briefly accompanied by Jacques de Lanchal, who subsequently became professed at Perseigne.

790919 RP ABBÉ, LA COLOMBE [PIERRE DE LA SALLE]   19 September 1679
TB 1137

Plurality of benefices wrong even for a very religious man.

791109 BISHOP OF GRENOBLE [ETIENNE LE CAMUS]   9 November 1679
TB 1145

Monchy has been two weeks at la T. and constantly talked of way Bp is being harried at Grenoble. R. so ill during visit that he received viaticum and unction. Worried about religious sent to Tamié.

The Jesuits, and others, were doing all they could to make life difficult for their ascetic bp.

791203   MARQUIS DE POMPONNE   3 December 1679
TB 1153; Gonod 209
He must learn to endure privation of worldly goods.
Pomponne had just lost his ministerial post owing to Louvois' influence.

791203a   JEAN FAVIER   3 December 1679
TB 1150; A 2106,f. 89
R. was so ill in September that after a week he received Extreme Unction and made his farewells. Denies allowing Statutes of la T. to be printed.
The first known edition of the Constitutions de la T. appeared in 1671, and was constantly reedited. R. was eventually obliged to issue an authorised version of what he called Règlements in 1690.

791205   RP PRIEUR, PERSEIGNE [ROBIN COUTURIER]   5 December 1679
Autographes Troussures, p. 540
Prior was kind to visit la T. when R. was ill, and it was a pity R. was too ill to see him. Sorry for Heisterbach monk ordered to find a house of Common Observance. Edifying death of dom Rigobert.
R. was first in contact with monks from Heisterbach in 1672, and this may be one of them. Rigobert Lévêque, R's secretary, died on 14 November.

791213   RP PRIEUR, PERSEIGNE [ROBIN COUTURIER]   13 December 1679
Autographes Troussures, p. 541
R's health is better and he looks forward to seeing prior.

791220   DUC DE MAZARIN   20 December 1679
TB 1154
Christian death of M. d'Albon [R's brother-in-law and friend of Mazarin].

791220a   COMTESSE D'ALBON   20 December 1679
TB 1155; A 2106, f. 158 vo. (wrongly dated 7 December 1688)
Condolences on husband's death.

791228   RELIGIEUSE   28 December 1679
A 2106, f. 90
Silence will never affect his friendship for her. She is fortunate in being forgotten by men and devoted to God.

80/1 CAPUCHIN [?1680]
Mug II/68

Cannot receive him without a brief from Rome.

Possibly Jean de Béthune, see 800124.

80/2 RP [CHAMPAGNE] [?1680]
Mug 11/102

'We have cause to thank God for his mercies when evil is so widespread.' Reference to fr René.

The only René known to have been in contact with R. was René Pasquier, the first monk professed at la T. after the reform in 1662, and then translated to Champagne, where François Gobin, professed at la T. in 1663, soon followed him. R. wrote to Champagne on 31 December 1680, which suggests very tentatively a date and address for this letter.

80/3 MONSIEUR L'ABBÉ [PERSEIGNE, PHILIPPE GUESTRE DE PRÉVAL] [1680]
TB 1159

Unlikely that God calls him to Barbeaux or Prières; Barbéry is in a poor state. At Prières they live well, with plenty of fish and entertain local dignitaries. He should become a regular and reform Perseigne.

The commendatory abbot of Perseigne since 1673 was Préval (1652–1708), a canon of Le Mans. Barbeaux was in commend, and Barbéry (diocese of Bayeux) had reverted to commend in 1677 (and was not so badly off), but the reference to Prières is odd, as it was always regular. Préval did not become a regular, but did a lot of good for Perseigne.

80/4 CARDINAL 1680
TB 1166, Latin

Congratulations on promotion.

80/5 R.P. SIMON GOURDAN 1680
TB 1170

Gourdan plans to visit to la T. soon and would like to stay.

80/6 MONSIEUR 1680
TB 1181

He will be most welcome.

80/7 MONSIEUR DAURAT, 1680
CONSEILLER DE LA GRANDE CHAMBRE
TB 1183

He has lost his wife and should prepare for his own death and give up his post.

80/8 TRP DE L'ORDRE [PRIOR OR ABBOT] 1680
TB 1190

He must give up his lawsuit against a gentleman; he is setting a bad example.

80/9 RP ALBERT, GUILLEMIN, LIÈGE 1680
TB 1193

He left la T. in a hurry, but R. is willing to let him try again.

The Guillemins (or Williamites) were founded in Italy in the twelfth century, but had mostly become affiliated to Benedictines by R's time. They died out in the eighteenth century, but the main rail station in Liège perpetuates the name Guillemins.

80/10 RP DE MONCHY, CONG.ORAT. 1680
TD C

Compliments.

80/11 DOM JEAN-FRANÇOIS CORNUTY, TAMIÉ [?1680]
Ms Chronique de Tamié; Burnier, *Hist. de Tamié*, 7

He must be patient and stay where he is [he wanted to come back to la T.]

800100 COMTESSE DE LA BARGE January 1680
TB 1203

Recommends Favier, who is nearby [at Thiers]. She needs a rule of life, and is on bad terms with her mother. Glad to know that she intends to work for her salvation and serve God better than hitherto.

The recent death of M. d'Albon no doubt accounted for renewed family tensions, but the Albons had never been a happy family.

800100a MONSIEUR [DU SUEL] January 1680
TB 1216

Will now only admit religious of other orders after careful inspection; they are more trouble than they are worth. Will see the religious mentioned if he comes.

This may be connected with the application in 800124 of the Capuchin from Béthune, in the diocese of Arras.

800100b RM ABBESSE [January] 1680
TB 1233

Encouragement.

800100c RP [? ALAIN MORONY], TAMIÉ January 1680
Carp,p. 454

R. is greatly distressed at bad reports of the way the monks he sent have alienated people by excessive fasting and abstinence.

On arrival Alain had been appointed prior, so that it was presumably to him that R. ad dressed complaints.

*800103 MARÉCHAL DE BELLEFONDS. 3 January 1680
BN na 12959 f.86,orig.; TB 1206

'I am too keenly interested, Mgr, in all that concerns you to fail to tell you so at the present juncture, and to testify that we shall ask God to look at you always with his accustomed goodness, and not to allow the engagements which you may contract to harm those you have to his service. As you know, Mgr, that here on earth no situation is assured and the human heart is in itself full of irregularity and inconstancy, I do not doubt that you watch yourself most diligently and vigilantly; indeed there is nothing which more invites God to stretch out his hand and concern himself with our conduct than the care we take to keep and strengthen ourselves in his ways. You found him in retreat, you appreciated him there, and this feeling must not now elude you or become dissipated in the world. God wishes us to keep a proper balance between him and men; he does not want to lose anything, and never tolerates us giving them anything which belongs to him alone. However, it is not impossible to render to him what we owe him and at the same time to acquit ourselves of whatever legitimate obligations we may have towards them, but for that one must consider him as our end in all things, turn everything towards him and make serve his glory any wealth and honours, prosperity and advantage that may accrue to us. I pray God, Mgr, not only that this will be a year of happiness for you, but that he will add many others, and not tire of pouring his grace and blessings on your person and your house. I am with every fidelity and respect yours etc.

PS Herewith, Mgr, a letter from the Bishop of Séez. I can assure you that no one could be more alive to all your interests than he.'

800106 RM LOUISE-HENRIETTE D'ALBON 6 January 1680
A 2106,f.90; TC II/245

Loss of her father; she must not allow her attachment for a world she has left to be too strong.

800108   NICOLAS PINETTE   8 January 1680
TB B

New Years greetings, also to the superior [of the *Institution de l'Oratoire*], RP Brézeau and the whole community.

*800113   RP ABBÉ, [CHÂTILLON, CLAUDE LE MAÎTRE]   13 January 1680
TB 1213

'My very dear Father, I am extremely sorry that your house has not been filled with good persons as quickly as you would like; I should not dare say to you that they are rare, because that causes you distress, but it is still true: piety is cold, few people are touched by true zeal for giving themselves to God, and the sort of conversions needed for embracing the life which you wish to be led in your monastery are not common. Do not lose heart on that account, never give up hope; God opens up his treasures when he pleases, and when one least expects it. I know what you think of me when I speak to you like that. I am really sorry for you, and as I share your desires I also share your sorrows deeply, and if I could put an end to them, it would give me immense joy.

Those who told you that my health was better were not mistaken, but it is still not restored, either because this is not the right season for it, or because God wishes me to remain unwell; his will be done in life as in death. The least we can do, who no longer belong to the world, is to hold ourselves in his hand and submit with perfect resignation to all his orders.

Dom Rigobert has gone to wait for us. The ways he walked in were very hard and painful, and one has scarcely seen greater pain, greater ills, and at the same time greater patience. Whatever good opinion you may have of God's mercy to him, do not fail to pray for him; one thing I can tell you is that God supported him up to the last moment of his life, which he ended full of peace and constancy.

The former abbot is as usual; he goes to matins every night without fail, and works twice every day like the rest of our brothers. I think that he will enjoy in this life already the gift of immortality. The good man is ashamed to live so long, and is full of envy for those who die before him. I think God is making him live in spite of himself as a punishment for his sins. He is certainly an example of extraordinary edification, and I cannot think of a greater in past ages.

Dom Arsène whom you saw quite twisted is walking as upright as though he were only thirty; it seems a sort of miracle. I am your' etc.

Rigobert Lévêsque, originally professed at Clairvaux, had been professed a second time at la Trappe in 1670 (he actually came to la Trappe four years before he changed stability). He had died on 14 November 1679, aged 46, after seven years sickness from 'rheumatism and excessive cold'. Jacques Minguet had been Abbot of Châtillon from 1656–69, but resigned and came to la Trappe as an ordinary monk in 1674, aged 77. He lived until 1681. Arsène Cordon, professed in 1672, aged 53, lived until 1685.

800118   RP. D'UN AUTRE ORDRE   18 January 1680
TB 1215

Thinks he can accept him, despite change of habit and observance. RP should come and see.

800120   RP ABBÉ, L'ETOILE [BERNARD DU TEILLÉ]   20 January 1680
TB 1225

Affairs of Reform going badly. Abbot did well to give up charge of Proviseur [of *Collège des Bernardins*].

As the one place where members of both observances lived together, the college was always an awkward assignment; the abbot was now visitor.

800122   RM THÉRÈSE [BOUTHILLIER]   22 January 1680
TB 1221

Mme de Tourouvre more ill than her mother but preparing for a christian death.

She died in 1710, her mother in 1690.

800122   FR BENOÎT CASTELLAIN, VAUCELLES   22 January 1680
TB 1226

He will be welcome. [Vaucelles was a house of the Common Observance in the diocese of Cambrai].

800124   RP JEAN DE BÉTHUNE, OSFC   24 January 1680
TB 1223

He would need a brief from Rome to join la T. and his superiors would never admit that life there was stricter. Admitting him would stir up trouble, and R. regrets that he cannot do so.

Cf. 80/1 and 800100a.

*800127   HENRI DUHAMEL   27 January 1680
TB/1239

'Monsieur, I knew nothing about your illness apart from what you tell me. God brought you through it, and you have not yet discharged the service you owe him. Faithful workers like you are met with so rarely that we must urgently pray God, once he has given such men to his Church, to preserve them for a long time. Apart from that general reason for wishing you a long life, you can be in no doubt that I also have particular ones, knowing, as I am sure you do, how much I honour you.

You did well to put all your affairs in order, and yourself in such a state as to be always ready to say to God *Loquere Domine quia audit servus tuus* [1K 3:9]. Most men, even those who profess piety and a regular life, leave this world in disorder and make their move in disarray because they did not see to it in good time.

I am not surprised that you were keenly touched by the death of poor Cardinal de Retz; it is really deplorable that with all the great plans he had for retreat, he did so little of what you and I maintained he should do. It is more than fourteen years since he opened his heart to me on the subject, and I am certain that he was not play-acting and was speaking sincerely. He had inestimable qualities for living in the world, and if he had completely turned towards God, as he wanted, he would have done great things. Yet I cannot believe that God has not had mercy on him, and I cannot accept that a man I loved and honoured with the utmost affection should be eternally wretched. He was to have come to see me four days before he fell ill, to let me know exactly how he stood, and take a final and decisive resolve with me, but God did not permit it.

I have carefully considered what you tell me about your plan for establishing a successor, and all my reflections show me no reason why you should not, if you find a worthy candidate to whom you can entrust the conduct of the souls with which you are charged. You are advanced in years, my very dear Monsieur, your health is uncertain, your occupation is very tiring, all the signs are that you have not got much further to go, and what is quite certain is that after your death *invadent gregem tuum lupi rapaces* [cf. Ac 20:29]; you are too clearsighted to doubt it. So why not forestall so great a disruption and provide for the salvation of those whom you love with the tenderness and affection of a father, by giving them in your lifetime a pastor who will do for them what you do and will, like you, be solely concerned with looking after them? If it was a desire for the quiet life, shedding your load so that you could end up in idleness and repose, and if eternity seemed further off for you than it is, then I should tell you that you must remain active and at work, but after weighing all your circumstances, I cannot agree with the arguments of those who are trying to dissuade you from your plan.

As regards the choice of persons, I can say nothing, except that if you do not find one capable of answering for you at God's judgement, it is better to die crushed beneath the load than to shed it, and I am sure that you are fully convinced of that, because God will not ask you to account for the consequences of your death and for any disorder that comes upon the house once he has removed its governance from you, and when you have done what depended on you while it was in your hands; but it would not be the same if you put in your place an unworthy minister. I do not know those whom you have in mind for this; but if they have the qualities you say, you cannot go wrong, and you will even have the consolation of setting them to work and giving them the plan of how you think they should behave, which seems a big point to me. M. Che[. . .]'s difficulty in singing high mass is rather a drawback, for that seems to be one of the main functions, but perhaps if he were engaged God would give him the facility he lacks and cure him of his timidity. I would not want to exclude him for that reason alone, so long as he has all the other attributes. If you are sure of the second one you have before your eyes, and know him for a man of solid virtue, disinterested as a christian priest should be and with a heart capable of loving those for whom he should take a father's place, it is beyond doubt that you may consider him; but as flesh and blood usually tend to magnify things, no matter how much one intends to judge men according to the truth, allow me to say that you must find more piety, more learning, more zeal, and more charity, in a word, more merit in him than another if you are to have no scruples about preferring him, and give no occasion to the world, to which we are responsible, to censure your action. There, my very dear Monsieur, you have my thoughts; I do not know if they concur with yours. However that may be, I pray God to give you all the guidance you may need and not to allow you to take any steps in so important a matter as this which are not according to his order and will.

I almost died three months ago. I received Our Lord and extreme unction, and as I am finding it hard to get well again, it may well be that my race has not long to run. Ask God, I beg you, to let me finish in a holy manner, worthy of a man who no longer belongs to the world, and was separated from it by his mercy so as to find the means of doing penance. Farewell, very dear Monsieur, I am unreservedly yours in time and eternity, *in aeternum et ultra.*

What you tell me about the late M. [. . .] is strange. A priest must be very blind to love material goods so dearly that he has no feelings for the holy and disinterested nature of his calling and thinks he can offer God an acceptable sacrifice with impure hands full of property which, strictly speaking, is the blood and heritage of the poor. For my part, I have always considered love of money in a priest as the ultimate abomination; it would be better for him to have forgotten the poor completely than to show he remembered them by the small share he let them have of his wealth.

I forgot to say that I do not think that when you resign you should give up the care of your flock, but should on the contrary watch over it all the more yourself, as well as through the intermediaries you put there, for a true disciple of Christ must die in his service and work, and I cannot approve the ideas of those who rid themselves of all cares and concerns, I mean those with which God has charged them, so as to die in what they call repose.'

Retz had died on 24 August 1679. R. had seen him in 1664 on his way to Rome, and again in Rome the next year. Retz's true feelings are open to question, but it seems most likely that he genuinely wanted to atone for a lurid past, though lacking the will to do so. R's judgement on him is quite without parallel for its strength of feeling and positive faith in the salvation of another, despite appearances. Since 1671 Duhamel had been back in his first parish of Saint-Maurice, near Sens. The second candidate was his nephew, and eventual successor, as 801120 shows.

801129 MADEMOISELLE   29 January 1680
        [GILLETTE DE CHALVET-ROCHEMONTEIX]
TB 1245

Glad to hear of family [of his late sister]. Eldest boy [Maximilien] promises well, the younger, the Chevalier [Antoine-Gilbert] can mention R's name to Bellefonds, who will surely help, though R. himself can do nothing because of his profession.

The Chevalier (1663–1720) was accepted as a Knight of Malta that same year. Maximilien (1662–1755) had a brilliant military career, becoming Lieutenant-General. After their father's death in 1673, his unmarried sister, Gillette, became their guardian, and R's brother, Henri, also took a close interest in the family, but was often abroad. There was also a daughter, Marie de Vernassal, to whom R. wrote about her religious vocation (which came to nothing).

800129a NICOLAS LE CAMUS,   29 January 1680
         PREMIER PRÉSIDENT DE LA COUR DES AIDES
TB 1247

RP Monchy had spoken of Président's brother, Bp of Grenoble: 'God will make him one of the greatest bps of our time'.

800129b DOM GUY, LA COLOMBE   29 January 1680
TB 1249

'God's elect will pass from peace in time into peace in eternity.'

800130 RP PIERRE DE MONCHY, CONG. ORAT.   30 January 1680
TB 1255

R. justifies himself against his critics.

*800131 RP ABBÉ, CHÂTILLON [CLAUDE LE MAÎTRE]   31 January 1680
TB 1251

'My very dear Father. I am delighted that you are beginning to wake up and set about the work. I do not doubt that as soon as it is known that you are working at forming your house, people will come forward and you will find men to carry out your good plans. I hope it will be so, for I can understand how painful it must be for someone who should do good, and ardently desires to do so, but cannot find the means to that end.

We will send you some small regulations concerning novices and professed religious which may be of some use for settling a number of things which would otherwise be done confusedly and uncertainly. As regards our major regulations, it will take time, as you know, to transcribe them, but we hope to finish it and send them to you like the others.

I will say nothing specific about dom Rigobert's death, except that it was peaceful and a comfort to those who witnessed it, as to myself. God rewarded him for his suffering already in this world by the great joy he gave him when he saw that he was being really called to God and was ready to go. I do not doubt that he is thinking where he is of those whom he loved and left behind. Men do not know what the sorrows of this life are worth, nor what good they are; if they did know, they would eagerly seek them out.

You wish me a long life, my dear Father, but I cannot believe that God will grant your prayer. You think that my life is some good, but God, who knows its usefulness, will, according to all appearances, soon cut down this barren tree, which is occupying a place that another could fill much more usefully, and indeed I cannot see my health improving much after four months sickness.

As for the former abbot, he is still the same, working, coming to matins and missing no exercise. He will not forget to ask God to give you all the protection you need to employ yourself successfully in establishing his service and glory. That is the only thing which we should set before us in this world, and anything that does not have that for its goal and end should be regarded as lost; that is, anyone who does not save up for eternity, whatever he may do, is merely wasting and destroying. Farewell, my very dear father, pray God for me, I beg you, and ask him to see that I make good use of the time it pleases him still to give me to live. I am yours with all my heart.'

R. is careful not to use such words as 'rule' or 'constitutions' to describe the domestic regulations laid down for la Trappe; he had had enough trouble with the unauthorised publication of 1671. The former abbot was Jacques Minguet (see 800113).

800131a   RP ABBÉ, 'NEWLY ELECTED' [? FOUCARMONT]   31 January 1680
TB 1253

Prior of Longpont should know situation in Rome. Greatest blessing for Reform would be unity of spirit.

Dom Joseph Cottin, Prior of Longpont, had accompanied Abbot Fleur de Montagne to Rome, where he died on 27 September 1678. His successor at Foucarmont was Jean-Edmond de la Teulle, to whom this letter is almost certainly addressed.

800200   MONSIEUR   [? February] 1680
TB 1271

Sends Scriptural maxims.

It was R's habit at the beginning of each year to send one or two maxims to his friends as subjects of meditation.

800201 JEAN FAVIER   1 February 1680
TB 1257

M. d'Albon left 100,000 livres of debts. Sorry about Favier's poor health and worries caused by abbey at Beauvais.

800208 DOM BERNARD BRAQUITI,   8 February 1680
        CHARTREUX, AVIGNON
TB 1264

Carthusians no longer deserve their reputation for austerity, but Braquiti cannot change his Order without scandal, and exchanges between Carthusians and Cistercians are specifically banned.

   Braquiti was severely censured in 1689 by his General for scurrilous pamphleteering, and seems to have been a natural malcontent.

800211 [? NICOLAS PINETTE]   11 February 1680
TB 1267

Brief granted for election of prior if la T. falls back into commend.

800211a MONSIEUR   11 February 1680
TB 1269

Forsake the world.

800218 MONSIEUR   18 February 1680
TB 1272

Encouragement.

800222 [? RM LOUISE-HENRIETTE D'ALBON]   22 February 1680
A 2106,f.92

Some people still in the world set an example that shames those in religion.

800312 RP, CONG. DE SAINT-VANNE   12 March 1680
TB 1274

His confrères have not always succeeded at la T. and he must think seriously about the austerities, obtain his superiors' permission and come to try his vocation.

800314 RELIGIEUX   14 March 1680
TD B (fragment)

God has saved R. from danger [? of illness].

*800314a   RM ABBESSE, LEYME [ANNE DE LA VIEUVILLE]   14 March 1680
TB 1276

'So many things, so different and so groundless, are said about us, RM, that the best thing to do is never to believe them. Among those who talk about it some have never seen us, others so misunderstand what goes on here and what they have been able to observe that in truth no one speaks justly about us, whether they speak good or ill. The ills which may be here are usually those which pass unnoticed, and it happens sometimes, though rarely, that good things are attributed to us which do not exist here.

My health since my serious illness is not entirely recovered, but there is no cause for regarding it as desperate. I am at almost all the exercises as if I had all the strength I once had and, most of the time, to see me in action, you would take me for someone free from any indisposition. You are too kind to take as much interest in it as you do, and I will say nothing about that, for I do not doubt that you believe my gratitude for that to be what it should be.

I did not see in your letter the fragment you mention; you must have forgotten to include it. I would like to walk as straight as you say in the true path. I confess that I sincerely desire it, but my actions and will are not always in agreement, and to my great regret I do most of the time what I condemn and know I should not do. God in his mercy has given me most pure principles, but I do not follow them with the fidelity he asks of me, and however much I resolve to watch myself carefully, I escape my own care, and all my vigilance is useless, or at least serves only to point out to me the defects of my conduct. My consolation, I assure you, is not in the sight of my works, but in my hope that God, having given me an upright heart, will not refuse me in the end the necessary firmness and strictness to express its impulses in the exercise of my duties and obligations. So, RM, when you believe that my intentions aspire to all that is best, you do me some justice, but you must go no further, for you would be mistaken.

It is true that the Abbot of [Septfons] and I have become real friends again, and I thought that God wanted to wipe the slate clean of things whose memory might be disagreeable. After much reflection, all that is clear to me is that the safest course, and the one most in accord with God's spirit, is to forget every reason one had to complain of people. Nothing would be less reasonable than constantly to have recourse to his mercies, as we are obliged to do by the infinite number of our sins, and to harbour resentment towards men. That, RM, is what I fundamentally feel, and I am sure that your feelings are too much the same for you not to approve. I do not fail, I beg you to believe, to commend you to Our Lord with all possible care; that is the only service I can render you, and the only sign I can give of the respect and sincerity with which I am yours' etc.

800325   CLAUDE NICAISE   25 March 1680
BN 9363,f.2 orig., TB 1416 (dated 1681); Gonod,53

R. recalls pleasure of their travel together in Italy. Nicaise had been reminded of it by seeing a letter R. had written to abbé Drouas.

R. and Nicaise had met in 1666 when they travelled from Rome to Florence, but this was apparently the first contact since then.

800408   RELIGIEUX [? OSB]   8 April 1680
TD B

Thanks him for a book. The Maurists' *St Augustine* was well received. R. has just read *Histoire des solitaires de l'Orient*.

The first two volumes of Augustine *appeared in 1679, the third in 1680.*

800411   RP PASQUIER QUESNEL, CONG.ORAT.   11 April 1680
U 1168 orig.; Tans 41

Thanks him for his *Jésus-Christ pénitent*.

800424   [LOUIS MARCEL] SAINT-JACQUES-DU-HAUT-PAS   24 April 1680
TB 1279

Annoyed with M. d'A[ngennes], a supposed convert who has published things against his bishop [of Séez]. Not the job of M. de Tourouvre to speak to him, but his confessor's [cf. 781006].

800516   MONSIEUR DE BONNEJOIE   16 May 1680
TB 1290

Many want to come to la T. but few persevere. If he really wants to come, first consult Cardinal d'Estrées [Bp of Laon].

800530   MONSIEUR DE BONNEJOIE   30 May 1680
TB 1292

Should not delay execution of his plans without taking into account steps taken for his ordination.

800602   DUC DE MAZARIN   2 June 1680
TB 1293; *Collectanea*, 28 (1966), 59–60

Has received 'gentleman from Madagascar' . . . A prodigy of God's mercy which seeks out men everywhere. Véretz is now solely in Mazarin's possession. Mazarin wanted to visit but R. was ill.

Mazarin had originally bought Véretz from R. jointly with his uncle, abbé d'Effiat, who had just resigned his share. The mysterious Madagascan is mentioned by Le Nain, but without any details. The version published (by dom Jean Leclercq) in Collectanea *was unable to include either Mazarin's name or that of Véretz, both erased in copy at la T. but legible with care.*

800607   [RM LOUISE ROGIER]   7 June 1680
A 2106,f.92vo.; TB 1211 (dated 10 January 1680)

Her present peace an indication that she has made the best of past events.

*800609   RM ABBESSE, LEYME [ANNE DE LA VIEUVILLE]   9 June 1680
TB 1295

'I should have answered your last letter sooner, RM, if I had been able, but I fell ill three days before Passion Week with a tertian fever which has lasted until now, and the attacks have been so long and violent that in a short time they have made me extremely weak; I was only just getting over a serious illness, and this one that followed has been no less serious. God be praised for all things; we must say like Job [10:9] that he who has begun us ends by reducing us to dust, and strikes us with all the force of his arm; may my consolation be that he lays his hand heavy on me without sparing me, but I shall never protest against his orders and wishes.

I have understood very well, RM, that I should not please men, and at the same time I adopted the attitude of paying little attention to their judgements and censure. They do not judge us in the last resort; we need only know that God will judge their judgements for us to worry very little about them and remain in profound peace, whatever interpretation they choose to put upon our actions and our conduct. I assure you that apart from my intimate friends, whom I value as I should, it is a matter of complete indifference to me whether other men speak good or ill of me. It is a great advantage for your whole region that you have a prelate full of zeal and diligent in his duties. We must ask God to add his protection to his care and vigilance, for if God does not bless our labours and take a hand in them there is not much point in having hopes of them.

Those who compare me to Monsieur de S. do me much honour, and scarcely know me. He is better than I in so many ways that it would be very difficult to draw fair parallels between us, but people have got to talk without knowing what they say, and without knowing the people or things which form the subjects of their conversations and reflections. Blessed is he who worships God in silence, and breaks off contact with men so as to have with God a contact as intimate and constant as human weakness makes possible. I will add nothing, RM, to this note, except to ask you to speak to God of me and say nothing to men, and to believe that it is not possible to be more genuinely and faithfully yours' etc.

Louis de Noailles had replaced Sevin as Bp of Cahors in 1679, but was translated to Châlons in June 1680. In the context 'M. de S.' could well be the much revered Alain de Solminihac, Bp of Cahors 1636–59, and previously regular abbot of Chancelade, Périgueux, beatified in 1981.

800613   RP SOUS-PRIEUR, CARMELITES, BESANÇON   13 June 1680
TD C

He has written twice asking to come to la T. Must ask permission from Rome. 'We sleep fully dressed; our monks have to learn the psalter by heart.' R. is not writing to fr Martin, and if he is a lay-brother there is no room left.

*800616   RP ABBÉ, CHÂTILLON [CLAUDE LE MAÎTRE]   16 June 1680
TB 1302

'My very dear Father. Your religious did not fail to come, but as he had no permission from his local superior, or from you, or from the visitor, I was not willing to accept him. There is another reason as well, which is that we have caused ourselves trouble by accepting religious here whose attitude was bad, like his. They have given wrong accounts of all the most edifying things they saw here once they left us, they have decried us by imputing to us facts, practices, and principles unknown to us, and what has given them some credibility is that no one doubted that, since they had stayed here, they were only saying what they had seen.

I am glad that you received the little regulations which we sent [on the education of religious], but I would be gladder still if you had people on whom to put them into practice. God will send them, and will doubtless take account of your good intentions and perseverance. Let people talk; they will tire of talking when they see that you do not tire of doing and do not base your conduct on their opinions and views.

For the rest, the former abbot is beginning to weaken; he can only go into the church now with support. He has been weak now for two weeks, and whatever we do, it is not very probable that he will regain his strength. His biggest trouble is his advanced age, eighty-four. He has no fever, is content with his lot and the spirit God gives him; he is clear and lucid, turned towards God; he is peacably awaiting eternity and eagerly desiring it. It may be said of him *spiritus promptus in carne infirma* [Mt 26:41].

Farewell, my very dear Father, may God give each of us a like fate, I do not mean as regards length of life, but its end. I am yours more than I can say.'

See 800131 on the regulations and on the former abbot.

800618   RELIGIEUX [? OSB]   18 June 1680
TD B

R. has been ill 3 months. Refers to Le Roy and St. John Climacus 'the greatest and most enlightened solitary ever'. Thinks neither St Benedict nor Cîteaux envisaged conferences, a later development. Question of diet and bedding in Rule.

800626   CLAUDE NICAISE   26 June 1680
BN 9363,f.3 orig.; Gonod 54

R. has received book from RP Boccone, Cistercian of Florence; he would not be suitable for la T., as Italians need very special qualities to adapt there.

800700   RP PIERRE DE MONCHY, CONG. ORAT.   [July] 1680
TD C; Mug I/7

Death of Bp of Châlons [11 June]. Praises him and the Bp of Grenoble. R. not as ill as people say.

800701   RP DE CHAMPAGNY   1 July 1680
TB 1304

Champagny wants a dispensation which he might get with help of Cardinal d'Estrées. The picture of St. Charles is interpreted as being that of Jansenius by those seeking to blacken R.

R. frequently quoted Charles Borromeo as the model prelate of recent times, e.g. in writing to and about Le Camus.

800718   RM ABBESSE, GIF [ANNE DE MONGLAT]   18 July 1680
TB 1306

Death of former Celestine on way to say mass [dom Claude d'Estrée, on 11 March]. She must stay where she is. Recommends Mlle X now at Gif whose family are friends of R.

800730   RP, CHANOINE RÉGULIER, LIÈGE   30 July 1680
TB 1310, Latin

He will be welcome. [cf 810629]

800730a   [RM LOUISE ROGIER]   30 July 1680
TB 1314; A 2106,f.93 vo. (partial)

Her tribulations and human injustice. Humiliation is the way to Christ. She is fortunate to be free of official posts.

Between two double triennates as superior she was free 1673–83.

*800730b RM ABBESSE, LEYME [ANNE DE LA VIEUVILLE]   30 July 1680
TB 1312

'I assure you, RM, that he who gives us life and health preserves it, for the trouble and care we take over it do not have the result and utility we imagine, and remedies often increase rather than cure ills. You have recently experienced that, from what you tell me, and perhaps I could say the same if I had thought about it. You complain that you are too sensitive, but for my part I think that you are much less so than you say, and that you know how to endure peacefully and patiently what God pleases to send down to try your virtue. Illnesses are usually the means he uses to punish and purify us, and we can say that they are remedies which he applies to our souls, either to preserve their health or to restore it when they have been unfortunate enough to lose it.

I confess that our brethren have been quite resigned to all God's wishes in their infirmities, harsh and painful as they have been, but at the same time you should know that I do not resemble them, and to my confusion I can say that they were much better than I.

So God has taken away the prelate he had given you. I do not doubt that the whole region is losing a great deal, for his intentions were certainly very pure and, although his ways were gentle and moderate, from what those who knew him told me, he had firmness and forcefulness when they were needed. I do not doubt that you have lost as much as others. I have nothing new to write, RM, my health is as usual, up and down, although I do not neglect it as much as you might think. I hope that yours improves, but I hope still more that Our Lord will increase in you the grace he has given you. All that comes to destruction and is reduced to dust is of little moment to those who ought to wait and sigh for eternity.'

R. must have learned of Noailles' translation after writing to Leyme in June; the new bishop was Henri le Jay (1680–93).

800806 RP DU [?]   6 August 1680
TB 1317

He is still young and can avoid proposed promotion. He should not move.

800828 JEAN FAVIER   28 August 1680
TB 1319

Rumours of R's death. May see his sister [Mme d'Albon] and will then discuss her daughter.

It is not clear how R. saw, if he ever did, Mme d'Albon, but she presumably came in the suite of some royal person, like Mme de Guise, who was allowed entry. The daughter could be Mme de Belin or any of the Albons.

800829   LOUIS-FRANÇOIS LEFÈVRE DE CAUMARTIN   29 August 1680
Autographes Troussures, p. 418

Reminds him of problem of dom Garreau [monk at Fontfroide wanting to come to la T.] Hopes to see Caumartin on latter's way to Brittany.

800900   M. L'ABBÉ   September 1680
TB 1335

Condolence's on brother's death.

800900a   RP ABBÉ, septfons [EUSTACHE DE BEAUFORT]   September 1680
TB 1343

R. asks if Septfons is now safe. Glad that la T. is an exception to Beaufort's decision never again to leave his monastery.

After two visits in 1679 Beaufort had been reconciled with R.

800900b   RP   [? September 1680]
Mug II/89

Br Pierre has just died [August 1680] and R. is happy that RP has safely arrived at [la] C[?olombe] where there is less outward austerity.

Pierre's death provides the date, and if la Colombe is a correct conjecture, this may be addressed to Guy, to whom R. wrote there.

800900c   DOM [ALAIN MORONY], tamié   September 1680
Carp, p. 454

Forbids him to return to la T.

800912   RP SIMON GOURDAN   12 September 1680
TB 1326

Death of Bishop Caulet of Pamiers, their mutual friend [7 August]. Novices should not be accepted too easily [at Saint-Victor]. Best to avoid new breviary, but submit rather than cause trouble. Should accept charge of 'vestiary' [issuing clothing].

*800914   MARÉCHAL DE BELLEFONDS   14 September 1680
BN na 12959 f.88,orig.; TB 1330

'I am sending you, Mgr, the passage from St Ephrem that I had promised you. It is so touching and consoling a subject that I wish he had given it wider treatment; I do not know whether it is the life or the death of these great saints that excites most admiration, but I do know that nothing gives a better idea of God's mercies and of what can be done by those who destroy in themselves every worldly feeling, let themselves be led by the movements of his grace, and put themselves so entirely in his hands. In truth we should not be surprised if men who during their life on earth have done only what angels do in heaven, that is, love God alone and worship him, have gone to him in such happy circumstances and if their death has been a blessed passage, a renewal and a true translation from one life to another.

That is a picture, Mgr, that one cannot have before one's eyes without being vividly impressed; but we have neither the grace, the strength, nor the detachment of these great saints, and if the affairs in which we are involved mean that God is not the perpetual subject of our thoughts, we must at least have none which are contrary to him, separate us from him or are unable to contribute to our sanctification and his glory, and cause us to bear constantly in our inner hearts what so easily escapes the attention of our minds.

The main concern of those who live in the world must be to rule their lives, their desires, their actions, and their conduct in such a way as to show in all things the conduct of God, and so that they may believe from the witness of their conscience that their occupations and the different affairs they treat are according to his order and the disposition of his will; otherwise, Mgr, it can be said that instead of serving God as every Christian is obliged to do, they are doing nothing but seeking their own interests and feeding their own passions and appetites. The examples of the saints are a great help in preserving us from such misfortunes, and it seems to me that at the sight of the great things they have done and the perfect sanctity in which they have lived, it is difficult, for anyone having any faith, religion, or care for his salvation, to let himself be carried along by whatever the corruption and vanity of the world may inspire, and to attach the least value to things for which the saints have felt such scorn and antipathy. The most evil temptations are feeble in the presence of those who have fought them and overcome so advantageously. That, Mgr, is something you have experienced thanks to the protection that God has accorded you for so long. I hope that he will continue to do so, and that as there is no limit to your intention of belonging to him, so he will put none to his grace towards you. I am with all possible respect and fidelity yours,' etc.

St Ephrem *was a fourth-century Syrian monk who wrote extensively on biblical subjects and, especially, on the Last Judgement. He is celebrated for his austerity and has been declared a Doctor of the Church.*

*800918   [? RP ABBÉ, CHÂTILLON, CLAUDE LE MAÎTRE]   18 September 1680
TB 1345

'My dear Father. I am amazed at the talk you have had with N. It is truly pitiful that a man of such importance and such a profession should complain at being given enlightenment and information about his calling that he did not have, and object to being told about obligations concerning which ignorance is inexcusable and never a defence against God's judgement. You did well to come out of it as best you could, because whatever reasons one may have for disagreeing with people, one never manages to persuade them. People who live in the world must think they have been strangely abandoned by God, since they cannot imagine a virtuous man living among them nor being able to preserve religion and piety while they receive both favours and rewards from the King. It is certainly wrong to desire and seek such things greedily and eagerly, but not to accept them when offered, and such an attitude may well exist with a most pure devoutness; I am speaking of those engaged in the world by God's order and their profession. Courtiers are unjust in what they think, always full of malice; they rarely open their mouths or speak, whether about those who belong to God or those who do not, except with the intention of denigrating and doing harm. They are like the devils who mutually detest each other, and only agree when it is a question of persecuting and oppressing the righteous.

I am very pleased that you already have two postulants, and hope that they will be joined by others. When I think that the Abbot of [Septfons] spent fourteen years doing nothing, and that now the life in his house is edifying and regular, that people go there, and that they have many applicants, I am convinced that one must never despair. God grants in the end what we ask him with persevering prayers. Farewell, my very dear Father, remember me before Our Lord and believe me yours' etc.

The address has been almost completely obliterated, but the final reference, and general tone, fit in with other letters to Châtillon. The person and situation discussed in the first part cannot be identified.

800920   MADEMOISELLE DE VERNASSAL   20 September 1680
TC I/26

She is going to consult God on her vocation, but must take care in choosing a convent. 'Leaving the world is to escape from the midst of a tempest in which it is almost impossible to avoid shipwreck.'

800930   JEAN FAVIER   30 September 1680
CF 344,f.83 orig.; Gonod 43

Sends a letter for his niece about her possible entry into religion. Not true that Pellisson is a close friend.

The enclosed letter must have been the preceding entry, and the date may be wrong. Pellisson was a distinguished scholar, converted from Protestantism, who had recently corresponded with R.

801000   COMTESSE D'ALBON   October 1680
TB 1353

She has married off her daughter [Marie-Claire, to Gilbert d'Hostun, comte de Verdun]. Refuses to find his brother [Henri] a benefice, as he is not a churchman. Would like to see her, but la T. is a long journey to see someone who is not worth it.

801000a   MONSIEUR DE CHENEVIÈRES   October 1680
TB 1358

Affairs in Rome have slowed up. Everyone wants peace in the Church.

801005   RELIGIEUX [? OSB]   5 October 1680
TD B

'Erudition is the reef on which humility founders, and vanity, the most usual product of study, has often caused a thousand fatal wounds in a scholar's heart.'

801010   MONSIEUR GOISDAN,   10 October 1680
         CURÉ D'A [? MIENS]À D[. . .]
TB 1349

Total renunciation required for peace in cloister, but he can come and see.

801015   MADAME DE SAINT-LOUP   15 October 1680
U 4279, orig. (part of last sheet and signature missing); U723; TB 1158 (2 last pages out of 8); BN 23497,f.40; Gonod 223

'You should not be surprised if you do not find in yourself the basic peace and quiet . . .' Ends: 'You are a woman, sinner, penitent . . . .'.

801027   BISHOP OF GRENOBLE [ETIENNE LE CAMUS]   27 October 1680
TB 1351

Compliments.

801031   DOM JOSEPH GARREAU, FONTFROIDE   31 October 1680
TB 1359

Come without delay.

801104   [? NICOLAS PINETTE]   4 November 1680
TD B

Sorry to hear M. Daurat is ill. 'Blessed is he who is forgotten by the world.'

801111   RM ABBESSE [? MAUBUISSON, LOUISE-HOLLANDINE]   11 November 1680
TB 1373

Has not given advice to RM Magdelaine because he defers wholly to abbess.

The identification is almost certain; R. regularly wrote to both the abbess and prioress (or sub-prioress) of Maubuisson under the same cover, and in these terms.

801114   RM PRIEURE, MAUBUISSON   14 November 1680
TC I/2; Gonod 210

Explanation of the Rule: inner precepts may never be changed, outer ones (vigils and abstinence) may be dispensed for good reason, but any infraction without such reason a mortal sin. Superior may dispense, and RM may rely on her. Obedience to superior must be total.

801115   MONSIEUR DE F   15 November 1680
         [? FONSAL/?FERRAND] MAÎTRE DES REQUÊTES
TB 1374

Glad to have seen him on recent visit. Has read treatise by Blessed RM du Saint-Sacrement; M. is fortunate to have known her so well.

Under heavy erasure, the name could be either Fonsal or Ferrand. There were so many Mères du Saint-Sacrement that without further detail this one eludes identification.

*801116   RP BRUNO FERRAND   16 November 1680
TD/C

'I praise God, my very dear Father, for giving you back your health. Almost nothing remains but to thank Our Lord for drawing you out from the danger to which he exposed you. These are visitations which he sends to those he loves. Illnesses, as you know, are tests, and God uses them to purify our hearts, by detaching them from love of life and any pleasure they might have in things here on earth, by making them feel that such things are always ready to escape them, and that there is never a moment when one may not lose them. I confess that the instability of earthly goods, if considered by itself, is so likely to disgust one with them, that I cannot understand that there can be people who seek after them and uselessly spend the time God has given them for quite contrary use, without making any worthwhile reflection which might make them really regret preferring a vapour, a shadow to the solid rewards promised by God to those who renounce the world for love of him. I understand even less, my very dear Father, that those who have left the world by their profession and calling busy themselves with it in their retreat as though they still had the affairs and commitments which they had left there. The name for that, if you will allow me to call things by the name they deserve, is aberration and scandalous profanation, for there is no other way to describe behaviour which dishonours the holiest of all professions. God grant us grace to respect it as fully as we are obliged to do, not by mere words, but by deeds and a fidelity worthy of it. It is easier than one thinks to have both a mind full of great truths and hands as empty as though one were deprived of all understanding and light. Farewell, my dear Father, I pray Our Lord to bless your efforts and give you grace to bring up and lead in his ways the flock whose education he has entrusted to you. I am with all possible cordiality and affection, yours' etc.

*801120   HENRI DUHAMEL   20 November 1680
TB/1382

'My very dear Monsieur,
I am delighted that you have finally made up your mind and chosen a successor to whom you can hand over the burden which it pleased God to impose on you. I am sure that all you had before your eyes was the sheer merit of the person, and that you paid no heed to the inclinations of nature and kinship. As it is the final and most important action of your life, you have done it just as you would wish to have done it when you appear before God to account to him for it. It must be a great consolation for you to have diverted from your flock the storm which threatened it from above, to have forestalled the misfortune which, to all appearances, would have come upon it, and to have been able to train in its leadership a pastor who is at one with you in attitudes and principles and will follow the plan you have drawn up. It is an inestimable boon for you to have only ordinary instruction left to do, and to have extricated yourself from a worrying situation which was no longer appropriate to your age or health; as for me, whatever anyone may say, I cannot believe that there is anything to condemn in the action of a priest who, after giving all his time and all his life to helping his neighbour, and exposing himself to the distractions inseparable from external duties, however holy they may be, beats a retreat before dying, so that he can prepare for that great journey by penitence, holy repose and meditation on things eternal.

I am very glad that you are reconciled with N., and without cost to yourself. You have spoken without persuading each other, and everyone remains with his own opinions; yours are so reasonable and well founded that I do not advise you to give them up. I should very much like to see N's dissertation, especially arranged as you tell me it has been. Farewell, my very dear Monsieur, come and see us when you can, and meanwhile pray God to have mercy on us. It is no small thing for persons as withdrawn as we are to respond to God's demands and account to him closely for their retreat, and it would be the greatest of misfortunes not to do so; I can say of my obligations as of my iniquities *supergressae sunt caput meum* [Ps 37:5]. The hand of God alone can draw me out of so deep an abyss; you can judge from that whether I need your prayers and ask you earnestly for them. I am with all my heart in life and death yours' etc.

801120a MONSIEUR LE [? FÈVRE], AMIENS   20 November 1680
TB 1387

Docility and submission essential to religious life.

801120b RP PRIEUR, PERSEIGNE [ROBIN COUTURIER]   20 November 1680
Tour, orig.; TB 1444

Prior did well to send away dom Julien [Kerviche], unable to lead strict life. Mentions fr Etienne [Romagné] and fr. Ernoud. 'God will judge murmuring as severely as blasphemy.... A community in which the superior is not loved and respected as he should be is . . . not a society ruled by God's spirit, but by a spirit opposed to him.'

801121   RM LOUISE-HENRIETTE D'ALBON   21 November 1680
A 2106,f.95 vo.; TC II/132

She does well to avoid contact with others. Talking is more often a cause for regret than silence.

801122   RP PRIEUR, PERSEIGNE [ROBIN COUTURIER]   22 November 1680
Autographes Troussures, p.541

Prior's health too weak for him to go elsewhere, but if his monks are incorrigible he would be justified in leaving. Fr Etienne wants to come to la T. and R. agrees. Afraid that Visitor may counsel compromise rather than force Perseigne monks into strictness. Nocey will bring news.

    This is probably Etienne Gruel, professed April 1680, a student at the Collège des Bernardins, and then prior at Perseigne 1717–30, an obviously good and able monk.

801124   LOUIS-FRANÇOIS LEFÈVRE DE CAUMARTIN   24 November 1680
Arch. Aude, Carcassonne, orig.

Abbot of Clairvaux authorises dom Garreau to leave Fontfroide for la T. The *lettre de cachet* is to be revoked.

    Garreau, former prior of Buzais (Common Observance, diocese Nantes) had been exiled to Fontfroide as a disciplinary measure.

*801126   BISHOP OF LUÇON [HENRI BARILLON]   26 November 1680
P f.768; TB 1374 (dated 13 November)

'I am infinitely obliged to you, Mgr, for the evidence you give me of your kindness and the honour of your remembrance. You certainly do me justice in believing that I take an interest in all that concerns you, for I can assure you that nothing touches me more deeply than to learn with what fidelity and perseverance you acquit yourself of what God asks of you, and at the same time the blessings he gives to your care and solicitude. Not only, Mgr, are all our hopes not disappointed, but God fulfills our expectations by the protection he grants you, and by the success with which he favours your diligent efforts to make the people he has committed to your charge according to his heart. We had much pleasure in talking to Monsieur Louis. It would be desirable, as you say, that the bishops should do something like what you and the Bishop of Grenoble have done regarding morals, but they would have to have your zeal, your views, and your principles, and that, as you know, is not the case. Never have faithful workers been more rare than they are, and never have men in every profession and situation been so empty of God and full of themselves. Each tries with unbridled passion to satisfy his own miseries, and as for the things of God, people live as though they did not know them or had no obligation to be attached to them. It is for him, Mgr, to inspire, inflame and soften their hearts. I pray him, and will pray him all the days of my life, always to hold your heart in his hand and be your light and strength. The greatest misfortune that can befall a bishop is not to be guided by his spirit and to have before his eyes anything but his glory and the service of his Church. I am with all possible affection, esteem and respect yours etc.

PS I am most grateful for your book. I have already read some of it on the subject of lawsuits. If people were to follow its views, disputes would be rare among men. As for me, I subscribe to it wholeheartedly, and am sure that it is almost impossible to have disputes without damage to charity and offence to God.

Father de Monchy has been here some days. We have talked about you a score of times. I do not need to say how much your person and your interests are dear to him, for he is sure, Mgr, that you are kind enough to be convinced of it.'

Barillon, like Le Camus, regularly held conferences for the diocesan clergy in which moral, and other, questions were discussed. Monchy had known Barillon since his youth, when Barillon made retreats with the Oratorians of St-Magloire. The book is presumably Les Conférences ecclésiastiques du diocèse de Luçon.

801128 MONSIEUR   28 November 1680
TB 1391

No longer willing to give advice on worldly affairs.

801129 RELIGIEUSE   29 November 1680
A 2106,f.96 vo.

He believes her sincere in her self-condemnation, but the way of tribulation is the right one.

*801130   RM ABBESSE, LEYME [ANNE DE LA VIEUVILLE]   30 November 1680
TB 1389

'It is true, RM, that I did not mention my health in the last letter I had the honour of writing to you, although I am sure that you take great interest in it, but as it is always in the same state, and nothing new is happening, it would be pointless always to use the same terms. God is not allowing things to go so quickly that I can believe that the end is very near, but I have no reason either to expect a complete cure. Thus, although there are exercises which my indisposition prevents me from discharging, it does allow me to fulfill the most important and essential duties. Everything is in God's hands, it is for him to decide and for us to submit.

I am delighted that you are beginning to feel a little better; do not break off what you may judge likely to help you recover, for being half well is as vexatious and inconvenient as being actually ill. It is even easier to resist a serious illness than a languor that goes on, and nothing, unless God provides quite exceptional assistance, is more intolerable than the apathy that goes with it.

I will say nothing of the bishop whom you have, for I do not know him. God grant that he will follow his predecessors in piety, as in their dignity and see. Right-minded people are becoming rarer and rarer and, as you say, there is a shortage of saints and truths grow weaker every day in the hearts of men. Blessed is he who is not of the world, but more blessed still he who hears no mention of it and knows nothing of what goes on there. It is enough to know that there is a world to know at the same time that it is worthy of pity, and one is strictly obliged to pray God for it without being informed in detail of its ills and disorders. Please keep for me, RM, the share you have given me of your friendship, and rest assured that no one will ever be with more esteem and sincerity than I yours' etc.

801200   [LOUIS-FRANÇOIS LEFÈVRE DE CAUMARTIN]   [December 1680]
Mug II/62

Now that dom N. has given the required resignation he is free to come and the *lettre de cachet* is revoked.

See 801124. This is a separate letter, but on the same subject. Caumartin had been enlisted to help because he was influential with the Abbot of Clairvaux.

801205   MONSIEUR DE FONSAL   5 December 1680
TB 1395

Sorry about Fonsal's poor health.

801212   CLAUDE NICAISE   12 December 1680
BN 9363,f.5 orig.; Gonod 55

Problem of inheritance of RP Bénigne Soyrot ODC from Dijon, now at la T., whose uncle claims the money.

Soyrot was professed in May 1680 as dom Bernard.

801212a   CHANOINE RÉGULIER   12 December 1680
TB 1404

No need to withdraw from the altar to purify his life.

*801212b   RM LOUISE-MADELEINE,   12 December 1680
           ABBESS OF MAUBUISSON [PRIORESS]
TD/C; TCII/131

'To reply to your last letter quite briefly, Reverend Mother, you must not be anxious or disturbed about the state in which you say you are. Sin alone should distress us, and as God bids us to love him but not to feel that we love him, as love is a precept but the feeling of love is not, you are doing nothing against his order, and consequently nothing to displease him, when you approach the sacraments without the emotions you would like to feel. The aridity which you experience in your confessions is not a sign that they are defective, and provided that you have prepared yourself and done what you can to hate sin and feel genuine repentance, out of the love you bear for Christ, stop worrying and regret all the thoughts which trouble you as scruples of which the only effect will be to fill your soul with bitterness, distrust, and weariness. Pass the same judgement on the aridity you feel in your communions, for, given that you want, as you say, to love Christ, that you regret your failure to acquit yourself of your duty as much as you are obliged to do, and that you take care to purify yourself of every sinful affection and all that you recognise as being displeasing to him, have no doubt that your feelings are such as are needed to please him. Do not think that because you do not have pious sensibility and lack a certain tenderness sometimes encountered by those participating in the sacred mysteries, you should stay away from them; that is indeed very painful, but it is not always a sign of our unworthiness. God often allows it to happen to us to try our faith and conscience, and make our efforts in his service more vigilant and strict. The best thing you can do in that, Reverend Mother, is to ask God to remove from you the occasion for so troublesome a temptation. But after all, if it should not please him to free you from it, remain in peace and await his will with perfect submission; for in the end, from the moment we want to love God and are distressed at not loving him as much as we should, we are already really loving him. I will add for your consolation these words of the Holy Spirit, from the Book of Tobit [3:21]: Anyone who professes to be your servant, Lord, must hold as a constant truth that if he lives in trials and temptations, you will not fail to crown him; if he passes his life in tribulations, you will deliver him in the end; if it pleases you to try him with chastisement, that is how you make him worthy of your mercy, for it does not please you to cause our downfall, but you make calm follow the storm and joy follow groaning and tears. I beg you to pray God for me as you promise, and believe me with much sincerity yours' etc.

The address is clearly wrong; the abbess was Louise-Hollandine, and it was the prioress (or sub-prioress) who was, as other letters show, tormented by scruples, and to whom this must refer.

801218   BISHOP OF LÉON [PIERRE DE LA BROSSE]   18 December 1680
TB 1399

Bp had written from Mortagne to say he did not want to be translated to Pamiers, but had deliberately not visited R. lest R. should be accused of causing him difficulties. R. sends compliments.

He was not translated. Mortagne was the nearest point to la T. on the bp's road to Versailles from Léon.

801219   MONSIEUR DE COURSELLES   19 December 1680
TD C

Does not know what to advise; ask M. Roulard [a doctor of the Sorbonne, friend of Gerbais, and connected with Saint-Victor].

801224   RP PRIEUR, PERSEIGNE [ROBIN COUTURIER]   24 December 1680
Autographes Troussures, p. 542

Rehallowing of cemetery in Order, approved by superiors. Professions must be recorded with witnesses. R. knew only through prior that Abbot of Prières' visit was delayed. Good wishes for New Year.

Hervé du Tertre, Abbot of Prières and Visitor, died on 8 December.

801230   RP PROCUREUR PRIÈRES   30 December 1680
TD C

Death of abbot announced three weeks ago, but grieved now to hear of it; praises deceased.

801230a   MGR [? DUC DE MAZARIN]   30 December 1680
TB 1409

New Year wishes. Finds new people difficult, will welcome Mgr but pleads reservations about his travelling companions.

801231   BISHOP OF GRENOBLE [ETIENNE LE CAMUS]   31 December 1680
TB 1411

Good wishes. Only darkness and confusion under those whose cause is other than that of Christ and his Church.

801231a   RP, CHAMPAGNE   31 December 1680
TB 1413

Glad to know that he is back. Champagne needs a good superior.

Ever since R's intervention during his novitiate at Perseigne, when he was sent to restore order, this small Reformed house in the diocese of Le Mans had given trouble. Two former monks of la T. were there, René Pasquier and François Gobin.

81/1   [DOM ALAIN MORONY] TAMIÉ   [late 1680, January 1681]
Carp p. 457

Glad to hear that things are now going well.

81/2   MONSIEUR DE POMMEREAU   1681
TB 1415

Asks protection for the religious of la Chalade, a poor ruined house, against their commendatory abbot.

Wars had ruined this Reformed house in the diocese of Verdun, and in 1670 the five remaining monks lived outside the enclosure in a house. Litigation dragged on for years before repairs were effected. Pommereau (1630–1702) had become a conseiller d'Etat *in 1680 and was Intendant in a number of provinces.*

81/3   RP SUPÉRIEUR, ORDRE DE SAINT-ANTOINE, PARIS   1681
TB 1420

One of RP's religious has come to la T. as to a stricter observance. Hopes he will not be forced to leave.

The Antonines originally ran hostels but now lived like Canons Regular. The religious was the Savoyard, Malachie Garneyin, professed November 1682, who became Abbot of Buonsolazzo.

81/4   RM LOUISE-HENRIETTE D'ALBON   1681
TB 1422

She must obey her superior in all things. If Mme d'Albon comes, R. will talk to her about Mlle de la Barge [his great-niece]. R. had never imagined marriage now proposed.

81/5   RM ABBESSE, ESSAI [FRANÇOISE TROTTI DE LA CHÉTARDIE]   1681
TB 1426

R's close friends, M. and Mme de Tourouvre, want one of their daughters to enter religion, and R. has recommended Essai. Praises the family's christian life.

81/6   RM ABBESSE, ESSAI [FRANÇOISE TROTTI DE LA CHÉTARDIE]   1681
TB 1455

Twenty-five of her nuns support her. Her [Augustinian] rule does not impose silence, but the general obligation to seek perfection suggests it. Sends wooden spoons and forks.

81/7   RP ABBÉ, SEPTFONS [EUSTACHE DE BEAUFORT]   1681
TB 1431

Beaufort's health now better. He must now remain in his monastery, having nearly died away from it, and away from his brethren who need a helping hand.

As one of the leaders of the Reform, Beaufort had been much involved in discussions in Paris.

81/8   M. L'ABBÉ SAZILLY   1681
TB 1433; Mug I/87

Sazilly is going home to Poitou without seeing R. He had planned to meet Bp of Luçon [Barillon] at Alençon. R's friendship persists 'despite silence, distance, and length of time'.

81/9   RP ANDRÉ DE LA CROIX, THEATINE   1681
TB 1435

M. Rousseau lacks the qualities of mind and body for la T. Asks RP to help soften the blow of rejection.

81/10   M. L'ABBÉ SAZILLY   1681
TB 1448

Glad to write despite profession of silence.

81/11   RM THÉRÈSE DE JÉSUS, VAL-DE-GRÂCE   1681
TB 1439

She is deprived of sacraments; R. offers consolation.

81/12 RP 'OF A HOLY AND REGULAR ECCLESIASTICAL CONGREGATION' 1681
TD C

RP is young and inexperienced. 'The reef on which the vessel of most ecclesiastics founders is abuse of their talents and satisfaction at their works.'

R. *usually calls such congregations as those of the Oratorians and Theatines ecclesiastics, and approved of very few of them, apart from those two.*

810100 BISHOP OF GRENOBLE [ETIENNE LE CAMUS] [January] 1681
TB 1442

M. Deslions [Dean of Senlis] has just been. Religious sent to Tamié have arrived back, claiming that their superior's lack of direction prevented them doing any good and justified their departure.

810100a SR LOUISE DE LA MISÉRICORDE [LA VALLIÈRE] January 1681
TB 1417
Respects.

810120 CLAUDE NICAISE 20 January 1681
BN 9363,f.7 orig; Gonod 56
Problem of dom Soyrot's money.
See 801212a.

810123 DUC DE BEAUVILLIER 23 January 1681
TB 1418

R. had seen him at la T. 'The life you lead in the midst of the court covers us with confusion in our remote retreat.'

*810123a MARÉCHAL DE BELLEFONDS 23 January 1681
BN na 12959f.90, orig; TB 1163

'I think you are sufficiently persuaded of my concern for all that regards you, Mgr, for me to have no need to tell you of it, and as I have no means of showing evidence of this, except before God, I shall not fail in the situation of which M. le comte de Saint-Géran has spoken to us to recommend to God with all possible care your person, your house, and all your interests; and I am all the happier to do so for being convinced that you relate all your interests to his glory and your salvation, and that the world has nothing to offer you to which you would become attached for a moment if you could only do so by displeasing him. You know that anything not established by him will not last or be blessed, and that according to his word he will tear up any plant not planted by his hand [Mt 15:13]. That is why men must behave most circumspectly and address themselves to him in all things, especially those concerning fortune, peace, and station in life. The reason why most of the things one undertakes, even with good intentions, have anything but the success one hopes for is that one either has not taken the trouble to enlist God on one's side or has neglected to keep him there by resorting to means and ways so irregular as to be unworthy of him and even inconsistent with the purity of the original intentions. We shall pray Our Lord not to allow you to fall into such misfortune, but, as you have had only him before your eyes from the beginning of the affair in question, that he will see that you have him alone before your eyes in the future and in every circumstance, so that nothing prevents him from letting you find all the benefits and consolations you seek, and finally so that, having thought as much as you are able of those whom he has entrusted to you, you have no one but yourself left to think about, and nothing left to do but make a last and holy use of the knowledge, feelings, and desires with which he has for so long filled your heart.

M. le comte de Saint-Géran was only here for a few hours. The joy we felt at seeing him here was soon replaced by our regret at losing him. In the brief conversation we had with him we did not find it hard to recognise all that you had told us about him. The consideration we have for you, Mgr. will always open the doors of la Trappe to all those who come from you, but it is also true that M. le comte de Saint-Géran has a powerful recommendation in himself and by his own merit. I am with more respect and fidelity than I can say yours etc.

PS Allow me to request you to be good enough to give M. le duc de Beauvillier the letter I take the liberty of addressing to you for him.'

Bernard de la Guiche, comte de Saint-Géran (1641–96), was Bellefonds' cousin and a distinguished soldier. Paul, comte de Saint-Aignan, became duc de Beauvillier in 1679 (1648–1714). In 1685 he was appointed tutor to the Dauphin's son, the duc de Bourgogne, and was a close friend of Saint-Simon.

810202   RP ABBÉ, PAIRIS   2 February 1681
TB 1458

Abbot had asked for help in reforming his ruined house [near Colmar, in Alsace] but it is too far to send monks from la T. and proposed financial arrangements are unacceptably onerous.

810206   RP PRIEUR, PERSEIGNE [ROBIN COUTURIER]   6 February 1681
TB 1460

Prior had asked Cîteaux for a visitor. R. will try to broach matter when he sees commendatory abbot, whose title is the beginning of a vocation, though insufficient in itself. Abbot should not hand over a cure of souls of which he is incapable, but should seek advice.

810213   RELIGIEUX [? OSB]   13 February 1681
TD B

'It is certain that by our profession and state we are not destined to be clerics' but he should accept. 'You are as dear to me as if divine providence had allowed you to complete with us what you had begun.'

810213a   [JEAN FAVIER]   13 February 1681
A 2106,f.97 vo.

Has just received a letter from [Mlle de Vernassal] after a long silence; she should follow Favier's advice. She had contemplated entering religion, and R. had advised deep reflection. Condemns marriage arranged for his niece.

cf. 800903, 81/4 and 801000.

810221   TRP ABBÉ, CLAIRVAUX [PIERRE BOUCHU]   21 February 1681
TB 1462

Visitor failed to find at Champagne acts of stabliity of three monks sent from la T. to reform house at prior's request. R. and Abbot of Prières had given written consent to the translation, and disappearance of the documents is rather suspicious.

The prior by now was Louis Alexandre (1681–84), but in 1684 he was censured for his treatment of René Pasquier, one of the monks from la T. whose papers had disappeared, and the Chapter of the Reform held in May 1684 refers to three and a half years vexation of René on that score [Stat. Cap. S.O.1684,91], which explains R's earlier letters to Champagne (cf. 801231).

*810309   RM MARIE-LOUISE [BOUTHILLIER]   9 March 1681
TD/A

'It is true, my dear sister, that we felt keenly the death of the Abbot of Prières. Fond of him as we were, we could hardly fail to be extremely grieved at losing him; I am sure that in the conversations you had with him you must have been well aware of his feelings towards us, and that is enough to show you how we felt and still feel about being deprived for ever of the consolation we had when he came to visit our monastery. Nothing here on earth is stable, my dear sister, everything passes with incredible rapidity, and our lives, when you really come down to it, are just full of loss and privation. What we imagine we are holding escapes from our hand without our thinking about it, and as God alone is immutable and we cannot lose him so long as we sincerely wish to keep him, it is also to him alone that we should become attached and whom we should regard as the fixed good of our affections. If we should happen to have affections for a good not made directly by him and in him, they must at least be so consistent with his order and so dependent on him that we are always ready to give them up when he asks. A heart which inclines and turns towards creatures is always agitated, because they have no reliable state or consistency, it follows all their movements and constantly changes its emotions according to the different dispositions of the creatures. We are fortunate in belonging to a profession which separates us from everything and unites us to Christ, because in giving us to him it gives him to us. He is the true example promised to those who renounce all for love of him, and choose him alone for their lot. I have no doubt, my dear sister, that you have already experienced that, but you will do so more keenly as you advance towards the goal you have set yourself, which is to belong totally to him, for if we wish to possess him without reservation, we must belong to him without reservation. He never fails to pour his grace copiously on souls which set no end or limit to the love they bear him and the care they render him. That means that your principal care must be to watch only over yourself, so carefully and closely that you tolerate nothing, not only which could fail to please him, but which is unworthy of the purity for which you know he has destined you. That is a blessed servitude, a yoke which does not weigh on those who know no other good in the world than that of loving him and being loved by him. I think that that is your whole ambition, and it cannot indeed be greater or more holy, since what is at stake is gaining his kingdom and reigning with him in his authority.

I did not know of your indisposition, and praise God that it is beginning to go. These are warnings he gives us when he makes us ill and the best thing we can do, however minor our ills, is to think them greater than they are, so as to make them useful to us and let us use them for the purpose for which he sent them. That is something which I am sure you do not fail to do. We shall continue, my dear sister, to offer him our prayers and ask him not to cease looking at you in his mercy, and be pleased to destroy in you all that could prevent you from being as acceptable to him as you should be and wish to be. Remember me too, I beg you, and all my miseries. I am more than I can say yours etc.

PS I do not know the hand of the person who was kind enough to commend herself to me in your letter. Assure her, please, of my gratitude and the care we shall have in commending her to Our Lord.'

Hervé du Tertre, Abbot of Prières and visitor of the province to which la Trappe belonged, died on 8 December 1680. As Jouaud's assistant he must have spent a lot of time in Paris on affairs of the Order.

*810312   RM ABBESSE, LEYME [ANNE DE LA VIEUVILLE]   12 March 1681
TB 1464

'I will say nothing more, RM, about Father [?]'s ideas, for I can see that I should have difficulty in persuading you, and you are not in a mood to accept my views. The main thing is that I am not so, and that people's opinion of me does not prevent me doing myself justice, and I admit that to fail in that I should have to be very blind, or live without reflection; from the fact that I still have eyes, and look at myself, I can scarcely not realise how mistaken are those who speak well of me. It is true that if a few people should happen to express favourable opinions of me, God, who is full of mercy, allows that to be destroyed or balanced by the great number who do not agree with them. I think I have already told you that praise is much more dangerous than calumny, and that it takes much less virtue to prevent oneself feeling the harmful effect of an insult than the pernicious impression of a eulogy. Those who approve of us usually do us harm, unless we are very much on our guard; it is not the same with those who condemn us. So, RM, profit from the opinion which you see me have, and abstain from praising me, whether because I am not worth it or because I have not sufficiently shaken off my self to take no pleasure in it. I agree with what you tell me, that it is difficult to find places where one has the necessary facilities and advantages to belong to God as much as one should, and serve him in the purity and detachment which he demands from those souls whom he wishes to separate from the mass of men in order to apply them solely to himself. I also agree that the observance and discipline established in our monastery give us unusual means of doing that; but I cannot agree that we make proper use of so great a protection, and, to speak frankly, every time we set our works beside our duties and all the signs of God's goodness that we receive, we see in ourselves only cause to feel humiliation and confusion. Grace weighs more heavily than people know, and we cannot tell how many people will be condemned for what should have brought about their sanctification. The most common and irresistible sin of men is ingratitude, for, looking at it properly, there is not an instant of our lives when God does not open the hands of his mercy upon us, and there is not one when we do not show him evidence of our hardness of heart. In a word the world is the kingdom of the ungrateful, and all God does is to send down rain and sow on rock.

The person whom you believe to be here did not come; the storm must have cast him upon another shore; his destiny is to be pitied, like that of his fellows. Our certainty that there is nothing that does not fall under God's providence, that his order guides everything, means that at all times and on all occasions we must preserve peace and quiet, and never have legitimate cause to lose it. Rightminded people are upset at public ills and calamities, but trouble and confusion never find a way into their hearts, because they belong to God, who brings wherever he is calm and tranquillity. That is the lot of his servants in this world, as it will be their reward in the next. With that trust one finds a consolation for everything. The saints once said that sadness was only for Jews and pagans, since Christians ought to live in joy. It is a joy that the world does not know, for it results from purity of conscience and the influence of the Holy Spirit. I wish it for you, RM, as for myself, knowing that without it we cannot serve God as we should.'

810421   PRINCE DE SOUBISE   21 April 1681
TB 1468

Prince should not only feel grief at his sister's death [Abbess of Malnoue, died 8 April] and should consider his own salvation without delay.

*810421a   MLLE DE GOELLO   21 April 1681
TB/1470

'I am sure, Mlle, that the loss of your sister has affected you as it should, by which I mean that it touched you deeply but that you did not cease, for all that, to submit to the orders of God, who disposes of the fate and governs as he chooses the life of all men. The unhappy event was quite unexpected, she was only ill for three days, but she had anticipated and prepared herself for it, from what I hear, by a general confession. God speaks to you and gives you special instruction through all these circumstances. What you may infer from them above all is that we must always be ready to be parted from the things and persons who are dearest to us, and as there is no hour or moment at which he may not demand the return of our souls, so there is none at which we should not be prepared to put them back in his hands. That is a most general and permanent truth, yet most people live as though they did not know it; others think about it, but so feebly and languidly that their thought is no use to them. If anything is likely to make such thought useful, it is when we see it in practice in moments of stress and occasions we feel keenly. I do not doubt, Mlle, that you are making holy use of this event, and that it increases the feelings that you have received up till now from God's goodness. He has given you so many gifts of grace that you should always have them before your eyes so that they occupy your mind, fill your heart and that there is never a moment, if possible, that you fail to tell him in gratitude that you are not worthy that he should look on you with mercy and compassion. I speak thus out of my interest in these things and out of my keen concern for all that affects you, and though I am not often privileged to assure you of it, do me the justice of believing that it is as it should be, and could not be greater, any more than the sincerity with which I am etc.

PS I am not writing to M. le [prince de Soubise ?]; he is in my heart. There is never a day when I do not present him to God several times, and the greatest joy I could have in this world would be to see him made by God such as I have wished for so long, or, more precisely, such as he wishes himself to be, as I am convinced that if he followed his light and the feeling of his heart he would be other than he is. I mean that he would show God the same rectitude and irreproachable loyalty he shows men.'

It was not the sister, but the niece, of Mlle de Goello who had just died. Marie- Eléonore de Rohan (1629–8 April 1681) had been Abbess of Caen, and then of Malnoue. She died at the dependent priory in the rue Cherche-Midi in Paris which she had set up. Soubise was the dead woman's brother, son of Mme de Montbazon, friend of R's youth. He was a distinguished soldier, but not conspicuous for piety. The allusions may well be, in view of 81042, to his son Louis, prince de Rohan.

810424   BISHOP OF MEAUX [J.-B. BOSSUET]   24 April 1681
TB 1473; Bossuet, *Correspondence*, II p.218

Thanks him for book received [*Histoire Universelle*].

810427   DUCHESSE DE LUYNES   27 April 1681
TB 1475

Death of her sister, Abbess of Malnoue.

810511   RM PRIEURE, LA CHAISE-DIEU-DU-THEIL   11 May 1681
TB 1477

She has asked for his prayers, unworthy as he is.

Not the great abbey in Auvergne, but a Fontevrist priory near Laigle (dioc. Evreux).

810519   RM LUCE, SAINTE-CLAIRE, ALENÇON   19 May 1681
TB 1479

She had asked R. for a novena to pray God to give them good water in their well, as they could not afford expense of digging a new one. R. agreed, but she must accept whatever God sends.

The prayers were answered.

810521   BISHOP OF SÉEZ [JEAN DE FORCOAL]   [21 May] 1681
TB 1424

R. will try to send an ordinand after Pentecost.

810525   JEAN FAVIER   25 May 1681
CF 344,f.85 orig; Gonod 44

R's niece, Mlle de Vernassal, is much to be pitied in her great uncertainty, but she must wait for a real vocation. Disclaims *Constitutions de la Trappe*.

This unauthorised book of rules continued to be reedited after first appearing in 1671.

810600 RP, CELESTIN [June] 1681
TB 1437

Dom Placide [Pérouse, a former Celestine] died a few days ago [24 May]. R. recalls incidents of humiliation of Paul Hardy [in 1671: cause of the dispute with Le Roy] of which RP had approved at the time.

The correspondent is one of two Celestines who left la T. when five others remained, in 1671.

810600a M. L'ABBÉ June 1681
TC I/176

He was right to cut himself down to a single benefice, as he had entered the most holy profession in a most profane way.

810602 RP BRÉZEAU, CONG. ORAT. 2 June 1681
TB 1481

R. has just written at Pinette's request to duchesse de Lesdiguières, niece of Cardinal de Retz, 'for whom I had inexpressible affection and respect'. Brézeau should pray for R. 'although places of solitude are refuges and haven, one can still suffer shipwreck there as in the open sea'.

810615 BISHOP OF GRENOBLE [ETIENNE LE CAMUS] 15 June 1681
TB 1483

Glad to hear that bp escaped an accident. Warm praise.

810622 JEAN FAVIER 22 June 1681
TB 1485

He should put in some good monks to his abbey at Beauvais. R. is not surprised that even the best of Favier's monks do not approve life at la T., though it is based on monastic fathers.

810629 RP PIERRE DE MONCHY, CONG. ORAT. 29 June 1681
TB 1446 (partially duplicated 1495)

Canon has arrived from Leège: good hopes for his success.

Cf. 800730. This is probably Arcise le Guay, professed 18 September 1682, died May 1684, aged 30.

810722 RP PASQUIER QUESNEL, CONG. ORAT. 22 July 1681
U 1168 orig.; Tans 42

Condolences on death of Quesnel's mother.

810725 [RM DE LA ROCHE]   25 July 1681
A 2106.f.101; BN 19324 (extract with name)

God brings storms on the heads of his elect but will never let them go under. Her life is full of tribulation but she should console herself that God thus shows his mercy.

810728 [RM DE LA ROCHE]   28 July 1681
A 2106.f.103 vo.; TC II/30; BN 19324 (extract with name)

Her present state is a preview of death. She should welcome it as the moment of deliverance. Right to be dissatisfied with herself, but she should strive for perfection.

The date of this, or the preceeding letter, must be wrong.

810800 ABBÉ-GÉNÉRAL DE L'ORDRE DE SAINT-ANTOINE, LYON   [August] 1681
TB 1499; Mug II/51

Asks permission for RP Garneyrin to transfer to la T., where he has been for some days.

[*Cf. 81/3*]

810800a BISHOP OF GRENOBLE [ETIENNE LE CAMUS]   August 1681
TB 1500

Recommends an ecclesiatic found unsuitable for la T. and unwilling to return to his diocese.

810800b M. LE CURÉ, PRÉPOTIN   [? August 1681]
TB 1506

Someone has been shooting the curé's pigeons; if it is one of R's people, he consents to his punishment and would see to it himself but for his profession.

Prépotin is a parish close to la T. and one whose curés were frequently in litigation with the abbey.

810800c RP, CELESTIN   August 1681
TB 1502

Dom Joseph [de Saint-Mesmin] the only one of his former confrères still alive. R does not know if they would have lived longer as Celestines, but 'they followed God's order in leaving and linked their salvation to their translation'.

Cf. 810600. Joseph was to die next year.

*810820   RM ABBESSE, LEYME [ANNE DE LA VIEUVILLE]   20 August 1681
TB 1503

'RM, I so much value the friendship with which you honour me that there is nothing I am less able to forget or fail to acknowledge. I declare that most sincerely, and beg you never to be tempted to think otherwise. I do not know why it is so long since I wrote to you, but I know that I wanted to fifty times or more, and your last letter anticipated me by only a few moments. I see from what you tell me that your health is not too good and that your usual state is that of someone infirm. That is a disposition of Providence to which, I am sure, you do not fail to submit. When ills occur one may take suitable means of relief, and yet await purely from God the decision affecting us, for death as for life. It is true that I am deeply obliged to God's goodness for withdrawing me from the agitations of the world, and putting me as it were in a shelter while all is in confusion and disturbance. That is a grace which I cannot sufficiently acknowledge, and whatever one may do to profit from such a great blessing, one is so far from using it as fully as one should, that one has every reason to fear that God will condemn as black ingratitude what men see as fidelity in our conduct. The weight of great mercies is something terrible, and few respond to God's designs as they are obliged to, and yet it is written that the hopes of the ungrateful soul will be dissipated as ice melts and is dissipated in the heat of the sun [Ws 16:29].

I do not know what to say about your question concerning your translation, except that there is nothing one should be more careful about than leaving the place to which God's order has attached us. I have always thought that to do so with conscience, his will had to be manifest, and our sanctification and his glory had to coincide in the change, since otherwise we act from human motives and considerations, either by yielding to the desires of those near to us or following the instability of our own spirit, and never find either the peace or consolation at which we aimed, and always find ourselves in a more awkward and tiresome situation than the one we are leaving. There are so few religious houses which live in strict piety and regularity that wherever you might go, you would have no fewer difficulties and obstacles than you have at home. Most of the time we change places without knowing why, and often we are no sooner in a new home than we have to leave, without having enjoyed for a single moment the peace and tranquillity we had sought. I am telling you my opinion; I do not claim that it is decisive, you must just pay it as much attention as you think right. Life is so short and our days speed by so fast that it hardly matters where we are, so long as we belong to God. As regards RM Prioress, let me say that as God has united you and bound you not only by blood but by his spirit and charity, she should not leave you lightly; she must probe her heart about it, and you and she must earnestly ask God to show you his will. It is a serious problem when those who are united become separated and disunited. I commend myself to your prayers and am yours' etc.

The Prioress was Anne's sister Marguerite, who left to become prioress of Laizières, a daughter house of few miles north of Cahors, in 1681 with a pension from her brother, Louis. The purpose of Anne's intended translation was presumably to bring her nearer the family home in Picardy.

810825   DUC DE BEAUVILLIER   25 August 1681
TB 1505

Promises his prayers.

810825a   RP PROVINCIAL, ORDRE DE SAINTE-CROIX   25 August 1681
TB 1507

Sends two letters from former religious of order now at la T.

Cf. 820707. Originally an order of comtemplative canons, mainly centered in Belgium and Holland, the 'croisiers' were by now much the same as other canons regular. They had been in Parish since 1258.

810825   FRANÇOIS DIROIS, ROME   25 August 1681
TB 1509

Complains that the Benedictines can give only one example of the translations against which they have secured briefs [Maur Aubert] and which they claim to have been so harmful. Denies that a small monastery like la T. can threaten them, but asks Dirois to speak to Sluze to try to reverse the decisions.

Jean Sluze, or Sluse, (1628–87), a friend of Nicaise, was promoted cardinal in 1686. A curial official born in Belgium, he was closely in touch with French affairs and not unfavorable to Jansenism. Dirois, a doctor of the Sorbonne, was theological advisor to Cardinal d'Estrées, French envoy in Rome. Although Maur Aubert was the only Benedictine (Maurist) actually professed at la T. up till then, many others had tried, and to stop further defections the Benedictines secured briefs prohibiting unauthorised transfers to la T. (see 700219).

810829   RP GÉNÉRAL   29 August 1681
         DE LA CONGRÉGATION DE CLUNY [PIERRE SIMON]
TB 1511

Monk destined for Saint-Martin-des-Champs, Parish, as novice-master has come to la T. and R. is so convinced of his sincerity that he would like to keep him.

Saint-Martin was the Paris headquarters for the Cluniacs; whoever the monk was, he did not remain at la T.

810830   JEAN FAVIER   30 August 1681
TB 1512

General sympathy for a godly house [? Beauvais].

810831 RP ABBÉ, LA COLOMBE [PIERRE DE LA SALLE]   31 August 1681
TB 1514

Is sending him a willing and docile monk. Comments on the action of the Abbot of Citeaux against proto-abbots. Only an extraordinary act of God can save the Common Observance.

In anticipation of the next General Chapter (1683) Abbot Petit of Citeaux was doing his best to outflank the proto-abbots who had caused such havoc in 1672, and in particular was trying to prevent any alliance between them and the Reform. The monk was probably fr Etienne Compagnon, professed at la T. 1674, died la Colombe 1716, aged 62.

810831a RELIGIEUX, LA COLOMBE   31 August 1681
TB 1516

Encouragement.

Presumably dom Guy; cf. 800129

810831b RM LOUISE-HENRIETTE D'ALBON   31 August 1681
TB 1518; A 2106,f.104 vo.

Dignity of religious life; exhortations.

810900 MONSIEUR C [?], CONSEILER D'ETAT   September 1681
TB 1522

He should be more aware of how transitory life is.

This could be either Caumartin or Courtin, both friends of R. and both conseillers d'Etat.

810908 JEAN FAVIER   8 September 1681
TB 1524

R. wonders whether Favier would not do better to resign his abbey if he can find someone suitable. Complains of criticism from those 'who walk in the broad ways'.

810911 RP ABBÉ, CHÂTILLON [CLAUDE LE MAÎTRE]   11 September 1681
TB 1527

'My very dear Father. I praise God that your religious are staying with you; that is a remarkable favour you have received, for which you should heartily thank God. You obliged me to write and express my thanks against all my inclinations, as I cannot imagine that I play the part you say in obtaining the consent you were sent, but I did so none the less since you wanted me so insistently to do it. I have nothing to tell you, except that I pray God to bless your designs and give you grace to establish in your monastery as much piety, discipline and regularity as you wish.

As regards Orval, my view is that it should be looked on as something considerable with regard to the attitudes of the region and nation involved, but I really think that if one looked closely at what has been established there, one would see major defects arising from the simple fact that they have not been sufficiently attached to the discipline of our Fathers. Perhaps it was not possible, but I am sure that their standards will never rise, and will go down much more in the future than up. When starting a work one says that one must go gradually, and in some respects that is true, but in others that is a dangerous principle, particularly in the observance of silence and the strict care to be taken in preventing the religious from communicating with each other, on the pretext of speaking words of edification. I am yours' etc.

The most likely explanation of the first part of the letter is that the devastated condition of Châtillon had prompted higher authority in the order to propose cutting down the number of monks resident there. R. was presumbably persuaded to write to the Abbot of Clairvaux, or Cîteaux, on his friend's behalf.

810913   RM SOURS-PRIEURE, MAUBUISSON   13 September 1681
TB 1531

Her idea of transferring to Carthusians a pure temptation; they are not as silent as she thinks. Persevere where she is. Since the age of twelve God has given her grace and will not now abandon her.

810913a   RM ABBESSE, MAUBUISSON [LOUISE-HOLLANDINE]   13 September 1681
TB 1533

Has received a virtuous ecclesiastic who has come from her. She must not resign unless she finds a worthy successor or she will always feel guilty. Refers to his letter to sub-prioress 'an over-scrupulous person who is nearer to God than she thinks'.

The abbess was fifty-nine and had been abbess since 1664.

810917   RP PIERRE DE MONSCHY, CONG. ORAT.   17 September 1681
TB 1535

Le Camus has been ill. R. would like to see Monchy: 'friendship is just a desire and affection of the heart, and one never ceases to desire those whom one does not cease to love.'

810920   RP ABBÉ, TAMIÉ[ANTOINE DE SOMONT]   20 September 1681
TB 1536

Seldom hears direct from abbot, but knows from elsewhere how hard he works to reform his house. Reminds him of written promise to that effect left with R. Dom Anselme wants to come back, but needs somewhere less austere than la T. Fr Antoine [R.'s former servant] must stay at Tamié, silence and seclusion of la T. too much for him. Dom Alain could well have stayed at Tamié, but is destined for elsewhere [Maubuisson, as chaplain]. Despite death rate, there are twenty-five professed monks and fourteen novices at la T.

810922   RM DE LA ROCHE, TOURS   22 September 1681
TB 1539; TC, I/105 (partial)

Glad to know of her peace of mind.

810923   RP PRIEUR, PERSEIGNE [ROBIN COUTURIER]   23 September 1681
Autographes Troussures, p.543; TB 1529; TC I/104 (dated 13 Sep)

All ordinary remedies permissible for prior's bad health, but he must not go to take the waters; wrong in itself and a bad example. He must try frequent purges. Asks for act of stability at Perseigne of dom Alexis, as that of some monks from la T. now at Champagne is being challenged.

Dom Alexis Nevoir came to Perseigne in 1658 from l'Etoile. On Champagne, see 810221.

810924   MONSIEUR L'ABBÉ DE [? LA MADELEINE]   24 September 1681
TB 1540

M's brother has died but posts remain in family. Reflections on transitoriness of life.

811005   RP PRIEUR, PERSEIGNE [ROBIN COUTURIER]   5 October 1681
Autographes Troussures, p.544

Thanks prior for sending acts [of stability]. Sorry that he is still ill and cannot write in his own hand, but R. still against his going to take waters. Peace can only be found in accepting God's will.

811009   RP PIERRE DE MONCHY, CONG. ORAT.   9 October 1681
TB 1550; TC I/106 (partial)

Hopes bad weather will not stop him coming.

811016   MONSIEUR   16 October 1681
TD C

R. cares little for men's praise or blame. Send young man if he seems suitable.

811022   RP PRIEUR, perseigne [robin couturier]   22 October 1681
TB 1552

R. has told commendatory abbot about his duties; administration, finance, possible entry as regular. Dom Al[?exis] caused another monk's death and should abstain from communion. Dom Jacques [de Lancahl] will be welcome. R. will speak more discreetly of Perseigne in future so as not to offend prior.

811102   RM ABBESSE, maubuisson [louise-hollandine]   2 November 1681
TB 1555

R. is not keen to advise sub-prioress, whom abbess knows better. Taking her off external duties might increase 'her melancholy humour and worries'. Perhaps it would be safe to dispense her from conferences and recreation. 'It is useful and even necessary to make allowances for people on many occasions.'

811115   RP SIMON GOURDAN, saint-victor   15 November 1681
TD B

His rule allows him to warm himself by the fire and it is doubtful whether he is robust enough to go without it. Dress should be in accordance with his delicate constitution. Avoid excess and conspicuous differences from others.

811123   RP PRIEUR, perseigne [robin couturier]   23 November 1681
Autographes Troussures, p.545

Dom Alain has already left; R. is confident that he will maintain discipline [at Maubuisson]. Suggests prior might try massage and standing in front of fire, but sickness has probably gone too far for such simple cures.

811128   CLAUDE NICAISE   28 November 1681
BN 9363,f.8 orig; Gonod 92

Two ecclesiastics sent by Nicaise left in such a hurry that R. never saw them.

811204   RELIGIEUSE   4 December 1681
A 2106,f.106 vo.; TC II/230

Her retreat should purify and detach her from all worldly impressions. God has given her a great grace in her love of solitude.

811208   RP PRIEUR, perseigne [robin couturier]   8 December 1681
Autographes Troussures, p.545; TB 1565; TC II/21

Hopes that plans to reform order will succeed but thinks laxity has gone too far. Prior should pay more attention to his own house than that of others; his responsibility is to the flock entrusted to him.

*811211   HENRI DUHAMEL   11 December 1681
TB/1567

'I am very sorry that your health is not returning as fast as we would wish. God, who does all things and takes special care in guiding those who love and serve him, has set limits to your ills and you should believe, as you no doubt do, that he only prolongs them because it would not be in your interest to be rid of them as your friends wish and according to what the affection they have for you makes them desire. The main thing, as I have already told you, is that your soul should be constant and calm, and if the subject of your reading and occupations wanders off into distraction, the disposition of your heart and your submission to God's orders remains firm and unshakable. That is a grace which God has granted you up to now, and your fidelity will win you its continuation in perseverance until he ceases to try you, either by giving you back the health of which he has for so long deprived you, or by giving you something better than the preservation of a life which he would grant you only for a time.

We do not know his plans, my dear Monsieur, yet we can say that the state in which he has put you is a very sure preparation for accepting his will, whatever it may be, in perfect resignation. Nothing gives us a truer idea of the miseries of this world and our own infirmity than illnesses, when they last a long time, and the distaste with which they fill us for things of the present can hardly fail to be accompanied by a feeling and ardent desire for those to come. We are only happy, strictly speaking, inasmuch as we desire and hope for those things, and this desire and hope is never more pure and vital than when we see nothing on earth to which we can become attached. Anyone who lacks health lacks everything except that he finds in God alone the remedies and consolations he cannot find in men. I pray Our Lord to confirm his grace on you and all your family, and make them as holy as you desire. We will not cease to offer you to him any more than we could cease honouring you with all the fullness and power of our heart. Always love me and believe that I am completely and unreservedly yours.'

811214   DOM JOSEPH GARREAU   14 December 1681
TB 1571

Garreau should have come straight to la T. and by breaking condition imposed will invite charge that he simply wanted to leave Fontfroide. He must give up affairs and interests of recent years of his life when he does come to la T. 'will be full of anxiety and languor'.

Garreau, former prior of Buzais and syndic of Brittany, had just been released from a lettre de cachet to come to la T. His interests were probably Jansenist.

*811214a   RM ABBESSE, LEYME [ANNE DE LA VIEUVILLE]   14 December 1681
TB 1569

'You will never persuade me, RM, that my letters, when I have the honour of writing to you, are such as you say. I certainly agree that they speak to you from the heart and are the most sincere expression of my feeling; I do not deny even that they may influence you in some way, since you say so positively that they do that I cannot doubt it, but I cannot grant you that they bear all the marks which your kindness towards me and the frame of mind in which you heed all that speaks to you of God makes you find there. He has given you a quite special grace, for nothing is so rare as to meet souls who hear with pleasure when one so often recalls their obligations and the rules of conduct they should observe, and it might be said that nothing is so common as to see those who are offended and feel importuned as soon as one touches on that kind of subject. As you love God alone, and wish to please him alone, you are sensitive to everything relating to his glory and the service you wish to pay him.

Although your opinion of the effect on you of your unavoidable contacts with the world is not as well founded as you would like to make us think, it is still of use to you. You will be more on your guard, and more reserved with those whom necessity obliges you to see. Indeed, external contacts always spoil something in persons who are made only for God, and should remain hidden in the secret of his countenance. Worldly people have a malign quality from which it is almost impossible to defend oneself, and the best thing for those who are united most closely to God, and best know the danger they run in meeting them, is to efface before God as soon as they have left them certain stains contracted simply by the atmosphere of their company. I am sure that that is something you do most carefully. You tell me that the respects you had had conveyed to Monsieur N. were not as well received as they should have been, and you adopt the only attitude about that which one should adopt on everything, which is to look to God, in whom we shall find what we cannot meet in men, even in those who look on us most charitably. We should summon that feeling to our aid on many occasions in our lives, otherwise we should often be deprived of all consolation. Do me the honour of believing that is is not possible to be more than I yours' etc.

811220 MONSIEUR   20 December 1681
TB 1574

Solitary life must be led strictly or one will find in it 'the trivialities and vanities of the world which one thought to leave for ever'.

811230 NICOLAS PINETTE   [late December] 1681
TB 1441

New Year greetings and prayers.

82/1 MONSIEUR DE LANCHAL   [? 1682]
TD A (fragment)

His son is at la T. [Dom Jacques was professed at Perseigne in November 1681. See 811022].

82/2 MADAME 1682
TC I/162

Until she puts all her trust in God for reasons found in her own heart she will never find such reasons in men.

82/3 RP SUPÉRIEUR DE CHANOINES RÉGULIERS 1682
TC II/278

Does not think RP should keep pension even if he gives it away in alms; not canonically correct and a bad example.

This may be to RP Claude de La Lane (prior 1681–4), Saint-Victor, to whom similar letters are later addressed.

82/4 RP [?1682]
BN 25080,f.48

As R. has not changed his mind since writing the letter to a German monk which RP has seen, 'I do not hesitate to say that it is almost impossible for you to render to God what he demands of you' where he is.

The German monk is probably the recipient of 7217. See also 7513.

820100 RP, DE LA COMMUNE OBSERVANCE January 1682
TC II/277

RP's entry into cloister 'a profanation' and his conduct and that of those who received him 'full of sacrilege and impiety'. He must make amends by genuine conversion and go to a reformed house.

820101 RM [DE LA ROCHE] 1 January 1682
TB 1576

Encouragement.

820101a MONSIEUR [DIRECTOR OF A SEMINARY] 1 January 1682
TB 1578

Praises priest recently dead. An ecclesiastic exercising a useful ministry should not give it up for retreat. R. no longer willing to accept ecclesiastics for more than two or three days on retreat, as obliged by hospitality, otherwise the monastery would always be full of them.

820104   BISHOP OF GRENOBLE [ETIENNE LE CAMUS]   4 January 1682
Carp p. 488

If R. accepted suggested improvements in diet two out of three monks would have to go and the poor would go empty. 'Seventy people live here, not counting guests' [i.e. workers, not monks].

820105   RM PRIEURE [? CARMELITES]   5 January 1682
TB 1585

New Year greetings.

820108   RM MARIE [-LUCE OR -LOUISE]   8 January 1682
TB 1590; TC I/5

She is ungrateful for God's goodness and must fight against pride, watch the small things.

820112   MONSIEUR D'ETRECHY, CHEZ PROCUREUR-GÉNÉRAL   12 January 1682
TB 1596

He has been at la T. Religious should avoid litigation.

820115   MONSIEUR [? DU SUEL]   15 January 1682
TB 1598; Mug I/96

M. has sent a young man to la T., rough and ready, but simple and docile. Another sent four years ago died a lay-brother. Heavy burden on priests with cure of souls who have to stay in the world without being corrupted.

   The most likely lay-brother is Simon Lambert, professed in 1679, died June 1681, who came from Arras, thus suggesting Du Suel (canon of Arras) as addressee.

*820125   RM ABBESSE, LEYME [ANNE DE LA VIEUVILLE]   25 January 1682
TB 1607

'The continuation of your indisposition causes me much anxiety; I doubt whether you do all you should to throw it off. God tries you in many ways, but I do not doubt that he supports you at the same time and preserves you from the evil effects of the temptations which are virtually inseparable from continuous and lasting illness. For although we know that we must in all things put ourselves in his hands and abandon our fate to him in time as in eternity, yet it is rare to keep enough virtue and firmness to stand up to the despondency and depression caused by ill health, when we see no sign of recovery. You say that my letters are a comfort, but if that is so, you owe it purely to your piety, for however much I may intend to be of use to you and contribute to the relief of your ills and troubles, I am hardly capable of doing so; I simply recall to your attention what you know, and practice better than I. I do however understand that it is not pointless to speak often about it, for the truths which it costs nature something to practice, which challenge our inclinations, which bring us to depend in all things on God's order, and make no other reflection in all that happens to us than about his pure will, such truths elude us so easily that it is not possible to take too much care and precautions to retain them and prevent them being effaced. What is strange is that although there is nothing to be gained when one forgets them, and on he contrary a great deal to lose, because the only consolation for someone who suffers is to look to God, yet usually, when afflicted in body or spirit, we behave as though these things were quite unknown to us and we had never had any inkling of them. We have much cause, RM, to ask God to animate our faith and be pleased to quicken his spirit in us, for when he leaves us to ourselves and we act from our own impulses, our whole life is nothing but languor, desolation, and a real death. I beg you always to remember me before God, and in doing so to have my needs before your eyes, as well as my sincere assurance that I honour you and am beyond all words yours' etc.

820129   RELIGIEUSE   29 January 1682
TC II/26

She is fortunate in having a job she would not have chosen herself.

820130   MONSIEUR F[...]ÀB[...]   30 January 1682
TB 1609

M. has decided to serve God, but there is danger of taking up again with the world. R. agrees when he says he does not want 'to commit a half-folly by leaving the world for Christ, for it is surely worth committing a total folly'.

820204   RP PRIEUR [? DE LA COUR]   4 February 1682
TC II/46 (the date 19 November 1687 also appears on the copy, but is almost certainly an error)

RP should refuse post offered, sure to be dangerous, and faithfully follow his rule, vigil, fasting, and silence.

820212   RM [? LOUISE]   12 February 1682
TB 1610; TC II/286

Would like to discuss her problems orally, but he cannot leave la T. 'I look on my monastery as my tomb.'

The address has been erased, but could be Marie-Louise or Marie-Luce.

820215   CLAUDE NICAISE   15 February 1682
BN 9363,f.9 orig; Gonod 58

The two ecclesiastics were amazingly misguided to come so far on such an unfounded idea. Dismisses letter sent on by Nicaise 'as a kind of jargon and way of talking peculiar to persons under direction', an enthusiasm understood only by their own kind. 'I do not know what this good woman intends for her director if life at la T. seems in her eyes to be too easy for him.'

820223   MADAME   23 February 1682
TB 1614; TC I/172

She is hardly in the world any more. 'One always does better to speak to God than of God.' Even pious people are to be avoided, otherwise one never leaves the self.

820300   RM ABBESSE [MAUBUISSON, LOUISE-HOLLANDINE]   [? March] 1682
TC II/276

R. is writing to sub-prioress telling her to stay calm and not heed her scruples. She is pleased with dom Alain 'an excellent man, much opposed to laxity and irregular conduct'.

*820300a   RM ABBESSE, LEYME [ANNE DE LA VIEUVILLE]   March 1682
TB 1618

'I am not pleased about your health, for apart from the fact that I doubt whether you are doing all you should to restore it, the weather is so bad and harsh that it makes me very much afraid; I hope however that God will give you back health, and, in a word, that you are neither at the end of your days nor at the end of your pains. You must endure patiently what that poor religious thinks of your condition. You became ill through obeying your rule, that is executing God's orders and conforming yourself to his will; are you not indeed fortunate? It can even be said that you are still fulfilling your rule, since it is as much for the sick as for those who are not sick, prescribing for the latter strict penitential ways and allowing to the former proper and necessary relief.

You do well not to allow your religious to withdraw to a place of disorder and irregularity. You must not feel her loss, if possible. However, since she is not to be corrected, and is able to do harm through her bad example, you should make no difficulties if she should obtain permission to go away. The Rule requires us to expel incorrigible persons, as you know, lest their wickedness is transmitted and the contagion strikes the whole flock (see Mabillon's note on St Bernard's *Letters*).

Your view is as just as it could be when you find it preferable for houses to be destroyed than to receive bad candidates, since superiors cannot, without displeasing

God and betraying their ministry, admit to a holy profession those who do not propose that sanctity as their aim, and it is strictly speaking to mock Christ by giving him brides whom he does not know, had not called, and who are not worthy of him. Nothing brings his curse more readily upon religious communities and those who rule them than such admissions. It must be agreed that that is precisely the origin of the general licence prevailing in cloisters. As most vocations involve self-interest, as the intentions of the people who present themselves are not pure, any more than the ideas of those who extend a hand to them, God has no place in a cursed alliance, and looks on such engagements and entries as profanations of his sanctuary. I am only surprised that with nothing more constant than this truth it is so little known and so universally neglected. Do me the justice of believing that no one in the world can honour you more than I, yours' etc.

820300b   RM [? SOUS-PRIEURE, MAUBUISSON]   March 1682
TB 1620

She is better; she must try to avoid the external duties which caused her harm and convince her superior.

820301   MONSIEUR FÉLIBIEN CHARTRES   1 March 1682
TB 1622

Instructions for dress of women entering religion. Avoid elaborate hair styles, bare arms and neck, 'costumes more fit for actresses than for persons living under rule'. 'I think most nuns are so convinced that this practice [of worldly dress] is so necessary that they would regard its absence as nullifying the clothing ceremony.'

This is probably Pierre Félibien; it is not known which religious house he was concerned with in this context.

820302   NICOLAS PINETTE   2 March 1682
Autographes Troussures, p. 546

R. regrets he cannot accept lad sent by Pinette, but he does not know Latin, and so cannot be a choir monk, nor a trade, so cannot be a lay-brother. Hopes to see Pinette.

820306   RP DE LA COUR, SAINT-JEAN DES VIGNES, SOISSONS   6 March 1682
TB 1624; TC II/178

RP has been to la T. Should accept proposed charge on condition that he can train novices properly.

This is the brother of dom Jacques, future abbot of la T., who left Soissons to become a Cistercian in 1674 (but joined la T. only in 1686 from le Pin).

820308 RM ABBESSE, ESSAI [FRANÇOISE TROTTI DE LA CHÉTARDIE]   8 March 1682
TC II/179
Death of Bp of Séez [Jean de Forcoal].
He died on 25 February.

* 820308a MADAME DE SAINT-LOUP   8 March 1682
TD/A

'The first words of your letter, Madame, kept me in suspense for a few moments, but I confess that their application seemed to me as appropriate and felicitous as possible, and in point of fact I could hardly be more delighted than by learning that God has thus moved someone with whom I have been bound by the most intimate links of friendship for more than thirty-five years. We must ask God to guide such an important affair, to give those concerned in it strength and fidelity, and so to rule the heart of the person on whom its success particularly depends, that it is not affected by any impression contrary to that which he has shown, for you cannot doubt that a campaign will be launched and every power unleashed to frustrate a plan whose execution will produce infinite benefits and advantages. What it seems to me is to be feared is some jealousy from Rome, which would be most vexatious, since a minor incident is sometimes capable of halting a major enterprise. This one needs much prayer, and the people who serve God are strictly obliged to turn to him for protection and support for men, whose wills in themselves have no firmness or consistency.

I cannot tell you my delight that the person you indicate was the prime mover in this great work; assure him, when you see him, of my affectionate honour and respect.

I do not want to say anything about N., except that he is much to be pitied. However, as there is not place so remote that one cannot return from it, we must not despair of his return nor tire of commending him to God.

There is no limit to man's weakness, and nothing, wise and enlightened though he may be, which he is not liable to do once he leaves God and abandons himself to himself. I assure you, as I believe I have often said, that the only course for a man rescued from shipwreck, who wants to make port and cease to be beset by storms, is to live in uncertainty and abasement in the eyes of God, who only casts his merciful countenance on humbled souls and does not tolerate elevation in the conversion of sinners, when it is sincere. We have become estranged from him through pride; it is humility alone which brings us close to him again, and if we are fortunate enough to win him back after losing him, it is humility that keeps him.

I praise God, Madame, that you love your retreat, and assure you that if God were not taking a hand, you would find it very onerous and would find anything but the peace and consolation which you tell me you are enjoying. We would be much consoled if divine providence so disposed things that you could once more in your life pass by our desert. You must not doubt that you are very much present to us here and that we offer you as fervently as possible to Our Lord. I pray him to make you happy all the more fervently for being sure that you put your happiness in him alone.

The poor Bishop of Séez has been ill for quite a long time, and I do not think that he is still alive at this moment. The close union between him and me can be criticised as much as people will, but that will not stop me feeling my loss with all possible grief, apart from the fact that God enjoins nothing more strongly than that we should love those to whom he has subjected us and whom he has given us as pastors and fathers. I can say that there never was a more cordial, faithful friend, nor one more devoted to all the interests of his friends. These qualities are so rare that one could not be too appreciative of those who have them.'

The reference to thirty-five years friendship goes back to 1647; R. is quite likely alluding to negotiations for reconciling the Jansenists, in which his very old friends Le Camus and Choiseul were involved, but a major obstacle to the return of Arnauld was another old friend, Harlay, Abp of Paris, and he is most probably the intimate friend in question. The Bp of Séez had indeed died on 25 February.

*820309   HENRI DUHAMEL   9 March 1682
TB/1626

'I am not surprised that you do not find much change in your health; the weather has been so trying and so unfavourable to its recovery that one might say that it was in the course of nature, as it was no doubt in the order of God, that you did not make faster progress, but from now on, as the season advances and we approach spring, I do not doubt that you will recover all your strength and will have the consolation of telling us that God has made you what we have been wanting for you for so long. The victim must, my dear Father [sic], be made fit and fat again, if possible, in order to be destroyed and offered as a fresh sacrifice which, to all appearances, will be the fulfilment of the work. At bottom one should live only in order to cease living, and receive life from God's hand only to have the pleasure and satisfaction of handing it back to him. Anyone not feeling like that would be living for himself and for the world, not for God, so that it would be for the world and not God to crown his race, and he would have no right to hope for anything and claim anything from one for whose love he had not lived. Have no scruples about being with people you like, and who show deference and consideration for you. That is a consolation which God will change when he sees fit, and you know from long experience that he knows how to mix bitterness and, if you like, imbibe with gall the sweetness that comes to us from men. He has thousands and thousands of ways of humiliating those whom he loves, and he seldom fails to let those whom he wishes to make fully accord with his heart feel the weight of his hand. We must believe that we belong to that number, and if we feel this keenly, not only can we endure with patience and resignation afflictions and setbacks, but we accept them joyfully when they befall us as the only signs and genuine characteristics distinguishing the true disciples of Christ from those who are not. I see that you do not find your spiritual exercises quite as easy as you would wish, and that you would like to say with the apostle *spiritus promptus in carne infirma* [Mt 26:41], but God, whose wishes in this are not the same as yours, moderates your impatience and zeal. The chief thing is that your heart should be fundamentally his, and I am certain that when you examine yourself that is what you find. You must be content with the fruits you have gathered in the desert; you are fortunate that the stocks you built up in solitude are not yet consumed and that you can use them with pleasure, and you must believe that if God were not taking a hand in it you would be saying like that ungrateful people: *Nauseat anima nostra super cibo isti levissimo* [Nb 21:5].

I wish you, my very dear Monsieur, an increase in ever sort of grace and benediction, and pray God that he will never let you tire of loving and serving him. A Christian is a creature to be deplored if his whole heart is not filled with this feeling. Do not forget us in your prayers, I beg you, and do not doubt that there is no one in the world who honours and cherishes you more than I.'

*820323   RM MARIE-LOUISE [BOUTHILLIER]   23 March 1682
TA orig; TB/1661 (dated 7 May)

'It is true, my dear sister, that God deprives us of our best friends, and we have lost one in the person of our bishop, whom we could not sufficiently mourn. It would be hard to have one who treated us as he did, for his cordiality and affection for everything that concerned us could not have been greater or more complete. It is very right that we should abandon those who love us to divine providence, since we are obliged to abandon ourselves also, and God disposes of our life and health as he pleases. You are right to want him to preserve poor Monsieur Pinette, for it would be difficult to find a heart like his. Faithful souls are so rare that when they leave the world it should give occasion for public grief and affliction. Detach yourself from men, my dear sister, since the bonds one contracts with them are not eternal, and when one comes down to it, Christ alone, whom one cannot lose so long as one wishes to keep him, is worthy of our attachment. It is hard when one has counted on someone's friendship, and even identified one's peace of mind with the consolation to be derived from it, to see oneself deprived of it for ever, and often when one least expected it. Such blows usually cause extreme disturbance. Thus, my dear sister, the best thing we can do is to depend solely on God and look at everyone and everything in him. He speaks to us through men, but when he withdraws them from us he hardly ever fails to speak to us himself.

You know only too well, my dear sister, what I told you in my last letter. I have nothing to add, except to exhort you to have confidence in God's mercy and be strictly faithful to him in all your duties. Your darkness will fade away, your heart will be warmed, you will feel the ice in it melt, and I do not doubt that what God has so far refused, he will grant to your perseverance. He wants to be sought after, he wants to be solicited and pressed, he yields to our importunities and we have never heard that they weary or repel him. Want him, desire him, tell him that you will not cease from prayer until he heeds you. Do not tire, although you see no obvious use in it, but be persuaded that a cry from the heart is the most powerful and effective prayer you can use. Do not withdraw from participation in the sacred mysteries unless your conscience reproaches you with something which obliges you to do so. Provided that your life is faithful and you have a sincere wish to progress in God's ways, this divine food will give you strength, and it will be through it more than any other means that you will overcome the difficulties of which you complain. Farewell, my dear sister, pray Our Lord Jesus for me and believe me yours' etc.

PS We shall not fail to commend to God the good religious whom he has taken away in so prompt and sudden a manner. She could not have been taken in a better disposition since she was ready to approach the holy table.'

820325   RP SIMON GOURDAN, SAINT-VICTOR   25 March 1682
TB 1632; TC I/93

His superior prevents reform. Obedience is owed when superior follows God's ways, but otherwise docility can be dangerous. 'You must accompany the resistance you are obliged to offer with external signs of deference to his rank.' Superior judges Gourdan's hair too short, his fasts too long. Accept preaching duty, but not that of confessions, usually dangerous.

This seven-page letter is part of Gourdan's campaign to lead at his own easygoing Saint-Victor the life he was not strong enough to lead at la T. The offending prior at the time was Claude de la Lane. Gourdan eventually won.

820400   DOM ROBERT HAR[DY], VISITOR, SAINT-MAUR   April 1682
TB 1640

Pressed to advise on choice of a new General, R. recommends someone of piety and virtue, acceptable at court, rather than someone firmer, less acceptable, and suspected of Jansenist sympathies.

Hardy had become Visitor for the province of France in 1681; it is odd that he should have asked R's opinion. The death of Vincent Marolles in September 1681, before the end of his term as General, precipitated a crisis. Eventually Benoît Brachet was elected in view of royal opposition to Claude Martin, his fellow Assistant and obvious candidate. It is clearly to these two that R. refers.

820400a MONSIEUR AMELINE, GRAND ARCHDEACON OF PARIS   April 1682
TB 1647; TC I/95
Ameline has recently visited la T.; value of solitude.

820413 ARCHBISHOP OF PARIS [FRANÇOIS DE HARLAY]   13 April 1682
TB 1650: TC I/1, TC I/94a
Praises abp's attempts to bring peace to Church; disastrous if current opportunity is missed. 'It is a plank thrown into the midst of a shipwreck, and to miss it is to lose all.' [See 820308a.]

*820423 MARÉCHAL DE BELLEFONDS   23 April 1682
BN na 12959 f.92,orig.; TB 1644: TC I/94

'If we gave ourselves the honour of writing to you, Mgr, every time we thought of it, you would often be hearing of us; but as no occasion presents itself, I content myself with remembering you before Our Lord and recommending to him your person and your needs. I say your needs because they must perforce be great, for as you have received much from God, you owe him much, and without special protection it would be difficult for you to respond with due fidelity to all the grace he has given you. I hardly know what is going on, but I learn with extreme pleasure that you continue to keep up the life you began, or rather that God keeps you up to it, and that everything in your conduct clearly shows that he is taking a hand in it, and that so far you have been inaccessible to the wickedness of the world. It is so rare that one escapes the traps that the world constantly prepares for those who live with its business and among those who live its distractions, vanities, and pleasures that you could not be too mindful of the gratitude you owe to God's goodness in separating you from the great mass of people who think so differently from you, whose views and principles are so opposed to yours, and who regard as their sole and principal business what you only look at in passing and as far as divine providence impels you. God's servants as well as those who do not serve him sometimes hold high rank among men, but with the distinction that some love those sorts of places for themselves and others only find themselves there by following God's order, and behave there with so much restraint and purity that it could be said that they are as much afraid of escaping from his hand and dependence on him as the others are afraid of falling into it. You know too well, Mgr, that all good comes from God, that it is he who effects it in us through his grace, and preserves it, that we are only what he makes us, that we walk only with the movement he gives us, that he is at once our light and our strength, that he shows us the way and leads us, not to humble yourself continually in his eyes in deep realisation of all the effects of his mercy heaped upon you, which is the real means of making him continue them. We lose God if we lack gratitude, and if those he loves were always careful, as they are obliged to be, to give him thanks for his goodness in regarding them as his, and if he saw himself in their heart as he should be, nothing could ever make him abandon a soul which showed by its gratitude its desire to please him. Piety consists of nothing but this continual relationship we have with God, and just as he gives himself to us at every moment by the operations of his Holy Spirit, so we must give ourselves to him by a perpetual response, so that this holy and intimate communication is never interrupted, since in truth it is no less essential to the life of grace than breathing to natural life.

I cannot refrain from speaking to you, Mgr, of a matter which is purely one of charity and concerns your nephew, the abbé de Villars. The Abbot of Clairvaux intends to establish good order and discipline in his abbey of Montiers, but this cannot be done unless he himself lends a hand and contributes; and as one of the principal means is to remove from the monks every cause of dissipation, it would be necessary for the abbé de Villars to let them have some rooms which are below their dormitory, and a large space opposite the windows of their cells in which to make a garden, which the abbots have used as a dependency of the abbatial lodging, although in fact it is not. The trouble about that is that the monks' windows have no other outlook than this large empty space, and so they are perpetually exposed to noise and commotion and have constantly before their eyes persons of both sexes, whether the abbot puts farmers in or is there himself. In other words, there is no kind of evil to which a religious is not exposed when his normal lodging is in such a situation, since men's minds, as you know, and especially those of persons in retreat are easily open to every sort of temptation. If you were good enough, Mgr, to speak to your nephew about it, and to draw his attention to the fact that the chief obligation of a commendatory abbot is to procure in every possible way the glory and service of God in the community expressly entrusted to his care by the Church, and make every sort of effort for the sanctification of those belonging to it, he will readily listen to the Abbot of Clairvaux's proposal on this subject. I do not doubt, Mgr, that you are as convinced as I am that he should regard his status and profession not according to the usual principles and views, but in God's truth and design, and that if you speak to him in this sense, the authority and respect you command will bring him to form proper plans and thoughts, should he not do so of his own accord.

The position of commendatory abbot has essentially nothing to justify or legitimise it before God but the diligence with which he works to see that God is served and honoured in his house, and the devotion with which he acquits himself of the duties imposed upon him by his original institution. I should be infinitely obliged to you, Mgr, if I could know that the abbé de Villars was disposed in this matter as I hope. Continue your accustomed kindness to me, I beg you, and do me the justice of believing that no one could honour or respect you more than I, nor be more faithfully yours' etc.

[A PS of six lines has been rendered completely illegible]

The abbé de Villars was not Bellefonds' nephew but the son of his aunt Marie, who had married the marquis de Villars, and whose elder son became the duc and maréchal. The monastery is Montier-en-Argonne, diocese of Châlons.

820430 JEAN FAVIER [30] April 1682
TB 1642
Favier's health is weakening and death approaches, but he has served God faithfully.

820500 DOM ALAIN [MORONY] [April/May 1682]
TC I/95a
Seculars should never be allowed into convents.

820500a RP PIERRE DE MONCHY, CONG. ORAT. May 1682
TB 1653; TC II/175
Monchy's health is getting worse; R. also not too well.

820500b RP May 1682
TC II/13
He will be welcome at la T.

820507 PAUL BARILLON, LONDON 7 May 1682
TB 1655
Condolences on death of Mme Barillon [Paul's mother], always very kind to R. [She died on 20 April.]

820507a BISHOP OF LUÇON [HENRI BARILLON] 7 May 1682
TB 1659; P f.602 (with date 16 November 1682)

'I was too well aware, Mgr, of your feelings for your mother and her affection for you, not to know that you would need all your virtue, and special protection from God, to bear the grief which her loss has caused you. For, though her already advanced age gave you no cause to believe that you could keep her for long, and you saw the moment approaching when she would have to pay the tribute which no one is excused, yet these are arguments to which nature does not listen when the wounds are deep, unless God gives nature a docility which she does not have of herself. It seems to me that this separation affects you in so many ways that God alone can make its weight tolerable. Finally, Mgr, your mother has gone to God full of good works and years. All her conduct was nothing but a constant practice of acts, each of which testified to and resulted from her piety and the purity of her faith. Her life was so christian and faithful that there is every reason to believe that God has granted her the rest accorded to his saints. I do not need to tell you, Mgr, how distressed I am at this event, knowing, as you do, how deeply involved I am in all that concerns you, and the respect which I was obliged to feel for your mother because of all the ways in which she showed me kindness. Fundamentally, God is the consolation of those who hope in him and remain' dependent on him. All men come from his hand, he entrusts them to the world for a few moments, and once these are past, the world has no right to retain them, but must give them back.

I wish you, Mgr all kinds of blessings, and pray that God may be at your right hand, that he may lighten and sustain all your steps on the slippery and difficult paths one has to tread, and not allow you on any occasion to have anything but truth before your eyes. Do me the honour of believing that no one in the world honours you more than I or could be more sincerely and respectfully yours' etc.

Barillon's mother died in Paris on 20 April 1682.

*820510 MADAME DE SAINT-LOUP 10 May 1682
TD/A

'You are so well aware, Madame, of my concern for you in all your troubles that there is no need for me to tell you of it at every occasion that presents itself. In a word, you must want what God wants you to be, and all your efforts and anxieties will not save you from the storm as long as it pleases him that you should stay in its midst. Give up to him in full confidence the care and running of your ship, knowing that he never sleeps and his eyes never close on those who love him; it is a saying of eternal truth that those who put their trust in him are happy; it is ordinary, but cannot be too often repeated, since none is more necessary and less put to use.

How fortunate the P[rincess] P[alatine] is to have her troubles and suffer them in peace, as you tell me. May she be strengthened in the feelings given her by God, may she extricate herself from the ills that come upon her and regard him as their real author. He afflicts her, as I think I have sometimes written to you, to make her more worthy of him. One day she will clearly know what at present she sees only through the obscurity of faith, that all her sorrows have resulted merely from his mercy. God does not fail doubtless to speak to her heart with words of consolation and in some sort justify his conduct towards her. I am most obliged at the honour she does me of thinking of me. I beg you to tell her, when you have a chance, how much care we take in offering her to Our Lord; we will pray him, as we burn on the altar the incense she was charitable enough to send, to fill and kindle her more and more with his love. I will not speak to you, Madame, of the affairs of the moment, since I know next to nothing of what is happening in the world. We only pray God for peace and agreement between Church and Empire, that is, for a union of these two powers, as must be the main obligation of persons in retreat.

Farewell, Madame, I hope that Our Lord will reward your patience with a peace and calm exempt from the inconstancy and revolution of the times. Think for your consolation that as everything passes away and is absorbed for ever in God's eternity, that perishable things are not worth considering.'

The Princess Palatine was Anne de Gonzague (1616–84), converted in 1672 with much publicity by Bossuet, and with support from R. A dispute had arisen between Louis XIV and Rome on the perennial problem of Gallicanism, whence the reference to Church and Empire.

820512   ARCHBISHOP OF PARIS [FRANÇOIS DE HARLAY]   12 May 1682
TB 1630

Condolences on death of abp's brother.

François Bonaventure de Harlay, marquis de Bréval, died 16 March.

820520   BISHOP OF GRENOBLE [ETIENNE LE CAMUS]   20 May 1682
TB 1664; TC II/177

Bp better after illness.

820523   RM THÉRÈSE [BOUTHILLIER]   23 May 1682
TB 1659

Death of Bp of Séez. She is better, R. has had a fever for three weeks.

820523a   RM MARIE-LUCE [PICOT], PRIEURE, ANNONCIADES   23 May 1682
TB 1663

Encouragement.

820524   MONSIEUR DE SAINT-GILLES   24 May 1682
TB 1666

His son granted King's permission to enter religion; not a deserter because he had been granted leave. M. should think again about what his son has done and be less worldly himself.

820524a   MONSIEUR BODEAU   24 May 1682
TB 1672

He has done well to keep only one benefice. Abbot of Pontigny will pay his pension, but if he does not need it, give it to the poor. His conversion must now equal his aberrations.

820524b   BISHOP OF SÉEZ [MATHURIN SAVARY]   24 May 1682
TB 1671

R's respects on Savary's appointment to see.

*820524c   HENRI DUHAMEL   24 May 1682
TB/1668

'Among all your news we observe that your health is gradually returning, and we hope that the stubbornness of the illness will yield to remedies and diets. I see that you have fully used God's visitation as you should, since you received it peacefully and your patience stood up to the distress which is almost inevitable in long illnesses, if one does not surrender as you do to the hand of God and if our will is not entirely submissive to his. My own prognostication of your condition is that if your body does not recover its former vigour, your soul will be quite rejuvenated and will have acquired fresh strength and liveliness. If, as you say, your outward economy has been turned upside down by the changes you have undergone, I am convinced that the inward good order subsists, that your heart is working perfectly, that all its movements are as they should be, and that the situation being, as it is, sent from God, remains firm and constant. Jesus Christ loves those who serve him and belong to him, nothing is dearer and more precious to him than the preservation of his elect, he allows them to be tempted, but he covers them with his protection and prevents them being overwhelmed by the attacks they experience. After all, Monsieur, the destruction of the body is nothing, and since faith teaches us that after its dissolution God will give us another which will never die, we must look on the perishing of this one not only without sorrow, but with joy and pleasure, *seminatur corpus mortale* [1 Co 15:44], since it necessarily has to pass through death to be reborn into a life which will no longer be subject to inconstancy, and will last as long as God's eternity. Ultimately we live only to die; God's design in giving us the enjoyment of light is to deprive us of it; he puts us into this world only as a passage; since the creation of the angels no one has been given a place in heaven without having had to journey on earth. That is how God prepares us and makes us worthy of the destiny allotted to us. The shorter our race, the sooner we shall enjoy the happiness awaiting us, and how can we value it as we should, desire it as it deserves, and still want to prolong our days, unless it is in order to submit to God's will, complete the time indicated and finish our course in full according to his eternal decisions? In short, God wishes men to die, and their will is not in conformity with his if they want to live out of their love and attachment to life. To tell the truth, anyone would be falling far short of loving Christ as much as he should who, faced with the option of dying or living, failed to prefer death to life. A Christian must constantly have on his lips the apostle's words: *Cupio dissolvi et esse cum Christo* [Ph 1:23], since such enjoyment of Christ is incompatible with the life of the world.

I am no less anxious, my dear Monsieur, than you are to see you at la Trappe, but I confess that I should not want it to be in the state in which we saw you, for we are sensitive to the ills and fatigues of our friends, and when these are incurable they cannot fail to make deep impressions on us. I do not despair after all that God will bring you back here, and with enough health and strength to share partially in our penitence, even if you cannot do so wholly. Farewell, my dear Monsieur, love me always and recommend our whole house to Our Lord, and me in particular, whose miseries, as you cannot have failed to see, are without end or limit.'

Duhamel was ill for two months while on a visit to la T. and had to be removed to the family home at Pithiviers, near Orléans, where he died.

*820608   MARÉCHAL DE BELLEFONDS   8 June 1682
BN na 12959 f.96,orig.

'You are too kind, Mgr, to have thought of me and been good enough to speak of me to the abbé Savary. I do not doubt that I owe to you the kindly feelings which he showed you he had for us. You can easily judge, Mgr, that it is more reassuring and advantageous for persons in retreat to enjoy favour in their bishop's eyes and have some claim on their friendship. I am declaring to him in the letter I am writing to him the care we took to recommend him to Our Lord as soon as we knew that God had given us him for our bishop. I am telling him too that I have begged you to assure him that no one under his authority will have more respect and submission for him and his orders than I.

I count M. de Villeneuve most fortunate in the retreat you have granted him at Vincennes. There he can serve God and live as much apart from men as God gives him a mind and heart to do. That is an obligation he imposes on those who serve him, whether they are in the world or not, and as it takes much virtue to detach oneself when one is living among them, those who find themselves engaged there should be very careful to ask God for the fidelity necessary so to behave towards men that they feel for them only what he wants them to give. We shall not cease, Mgr, to commend to God your person and your house. I beg you to believe that there is nothing that we more frequently have before our eyes and of which we can speak to him with more fervour, having all the respect I have for you, and all the attachment to all that concerns you.'

Mathurin Savary had just been appointed Bp of Séez in succession to the harassed Jean de Forcoal who died in February 1682. R attached the greatest importance to having good relations with his diocesan. Villeneuve cannot be identified, but was probably a former army officer. Bellefonds was Governor of Vincennes, just outside of Paris.

820613   PRINCESS D'HARCOURT   13 June 1682
TB 1674; TC II/31

She must continue serving God as she has begun.

820613a   FRÈRE THÉODORE, l'etoile   13 June 1682
TB 1676

He had tried vocation at la T. but was dismissed by R. Can build at l'Etoile on foundations laid at la T. He did well to obey and leave, and R. still feels responsible for his welfare.

820620   BISHOP OF TOURNAI [GILBERT DE CHOISEUL]   20 June 1682
TB 1678

R. remains faithful friend.

820627   BISHOP OF MEAUX [J.-B. BOSSUET]   27 June 1682
TB 1684; Bossuet, *Correspondance*, II p.256

R. asks him not to divulge MS of *Sainteté*.

R. *always maintained that the* MS *of* De la Sainteté et des Devoirs de la vie monastique *had been shown outside la T. without his consent, and that he only agreed to publication (March 1683) under pressure, especially from Bossuet. He invariably referred to his book as* 'de la vie monastique' (*on monastic life*).

*820627b   RP ABBÉ, LA COLOMBE [PIERRE DE LA SALLE]   27 June 1682
TB 1685

'I will simply tell you my opinion as you ask, without being prevented by the thought that you would easily find within yourself what you are seeking elsewhere. To answer precisely, I think that when one finds oneself in irregular assemblies, where one sees things neither conducted nor decided by the spirit of God, and there is no hope of profitably or successfully resisting the torrent, the best thing to do is to avoid charges and offices, especially those obliging us to speak or write in the name of the whole body. For my part, considering the present state of the Order, and the way matters are treated in General Chapters, I would not for anything in the world accept the post of notary, or secretary. That is the real way to avoid exposing oneself to anything which might wound one's conscience. Someone who does not want a post is not compelled, and even if pressure is put on him, and with some insistence, that is when one must stand firm and not give up one's point of view. Always keep the honour of your friendship for me, and believe me, I beg you, to be yours' etc.

Although official summons to the Chapter of May 1683 did not go out until August 1682, La Salle must have anticipated that he would be forced into a prominent role (in the event he became one of the definitors and visitor).

*820627c   RP ABBÉ, CHÂTILLON [CLAUDE LE MAÎTRE]   27 June 1682
TB 1680

'You must resolve to suffer patiently whatever men may say about you if you want to establish God's work in your house, and the first thing you ought to have reckoned with is that your conduct would be regarded as something novel and impractical, and thus exposed to public censure. So you must go your way and follow up what you have begun, without paying attention to their judgements. Do not be surprised if few remain from the many who present themselves for entry into your monastery; the number of the elect of God is small, and as well regulated cloisters are places in which he prepares them and makes them worthy of being chosen by him, there is nothing to be amazed at if many embark on the road, while only a small number persevere. You must hope that if you make yourself worthy of God's designs, he will not fail to sustain you and give blessing and success to what he has inspired in you for so long. There cannot fail to be squalls and tempests, since we all sail on a stormy sea, but we know to our consolation that when it pleases him who is the master of the elements to bid the wind and sea to be calm, all obey his voice, and the way to induce him to utter this command is to tell him often, not in a spirit of timidity but of trust: *domine salva nos, perimus* [Mt 8:25], Lord if your almighty hand does not steer our ship, we shall perish.

'I would say about the religious of whom you speak that in the sickness with which he is assailed you should not make any difficulty about giving him meat to restore his strength and constitution, and in so doing you will not be doing anything against the spirit of the Rule; and if after having made his health better, you find him unable to live on vegetables, you will do well to dispense him and relieve him of an austerity of which he is not capable; and with that difference, if he continues to show piety and religion, and give edification and example, you should not think of sending him to another monastery, especially if you judge that this concession is not causing any untoward impression on the spirit of the rest of his brethren.

'As for our lay brothers, those who work a lot in the heat of the summer, are given the *mixtum* in the morning, and some are allowed to drink water when their thirst is great and their need real and pressing. I would grant the same permission to a choir monk in the same case. One must not make concessions to laxity, but one must also not be too firm when needs are real. The surest way to prevent religious giving way to sleep is to make them read in the cloister or chapter house in common, according to the ancient uses. It would be against all good order to allow those who have rested in the morning to do so again in the afternoon, unless there is some quite unusual necessity.'

820700   BISHOP OF GRENOBLE [ETIENNE LE CAMUS]   July 1682
TB 1686

People criticise bp's austerity and blame his poor health on it, but that is no justification for the sort of mitigation they propose. He could allow himself eggs, a little wine, fewer sermons and vigils. Even taking meat would not harm edification. R's advice is not prompted by selfish fear of losing a friend. 'That would not impair your desire to lead a monastic life.'

In 1681 Le Camus had taken vows as an oblate in a local benedictine house, and scrupulously observed the Rule.

820704 BISHOP OF GRENOBLE [ETIENNE LE CAMUS]   4 July 1682
TC I/10

R. is anxious to see bp's health restored. His austerity is widely disapproved. 'You can diminish your austerities but cannot prolong your days.' He could eat meat again without denying edification to the Church.

This and the preceding letter are different, and both seem to have been sent, though it is not clear in what order.

820704a RM DE LA ROCHE, TOURS   4 July 1682
TB 1691; TC II/219

RM Louise [Rogier] is recovering from illness. Always best to condemn oneself before God.

*820704b RM ABBESSE, LEYME [ANNE DE LA VIEUVILLE]   4 July 1682
TB 1693

'I have not heard from you for an extremely long time, and I find it hard to go any longer without asking for your news, although I imagine that nothing unusual has happened, since you have not written. I must tell you that I realise that I have been deprived of a real consolation, in having been deprived of the marks of a friendship as cordial and sincere as yours. And then your health is so uncertain, and your infirmities are so frequent, that one is never free from fears about your preservation. I very much doubt whether you think about it as much as you should, but although life has nothing attractive about it to make us become attached to it, it must none the less not be so neglected that one takes no care over it, since some care is permissible and comes within God's order. Although a Christian who is as moved as he should be by things eternal has nothing but contempt for those which are transitory, and looks with pleasure towards his end, he still often does what those who have contrary feelings do, that is he takes steps and adopts courses of action to avoid dying, although he really does not wish to live. All our inclinations and bias, if our faith is a live one, should impel us on to the side of death, and God's will alone should make us feel the opposite. In sickness a Christian thinks of his recovery in profound peace, because he wants it only in so far as God wants to give it, and anyone who is not christian is anxious and troubled, because he wants to recover, cost what it may. Happy are those who abandon their fate into God's hand and leave entirely to him the decision as to what concerns them. It is a fixed truth, and one which it is so necessary to practise, that without it life is just a series of random movements and perpetual agitation, through the numerous actions and over zealous precautions with which it is filled, and which cause nothing but trouble, with none of the fruits and utility hoped for from them.

I will not ask, RM, if people are still speaking ill of me in your part of the world, for

I can easily imagine that there has been no change of mind, and that people who still have the same attitudes and principles will always form the same judgement regarding our conduct. God confers a great grace on those who love him when he does them good, but a still greater one when that good is contradicted and censured by men. They were never less equitable than they are at present, and their eyes are so closed that they indiscriminately condemn anything which deviates in the slightest degree from usual ways, without realising that the narrow way, which is that which Christ taught, is not the usual way, that few walk in it and that the broad way, which he always denounced, is that of the majority.

I will say no more about the desire people had, and still have, to recall you to your native parts. There are obstacles and barriers everywhere, and often, as I believe I have told you, in those places where one had imagined one would enjoy perfect tranquility one finds only trouble and bitterness.

You are very right when you say that in most monasteries the education given to young women is less christian than it is in the world. Vanity reigns, and self-love, and not only are the religious virtues unknown, but people pride themselves on not being ignorant of the manners, disorders, and malice of people living in the world. Yet that is so general and so authorised that the contrary ideas are regarded as new and suspect principles. I pray God to strengthen those which he gave to you, and for my part I consider them as resulting purely from his mercy and requiring of you acknowledgement and gratitude of no ordinary degree. I wish you, RM, all kinds of blessing, and beg you to believe that the interest I take in all that affects you is beyond all I can express....

PS Please tell the RM, your sister, that she has no legitimate cause for complaint against me; I honour her as I should and no one could value more the honour of her remembrance and friendship.'

On the proposed move near home, see letter 810820.

820705   RP, CHANOINE RÉGULIER   5 July 1682
TC I/38
Question of pension paid by a mother for her son in religion.

820706   RM ABBESSE, MAUBUISSON [LOUISE-HOLLANDINE]   6 July 1682
TB 1697
Praises training given to novices.

820706a   RM, [SOUS-PRIEURE], MAUBUISSON   6 July 1682
TB 1698
Dom Alain is more pleased with her than she thinks. She should not worry about all her minor faults.

820706b MONSIEUR DES CHASSAY   6 July 1682
TB 1696; TC II/341

Condolences on death of son.

820706c BISHOP OF GRENOBLE [ETIENNE LE CAMUS]   6 July 1682
TB 1699

Perhaps R. should have insisted that bp be fully recovered before resuming austerity, as St Benedict's Rule prescribes. He must take care.

820706d ARCHBISHOP OF PARIS [FRANÇOIS DE HARLAY]   6 July 1682
TB 1701

Regrets that opportunity for peace has passed. Has received abp's message through Muguet [his publisher].

This, and 820413, seem to refer to a specific initiative for reconciling Arnauld and the Jansenists in which the abp would have played a key part.

820706e RP TACONNET, PRIEUR, SAINT-VICTOR   6 July 1682
TB 1703

RP has been at la T. Better to renounce his pension to avoid sense of ownership, unsuitable in a religious.

Taconnet ceased to be prior in 1678. La Lane was prior in 1682, but it is more likely the title than the name that is wrong.

820706f PAUL BARILLON   6 July 1682
TB 1705; TC II/58

Has seen Pinette at la T. 'Probity must be joined to piety and religion, otherwise it is a mere cloud, with colour, light, and brightness, but dissipated in a moment.'

820706g SOEUR ÉMÉLIE [DE BOUILLON]   6 July 1682
TB 1707; TC II/220

Has spoken about her to RP Aveillon, Cong. Orat. She must repair her shameful past conduct, submit to superiors, practise self-denial, forget her birth and be humble.

Aveillon (1620-1713) was superior of the Paris house of the Oratory in 1686, but not superior of the Carmelites, though he may well have been one of their confessors.

820707 RP JÉRÔME, SAINTE-CROIX, PARIS   7 July 1682
TB 1709

He has no cause for self-reproach, being prevented by health from staying at la T., but should now try to base his life on what he saw there.
Cf. 810825.

820713 RP PRIEUR, BARBEAUX   13 July [1682]
Tour. orig.

R. was glad to see him at la T. Dom Alain will tell him how to send the books he bought. Details of new seal for abbey.

Dom Alain at Maubuisson was on the other side of Paris from Barbeaux; presumably they met in Paris.

820715 DOM JEAN-FRANÇOIS CORNUTY, TAMIÉ   15 July 1682
MS *Chronique de Tamié*, Burnier *Hist. de Tamié*, 8

Sorry that Cornuty has such cares. His abbot has gone in obedience to orders.

Abbot Somont had been appointed Procurator-General in Rome for the whole order in January 1682, as a gesture to the Reform, but it made of him a virtually permanent absentee and Cornuty was left to run the abbey.

820718 MADAME JOLY   18 July 1682
TB 1711

Condolences on brother's death; clearly not suicide, whatever people may say.

820720 MARQUISE D'ALÈGRE   20 July 1682
TB 1713; TC I/6

She wants to serve God; she can respect conventions and still remain pious. 'One must be right but not extreme.' She may take the waters for her health, and make concessions to those with whom she has to live.

*820723 MLLE DE GOELLO   23 July 1682
TB 1719

'Your letter made me reflect a great deal, all the things of the past crowded back into my memory, and when I put them beside the things of the present I can only feel wonder and worship God's providence; his dispositions are impenetrable and he leads by ways we cannot understand those whom he deigns to look upon mercifully towards the ends he has destined for them. I confess that it would be very difficult for me to acquit myself before him of the prayers I owe to M. and my obligations in that respect seem so great to me that, whatever I do, I can scarcely satisfy them. I cannot think about it without that memory making a deep impression on me, and would to God that I were sufficiently a man after his own heart to be in a position to render useful help, in case there should still be need of assistance from the living. There is no one, Mlle, better able than you to arouse my feelings on this matter, since, as you say, you witnessed the desires of the one and the resolutions of the other. I am too convinced that nothing escapes God's wisdom, that it governs even the least events, and I perceive his order in this one as manifestly as if I had seen it written by his hand.

The thoughts that came to you on the death of M. [your niece] are thoroughly right and christian, for, in truth, from the fact that persons and fact are capable of not existing, they should in our eyes be as though they no longer did exist. We may say that their span is so short and uncertain that they are much more suited for causing grief than joy. Yet we become attached to our friends as though they were to be immortal, and when it happens that God takes them away, they leave us with as much regret at the parting as if we should never have had to lose them. There is nothing odder than to see that our daily experience of the instability of human things, and of the vanity of everything transitory, is unable to detach our affections from them, and despite all the reasons we have for behaving towards creatures with reserve and precaution, we contract commitments to them which never produce the pleasure, the advantages, the delights and the usefulness hoped for. Although you found in [Mme de Malnoue] all that you tell me, I am sure that there was a void in your heart which she did not fill; in a word, a creature who should not and cannot be content except by possessing God alone will find nothing beside him capable of giving satisfaction. One has only to be a Christian and follow the eyes of faith to notice that men are merely weak and impotent, that peace, calm, and true happiness come so purely from God that apart from him all is confusion, restlessness, and sorrow. It is for him alone to make us happy in time as in eternity. All our fortunes and destinies are entirely in his hands; he creates our winters and our springs, and the greatest consolation we can have is to think that he decides absolutely all that affects us.

There, Mlle, are some very constant truths which ought to be the usual subject of our meditations; you are fortunate in that God has made you capable of such meditation, and when you think by what changes and revolutions you became what you are, you must be deeply grateful, for it is true that nothing could be more contrary to the steps you took for your salvation and your ardent desire to belong to God than the careless, languid way in which you used to spend your days. It could be said that he melted mountains of ice before giving you a spark of his love.

I remind you of all this to make you realise that although you may be right to complain of yourself, and to reproach yourself for not going as fast as you would like, still you should have great confidence in God's goodness and sustain yourself in lively hope, without ever allowing the smallest foothold to anything that might shake it.

He did not go so far to seek you only to abandon you once found, and he did not give you his hand only to withdraw it. You do well to judge yourself severely, so long as the strictness with which you treat yourself animates your zeal and makes your piety stronger and more ardent. You seem to me so inclined to speak ill of yourself that I cannot take literally what you say of yourself, and your resignation before all God's wishes is a sign that you are not as sick as you imagine. You know that the souls which serve God often change their state and situation, that they are sometimes in darkness, in depression, in apathy and insensibility, and that he tests them in hundreds of different ways, but so long as they stand firm, and the two principal foundations remain, that is conscience and submission, they make much more progress in a disposition which seems to them a real desolation, than if they enjoyed constant serenity. The main thing is that when you feel thus abandoned and deprived, you should be particularly careful to awaken your piety, and arouse all your strength against temptations that may assail you. Spare no effort in your prayers, your reading, and your other exercises, and tell God often that you accept his orders and all his dispositions regarding your person, let him take and remove whatever he pleases, so long as he sees that you remain faithful to him and that nothing prevents you from loving him. We shall not cease to pray that he pour his blessings on you more and more, and makes you as conscientious as he wishes in the use of his grace. I beg you to believe that my interest in this could not possibly be greater or keener, any more than the sincerity and respect with which I am yours' etc.

This strangely evocative letter can only refer to the memory of Mme de Montbazon, who had died just twenty-five years earlier, on 28 April 1657. The notes given in square brackets are marginal comments of the copyist. The nature of R's obligation to the late Abbess of Malnoue (daughter of Mme de Montbazon and a girl of eighteen at her mother's death) is quite unknown, but surely connected with R's conversion, to which Mlle de Goello had presumably alluded.

820725   LOUIS-FRANÇOIS LEFÈVRE DE CAUMARTIN   25 July 1682
Autographes Troussures, p.418
Would like him to talk to Pinette about la T. after R's death.

820730   RP PRIEUR   30 July 1682
      [SAINT-VICTOR,? CLAUDE LA LANE *or* NIC. TACOUNET]
TC II/38
R. thought RP would agree with him about pension. Could accept alms from superior, but better not [cf. 820706e].

820730a   COMTESSE D'ALBON   30 July 1682
TB 1724
Would like to see her and help her out of the pains of those who live in the world.

820730b   MONSIEUR FÉLIBIEN, CHARTRES   30 July 1682
TB 1725

M Aubert has visited, spends his time in hospitals visiting the sick. He has no need to change his status or place. 'The world does him no harm.'

Aubert was canon of Beauvais and a correspondent of R.

*820806   HENRI DUHAMEL   6 August 1682
TB 1727

'I see, my very dear Monsieur, that your ills are not at an end, and that God is not yet content with what you have suffered up till now; but I see that your patience is renewed and that neither your faith nor your constancy have been shaken by the length of your sufferings. You see them too clearly in their true light, and you know too well that the sovereign master is using in your case the right he has over all creatures for you not to adore his conduct and accept all its moves with profound submission. Most men, that is, those whose conduct follows natural inclinations, grow weary and forget to suffer as their sufferings progress; but those who live by faith learn this knowledge of the saints by suffering, and the feeling given them by God increases proportionately to their afflictions. You will agree, my very dear Monsieur, that we have cause to say, whatever the state in which we find ourselves, *non sunt condignæ passiones etc* [Rm 8:18], that everything we endure on earth is unrelated to the goods and advantages we hope for. God's eternity will console us for everything, and the faith which teaches us that affliction and pain are the means whereby we open its doors to ourselves should make all our ills, however great they may be, tolerable. Our souls must be purified in the fire of tribulations to become worthy of the happiness God prepares for us, and our bodies will only be clothed in immortality after they have been reduced to dust and ashes. Finally, since the whole man had the misfortune to separate himself from God and displease him, it is only right that his reconciliation should take place in due form and that he should only recover the good graces of God, which he lost so miserably, after being punished for his errors, ingratitude, and sin. I do not doubt that you fully study all these truths, that they are present before you, and that they are your chief source of comfort.

You say that you find yourself depressed, and that you are not doing what you would like to do with your spirit. I realise that that is not the least of your trials. Yet I am sure that if you do not find God at such times by the action of your spirit, you none the less have him in your innermost heart, and are no less agreeable to him in such a passive disposition than if you had him before your eyes as a result of vigorous and lively intellectual effort. It was a great help for you to go to church and communicate every Sunday and feast day, but as your weakness prevents you, you must suffer that deprivation in peace, however hard it may seem to you. To go away from God by God's order is to approach him, and we are never more intimately united with him than when our will conforms to his and we desire exactly nothing but what he desires. That, I believe, is your disposition, and that is the situation in which you will receive from his hand both life and death with perfect submissiveness and unshakable equanimity.

We shall not cease, my very dear Monsieur, praying God for you and recommending to him all your needs as though they were our own. I can imagine that visits and conversations, if you were in a place where you could have them, might relax your spirit at certain times, but it is hardly probable that they could achieve as much as people say in restoring your health; and then, as you say, God has so disposed things, and put you in a position which deprives you of that relief. His goodness will make up for everything, and your trust in him will be the great remedy for bodily as for spiritual ills. Farewell, my very dear Monsieur, remember me in your prayers and believe me without reserve' etc.

820806a   [JEAN FAVIER]   6 August 1682
A 2106,f.108 vo.

Presses him to take more care of his health.

820810   BISHOP OF GRENOBLE [ETIENNE LE CAMUS]   10 August 1682
TB 1730; TC I/135

'I would gladly shorten my days to prolong yours.' The Pope has told Le Camus to cease his ascetic life for a while. He is like St Charles. One should not rule one's life by medical advice. When he is better he can go back to roots and vegetables, with a little wine and two fresh eggs a day.

820813   RP   13 August 1682
TC I/140

Only royal princesses are exempt from rules about enclosure for women, because of their rank, and duchesses are not so entitled. Nuns should not go into parks and gardens open to the public.

820816   MADAME DE LA [? BARGE]   16 August 1682
TB 1732

Advises her to make herself worthy of frequent use of the sacraments and not to trust men's opinions.

820822   RM ABBESSE, ESSAI [FRANÇOISE TROTTI DE LA CHÉTARDIE]   22 August 1682
TB 1734; TC I/151

Her recent illness has done her spiritual good; 'life is but a shadow and a vapour'.

820825 RM LOUISE [ROGIER], TOURS   25 August 1682
TB 1736; TC II/64
She is better after illness.

820827 RP SIMON GOURDAN, SAINT-VICTOR   27 August 1682
TB 1745; TC I/81; TC I/168
Precious relic of St Bernard's cowl at Saint-Victor. Councils forbid entry of women to cloister, queens and princesses excepted, but even then religious would do better to stay in cells during visit. Certainly no female friends or family. Superior has no right to abrogate the law [cf. 820813].

820830 DOM JEAN MABILLON, OSB   30 August 1682
BN 19656, f.186, orig; TB 1741 *Revue Mabillon*, 45 (1955) pp. 29-35
Mabillon had asked whether St Bernard preached in Latin or in French subsequently translated. R. thinks normally in French.

820831 MONSIEUR LE [? FÈVRE]   31 August 1682
TB 1754; TC II/25
In view of his health it is unlikely that God wants him to come to la T. He should take advice of Bp of Grenoble.

*820831a RM ABBESSE, LEYME [ANNE DE LA VIEUVILLE]   31 August 1682
TB 1749

'I do not deserve all the signs you give me of your kindness, but the only thing that may prevent you regretting that you have granted me as much of it as that which you show I enjoy, is that I respond with gratitude which could not be keener or more sincere. I agree with you, RM, that one of the greatest delights we have in this world is that which we find in our true friends, when we look on them in God's order and consider in them the qualities which he has set in them and by which he has wished to distinguish them and make them preferable to so many others. Loving them in that way makes our feelings for them refer to him, and strictly speaking it is God who is loved in that way. You know very well that the emotions of our heart must rest in him alone, and not in creatures. Any affections which might be encountered which did not conform to this rule would be defective, and would not have the purity which God demands of christian souls, especially of those who should no longer live except for him. You are so fully informed of all this that it would be hard to tell you anything on the subject which you do not know and observe in all your conduct.

I am learning like many others that there is nothing so easy as to destroy one's health, and nothing harder than to restore it when it has been impaired; yet you should still use suitable remedies, like drinking the waters. I would never advise you to leave your monastery to go and take the waters on the spot, for I believe that that is not permissible for a nun, but as for taking them at home, that you should do; it is an innocent remedy which sometimes has very successful results. We must not love life, we must be convinced that it does not merit our attachment, but God is willing for us to use certain means by which we can either maintain our health or restore it once it is lost. Someone living in dependence on God does things without anxiety, awaits success from his hand, and when such a person has done what he thought he could do, he receives with perfect resignation good and ill, according to how it pleases God to order his fate. Apart from the fact that our fears would be pointless and would not change his orders in any single detail, it is our essential duty to embrace those orders with sincere submission and govern all our wishes by this. That is a double obligation which we have contracted both by the birth of baptism and that of our vows. Thus, RM, nothing should occupy us so much as studying his designs, knowing his inclinations and following them. On that depends our peace of mind, and those who do not live in such piety and religion will never enjoy true and constant peace in this world. When it is written in Scripture that there is no peace for the ungodly [Is 48:22, 57:21], that does not just mean villains and those who do not believe in God, but those who have belief and faith, but do not take the trouble to express their feelings in their works and, failing to render to God all that they should, and that he asks of them, spend their days in confusion, trouble, and all the ill effects of an uneasy conscience. You are fortunate to look as you do on all earthly things, and God has shown you great mercy in giving you such indifference and scorn for all that fills the spirits and carries away the hearts of people in the world. What they have for perishable things is not just simple affection, but real adoration, since they become attached to the things that pass away as though they were never to pass away, and were, as far as they are concerned, in the place of things eternal. That is making an eternity of time, and to have through pathetic blindness for creatures what it is only licit to have for God. As those who have such attitudes are guided only by false principles and argue only from falsehood and not from truth, we should not be surprised that their ideas are so extravagant and their views so pitiful, for they normally esteem what they should condemn and criticise what is worthy of esteem and praise. That is why they have feelings and speak a language which those who serve God could never understand.

People say so many things about us which have no basis that I should find it hard to conceive where they come from if I did not know that the human head is a fearful vacuum which receives every kind of illusion endlessly and wildly. Someone dreams up an idea, someone else receives it as a firm truth, then it multiplies infinitely. That is something which we have long experienced and to which are exposed all who live in a way which is not to the taste of the world and who care more about pleasing God than men.

People are worried as to whether la Trappe will last or not. God alone knows what is to come of it. We have no prophets in our time to penetrate the future, but a lot of people anticipate and make rash decisions about future events. Our destiny is in the hand of God. I dare to say that la Trappe is his work, and if I did not believe that, I should not stay there a moment. It will last just as long as it is meant to according to his eternal decisions. If in bygone ages people had behaved on the principle that there is nothing that does not change and become subject to decadence, people would have remained without doing or undertaking anything. The field of Christ's Church would be an arid, sterile desert, deprived of all the great works which adorn it and are its sanctification and beauty to the end of time. It is not true, as you have been told, that I can no longer speak in public; only today I talked for an hour and a quarter. It is not that my health is as it was seven or eight years ago. Some people say, and try to persuade me, that it will last a long time, but as for me, I think they are wrong. However that may be, God's will will always be mine, and I receive with profound resignation whatever he is pleased to ordain regarding my death and my life. Pray God, I beg you, to increase such feelings in me always, and never to allow me to have others. I am with too much sincerity and respect to be able to express it yours' etc.

820906   DOM PAUL, BARBEAUX   6 September 1682
TB 1756; TC II/155

'I cannot bring myself to do as you wish and take you with no other hope but that of burying you.' Will pray for him just as though he were one of R's brethren.

820906a   DUCHESSE DE LUYNES   6 September 1682
TB 1758; TC I/141

Those who seek God are always dissatisfied with their efforts. Marriage of her daughter to duc de Bournonville a blessed union.

Charlotte-Victoire (died 1701) had just married Alexandre-Albert, duc de Bournonville (1662–1705).

920906b   MARQUISE D'ALÈGRE   6 September 1682
TB 1761; TC I/142

She must accept her dependent situation and moderate her desire for God's deliverance from a shared existence. So young [24], so recently touched by God, so little progress yet in his service. 'You must not aspire to things that are not feasible. Do what good is appropriate to you.'

820906c   DOM ANDRÉ FERRAND, osb   6 September 1682
TC II/155; TD E (dated 10 October)

Follow Rule without making oneself conspicuous; if superior does not inspire confidence one may look elsewhere.

The reading Ferrand is clear, but may well be an error for 'Jannel'; there was no André Ferrand either in the Maurist or Vannist congregations, though he could have been a Cluniac.

820910   RM ABBESSE, essai   10 September 1682
         [FRANÇOISE TROTTI DE LA CHÉTARDIE]
TB 1765

He has done the novena to St Bernard for which she asked.

*820911   MARÉCHAL DE BELLEFONDS   11 September 1682
BN na 12959 f.98, orig.

'M. le marquis de Lassay has been to see us and spent three days with us. I confess, Mgr, that I found him so detached from the world, so genuinely anxious to belong to God and occupy himself solely with his salvation, that it is not possible to talk to him without being much edified. The secrets of God are impenetrable, and the ways he uses most of the time for men's sanctification are incomprehensible. He suffers evil that good may come of it and allows us to stray so that we may later return to the right path.

We eagerly look forward to the honour you make us hope for, Mgr. I do not need to tell you the consolation it will be for us to see a family whose chief and main blessing you are. It means that you are going to have a change of air and take a few moments' rest to restore yourself after the tumult and agitation of the outside world, and although you are one of those on whom it has least grip, and who most defend themselves against its evil impressions, you cannot fail to realise that one cannot be there without being exposed and losing something; one fights and after surviving numerous occasions, it can hardly be that something does not take us unawares and that in the midst of so many dangers one is ever watchful enough to remain always intact. God even, who protects those who serve him, sometimes leaves them so that they should know and realise how necessary his protection is. I hope that nothing impedes your plan, and that once more in my life I have the joy and happiness of telling you that there is no one in the world more respectfully and faithfully yours' etc.

Armand de Madaillan, marquis de Lassay (1652–1738), was a Norman who became aide-de-camp to the King.

820913   RP PRIEUR, SAINT-JACQUES, PROVINS (OSA)   13 September 1682
TB 1766; TC II/156

Three of his ecclesiastics want to come to la T. 'The mortification practised here is more spiritual than corporal.'

If any of them came, they did not stay.

820913a   DUC DE MAZARIN   13 September 1682
TB 1768; TC II/282

Question of duke's daughter and her intended marriage. R. is not competent to advise; try Le Camus or Monchy [cf. 820921a].

*820916   RM MARIE-LOUISE [BOUTHILLIER]   16 September 1682
TB 1769

'It is God alone, my dear sister, who makes you find in my letters something useful and comforting, and I do not doubt that if they have on you all the effect which you say, it passes into your works, and you take care to practise truths of which you are convinced. God grants you a very special grace by visiting you at certain moments and arousing in you the feeling that it is he who is speaking to you, but that would not be enough unless you were faithful in responding and profited from those moments, which should be so dear and precious to souls who seek him alone and whose chief aim is to serve him. The way to ensure that God does not keep silence with us is to conduct holy exchanges with him, to prove to him what his word can do to us by executing what it prescribes and doing scrupulously and religiously what he wants us to do to please him. Our fidelity is our thanksgiving, and nothing impels him to continue to show us marks of his goodness more than effective gratitude, which consists in embracing his will in all things and taking it as the rule for our conduct. God is liberal and gives abundantly to those souls who keep and turn to good account what they receive from his mercy, and he hands over no goods to those who, instead of husbanding them and using them in holy ways, neglect and dissipate them. You know, my dear sister, what he wants from you; his intentions have been shown to you, you are not unaware of the obligations of your state, it is up to you to fulfill them. You will no doubt not fail to work at it with all possible effort if you are persuaded, as you should be, that God will call you to account for the feelings and understanding he has given you, all these secret inspirations, all the impressions of his grace, so many impulses which he has formed in your heart. Unless you submit to them and follow them, you will never be content, you will never have anything but bitterness and disgust at every moment of your life, and all men together will be unable to make you find that peaceful and tranquil state which you so ardently desire, and which God grants only to those who serve him with pure religion and strict piety. Otherwise, my dear sister, your conscience will always tell you something displeasing, and there will be no other way to calm your anxieties than to renounce yourself and walk in that narrow way which you know perfectly.

You should not doubt, my dearest sister, that any Christian, and especially someone consecrated to God, is doing very well when he can and has occasion to practise acts of inner mortification and deprive himself of licit things. One cannot refuse too much to nature in order to give to God, but one must do it freely and without scruples, like a child seeking to please its father, not like a slave. You should also believe that there are things which God wants from us to which he inclines us by an inner feeling. Sometimes he demands from some what he does not demand from others, although they are in the same situation and the same condition, and we must not doubt that we are obliged to follow the movement of his spirit; and when we resist it after recognising it, that is a sin of which we should accuse ourselves. However, we must avoid over-scrupulous behaviour, for it is no less wrong to make one's ways too narrow than too broad and spacious, for if latitude leads to laxity and licence, too much restriction throws one into trouble, anxiety, pusillanimity, dejection, and entirely removes that holy and filial freedom in which one can do nothing that is not pleasing to God.

So I think you should not observe yourself too rigorously, but be content to avoid what is not according to your rules and constitutions, and in case God sometimes inspires you to do, or to abstain, be faithful. There are omissions of so little importance that they should not be confessed; it is enough simply to acknowledge them before God, and there are others to be taken more seriously, and which it is useful to submit to confession, although they are not mortal. You ask my advice on praying, but it would be very difficult to satisfy you in a letter, and then there is no subject on which more instruction is to be found. The first and most common, it seems to me, is to spend the days as faithfully as possible in the exercise of one's duties, to present oneself to God in a spirit of profound humility, recognition of one's wretchedness, total detachment from everything we should not love and genuine desire to learn his will and follow it. You should believe that a soul which comes before God in such a disposition will not lack protection and will receive all the consolations it needs for the conduct of its life.

There, my dear sister, is all I can say in a few words. We shall commend you to Our Lord with care, do not doubt that, I beg you, and believe me with all imaginable affection yours' etc.

*820921   MARÉCHAL DE BELLEFONDS   21 September 1682
BN na 12959 f.99, orig.

'Seven or eight days ago, Mgr, I received a letter from the duc de Mazarin telling me that he was being pressed to arrange the marriage of his daughter on conditions to which important considerations prevented him consenting, that all his family were pressing him, that the King even had heard of it, and that he did not want to take any decision except on the advice of three persons whom he trusted, of whom I was one. I answered, begging him not to cast his eyes on me on this occasion, and saying that apart from the fact that the matter was not consistent with my profession and the life of retreat I lead, I was so little informed about the affairs and interests of the world that there was no cause to ask my advice, nor to follow it if I should offer any. I wrote that so positively that I do not think he will mention it again. You can see, Mgr, that if, after making such a declaration to him, I were to give my opinion on the memorandum you sent me, he would take no notice of it if he did not find it in conformity with his own, and would consider it as the idea of a man who had been canvassed and prejudiced against him, all the more so as I would have explained myself without hearing him, although he said it was absolutely necessary for him to speak to me and for me to hear his reasons from his own mouth. I am sure, Mgr, that you will agree with me, and see that I cannot do what you wish. However, if the duc de Mazarin comes here, as he has promised, I will say all in my power to make him adopt reasonable conduct and give up the preconceived notions he may have. I cannot see, from the memorandum you sent me, what reasons he can have for no longer wanting what he did want, since the person has the wealth and all the main qualities. We impatiently await the end of the month. M. le marquis de Tourouvre has not been at home for two months, but you will always find his house open. A day is, as you say, very little, but there are some necessities one cannot avoid, and God who knows the purity of our wills and our innermost hearts supports our weakness against the world's torrent, otherwise who could live there and preserve the slightest hope amid all the obstacles to the good one wants to do, almost infinite as they are? We shall not fail, Mgr, to recommend you to God as much as we are able. It is the only means we have in this world of giving you marks of the respect we have for you.'

Mazarin's daughter, Marie-Charlotte, had eloped from the convent at Chaillot (where she was living) with the marquis de Richelieu (great-nephew of the great cardinal) and fled to England, where Mazarin's estranged wife had already been for some time. Mazarin incurred public ridicule and consulted R., Le Camus and Henri Arnauld, Bp of Angers. The couple eventually married in 1683. Bellefonds' only son had married another of Mazarin's daughters, Marie-Olympe, in 1681.

*820921a   BISHOP OF LUÇON [HENRI BARILLON]   21 September 1682
P f.769

'I am sorry, Mgr, that your indisposition prevented you from honouring our desert with your presence. I am consoled by the fact that the visit is only put off till later. I hope more than I can say that no obstacle comes to hinder the execution of your plan and that your affairs come to a swift conclusion and with all the success you hope for. I see that your stay in Paris hardly accords with your inclinations, and that you only like to be where your duty calls you. There are, however, necessitities to which one is obliged to yield, and when your absence is of use to your diocese, it is in accord with God's orders. So you should be satisfied since you are where he wants you to be. The curé of Saint-Jacques will be able to tell you our news and for my part, Mgr, I will content myself with assuring you that I fully realise all your kindness towards me, and nothing could be added to the gratitude and respect with which I am yours' etc.

Louis Marcel, curé of Saint-Jacques-du-Haut-Pas, was Barillon's close friend and one-time confessor.

821001   MADAME DE LA HOUSSAYE   1 October 1682
TB 1773

Praises her son, whom he has advised not to study Theology but Scripture and ethics.

821001a   MONSIEUR L'ABBÉ SAZILLY   1 October 1682
TB 1775; TC II/158

Make good use of illness.

821005   BISHOP OF MEAUX [J.-B. BOSSUET]   5 October 1682
TB 1777; TC II/159; Bossuet, *Correspondance*, II p. 259

Thanks him for two books received. [*Traité de la Communion sous les deux espèces* and *Conférence avec M. Claude.*]

821012   RM [? LOUISE]   12 October 1682
TC II/161

She makes the best of all God sends and is always submissive to his will.

821012a   RM MARIE-LUCE [PICOT], PRIEURE, ANNONCIADES   12 October 1682
TC II/160

Wishes he could help her. Has reminded his sister of her obligations to live by the rule.

*821012b   RM MARIE-LOUISE [BOUTHILLIER]   12 October 1682
TC II/161a

'As your needs are always the same, my dear sister, I have almost nothing new to tell you. However, I see from your last letter that you are suffering a quite new kind of trial and trouble. I sympathise deeply, for I understand that the situation in which you find yourself is most distressing. For all that, so long as you do God's will, you should be content. I do not think he wants anything else of you, in case you should be one of the four nuns of whom you speak, than to say what you think, following the movements of your heart in truth and justice, bringing to it so much moderation and humility that it should appear that what makes you speak out is charity and love of the rule. If you are not listened to, and there arise disorders which trouble the good order of your community and harm the regularity which ought to be observed there, you have a [male] superior to whom you can tell your troubles and open your heart about anything likely to harm or serve the interests of your house. One must be very respectful towards one's [female] superiors, avoid all disputes, but there are none the less cases and occasions when one cannot think like them because one could not do so without offending one's conscience. Then one is free once one points out these things to the man to whom God has given authority and whose duty it is to watch over the conduct of the monastery and prevent the introduction of abuses, whether from the superiors or from the religious.'

With the death of J.-B. de Contes, Dean of Notre-Dame, who had been superior from about 1647 until July 1679, a new superior, Courcier, had taken over. At much the same time the immensely experienced Marie-Christine died, after fourteen years as prioress, and was succeeded, in 1681, by Marie-Ursule Polard (died 1694), who served only one triennate and may not have been very successful, since she was not reelected. The exact nature of the dispute is unknown, but as Marie-Louise spent much of her time in charge of the door and visitors, it had probably to do with the perennial problem of enclosure.

*821014   RM ABBESSE, LEYME [ANNE DE LA VIEUVILLE]   14 October 1682
TB 1779

'I think I have already told you many times, RM, that you have too good an opinion of us; I confess that we do not lack the will to be as you believe us to be, but you know that wishes are not always effective, and it often happens that one wishes and desires what one does not do. I hope however from God's mercy, although our works are very different from what they ought to be, that he will still look upon them in his goodness, because he sees our innermost hearts and knows that our intentions are sincere. As there are some which he rejects, so there are others which he accepts and which will subsist at his judgement since their purity and sincerity will comprise all their merit and distinction.

What you say of the diligent efforts with which people try to weaken evangelical truths is only too true. Everyone wants to walk in the broad and spacious paths, although the Son of God condemns them and teaches us that it is the narrow ways which lead to his kingdom. Men try to be ignorant of what is as clear as day, and because they cannot help agreeing that the need to bear one's cross is for everyone, since nothing is more expressly stated in Christ's words, they alter that obligation by their explanations so that they reduce it to nothing, they ruin all that is difficult and painful in it, and consequently all its merit, value, and reward. Yet that expression "to bear one's cross" is something so hard, its significance is so vivid, that I cannot understand how people can maintain that love of pleasures, abundance, joys, luxury, amusements, and the other delights enjoyed by worldly people are compatible with a duty so opposed to them. Christ came precisely to detach them from natural inclinations and destroy them, he told them above all that we must live in self-denial and privation, that self-denial was a quality without which we could have no share in his true riches, that he would share them only with those who followed him. Yet people behave in such a way that it seems that this precept, indispensable as it is, has made no impression on their minds, and that they care about nothing less than becoming worthy of his promises. Once truth has been abandoned, that is not enough, people want at any price to substitute error in its place, they seek arguments to justify and authorise themselves, as if they were afraid of being disabused and wanted to do evil without being able to be convicted of it. The most pitiful of such arguments, although the most common, they take from the almost countless multitude of those who have no other rules than usage and custom, without bothering whether they are contrary to or consistent with their principles. To be exact, at the present time truth is only maintained despite the corruption of the age and in the conduct of a small number of chosen souls, like a stream running through a great lake, full of filth and dirt, but keeping all the purity and cleanliness of its source.

I will say no more about your health, except that you must take care of it. Although we must not love life or become attached to it, God wishes us to use certain means and remedies to preserve it. Those who lived in deserts and remote solitudes gave themselves up to his providence, and awaited from that alone, when they were ill, the end of their lives or the restoration of their health. Those who lived in communities, although their hearts were perhaps no less detached from things of this earth, have been more moderate, as we see, not only in St Benedict's and St Bernard's time, but even in the first centuries of the Church. So we must treat life as those who love God treat earthly goods; they use them, but put no affection in them. Everything which one loves apart from God, and is not relevant to him, can only soil our souls and make them less fine and pure. As they are solely for him, we must preserve them for him in their integrity, if possible without their being separated or destroyed by any inclination or feeling of which he is not the object and the end. Thus we must live only in him and for love of him, and that can only be done if he is fully in us and lives in us himself.

Although your infirmities prevent you instructing by your own example, do not fail to do so by your words, and do not fail to say what your incapacity alone does not allow you to do. I know that nothing is more painful to those in authority, when they have piety and zeal, than to teach what they do not practice. That is a humiliation which they must patiently suffer, while making themselves all the more scrupulous to guide by their vigilance and care since they are less able to do so by deeds. As for the admission of your young women, in God's name do not accept any in whom you do not find the needful qualities, for apart from the fact that all they would do in your community would be to cause trouble, you would be accepting them against God's order and opening the gates of his house to souls he had not called, and you would thus be charging yourself with all the drawbacks arising from a vocation in which he had no part, which is an infinite account to bear. Above all, take care that your admissions are pure, never demand anything. You may represent the needs of your house, in case, as I believe, it has real needs, and receive what may be given to you as charity and alms, without even making a contract to assure yourself of what may have been promised. What has banished God's spirit from most religious communities is that the admissions are not legitimate and are almost never granted except against the Church's rules. There is a principle from which you should never depart, which is never to reject anyone whom you find worthy, for the only interest you should have before your eyes is the service of God and your own sanctification. I am yours' etc.

821019   RP DE LA COUR,   19 October 1682
          SAINT-JEAN DES VIGNES, SOISSONS
TB 1783; TC II/163

Saint-Jean is so evidently disorderly that R. advises him not to stay. 'The young professed religious whom you should rule do not believe in you . . . your efforts are useless.' He can come to la T. if health permits, otherwise to le Pin [where his brother still was].

821029   MONSIEUR [? DE TRÉVILLE]   29 October 1682
TB 1787

He has calumniated R., despite the latter's fidelity and moderation.

821102   RM LOUISE-HENRIETTE D'ALBON, TOURS   2 November 1682
TB 1789

Encouragement.

821102a RM DE LA ROCHE, TOURS   2 November 1682
TB 1791; TC II/164 (dated 31 October 1682); A 2106,f.93 vo. (dated 30 October 1680)

R. thinks she is much better off in calm than agitation. 'I say that because some people find storms helpful.'

821107   HENRI DUHAMEL   7 November 1682
TB/1793; *Vie de M. Duhamel* [S. Treuvé], both with note: 'this is the letter that M. Duhamel read a few moments before his death and the last he received from the Abbot.'

'I can hardly believe, my dear Monsieur, that your ills have diminished since your last letter, for from the way you spoke to us about it, your condition was progressive; I do not mean that you are going from bad to worse, for no doubt the best thing that can happen to a Christian, and especially a priest, is to approach the final point of his race and leave men for eternal union with Christ. I think that this feeling fills your heart, and that the greatest pleasure one can give you is to say that time is no longer worthy of you, that it must be forgotten, with all other passing things, so as to think of nothing but things eternal. In his great goodness God has been preparing you for more than a year, and if after calling you, when he made you ill, he delayed taking you, it has only been an act of mercy so as to give you better means of disposing yourself for this great passing. Finally, it is a question, my dear Father, of closing a career full of ills, miseries, and afflictions by a blessed end. Let the world pity as much as it may those who are separated from it, let them regard their death as cause for grief. Truly they must not persuade us if we have faith, for it must surely give us quite contrary feelings and attitudes, since it teaches us that we must cease to be in order to be something, and that what is deemed a misfortune is exactly what makes us eternally happy. Life, whatever it may be, would not be tolerable if we did not know it had to end, and nothing can comfort that bitterness which is spread so widely over everything here on earth except the hope of changing our situation and abode and the trust of finding in God's goodness what all men together, even if they were to conspire to favour our inclinations and satisfy us, are incapable of giving us. God alone contains those goods which are proper to us, he is himself our true riches; apart from him, whatever opinion one may have, the whole universe is a mere nothing, a true abyss of poverty and indigence. And if we belong to Christ as much as we should, and I am sure you do, each of us should say to him from the depths of his heart, *Regnum meum non est de hoc mundo* [Jn 18:36], all the more as we have his word and he himself has promised to his elect, who are his disciples, to give them his kingdom. That above all is what I wish for you, my dear Monsieur, for though we urgently desired the recovery of your health, yet we know that it is much better for you to be living among the living than not living among the dead. We shall continue to recommend you to Our Lord, and pray him to give you the protection you need in the state in which he has put you. I am in him more than I can say,' etc.

*821107a ECCLESIASTIC 7 November 1682
TC II/285

'In answer to your letter, Monsieur, I would say that if the good man on whose behalf you write could only read Latin with edification, though being otherwise unlearned, we should not fail to accept him as a choir monk. It seems to me, from what I can judge from the letter he wrote me, that that status would suit him better than that of lay brother, unless he has no aptitude for reading Latin.
 The life of the lay brothers, since you wish to know, is hard and laborious. They

spend their days in manual work, some in the garden, others in the kitchen, the bakehouse, and the cowsheds, and in general are employed in all the tasks required in the monastery. They speak only to the superior, to the person who directs their conscience, and to the cellarer who gives out their work. They never leave the enclosure, and if they have to go outside, it is not to the villages or farms, for they never go there, but only for work which may come up in the neighbourhood, and then never except on express orders. Those given to the inner life preserve a high degree of meditation in the course of their occupations, and lose God's presence as little as possible. Silence and separation from seculars afford them many opportunities of concerning themselves with God. Their profession requires physical strength above all, because their main task is manual labour. They rise on feast days and Sundays like the choir monks at 1 a.m. and attend all the offices. On ferial days, as they go to bed later, they rise at 3.30, and stay in church until 5.30. They say their office, which consists of a certain number of *Paters* and *Misereres*, and hear Mass, after which they all go about the tasks assigned to them the previous evening. The rest of the day, at every hour when the office is sung in the church, they stop work briefly, and say the prayers prescribed for them in the place where they are. They hear Compline every day and are present at the spiritual reading which precedes it. They have a separate choir in the church, and a separate dormitory, in which the cells are divided only by cloth partitions. They eat in the monks' common refectory, and have the same food, keeping the same abstinence and fasts, unless dispensed on account of exceptional work. They observe such rigorous silence that they never break it.'

Their number was originally limited by shortage of accommodation, but even when there was more room, R. was adamant in restricting their number lest they form a faction within the community.

821110   RM LOUISE [ROGIER], TOURS   10 November 1682
TB 1795

She is better.

821110a   MADEMOISELLE DE VERTUS   10 November 1682
Dubois, II p. 342

Her pains continue but her faith grows stronger.

821115   MARQUISE D'ALÈGRE   15 November 1682
TB 1796; TC II/166

She wants to serve God more perfectly. 'Take upon your mind and heart what you cannot take on your flesh and senses, and believe that secret and inner mortification is incomparably greater in God's judgement than external mortification, which catches the eye and is noticed by men.'

821119 DUCHESSE DE GUISE   19 November 1682
TB 1798

She has had a coach accident near Tourouvre; she should profit from the lesson and strive for sanctification in Christ.

*821119a RM ABBESSE, LEYME [ANNE DE LA VIEUVILLE]   19 November 1682
TB 1800

'I had no difficulty, as you may imagine, RM, in finding out the origin of the letter of which you sent me a fragment. I do not doubt that they lived very piously and religiously in the monastery of N., but I know that there were practices and principles there which were far removed from the poverty and simplicity in which those who embrace the Rule of St Benedict should live, and that it was not understood in its main features, like that of humiliations, stability, and the quality of the food normally eaten, in the observance of silence and other similar matters. There is no better way of learning St Benedict's mind on these points than from the way the first religious of Citeaux practised them, since they were full of God's spirit, and what they had resolved, that is, what God had put into their hearts, was to take up and observe St Benedict's Rule with literal exactness. St Bernard declared that so precisely that there is no room for disagreement, and for my part I do not see that there is anything to weigh against the opinion of that great saint and for those who put out opinions so contrary to his. The first Constitutions of Citeaux are most holy, and if they added to the Rule, that is because the Rule had not provided for everything and supplements were necessary. As for us, we have tried to follow it as closely as possible, yet we see differences which fill us with confusion, and the life we lead is so small a thing that I am surprised that anyone pays attention to it or notices it.

It is true that our Fathers left the jurisdiction of the bishops, but the sanctity of their conduct in the early days was the reason for that, and the bishops voluntarily surrendered the authority they had over them, thinking it was of more use to them to look after themselves than be dependent on someone further away. Originally that took place with the agreement and goodwill of the bishops, and to tell the truth we cannot see that the congregations over which they retained their authority are better disciplined or less irregular than others. I had two abbeys apart from this one of which bishops were the superiors; in the one, which belonged to the Order of St Benedict, there was no shadow of piety, although it was next to the walls of an episcopal city and the bishop was a prelate of great conscientiousness. The other was full of scandals and disorders. There are drawbacks on every hand. After all we do not see much regularity in chapters which come under the authority of the ordinary.

I want to say nothing about the admission of women, except what you tell me; it is certain that they cannot become perfect all at once, and one cannot desire it of them, but there is a basis which they must have, and that is the will to become perfect, and to that end embrace all the means and instructions contained in the Rule.

There is nothing better one can do than judge that from what St Benedict teaches us about the attitudes that should be found in those engaging in Christ's service in his institution. Love and patience in humiliations is the chief one, and he implies that it should at least be in the affections and feelings of their hearts before they are allowed to come inside the house. People can argue as much as they like about it, there is no gainsaying the fact that St Benedict knew better than anyone what qualities were necessary to someone who was to be admitted to his congregation. We must certainly put up with the weakness and infirmities of those who are beginning, for virtue is only acquired through progress; none the less there is an essential will and preparation, such as docility and gentleness, and if that is missing, it is most unlikely that there is a true vocation.

That poor English gentleman is much to be pitied for suffering as he has deprivation of home and property, and not being able to endure the inevitable results of that. It seems to me that having received the grace of losing everything, rather than lose Christ, it is a glory to live poor and a stranger on earth, and to need the help and charity of men for one's survival. We must not be half-Christians, and Christ, who gave every thing in order to have us, wants no restriction and reservation, which is exactly what the world does not want to hear. I will add nothing to this note, except to say that I am beyond all I can express yours' etc.

The two abbeys referred to are Saint-Symphorien at Beauvais, under the jurisdiction of the much respected Bp Choart de Buzenval, and the Abbaye du Val, under Bayeux.

821130   MADAME DE SAINT-LOUP   30 November 1682
TC II/320

Hopes God will restore harmony among men.

821207   BISHOP OF GRENOBLE [ETIENNE LE CAMUS]   7 December 1682
TB 1804

Would reproach himself for denying a monk rest after night office if needed, all the more so a bp like Le Camus. Praise of Bp of Luçon.

821209   RP SIMON GOURDAN, SAINT-VICTOR   9 December 1682
TB 1806; TC I/48

Gourdan has no reason not to celebrate mass. When of use, talking is quite permissible at Saint-Victor, where silence is not observed. Novice can give his goods to the poor without keeping a pension, and they should not study.

821214   RP PIERRE DE MONCHY, CONG. ORAT.   14 December 1682
TB 1809

R. has not seen him all the year since ill health has kept him in Paris.

821214a RM [? SOUS-]PRIEURE, MAUBUISSON   14 December 1682
TB 1811
Praises her abbess. General advice.

821215 RM ABBESSE, MAUBUISSON [LOUISE-HOLLANDINE]   15 December 1682
TB 1813
If the nuns are upset at her proposal to move her abbatial throne to a humbler place, leave it where it is. She has already renounced her rank and royal birth.

821217 MONSIEUR LE CURÉ, SAINT-LOUIS-EN-L'ILE   17 December 1682
TB 1814
Encouragement.

The curé from 1662–93 was Pierre Grave.

821220 MONSIEUR   20 December 1682
TB 1816
Death of M. Duhamel. R. has learned that his letter of 7 November arrived just before he died.

The erased address may well be that of Simon Treuvé, a friend of R. and Duhamel's subsequent biographer.

821222 MONSIEUR DUHAMEL   22 December 1682
       CURÉ SAINT-MAURICE, SENS
TB 1818
Death of his uncle, M. Duhamel, who had been at la T. for three months seriously ill, always edifying. He died happily.

*821222a BISHOP OF LUÇON [HENRI BARILLON]   22 December 16[82]
P f.614 (wrongly dated 1673)

'I have received, Mgr, the two books you did me the honour of sending. It would be a great advantage to have all the principles of morality treated so clearly and purely. As we do not doubt that you intend to continue a work of such public usefulness, we await the sequel with impatience.

I am sure, Mgr, that your affairs are making progress and, with God granting you always the favour of his protection, you will soon be in a position to take the road back to your diocese. The success you have enjoyed through God's goodness during your absence will enable you to resume your activity and functions with renewed vigour. Your fidelity and faith will obtain everything from him, for his hands, as you know, are always open for those who have only his glory before their eyes and never tire of hoping and waiting.

The Bishop of Grenoble wrote to me two or three days ago. He says he has read the manuscript and praises it more than it deserves. Only the discussion on parents is not to his way of thinking. He says again that all theologians have not thought as I do, yet I based myself on St Basil, St Gregory, St Bernard, and St Thomas, who spoke about it quite positively and clearly, as you have observed in the work. It is a question which has never been examined closely, but treated superficially and on commonplace principles. It seems to me, all things considered, that both God and man have their due in the opinion I have explained, since the religious remains in the monastery according to his vow, and the father receives through the community all the help he needs, and perhaps much better than he would have done through the presence of his own son. The manuscript that you have seen is defective on many points and many additions and corrections have been made to it. You will easily judge, Mgr, how much your opinion and approval are valued. I hope that you will not find it unworthy. I am with more respect than I can say yours' etc.

The books received from Barillon were probably his Statuts synodaux *of 1681. The* MS *was that of* Sainteté. *The question of helping indigent parents had already provoked controversy (with Floriot; see 73/7) and as represented in ch. XVI was to provoke still more. R. absolutely denied any obligation on the part of the individual religious to leave his monastery to help parents, but, as here, fully recognised the corporate duty of the monastery to provide such help.*

*821225 BISHOP OF LUÇON [HENRI BARILLON] 25 December 16[82]
P f.615 (wrongly dated 1673)

'Now, Mgr, you have read the manuscript and I wish it were just as your charity and favourable predisposition towards us make it appear to you. Orders have been given for toning down the passages you indicate, and I think the printer will do all in his power to correct them.

As regards the miracle of St Columban, because it is used as a powerful argument in support of the view opposed to our own, I have only put in that of St Gontier in opposition, and I think that neither of them may enjoy great authority. However, it seemed to me quite an appropriate idea to answer one miracle with another.

As regards St Theonas I only quoted him as an example so extraordinary as not to be of much consequence, and if it cannot be taken out, it will be precisely indicated in the margin.

It is true that the Bishop of M[eaux] made some remarks, as he told you and as I think said too, to tone down some expressions, and we have followed all his advice most scrupulously.

I think, Mgr, that it will be very suitable, as the Archbishop of R[eims] thinks, that your statements of approval should be in common, since they will all be dated from the same place. I am waiting for that of the Bishop of Grenoble.

I do not doubt that the book will find people to censure it, and many at that, but there will perhaps be some souls which will be moved by it and will adopt views and resolutions about their profession which they did not have before.

I praise God, Mgr, that your affairs have concluded so profitably. It remains a lot that fourteen Protestant assemblies should be reduced to one. God will one day grant more to your prayers, your fidelity, and your perseverance. We do not fail to commend to him with fervour your person and all that concerns you, and you must believe that we count that one of our chief obligations. Remember me always, I beg you; and rest assured that no one in the world is more affectionately and respectfully yours' etc.

References to Columban and Gontier occur in Sainteté, (*1683 ed.*) *vol. II, ch. XVIII, p.216, to Theonas, ch. XVI, p.94. As pressure on Protestants increased their rights of assembly were being rapidly and drastically curtailed.*

821229 MONSIEUR [DE MONTHOLON]   29 December 1682
Charavay, orig, catalogue November 1960 and June 1965; published in *Bulletin du Bibliophile*, 1872, p.387, with incorrect date 19 December 1686.

Promises to do what he can for M.'s son, whose abbey is in a state of decadence.

François de Montholon was commendatory abbot of Saint-Sulpice-en-Bugey (dioc. Belley) and evidently wanted a good prior.

*821231 BISHOP OF LUÇON [HENRI BARILLON]   [31] December 1682
TB 1820; P f.603 (with the impossible date 31 November 1672)

'It is for us, Mgr, to tell you how much consolation you gave us during the short time you were good enough to spend in our desert; and indeed your person and all that we saw and heard of you is so prominent in our hearts and memories that it could never possibly be effaced. How happy we should be if we should sometimes happen to be on your way, but God has not judged us worthy of it and all we can do is to preserve in our minds and desires a happiness of which we must, despite ourselves, be deprived. I am sure you would allow us to join to that, I will not say, the hope, but the certainty, of enjoying the full share you have given us in the honour of your friendship and being remembered by you before God.

'I confess, Mgr, that when I consider the grace and understanding you have received from God, the care and fidelity with which you work to follow them, I can never tire of wondering at the severity with which you condemn all your ways, and nothing gives me a better idea of what God wants to make of you than the poor opinion you have of yourself. You know that to be small in one's own eyes is the way to become great in the eyes of God, and that he exalts us in proportion to the care we take to abase ourselves.

Above all, Mgr, set yourself no limits. God does not say all at once, or all of a sudden, what he means to say; he explains himself gradually, and often leads and raises those who love him and abandon themselves to his hands where they would never have imagined he would have led them. Can we ultimately do better than leave to him, without restriction or reserve, the decision about what affects us in time as in eternity?

It is true that we are more than moderately sorry to see Monsieur de Morangis taken away from us, not only because of the help and support we had from him when the injustice and wickedness of men obliged us to resort to him, but also because he was a reason for you to come near our part of the world, and now we can no longer hope to see you there.

I am much obliged to the Ar[chbishop] of [Reims] for all that you tell me he said about us. I should be very glad to excuse myself from writing to him, for having been more or less committed to letting the work that you know become public, I should like to write nothing to indicate that I had any part in it. Be good enough to tell me what you think. For my part, I am very much afraid that the matter may be divulged before it is time, and that that might hinder its accomplishment. I do not think that my fears on that score will seem to you ill-founded.

I must beg you, Mgr, in case you see Father de Monchy, to tell him that the Bishop of M[eaux] is looking after the affair and the privileges [for printing], and that but for him it would never have come into my mind to allow it to see the light of day. Tell him too to keep this absolutely secret; I should be most upset if he were to think that there was any intention of keeping it secret from him.

I hope that your affairs end as successfully as you hope. Your cause is the cause of God; he will not abandon it. I beg you to believe that we shall continue to commend it to him insistently, apart from the fact that his service and the glory of his house obliges us to do so. Your interests are ours, I beg you not to doubt it, any more than the respect and perfect sincerity with which I am yours etc.

PS I am delighted that our thoughts appeal to the Bishop of Gr[enoble] and that he deems them worthy of his approval. The Bishop of M[eaux] will give them to you when he returns.

Monsieur Maisne humbly thanks you for doing him the honour of remembering him.'

Barillon had spent six days at la T. on his way back from Grenoble and Paris. His brother, Antoine de Morangis, moved as intendant to Caen in December 1682. The Abp must be that of Reims, involved like Barillon and Bossuet in the publication of Sainteté. *R. always maintained that only irresistible pressure from Bossuet persuaded him to allow publication of conferences intended only for his own monks.*

83/1   RP, SAINT-JEAN DES VIGNES, SOISSONS   [1683]
TC I/114

RP is prieur-curé of a small town and has just been appointed claustral prior during which time he wants to put a vicar in his place. 'Would you be a shepherd in two places and guide two churches at the same time?' He must refuse.

This letter is probably addressed to Nicolas de Brie, curé at la Ferté-Gaucher. On 31 December 1683 Bossuet wrote to R. and mentioned a letter R. had written to the otherwise unknown Nicolas, who is almost certainly the Canon Regular of other, unidentified, letters. R. corresponded also with RP de la Cour at Soissons, and there is no way to distinguish between his correspondents there except on this occasion. A prieur-curé was a Canon Regular in charge of a parish, a claustral prior the head of the mother-house.

83/2   BISHOP OF GRENOBLE [ETIENNE LE CAMUS]   1683
TC II/302

R's health is weaker. He is trying to atone for the past as he waits for death.

83/3   RM ABBESSE   1683
TC II/203, TC II/304

Her desire to belong wholly to God sign of exceptional grace, but she must be patient.

830101   BISHOP OF GRENOBLE [ETIENNE LE CAMUS]   1 January 1683
TB 1822

New Year greetings. Bp of Luçon has visited. Bossuet has toned down some passages in *Sainteté*, which Le Camus is now reading.

830104   NICOLAS PINETTE   4 January 1683
TB 1824

New Year greetings.

830106   DOM ALAIN [MORONY]   6 January 1683
TB 1825

He is doing his best. Reference to unnecessary move of abbatial chair.
Cf.821215.

*830112   RP ABBÉ, CHÂTILLON [CLAUDE LE MAÎTRE]   12 January 1683
TB 1828

'I do not think that you can dispense yourself from attending the Genereal Chapter, since no legitimate cause prevents you, although there is no hope either of procuring any benefit for our observance, or even of averting the harm that people would like to do to it. In that respect we enjoy neither consideration nor credit, and I always come back to my first principle, which is that we have no one to blame for our ills but ourselves. You know our observance, and you know that we do not deserve that God should give us the necessary protection for survival. The narrow ways, which are his, have been abandoned, and apart from a very small number of individuals, everyone makes his ways as broad and spacious as he can. Such complaints are no use, for we shall not cure our sickness by talking about it. People must be persuaded that they are sick if they are to be induced to want the recovery of their health, and that is what all our arguments will never achieve. So we must limit our knowledge and opinions to quite simple and useless complaints. Conduct yourself in that assembly in such a way that, without departing from terms of respect and moderation, you neither say nor do anything which is not worthy of a man who has the fear of God before his eyes. Although decisions have to be made on the spot, it is still a good thing to have premeditated them and in all things act in the light of one's duty.

The Abbot of Vauclair must have been easily led and not much attached to the primitive discipline to have given it up so easily. It is true that having abandoned it on so many main issues, even if he had kept this one point, it would not have been much use to him. I have sometimes heard people talk about the regularity of that monastery, and some others like it, but seen more closely and in detail, what goes on there is pitiful. How can one see the ground there filled with the bodies of saints, and then trample underfoot without scruple or hesitation their examples and instructions like their ashes? And how can one not apply these words to oneself: *viri ninivitae surgent in judicio* [Mt 12:41]? When men reach a certain point, they have eyes and ears, but not to use in a legitimate and genuine way. God grant us grace to make good use of what we know to be reprehensible in others.

I will always look on what the Abbot of Orval has done as a remarkable thing for the region in which he is, although I think that the regularity observed in his monastery is not absolutely strict, since that is hardly possible with the communications he permits there. As he has much piety and virtue, there is every reason to believe that God will bless his work and maintain it; that is what all those who love his glory must wish.

The Bishop of Meaux only saw the surface; the outward man may have pleased him, but if he had seen the inner, he would not have spoken as he did. Very charitable persons are easily prejudiced in favour of those whom they believe to desire good. That is a cause for infinite humiliation for those who know themselves to be so different from what they are thought to be.

As regards the income of our abbeys, small as it is, let us be content with it, and not look at those who have more. Our poverty is our wealth, it is our glory; let us say like Tobias: *pauperem quidem vitam gerimus, sed bona multa habebimus, si timuerimus Deum, et recesserimus ab omni peccato, et fecerimus bene* [Tb 4:23].

Farewell, my very dear Father, I pray Our Lord to give you many years, that you may long serve him, that this may be a happy one for you, and that he will add many more like it. Remember us when you are in his presence and believe me without reserve yours' etc.

R. himself did not attend this, or any other Chapter after 1667, always pleading ill health. Louis Brulart had been Abbot of Vauclair from 1680 (and coadjutor from 1673) until his death in 1705. Much damaged by war, Vauclair was one of the early reformed houses, and despite R's strictures had a good reputation. Bossuet, Bp of Meaux, had paid his first visit to la Trappe in October 1682.

830114   CLAUDE NICAISE   14 January 1683
TB 1831; TC II/312

Hopes for peace in the Church, extinction of heresy or reunion of Church's enemies. The King is doing great things to that end.

830114a   RM ABBESSE,   14 January 1683
          ESSAI [FRANÇOISE TROTTI DE LA CHÉTARDIE]
TB 1833; TC II/318

New Year greetings.

A Biographical Index of Addresses and
a General Index will appear in Volume Two

CISTERCIAN PUBLICATIONS INC.

TITLES LISTING

THE CISTERCIAN FATHERS SERIES

THE WORKS OF BERNARD OF CLAIRVAUX

Treatises I: Apologia to Abbot William,
On Precept and Dispensation..........CF 1
On the Song of Songs I-IV........CF 4,7,31,40
The Life and Death of Saint Malachy
the Irishman......................CF 10
Treatises II: The Steps of Humility,
On Loving God....................CF 13*
Magnificat: Homilies in Praise of the
Blessed Virgin Mary [with Amadeus
of Lausanne]......................CF 18
Treatises III: On Grace and Free Choice,
In Praise of the New Knighthood.......CF 19
Sermons on Conversion: A Sermon to Clerics,
Lenten Sermons on Psalm 91..........CF 25
Five Books on Consideration:
Advice to a Pope..................CF 37

THE WORKS OF WILLIAM OF SAINT THIERRY

On Contemplating God, Prayer,
and Meditations...................CF 3*
Exposition on the Song of Songs........CF 6
The Enigma of Faith.................CF 9
The Golden Epistle..................CF 12
The Mirror of Faith.................CF 15
Exposition on the Epistle to the
Romans..........................CF 27
The Nature and Dignity of Love.........CF 30

THE WORKS OF AELRED OF RIEVAULX

Treatises I: On Jesus at the Age of Twelve,
Rule for a Recluse, The Pastoral Prayer....CF 2
Spiritual Friendship..................CF 5
The Mirror of Charity................CF 17†
Dialogue on the Soul.................CF 22

THE WORKS OF GILBERT OF HOYLAND

Sermons on the Song of Songs I-III..CF 14,20,26
Treatises, Sermons, and Epistles........CF 34

THE WORKS OF JOHN OF FORD

Sermons on the Final Verses of the Song
of Songs I-VII......CF 29,39,43,44,45,46,47

OTHER EARLY CISTERCIAN WRITERS

The Letters of Adam of Perseigne, I.......CF 21
Alan of Lille: The Art of Preaching........CF 23
Idung of Prüfening. Cistercians and Cluniacs:
The Case for Citeaux................CF 33
The Way of Love...................CF 16
Guerric of Igny.
Liturgical Sermons I-II.............CF 8,32
Three Treatises on Man: A Cistercian
Anthropology....................CF 24
Isaac of Stella. Sermons on the
Christian Year, I..................CF 11
Stephen of Lexington. Letters from
Ireland, 1228-9...................CF 28
Stephen of Sawley, Treatises...........CF 36

THE CISTERCIAN STUDIES SERIES

MONASTIC TEXTS

Evagrius Ponticus. Praktikos and
Chapters on Prayer.................CS 4
The Rule of the Master................CS 6
The Lives of the Desert Fathers..........CS 34
The Sayings of the Desert Fathers........CS 59
Dorotheos of Gaza. Discourses
and Sayings......................CS 33

Pachomian Koinonia I-III:
The Lives........................CS 45
The Chronicles and Rules.............CS 46
The Instructions, Letters, and Other
Writings of St Pachomius and
His Disciples.....................CS 47
Besa, The Life of Shenoute............CS 73

* Temporarily out of print   † Forthcoming

Symeon the New Theologian. Theological
and Practical Treatises and Three
Theological Discourses . . . . CS 41
Guigo II the Carthusian. The Ladder of
Monks and Twelve Meditations . . . . CS 48
The Monastic Rule of Iosif Volotsky . . . . . . CS 36

CHRISTIAN SPIRITUALITY

The Spirituality of Western
Christendom . . . . CS 30
Russian Mystics (Sergius Bolshakoff) . . . . CS 26
In Quest of the Absolute: The Life and Works
of Jules Monchanin (J.G. Weber) . . . . CS 51
The Name of Jesus
(Irénée Hausherr) . . . . CS 44
Entirely for God: A Life of Cyprian
Tansi (Elizabeth Isichei) . . . . CS 43
The Roots of the Modern
Christian Tradition . . . . CS 55
Abba: Guides to Wholeness and
Holiness East and West . . . . CS 38
Sermons in a Monastery
(Matthew Kelty–William Paulsell) . . . . CS 58
Penthos: The Doctrine of Compunction in
the Christian East (Irénée Hausherr) . . . . . CS 53
Distant Echoes. Medieval Religious Women,
Vol. 1 . . . . CS 71

MONASTIC STUDIES

The Abbot in Monastic Tradition
(Pierre Salmon) . . . . CS 14
Why Monks? (François Vandenbroucke) . . . CS 17
Silence in the Rule of St Benedict
(Ambrose Wathen) . . . . CS 22
One Yet Two: Monastic Tradition
East and West . . . . CS 29
Community and Abbot in the Rule of
St Benedict I (Adalbert de Vogüé) . . . . . . CS 5/1
Consider Your Call: A Theology of the
Monastic Life (Daniel Rees et al.) . . . . CS 20
Households of God (David Parry) . . . . CS 39
Studies in Monastic Theology
(Odo Brooke) . . . . , ... CS 37
The Way to God According to the Rule
of St Benedict (E. Heufelder) . . . . CS 49
The Rule of St Benedict. A Doctrinal
and Spiritual Commentary
(Adalbert de Vogüé) . . . . CS 54
As We Seek God (Stephanie Campbell) . . . . CS 70

CISTERCIAN STUDIES

The Cistercian Way (André Louf) . . . . CS 76
The Cistercian Spirit
(M. Basil Pennington, ed.) . . . . CS 3
The Eleventh-Century Background of
Cîteaux (Bede K. Lackner) . . . . CS 8
Contemplative Community . . . . CS 21
Cistercian Sign Language
(Robert Barakat) . . . . CS 11
The Cistercians in Denmark
(Brian P. McGuire) . . . . CS 35
Saint Bernard of Clairvaux: Essays
Commemorating the Eighth Centenary of
His Canonization . . . . CS 28
Bernard of Clairvaux: Studies Presented
to Dom Jean Leclercq . . . . CS 23
Bernard of Clairvaux and the Cistercian
Spirit (Jean Leclercq) . . . . CS 16
Image and Likeness. The Mystical Theology of
William of St Thierry and St Augustine
(D.N. Bell) . . . . CS 78
Aelred of Rievaulx: A Study
(Aelred Squire) . . . . CS 50
Christ the Way: The Christology of
Guerric of Igny (John Morson) . . . . CS 25
The Golden Chain: The Theological
Anthropology of Isaac of Stella
(Bernard McGinn) . . . . CS 15
Studies in Cistercian Art and Architecture, I
(Meredith Lillich, ed.) . . . . CS 66
Studies in Cistercian Art and Architecture, II
(Meredith Lillich, ed.) . . . . CS 69
Nicolas Cotheret's Annals of Cîteaux
(Louis J. Lekai) . . . . CS 57
The Occupation of Celtic Sites in Ireland
by the Canons Regular of St Augustine and
the Cistercians (G. Carville) . . . . CS 56
The Cistercian Way (André Louf) . . . . CS 76
Monastic Practices (Charles Cummings) . . . . CS 75
The Letters of Armand-Jean le Bouthillier,
abbé de Rancé (A.J. Krailsheimer) . . . . . CS 80,81

Studies in Medieval Cistercian
History sub-series

Studies I . . . . CS 13
Studies II . . . . CS 24
Cistercian Ideals and Reality
(Studies III) . . . . CS 60
Simplicity and Ordinariness
(Studies IV) . . . . CS 61
The Chimera of His Age: Studies on
St Bernard (Studies V) . . . . CS 63
Cistercians in the Late Middle Ages
(Studies VI) . . . . CS 64
Noble Piety and Reformed Monasticism
(Studies VII) . . . . CS 65
Benedictus: Studies in Honor of St Benedict
of Nursia (Studies VIII) . . . . CS 67
Heaven on Earth (Studies IX) . . . . CS 68

* *Temporarily out of print*   † *Forthcoming*

THOMAS MERTON

The Climate of Monastic Prayer...........CS 1
Thomas Merton on St Bernard...........CS 9
Thomas Merton's Shared Contemplation:
A Protestant Perspective
(Daniel J. Adams)..................CS 62
Solitude in the Writings of Thomas Merton
(Richard Anthony Cashen)...........CS 40

The Message of Thomas Merton
(Brother Patrick Hart, ed.).............CS 42
Thomas Merton Monk (revised edition/
Brother Patrick Hart, ed.).............CS 52
Thomas Merton and Asia: A Quest for
Utopia (Alexander Lipski)............CS 74

THE CISTERCIAN LITURGICAL DOCUMENTS SERIES †

The Cistercian Hymnal: Introduction
and Commentary...................CLS 1
The Cistercian Hymnal: Text and
Melodies.........................CLS 2
The Old French Ordinary and Breviary
of the Abbey of the Paraclete: Introduction
and Commentary..................CLS 3
The Old French Ordinary of the Abbey of
the Paraclete: Text.................CLS 4

The Paraclete Breviary: Text..........CLS 5-7
The Hymn Collection of the Abbey
of the Paraclete: Introduction
and Commentary...................CLS 8
The Hymn Collection of the Abbey of the
Paraclete: Text....................CLS 9

FAIRACRES PRESS, OXFORD

The Wisdom of the Desert Fathers
The Letters of St Antony the Great
The Letters of Ammonas, Successor of
St Antony
A Study of Wisdom. Three Tracts by the author
of *The Cloud of Unknowing*
The Power of the Name. The Jesus Prayer in
Orthodox Spirituality (Kallistos Ware)

Contemporary Monasticism
A Pilgrim's Book of Prayers
(Gilbert Shaw)
Theology and Spirituality (Andrew Louth)
Prayer and Holiness (Dumitru Staniloae)
Eight Chapters on Perfection and Angel's Song
(Walter Hilton)

Distributed in North America only for Fairacres Press.

DISTRIBUTED BOOKS

La Trappe in England
O Holy Mountain: Journal of a Retreat on
Mount Athos
St Benedict: Man with An Idea (Melbourne Studies)
The Spirit of Simplicity

Vision of Peace (St Joseph's Abbey)

The Animáls of St Gregory (Paulinus Press)
Benedict's Disciples (David Hugh Farmer)
The Christmas Sermons of Guerric of Igny
The Emperor's Monk. A Contemporary Life of
Benedict of Aniane
Journey to God:. Anglican Essays on the
Benedictine Way

* *Temporarily out of print* † *Forthcoming*